TROUBLE WITH STRANGERS

In memory of Charles Swann
Endless kindness, endless courage

TROUBLE WITH STRANGERS

A Study of Ethics

TERRY EAGLETON

WILEY-BLACKWELL

A John Wiley & Sons, Ltd., Publication

This edition first published 2009
© 2009 Terry Eagleton

Blackwell Publishing was acquired by John Wiley & Sons in February 2007. Blackwell's
publishing program has been merged with Wiley's global Scientific, Technical, and Medical
business to form Wiley-Blackwell.

Registered Office
John Wiley & Sons Ltd, The Atrium, Southern Gate, Chichester, West Sussex, PO19 8SQ,
United Kingdom

Editorial Offices
350 Main Street, Malden, MA 02148-5020, USA
9600 Garsington Road, Oxford, OX4 2DQ, UK
The Atrium, Southern Gate, Chichester, West Sussex, PO19 8SQ, UK

For details of our global editorial offices, for customer services, and for information about how
to apply for permission to reuse the copyright material in this book please see our website at
www.wiley.com/wiley-blackwell.

The right of Terry Eagleton to be identified as the author of this work has been asserted in
accordance with the Copyright, Designs and Patents Act 1988.

All rights reserved. No part of this publication may be reproduced, stored in a retrieval system,
or transmitted, in any form or by any means, electronic, mechanical, photocopying, recording
or otherwise, except as permitted by the UK Copyright, Designs and Patents Act 1988, without
the prior permission of the publisher.

Wiley also publishes its books in a variety of electronic formats. Some content that appears in
print may not be available in electronic books.

Designations used by companies to distinguish their products are often claimed as trademarks.
All brand names and product names used in this book are trade names, service marks,
trademarks or registered trademarks of their respective owners. The publisher is not associated
with any product or vendor mentioned in this book. This publication is designed to provide
accurate and authoritative information in regard to the subject matter covered. It is sold on the
understanding that the publisher is not engaged in rendering professional services. If
professional advice or other expert assistance is required, the services of a competent
professional should be sought.

Library of Congress Cataloging-in-Publication Data

Eagleton, Terry, 1943–
Trouble with strangers : a study of ethics / Terry Eagleton.
    p. cm.
Includes bibliographical references and index.
ISBN 978-1-4051-8572-1 (pbk. : alk. paper)—ISBN 978-1-4051-8573-8 (hardcover : alk.
paper) 1. Ethics. I. Title.
BJ1012.E23 2008
170—dc22
2008011376

A catalogue record for this book is available from the British Library.

Set in 10.5/13pt Minion by SNP Best-set Typesetter Ltd., Hong Kong
Printed in Singapore by Fabulous Printers Pte Ltd

1 2009

Contents

Preface

The argument of this book is fairly straightforward. It consists in the claim that most ethical theories can be assigned to one of Jacques Lacan's three psychoanalytical categories of the imaginary, the symbolic and the Real, or to some combination of the three. Using these registers rather broadly, I try to weight the strengths of each of these types of ethical thought alongside their defects, and to contrast them with what seems to me the richer ethics of socialism and the Judaeo-Christian tradition.

Some of my friends and readers will be dismayed to see me wasting my time yet again on theology. It is true that religion has proved one of the most noxious institutions of human history; but that squalid tale of oppression and superstition stands under the judgement of the version of Christianity advanced in this book. It is a paradox of our times that while it has bred various lethal brands of religious fundamentalism, it has also given birth to a current of radical theology – one which, ironically, represents one of the few surviving enclaves of materialist thought in these politically patchy times, and which is often more revolutionary in its political implications than much secular leftist thought. It may well be a dismal sign of the times that it is to the science of God, of all things, that we must look for such subversive insights. But there is no reason to look a gift horse in the mouth.

'If a man could write a book on Ethics which really was a book on Ethics,' comments Ludwig Wittgenstein, 'this book would, with an explosion, destroy all the other books in the world.'[1] I am pained to report that when I glanced up from the last sentence of my text, the volumes on my bookshelves were still intact. I trust, even so, that this work makes an original contribution to ethical theory, if only because few such studies investigate both Hume and Levinas, Burke and Badiou. My hope is that

[1] Ludwig Wittgenstein, 'Lecture on Ethics', *Philosophical Review*, 74 (January 1965), p. 7.

the book will be disliked by Anglo-Saxon philosophers for taking Parisians seriously, and scorned by Parisians for finding something of value in English thought. As ever, my philosophical minders, Peter Dews, Simon Critchley, Peter Sedgwick and Slavoj Žižek, have rescued a rank amateur from some of his customary errors and howlers, and I appreciate their kindness in taking the trouble to do so.

In case anyone assumes that only those of impeachable moral stature have the authority to write on ethics, I can only recall, *mutatis mutandis*, Marx's comments on his own labours, when he remarked that nobody had written so much on money and had so little.

TE
Dublin, 2007

PART I

THE INSISTENCE OF THE IMAGINARY

Introduction: The Mirror Stage

No piece of leftist cultural criticism of the 1970s and 1980s seemed complete without an account of Jacques Lacan's theory of the mirror stage – that moment in the development of a small child when, contemplating its own reflection in a mirror, it delights in the magical correspondence between its own movements and those of the image before its eyes.[1] Magical correspondences and miraculous affinities are the stuff of myth; and if Lacan's essay 'The Mirror Stage' investigated such a myth, it rapidly became one in its own right. The boundaries between reality and make-believe, so Lacan argues, are blurred in this early phase: the ego, our window on the so-called real world, is really a kind of fiction, while the child before the mirror is said to treat its image as real even though it knows it to be illusory. A similar ambiguity applies to the word 'imaginary', which for Lacan means 'pertaining to an image' rather than fantastic or unreal, yet which (like the theory of ideology which Louis Althusser was famously to derive from it) involves delusion and deception even so.

In a mirroring kind of way, the fictional or real-life status of Lacan's argument itself came into question. Was the mirror stage meant to be literal or metaphorical? Was this most mandarin of French intellectuals really talking about something as embarrassingly empirical as toddlers? How on earth could one actually know what a child might experience in this situation? What – to raise the kind of commonsensical objection of which only the English are capable – about societies which did not enjoy the privilege of possessing mirrors? Would ponds or rivers do just as well?

---

[1] See 'The Mirror Stage as Formative of the Function of the I as Revealed in Psychoanalytic Experience', in Jacques Lacan, *Écrits: A Selection* (London, 1977).

Or is the true mirror of the child its parent or carer, who by investing different parts of its body (face, orifices, etc.) with variable degrees of intensity, builds up for the infant a somatic self-portrait? Are our bodies, like our desire, constituted by the Other? How odd, in any case, that such a momentous piece of theorising should be based on that most fictive and primitive of all human activities, play and play-acting! Play-acting, to be sure, as well as play – for the child jubilantly imitating its own motions in the mirror is a mimic, a miniscule magician who can alter reality simply by raising his hand, an actor performing before an appreciative audience of one, a pocket-sized artist who revels in his ability to shape and transform his product at the flick of a finger or the turn of a head. To perform in front of a mirror involves a kind of infinite regress or *mise en abyme*, as the *Gestalt* in the glass beams approvingly at the child's endeavours, thus provoking his smile, which in turn cues another supportive sign of delight from the reflection, and so on. We shall see something of the same dialectic later, in – of all things – eighteenth-century moral philosophy.

It was not, to be sure, as though the cultural theorists of the time were particularly enthralled by the topic of child development. The importance of Lacan's lecture lay in its illustration of the imaginary – that strange realm of the human psyche in which subjects and objects (if we can even speak of such a division at this early point) appear constantly to exchange places and live each other's lives. In this play of projecting and reflecting, things seem to pass in and out of each other without mediation, feel one another from the inside with all the sensuous immediacy with which they experience their own interiors. It is as though you can put yourself in the very place from which you are being observed, or see yourself at the same time from the inside and outside. Psychology is only just beginning to understand the neural mechanisms by which a very small infant can playfully imitate an adult's facial expression, in a complex set of reflections from outside to inside to outside again.[2] As Maurice Merleau-Ponty writes:

> A baby of fifteen months opens its mouth if I playfully take one of its fingers between my teeth and pretend to bite it. And yet it has scarcely looked at its face in a glass, and its teeth are not in any case like mine. The fact is that its own mouth and teeth, as it feels them from the inside, are immediately, for it, an apparatus to bite with, and my jaw, as the

---

[2]   See Sandra Blakeslee, 'Cells That Read Minds', *New York Times*, 10 January 2006.

baby sees it from the outside, is immediately, for it, capable of the same intentions.[3]

The imaginary is a realm in which things give us back ourselves, if only we had a determinate enough self to appreciate it. It is a prelapsarian domain, in which knowledge is as swift and sure as a sensation.

In this peculiar configuration of psychic space, where there is as yet no clearly organised ego or centre of consciousness, there can be no genuine otherness. My interiority is somehow 'out there', as one phenomenon among others, while whatever is out there is on intimate terms with me, part of my inner stuff. Yet I also feel my inner life as alien and estranged, as though a piece of my selfhood has been captivated by an image and reified by it. This image seems able to exert a power over me which both does and does not spring from myself. In the domain of the imaginary, then, it is not apparent whether I am myself or another, inside or outside myself, behind or before the mirror. One can imagine this as capturing something of the experience of the small infant nursed by its mother, who uses her breast as though it were its own organ; but it is also, as far as objects which are ambiguously inside and outside us goes, a matter of those 'part-objects', bits of the body extruded into the external world (faeces, breast milk and the like), which Melanie Klein portrays as transitional between self and other, subject and object, and which Lacan himself describes as the very stuff, lining or imaginary filling of the human subject.

This is why the imaginary involves what is technically known as transitivism, in which, as in some primitive bond of sympathy, a small child may cry when another child takes a tumble, or claim to have been struck himself when he strikes a companion. The eighteenth-century philosopher Adam Smith is much taken with this phenomenon, writing as he does in his *Theory of Moral Sentiments* of how, 'when we see a stroke aimed and just ready to fall upon the leg or arm of another person, we naturally shrink and draw back our own leg or our own arm'. Transitivism is just a peculiarly graphic instance of sympathetic mimicry as such, which remains to some extent a bodily affair even for those who have managed to travel beyond the seductions of the mirror stage. This is why smiling is contagious, or why, as Smith observes, 'the mob, when they are gazing at a dancer on a slack rope, naturally writhe and twist and balance their own bodies, as they see him do, and as they feel that they themselves must do

---

[3] Maurice Merleau-Ponty, *Phenomenology of Perception* (London, 1966), p. 352.

in his situation'.[4] Smith seems to suppose that this spontaneous mimicry is a result of what Lacan calls imaginary transposition, as we project ourselves imaginatively into the body of the dancer. But these spectators are also would-be magicians, involuntarily seeking to control the dancer's movements by their own sympathetic swaying, as the toddler in the mirror stage exuberantly masters his own reflection at the very moment he is in thrall to it. Smith's spectators remain themselves at the very moment they assume the identity of another; and this conflation is typical of the imaginary register.

Transitivism, then, is a kind of chiming or resonating of bodies. Those with delicate fibres, Smith observes, feel itchy or uneasy sensations when they gaze on the ulcers of a beggar, while looking at the sore eyes of someone else is likely to make your own eyes feel tender. In the end, the only satisfactory image of this condition would be that of two bodies folded into one, as Clym Yeobright and his mother in Thomas Hardy's *The Return of the Native* speak to one another as though 'their discourses were . . . carried on between the right and the left hands of the same body'. Jude Fawley and Sue Bridehead in Hardy's *Jude the Obscure* achieve 'that complete mutual understanding in which every glance and movement was as effectual as speech for conveying intelligence between them, (and) made them almost the two parts of a single whole'. The affection between Laurence Sterne's Walter Shandy and Uncle Toby, a matter of gesture, intuition and wordless communion, is another case in point. We shall have occasion to return to this idea of the body as language later in the book.

There is a sense in which the adult version of the imaginary is friendship. In friendship, as Aristotle notes in the *Ethics*, the other is both you and not you – so that this merging and mingling of identities re-creates the mirror phase on a higher level. 'The only joy I have in his being mine', writes Montaigne in his great essay on friendship, 'is that the *not mine* is *mine*.'[5] His relationship with his dearest friend, he adds, left him nothing that was their own, nothing that was either his friend's or his own. 'If I were pressed to say why I love him', he comments, 'I feel that my only reply could be: "Because it was he, because it was I" . . . Such a friendship has no model but itself, and can only be compared to itself.'[6] The imaginary resists being

[4]   Adam Smith, 'The Theory of Moral Sentiments', in L. A. Selby-Bigge (ed.), *British Moralists*, vol. 1 (New York, 1965), p. 258.

[5]   Montaigne, *Essays* (Harmondsworth, 1979), p. 98.

[6]   Ibid., p. 97.

translated into rational or comparative terms. Unlike the symbolic, in which, as we shall see, exchange and commensurability are of the essence, all its elements are irreducibly specific.

On the whole, the cultural left of the 1970s evoked the imaginary only to demonise it. For one thing, for theorists for whom discourse had become a veritable obsession, pre-linguistic states were scarcely more popular than babies. For another thing, the imaginary was a matter of unity, stasis, resemblance, correspondence, autonomy, mimesis, representation, harmony, plenitude and totality; and no terms could have been less *à la mode* for an avant-garde whose buzz words were lack, absence, difference, conflict, fissure, dispersal, fragmentation and heterogeneity. The left of the day would tolerate the idea of representation only if the means and conditions of representation were given along with it; and all this, in the mirror stage, is ominously suppressed.[7] Even worse, the representation in question is a false one. The image in the mirror is a deceptively unified version of the child's actual, uncoordinated body, and his delight in it springs from contrasting this idealised whole with his dysfunctional state. The mirror allows him an autonomy which he lacks in real life. One might speculate, too, that he contrasts this agreeably coherent appearance with certain Kleinian fantasises of his own body as torn, mutilated, pounded to pieces.

The pre-egoic innocence of the mirror stage, then, seemed ripe for deconstruction, turning as it did on what was really an iconic notion of identity. This mirror is a glass in which, in St Paul's phrase, we see only darkly. The dysfunctional toddler enraptured by his own image was as much a case of false identification as the idea that every signifier, as with an icon, is leashed by an internal bond to a single signified, which can be said to represent its meaning. In the mirror, remark Jean Laplanche and J.-B. Pontalis, 'there is a sort of coalescence of the signifier with the signified'.[8] The other place where this is supposed to happen is known as poetry, in which, by a kind of verbal *trompe l'oeil*, these two aspects of the sign appear indissociable.[9] But it will not do either to think of words and meanings as separate, as long as one still imagines that they are roughly the same kind of entity. 'Here the word, there the meaning',

---

[7]   The British film journal *Screen*, which published some remarkably pioneering work, is characteristic of the cultural avant-gardism of the time.

[8]   J. Laplanche and J.-B. Pontalis, *The Language of Psycho-Analysis* (London, 1980), p. 210.

[9]   See Terry Eagleton, *How To Read A Poem* (Oxford, 2006), Ch. 2.

remarks Ludwig Wittgenstein sardonically. 'The money, and the cow that you can buy with it. But contrast: money and its use.'[10] A word for Wittgenstein acquires meaning through its use; and this involves it entering into rule-governed relations with other signs in a specific form of life. This, one might suggest, is his version of what Jacques Lacan will term the symbolic order. It is just that Lacan shows that what goes for signs goes for human subjects too. The toddler who imagines that his mirror image is the tangible incarnation of his selfhood is an old-style pre-structuralist who has not yet grasped that human identity, like signs, is a differential affair – that it is a question of assuming a place in a symbolic order, a system of roles and relations in which you are an exchangeable function rather than a unique, irreplaceable, living and breathing animal. Elated by the fantasy of being wholly at one with himself, the infant has yet to recognise that, as Wittgenstein comments in his *Philosophical Investigations*, there is no more useless proposition than that of the identity of a thing with itself. The small child has fallen prey, so to speak, to the philosophical error that there is a special kind of certainty and accessibility about human selfhood.

So it is that the child's self-recognition in the imaginary sphere is in fact a misrecognition – one which acts as a prelude to the rather more momentous form of misrecognition which it shall encounter in the symbolic order. Its identity is also an alienation, as the *je*, or subject, mistakes its elusive being for that of a mere *moi*, a determinate thing in the glass of its self-reflection. The truth of the subject accordingly eludes it – the fact that, in Lacan's flamboyant rewriting of Descartes, 'I think where I am not, therefore I am where I do not think.' The infant has yet to learn that a subject which coincides with itself is no sort of subject at all. The selfhood which (so one assumes) the young Narcissus of the mirror stage regards as fixed and determinate is in fact fissured and imperfect. Like the process of signification itself, it is driven on by its own incompleteness.

The opposition of the imaginary, in which each term (infant and image) depends symbiotically on the other, must eventually be prised apart or triangulated. And this, for Lacan, is the Oedipal moment. The imaginary enclosure must be thrown open to the play of difference and otherness. The small child must break through the mirror of its own misrecognition to emerge on the terrain of the intersubjective, where it may alone negotiate some poor scraps of truth. For Hegel, from whom much of Lacan's thought

---

[10] Ludwig Wittgenstein, *Philosophical Investigations* (Oxford, 1963), p. 49.

derives, the transition from the one state to another has an ethical dimension. The subject must be weaned from mistaking itself for an autonomous entity and come instead to confess its dependence upon others in the domain of the intersubjective – a domain which Hegel names *Geist* and Lacan calls the Other or the symbolic order. In Lacan's words, this involves at its most complete the 'total acceptance of the subject by the other subject'.[11] It was not an ideal of human reciprocity he was to maintain for very long. We must cease to derive our self-image from the other, as we do in the imaginary, and come instead to take it from the Other (the realm of sociality as a whole), as we do in the symbolic. For Hegel, the most elementary forms of human life involve a non-reflective absorption in a closed social order, one which is not far removed from Lacan's imaginary. Only when one ventures upon the intersubjective exchanges of the symbolic can one become conscious of oneself as an individual. We shall see later, however, that this achievement is, in Lacan's eyes, never far from catastrophe.

For the cultural avant-garde of the 1970s, this shift of ontological registers was more political than ethical. The point was not to bolster the bourgeois subject by holding a looking-glass to its self-satisfied gaze, but to pitch it into permanent crisis. The former was a matter of ideology, while the latter was a question of revolutionary cultural practice. What made us what we were – lack, the Real, repression, castration, the Law of the Father, the invisible laws of the social formation – lay quite beyond representation. They were the fractures and blind spots in the mirror of consciousness – a phenomenon which itself was traditionally conceived of in specular terms ('reflection', 'speculation', 'contemplation'). As the Earl of Shaftesbury puts it: 'Every reasoning or reflecting creature is, by his Nature, forc'd to endure the review of his own mind, and actions; and to have representations of himself, and his inward affairs, constantly passing before him, obvious to him, and revolving in his mind.'[12] Self-reflection is in this sense a kind of inward imaginary – a matter of contemplating ourselves in the mirror of our own minds, a mental theatre in which we pass like actors before our own spectatorial gaze as though we were someone else. It was this rather smug self-enclosure which in the left's view needed to be shattered, and

---

[11] Jacques Lacan, *Le Séminaire Livre 1: Les Écrits Techniques de Freud* (Paris, 1975), p. 242.
[12] Shaftesbury, *An Inquiry Concerning Virtue or Merit,* in L. A. Selby-Bigge (ed.), *British Moralists* (New York, 1965), vol. 1, p. 45.

the imaginary subject decentred, if something of the real determinants of our existence was to be exposed.

'A *picture* held us captive', Wittgenstein writes in the *Philosophical Investigations*. 'And we could not get outside it, for it lay in our language and language seemed to repeat it to us inexorably.'[13] If Lacan's toddler is captivated by an image or ideal ego, beguiled like Marx's alienated labourer by a power he fails to recognise as his own, Wittgenstein's verbally bewitched adult has fallen victim to the inherently reifying structures of our grammar, which forge spurious identities out of what is really no more than a tissue of differences. Friedrich Nietzsche was of much the same opinion, writing of thought as being caught up in 'the spell of certain grammatical functions'.[14] For Wittgenstein, this is a chronic form of false consciousness, language being the homogenising way it is – rather as the imaginary for Lacan is not simply a phase we can outgrow, like thumb-sucking, but the very inner structure of the ego, and thus an ineradicable dimension of all human experience. This infantile crowing and cavorting before the looking-glass lives on in all of our later libidinal investments, as we identify with the sort of objects which bear some reassuring resemblance to ourselves. 'It is around the wandering shadow of his own ego', Lacan suggests, 'that will be structured all the objects of (the human) world.'[15] What the child of the mirror stage needs to become a person is what we linguistically bamboozled adults require as well – a requirement summarised in the quotation from *King Lear* which Wittgenstein thought of using as an epigraph to his *Investigations*: 'I'll teach you differences.'

The interminable talking cure which Wittgenstein knew as philosophy is what enables us to de-fetishise our meanings. Philosophy for him is a kind of therapy, which allows us to free up those rigid, isolated, portentous signifiers on which we have become stuck like so many neurotic symptoms, returning them to the play of differences which constitutes a form of life. Or, as Wittgenstein puts it elsewhere, returning us from the pure ice to the rough ground. 'When philosophers use a word – "knowledge", "being", "object", "I", "proposition", "name"', he admonishes, 'and try to grasp the *essence* of the thing, one must always ask oneself: is the word ever actually used in this way in the language-game

---

[13]   Ibid., p. 48.

[14]   Quoted in Manfred Frank, *What is NeoStructuralism?* (Minneapolis, 1989), p. 208.

[15]   Quoted in Peter Dews, *Logics of Disintegration* (London, 1987), p. 59.

which is its original home? – What *we* do is to bring words back from their metaphysical to their everyday use.'[16]

There is, to be sure, a world of difference between the homespun musings of a Wittgenstein, which at their least impressive merely consecrate the commonplace, and the baroque lucubrations of a Lacan. Yet the aim of the psychoanalyst, too, is to restore the lost signifieds to those who have become stuck in a hard place, and whose discourse has consequently grown rigid and repetitive. To unpick the knot of a neurosis, and to unravel a reified piece of signification, are not dissimilar activities. In the scene of analysis, they may form aspects of a single practice. One of the roles of psychoanalysis is to free us from a fantasy or compulsive repetition on which we have become impaled, converting this stuckness or stumbling-block at the core of one's being into the cornerstone of a new form of life.[17]

The mirror stage, then, was never exactly a state of Edenic innocence. On the contrary, there is a sense in which it is a snapshot of the Fall in the act of taking place. For one thing, narcissism itself involves a certain self-loathing and self-aggression. For another thing, the blurring of boundaries between subjects makes for rivalry as much as for harmony. It is the kind of identity-cum-antagonism we can observe in the paranoid state, in which the persecutory figure is both oneself and some shadowy alter ego. It is what Kierkegaard refers to as 'antipathetic sympathy' in *The Concept of Dread*. One's neighbour, Freud remarks in his *Project for a Scientific Psychology*, thinking chiefly perhaps of one's sibling, is both our first gratifying object and our first hostile one. Some of her features (her face, for example), Freud argues, will be strange and threatening, but others – such as the motion of her hands – will evoke similarity. It is interesting in this respect that the word 'emulate' means both to rival and to mimic, to equal and to excel. 'The one you fight is the one you admire the most', remarks Lacan, unconsciously quoting Oscar Wilde.[18] The ideal ego, which is how the infant's reflection looms up for it, is what you have to kill.

Sunk in mindless collusion with its own image and the objects surrounding it, the small child seeks to dissolve this state of inertia through aggression. One can imagine the infant under the sway of transitivism shifting ceaselessly from the role of hunter to that of hunted, or assuming

---

[16]   Wittgenstein, *Philosophical Investigations*, p. 48e.

[17]   See Eric Santner, *The Psychotheology of Everyday Life* (Chicago, 2001), for an illuminating discussion of this point.

[18]   Jacques Lacan, 'Desire and the Interpretation of Desire in *Hamlet*', *Yale French Studies*, 55/56 (New Haven, CT, 1997), p. 31.

both positions simultaneously.[19] Max Horkheimer and Theodor Adorno speak in *Dialectic of Enlightenment* of the mimetic desire to merge with the world, but also of the fear of being possessed by alien forces which this desire can engender. In a curious, rather sinister passage, Martin Heidegger writes of how, in the First World War, troops on both sides of the conflict were able to encounter each other face to face on the front, and came thereby to identify with each other, 'melding into a single body' (the words are Ernst Jünger's).[20] No such imaginary encounter, Heidegger laments, was possible in the mechanised context of the Second World War. A spot of hand-to-hand fighting is more satisfyingly symbiotic than the ignobly impersonal business of slaughtering each other at long range.

In Lacan's view, the mirror stage marks the first emergence of the ego, a function which is no more than a form of self-estrangement. Consciousness itself is a structure of misrecognition. The child's reified reflection in the mirror becomes the prototype of all the later narcissistic identifications which go to make up the ego. 'The ego of which we speak', Lacan remarks, 'is absolutely impossible to distinguish from the imaginary captivations which constitute it from head to toe.'[21] This 'rigid structure', as intimate yet external to us as a suit of chain mail, is a mirage of unity and solidity, and as such serves to mask the truth that the subject is more non-being than being. The imaginary, in short, is a kind of ideology.

It is in just this way that Lacan's most spectacular failure of a patient, the Marxist philosopher Louis Althusser, interprets the imaginary realm, using the term in the broad sense we shall be adopting in this study.[22] Ideology for Althusser is a form of imaginary misrecognition, in which subject and object, or self and world, seem tailor-made for one another. Rather than being stonily indifferent to our ends, the world appears to be on familiar terms with us, conforming obediently to our desires and bending to our motions as obsequiously as one's reflection in the glass. Yet since this image is a consolingly coherent one, as in the case of the Lacanian infant, both self and social reality are misperceived at a stroke. Viewed theoretically, the human subject is as much a decentred entity as the shambolic toddler before the mirror, the mere function of this or that social structure. But since such dishevelled creatures would be incapable

[19] See Frederic Jameson, 'Imaginary and Symbolic in Lacan', *Yale French Studies*, 55/56 (New Haven, CT, 1997), p. 356.
[20] See Jacques Derrida, *The Gift of Death* (Chicago and London, 1996), p. 16.
[21] Quoted in Dews, *Logics of Disintegration*, p. 57.
[22] See Louis Althusser, 'Ideology and Ideological State Apparatuses', in *Lenin and Philosophy* (London, 1971).

of purposive action, the imaginary realm of ideology intervenes to endow them with a sense of unity and autonomy. Only thus do they become historical agents, of whatever political stripe. From this viewpoint, the Bolshevik revolution involves the sphere of ideology quite as much as a St Patrick's Day parade.

To call the subject of ideology 'imaginary' is to claim that, like the child before the Lacanian looking-glass, it feels the world to be part of its own inner substance, centred upon it, spontaneously given to it, leashed to it by an internal bond. Ideology in this view is a rather bovine kind of anthropocentrism. 'We are all born in moral stupidity,' writes George Eliot in *Middlemarch*, 'taking the world as an udder to feed our supreme selves.' Ideology reinvents the imaginary at the level of society as a whole, for those fully evolved human subjects who might otherwise realise with a *frisson* of alarm that the world does not owe them a living and is as indifferent to them as the weather. Caught in this comfortable delusion, the subject can rest assured that society lays special claim to it, singles it out as uniquely precious and addresses it, so to speak, by its name. In beckoning us from the ruck of faceless citizens around us and turning its visage benignly towards us, the super-subject of ideology fosters in us the flattering faith that reality could not get along without us and would be inconsolably distressed to see us lapse from existence, rather as we can imagine the infant at the breast believing in some Berkeleyan fantasy that if it disappeared, then everything else would vanish in a thunderclap along with it.

There are some thorny problems with Althusser's theory. But I do not intend to pursue them here.[23] I want instead to explore the parallels between these modern psychoanalytical ideas and what one might call the imaginary ethics of some eighteenth-century English moralists. Before we come to that, however, we must take a detour through the topic of eighteenth-century sentimentalism.

---

[23] For a critical discussion, see my *Ideology: An Introduction* (London, 1991), Ch. 5.

1

Sentiment and Sensibility

It is commonplace nowadays to acknowledge that the eighteenth century was as much an age of sentiment as of reason. Certainly there was a good deal of fashionable snivelling, swooning, twitching, tingling, snuffling, gushing, glowing and melting.[1] Sensibility, that key term of the age, represents a kind of rhetoric of the body, a social semiotics of blushing, palpitating, weeping, fainting and the like. It is also the age's riposte to philosophical dualism, since for the ideology of sentiment body and soul are on as cosy terms with each other as a jerkin and its lining. As a kind of primitive materialism, eighteenth-century sensibility is a discourse of fibres and nerve endings, vapours and fluids, pulses and vibrations, excitations and irritations. 'Feelings', remarks Vicesimus Knox, 'is a fashionable word substituted for mental processes, and savourying (*sic*) much of materialism.'[2] Indeed, the very word 'feeling', which can mean both physical sensation and emotional impulse, the act of touching and the event of experiencing, provides the age with a link between the excitation of the nervous fibres and the subtle motions of the spirit.

The Irish novelist Sydney Owenson (Lady Morgan) bemoans in her memoirs her 'unhappy physical organisation, this nervous susceptibility to every impression which circulated through my frame and rendered the whole system acute',[3] but she is really just boasting of how compassionate she is. Her husband Sir Charles Morgan wrote a treatise on physiology, perhaps influenced by observing his exquisitely impressionable wife. Isaac Newton's *Principia*, not unlike Bishop Berkeley's eccentric work *Siris*,

---

[1]   I have written more fully on this subject in *The Rape of Clarissa* (Oxford, 1982), and in 'The Good-Natured Gael', Ch. 3 of my *Crazy John and the Bishop* (Cork, 1998). I have reused some of the latter material in somewhat altered form for the present chapter.

[2]   Quoted by G. J. Barker-Benfield, *The Culture of Sensibility* (Chicago and London, 1992), p. 2.

[3]   Lady Morgan, *Memoirs* (London, 1862), vol. 1, p. 431.

regards the whole of creation as permeated by the subtle spirit of ether, which creates sensations by vibrating the nerves. Sensibility is the spot where body and mind mingle. It is now the nervous system rather than the soul which mediates between material and immaterial realms. Morality is in danger of being superseded by neurology. Laurence Sterne sends up sensibility as a kind of social pathology in *A Sentimental Journey*, despite purveying the stuff himself in plenty. For its abundant critics, the cult of sentiment is a mark of the neurasthenically overcivilised.[4] The Man of Feeling is a moral pelican who feeds off his own fine emotions.

In contrast to the frigid *hauteur* of the patrician, a middle-class cult of pity, benevolence and fellow-feeling was sedulously fostered. Richard Steele writes:

> By a secret charm we lament with the unfortunate, and rejoice with the glad; for it is not possible for a human heart to be averse to any thing that is human: but by the very mien and gesture of the joyful and distress'd we rise and fall into their condition; and since joy is communicative, 'tis reasonable that grief should be contagious, both of which are seen and felt at a look, for one man's eyes are spectacles to another to read his heart.[5]

We have here some of the primary elements of the imaginary: a projection or imaginative transposition into the interior of another's body; the physical mimesis of 'by the very mien and gesture (of the other) we rise and fall into their condition'; the 'contagiousness' by which two human subjects share the same inner condition; the visual immediacy with which the other's inner state is communicated, so that the inside seems inscribed on the outside; and the exchange of positions or identities ('one man's eyes are spectacles to another').

Or consider this statement from Joseph Butler's *Sermons*:

> Mankind are by nature so closely united, there is such a correspondence between the inward sensations of one man and those of another, that disgrace is as much avoided as bodily pain, and to be the object of esteem and love as much desired as any external goods . . . There is such a natural principle of attraction in man towards man, that having trod the same tract of land, having breathed in the same climate, barely having been born in the

---

[4] See John Mullan, *Sentiment and Sociability: The Language of Feeling in the Eighteenth Century* (Oxford, 1988), Ch. 5.

[5] Richard Steele, *The Christian Hero* (Oxford, 1932), p. 77. Steele is said to have written this tract while on guard duty at the Tower of London.

same artificial district or division, becomes the occasion of contracting acquaintances and familiarities many years after . . . Men are so much one body, that in a peculiar manner they feel for each other, shame, sudden danger, resentment, honour, prosperity, distress . . .'[6]

Once more, we are offered some of the chief components of the imaginary: correspondence, the exchange of inward sensations, the merging of two bodies and a quasi-magical principle of magnetism, along with a rather clubbish disregard for difference which assumes that others are of much the same inner stuff as oneself. Indeed, for Aristotle's *Nicomachean Ethics*, such affectionate sentiments are due as much to oneself as to others. Only those who are amicably disposed towards themselves, Aristotle argues, are truly capable of love for others, while those who feel no affection for themselves 'have no sympathetic consciousness of their own joys and sorrows'.[7] The necessary corollary of treating others as oneself is to treat oneself as another. For Aristotle, the condition in which each takes place in terms of the other is known as friendship.

Before we delve more deeply into Butler's idea of inward correspondences, however, we need to investigate its social context a little further. In the culture of sentiment, the virtues of civility, uxoriousness and blitheness of spirit seek to oust the more barbarous upper-class values of militarism and male arrogance.[8] They are aimed equally at the unpolished earnestness of the petty-bourgeois puritan. 'The amiable virtue of humanity', Adam Smith observes, 'requires a sensibility much beyond what is possessed by the rude vulgar of mankind.'[9] The delicacy of your nervous system is now a reasonably reliable index of social class. A new kind of anti-aristocratic heroism, one centred on the man of meekness, the chaste husband and the civilised entrepreneur, becomes the order of the day, to reach its consummation in that ineffably tedious prig Sir Charles Grandison, last and least of Samuel Richardson's protagonists and a kind of Jesus Christ in knee-breeches. There is a general embourgeoisement of virtue: Francis Hutcheson offers as types to be commended not only the prince, statesman and general but 'an honest trader, the kind friend, the faithful

---

[6]   Joseph Butler, *Sermons*, in L. A. Selby-Bigge (ed.), *British Moralists* (New York, 1965), vol. 1, pp. 203–4.

[7]   Aristotle, *Ethics* (Harmondsworth, 1986), p. 295.

[8]   See R. F. Brissenden, *Virtue in Distress: Studies in the Novel of Sentiment from Richardson to Sade* (London, 1974).

[9]   Adam Smith, *The Theory of Moral Sentiments*, in Selby-Bigge, *British Moralists*, vol. 1, p. 279.

prudent adviser, the charitable and hospitable neighbour, the tender husband and affectionate parent, the sedate yet cheerful companion'.[10] It is, in Raymond Williams's phrase, 'the contrast of pity with pomp'.[11] Mildness, gallantry and joviality are weapons to wield against both the hatchet-faced Dissenters and the bellicose ruffians of the old-style squirearchy. Adam Smith sees economic self-interest as a kind of displacement or sublimation of the lust, power-hunger and military ambition of the ancien régime, while Francis Hutcheson distinguishes a 'calm' desire for wealth from the more turbulent passions. The Earl of Shaftesbury speaks with remarkable blandness of the possession of wealth as 'that passion which is esteemed particularly *interesting*';[12] while Montesquieu, whose *Esprit des Lois* is the source of much of this philosophy of *le doux commerce*, has a touching faith in the civilising power of bills of exchange.

One thinks, too, of Samuel Johnson's celebrated remark that a man is never as harmlessly employed as when he is making money – a comment which goes to show that a falsehood authoritatively enough proclaimed ceases instantly to sound like one. As far as economic life goes, the Scottish Enlightenment philosopher John Millar even ropes the proletariat into the sentimentalist project, incorporating them into a single social sensorium or community of sentiment. When labourers are massed together by the same employment and the 'same intercourse', he asserts, they 'are enabled, with great rapidity, to communicate all their senses and passions', and the basis for plebeian solidarity is accordingly laid.[13] For the English middle classes of a later historical era, such solidarity would prove more a source of anxiety than edification.

In this pervasive feminisation of English culture, pathos and the pacific were now the badges of a bourgeoisie whose commercial ends seemed best guaranteed by social decorum and political tranquillity. Sensibility was among other things a response to the bloody sectarianism of the previous century, which had helped to fashion the political status quo but which now, having accomplished its subversive work, was like many a revolutionary heritage to be erased from memory and thrust into the political unconscious. Within a still despotic patriarchy, there were calls for a deepening

---

[10] Francis Hutcheson, *An Inquiry Concerning Moral Good and Evil*, in Selby-Bigge, *British Moralists*, vol. 1, p. 17.
[11] Raymond Williams, *Modern Tragedy* (London, 1966), p. 92.
[12] Quoted in Albert O. Hirschman, *The Passions and the Interests* (Princeton, NJ, 1977), p. 37.
[13] Quoted in ibid., p. 90.

of emotional bonds between men and women, along with the emergence of 'childhood' and the celebration of spiritual companionship within marriage.[14] A cheerful trust in Christian providence was to oust an old-style pagan fatalism. A style of mannered moderation was fashioned by social commentators such as Joseph Addison and Richard Steele, one which would seem to succeeding generations the very essence of Englishness. Properly indulged in, sentimentalism allowed you to be ardent or enraptured, lively or lachrymose, without for a moment violating decorum. It is this which Jane Austen's emotionally unkempt Marianne Dashwood of *Sense and Sensibility* has yet to learn.

In the domain of ideas, a militant empiricism sought to discredit rationalist systems with too little blood in their veins, embracing instead the raw stuff of subjective sensation. Concepts were to be rooted in the rough ground of lived experience, where the honest burgher felt rather more at home than on the pure ice of metaphysical speculation. It was a style of philosophising appropriate to an age which witnessed the rise of the novel. Perception and sensation – the human body itself – lay at the source of all our more elaborate speculations. Meanwhile, buoyed by the nation's economic prosperity and political triumphs, many of the intelligentsia felt free to cultivate a sanguine trust in the beneficence of human nature. An oozy, self-satisfied air of benevolence and humanitarianism suffused the clubs, journals and coffee houses. Despite the prevalence of malice, envy and competition in society, the Scottish philosopher Adam Ferguson was still able to believe that 'love and compassion [were] the most powerful principles in the human breast'.[15]

Sensibility and sentimentalism were, so to speak, the eighteenth century's phenomenological turn – the equivalent in the realm of the emotions of that turn to the subject which was Protestant inwardness and possessive individualism. In such extraordinarily influential journals as the *Tatler* and *Spectator*, sensibility took on programmatic form, as the uncouth reader submitted himself to a crash course in civility. This brand of journalism,

---

[14]   See Lawrence Stone, *The Family, Sex and Marriage in England 1500–1800* (Harmondsworth, 1979), Ch. 5; but also the challenge to Stone's main thesis in Ruth Perry, *Novel Relations* (Cambridge, 2004); Philippe Ariès, *Centuries of Childhood* (London, 1962), especially Part 3; Jean H. Hagstrum, *Sex and Sensibility: Ideal and Erotic Love from Milton to Mozart* (Chicago and London, 1980); David Marshall, *The Surprising Effects of Sympathy* (Chicago and London, 1988) and Markman Ellis, *The Politics of Sensibility* (Cambridge, 1996). See also Terry Eagleton, *The Function of Criticism* (London, 1984) and *The Ideology of the Aesthetic* (Oxford, 1990), Chs 1 & 2.

[15]   Adam Ferguson, *An Essay on the History of Civil Society* (Dublin, 1767), p. 53.

with its adroit blending of grace and gravitas, represented a new form of cultural politics, consciously educating the reading public in the virtues of meekness, simplicity, decency, non-violence, chivalry and connubial affection. 'I have long entertained an ambition to make the word Wife the most agreeable and delightful name in nature', Steele writes in the fortieth number of the *Spectator*. He was hardly a cynosure of virtue himself: he drank too much, killed a man in a duel, was familiar with the inside of a debtor's prison, married a widow for her money and was arraigned for sedition before the House of Commons. Yet the writ of his and Addison's cultural authority ran all the way from the reform of dress to homilies against duelling, from modes of polite address to eulogies of commerce.[16] Among their journalism's gallery of exemplary social figures were Cits, Snuff-Takers, Rakes, Freethinkers, Pretty Fellows and Very Pretty Fellows.

Moral codes were to be aestheticised, lived out as style, grace, wit, lightness, polish, frankness, discretion, geniality, good humour, a love of company, freedom and ease of manner, and courteous self-effacement. Francis Hutcheson recommends as quasi-moral virtues in his *An Inquiry Concerning Moral Good and Evil* 'a neat dress, a humane deportment, a delight in raising mirth in others', along with sweetness, mildness, vivacity, tenderness, certain airs, proportions and '*je ne sais quoys* [*sic*]'.[17] It is a far cry from the moral philosophy of Plato or Kant. As in the fiction of Richardson or Austen, stray empirical details can prove morally momentous: it is in the crook of a finger or the cut of a waistcoat that virtuous or vicious dispositions may be disclosed, a notion which would have seemed absurd to Leibniz. Bodies, and countenances in particular, are for Hutcheson directly expressive of the moral condition of their possessors, so that in the manner of the imaginary, interiors and exteriors are easily reversible and seamlessly continuous. In this unity of manners and morals, states of consciousness are well-nigh material affairs, visibly inscribed on the surfaces of human conduct, incarnate in too servile a gait or too haughty a tilt of the head. Dickens will inherit this brand of anti-dualism. The most admirable of Jane Austen's characters reveal an inward sense of outward propriety, dismantling the opposition between love and law, spontaneity and social convention.[18] *Politesse* goes all the way down: civility means not just

---

[16] See Eagleton, *Function of Criticism*, Ch. 1.
[17] Selby-Bigge, *British Moralists*, p. 148.
[18] See Terry Eagleton, *The English Novel: An Introduction* (Oxford, 2005), Ch. 5.

not spitting in the sherry decanter, but not being boorish, conceited or emotionally tactless as well.

The cult of sentiment was the feel-good factor of a successful mercantile nation, but it was a social force as well as a state of mind. Feeling could oil the wheels of commerce, allowing the Irish-born poet and novelist Henry Brooke to write rhapsodically of how the merchant 'brings the remotest regions to converse . . . and thus knits into one family, and weaves into one web, the affinity and brotherhood of all mankind'.[19] (As a rapaciously mercenary character who wrote pro-Catholic pamphlets for profit despite his robustly anti-Catholic views, Brooke knew a thing or two about the market.) Here, in a nutshell, is the ideology of so-called commercial humanism, for which the proliferation of trade and the spawning of human sympathies are mutually enriching.[20] Laurence Sterne uses the phrase 'sentimental commerce' with the economic meaning well in mind. Economic relations between men deepen their mutual sympathies, polish their parochial edges, and render the conduits of commerce more frictionless and efficient. Trade, as a kind of material version of civilised conversation, renders you more docile and gregarious, a doctrine that the associates of Defoe's Moll Flanders or Dickens's Mr Bounderby might have had trouble in believing. Commercial wealth, being diffusive and mercurial, has an affinity with the ebb and recoil of human sympathies; and the same quicksilver quality provides a mighty counterweight to the insolence of autocratic power.

Yet these rituals of the heart had their utopian aspect as well as their ideological one. Sensibility, of all things, was perhaps the most resourceful critique of Enlightenment rationality which pre-Romantic British culture was able to muster. Feeling may have oiled the wheels of commerce, but it also threatened to derail the whole project in the name of some less crassly egocentric vision of human society. The man of sentiment, Janet Todd comments, 'does not enter the economic order he condemns; he refuses to work to better himself or society'.[21] There is a smack of the Benjaminian *flâneur* about the Man of Feeling, whose lavishness of sensibility, and smug or generous-hearted refusal to calculate, cut against the grain of a crassly utilitarian order. His cavalier carelessness of proportion, as well as his habit

---

[19]   Henry Brooke, *The Fool of Quality* (London, 1765–70), vol. 1, p. 41.

[20]   The classic account is J. G. A. Pocock, *Virtue, Commerce, and History* (Cambridge, 1995).

[21]   Janet Todd, *Sensibility: An Introduction* (London and New York, 1986), p. 97. Todd's claim is perhaps a little unnuanced.

of giving for the sheer sake of it, represent an implicit assault on the doctrine of exchange value, rather like the later extravagances of an Oscar Wilde. At the same time, carelessness of proportion was just what the critics of sentimentalism find hard to stomach: an excess of sensibility means a failure to sort the central from the marginal, since 'feeling' itself will yield you no clue to such vital distinctions. Sentimentalism, and the literature produced by it, tends to be whimsical, digressive and idiosyncratic, preferring the pale sheen of a snowdrop to prison reform. It is in every sense a luxurious ethics.

There is, however, a need for such affective *rapport* in a social order no longer held together by an absolutist state. An individualist society requires a framework of solidarity to contain its anarchic appetites. Otherwise, those appetites are in danger of subverting the very institutions which permit them to flourish. It is, however, a concord increasingly hard to come by, given that social relations are in danger of being reduced to the purely contractual, political power to the instrumental, and individuals themselves to isolated monads. Adam Ferguson, in his *Essay on the History of Civil Society*, gloomily contrasts the solidarity of a tribal culture with the 'detached and solitary' individuals of modern life, for whom 'the bands of affection are broken'. In these conditions, it is not surprising that men and women should fall back on the natural affections to secure themselves a degree of fellowship, given its shrinking availability in the social world. What cannot be found in human culture must now be located in human nature.

In a self-interested social order, the springs of public virtue are likely to appear obscure. As Alasdair MacIntyre has argued, it is no longer possible in such conditions to provide an account of social roles and relations in ways which make implicit reference to moral obligations and responsibilities.[22] Such obligations are accordingly left hanging in the air – rather as, for the more immoderate of the sentimentalists, feelings have come loose from the objects with which they are supposed to be bound up, to become strange, quasi-objective entities in their own right. Since there seems nothing in the constitution of society which might prompt its members to mutual aid and affection, the sympathetic faculty must be relocated instead in the interior of each man and woman, naturalised as an instinct akin to hunger or self-preservation. We are as much delighted by benevolence as we are gratified by the scent of perfume or nauseated by a foul stench. It is in this sense that an age of reason, for which utility, technology and

---

[22] See Alasdair MacIntyre, *After Virtue* (London, 1981).

rational calculation are increasingly paramount, is also a culture of the heart, of tearfulness and *tendresse*. In the kingdom of possessive individualism, love and benevolence are forced to migrate from the private sphere of the domestic hearth to become metaphors of broader public significance. On the most dismal of estimates, sentiment – the quick, whimsical, wordless exchange of gestures or intuitions – is now perhaps the sole form of sociality left in a world of bleakly isolated individuals. Sterne's *Tristram Shandy* might be taken to intimate as much.

The turn to the subject is a canny move, but also a perilous one. For to anchor political community in the natural affections is in one sense to furnish it with the strongest foundation imaginable, and in another sense to leave it alarmingly vulnerable. For David Hume, human society is held together in the end by habits of feeling; and if nothing could be more spiritually coercive, nothing could be less rationally demonstrable. Feelings matter because they provide motives for behaviour in a way that mere rational precepts may not. The same is true for modern-day rationalism: as J. M. Bernstein points out, Jürgen Habermas's communicative ethics are strongly decontextualising; but if their universal norms are to be fleshed out as persuasive motives, they must be re-anchored in everyday practice.[23] The drawback is that there can now be no rational justification for compassion or generosity, as there could be for Spinoza. There is no pragmatic rationale for it either: as the fiction of Henry Fielding suggests, such softheartedness is more likely to land you up at the end of a rope than to secure you a country estate or a government ministry. This is why Fielding commends his heroes' virtue while at the same time satirically sending it up, since in such a predatory society it can only appear naïve.

Yet there is no rational justification for tasting a peach or smelling a rose either, experiences which (like a sudden upsurge of pity or moral revulsion) seem to carry their justifications on their faces, writ large in their very immediacy and incontrovertibility. If we cannot furnish the virtues with a rational foundation, as eighteenth-century moralists like Samuel Clarke and William Wollaston still sought to do, perhaps this is because they are themselves foundational, as built into the body as the liver or pancreas. Maybe in this sense they resemble aesthetic taste, a *je ne sais quoi* which – who knows? – we may need to know no more of after all, since there may be nothing more to know. Perhaps taste and moral judgement, like God and the work of art, provide their own *raison d'être*. Francis Hutcheson

23   J. M. Bernstein, *Adorno: Disenchantment and Ethics* (Cambridge, 2001), p. 83.

certainly seems to have believed so: if he is asked, he writes, why we approve of public good, 'I fancy we can find (no reasons) in these cases, more than we could give for our liking any pleasant fruit'.[24] Explanations, as Wittgenstein comments, have to come to an end somewhere; and Hutcheson's spade hits rock bottom, in a Wittgensteinian phrase, when it arrives at the idea of a moral sense which is as much part of our material nature as sneezing or smiling.

In any case, 'good' and 'bad' seem to be terms which go all the way down, in the sense that even if we could back such judgements up with non-moral reasons, as the rationalists claim we ought, it might always be possible to push the question back a stage and ask why these reasons should in turn be regarded as good ones, or why it should be thought good to be guided by them. The question is partly one of motivation, as the etymology of the term 'benevolence' would suggest. Hutcheson, Hume and their colleagues are addressing a civilisation in which what is thought to be real is by and large what is felt on the pulses or the eyeballs, and which thus feels a natural scepticism of acting on abstract principle. 'Virtue placed at such a distance', Hume remarks of images of ancient virtue, 'is like a fixed star, which, though to the eye of reason it may appear luminous as the sun in his meridian, is so infinitely removed, as to affect the senses, neither with light or heat.'[25] Such bloodlessly admirable ideals lack psychological force. As far as a concern with motive goes, the philosophy of Hutcheson and the fiction of Defoe belong to the same cultural milieu. If one wished to pursue an inquiry into human motivations in all their pragmatic intricacy, one which delves into the most elusive recesses of the psyche, one would probably end up writing a novel.

Besides, in a society where virtue appears in scant supply, and where what little of it exists is scarcely beguiling (thrift, prudence, chastity, self-discipline, obedience, abstinence, punctuality, industriousness and so on), men and women are likely to demand some rather more robust motivation for acting well than a rational appreciation of cosmic harmony. Once morality grows drearily bourgeois, in short, one needs extra incentives for adhering to it. In any case, what would it mean to claim that the reasons for virtue advanced by the rationalists have a specifically *moral* force? What is so splendid, for example, about conforming to the nature of the cosmos? Plenty of moralists have imagined that the good life consists precisely in not doing so.

---

[24] Francis Hutcheson, *Illustrations on the Moral Sense* (Cambridge, MA, 1971), p. 129.
[25] David Hume, *An Enquiry into the Principles of Morals* (Oxford, 1998), p. 45.

Hutcheson himself deploys just this line of reasoning in his *Short Intro-duction to Moral Philosophy*, arguing that rationalism presupposes the very moral sense it seeks to explain. It is a dilemma familiar enough to modern ethical theory: either we hold, like Hutcheson and G. E. Moore, to an intui-tive or non-naturalistic notion of the good, in which case we buy a founda-tion of sorts at the cost of its utter mysteriousness; or we translate the idea of the good into some set of natural properties, which demystifies the notion only at the expense of laying the explanation itself open to further explanation, thus depriving it of the very foundational function it was required to fulfil.

The so-called moral sense of Shaftesbury and Hutcheson, which as we shall see a little later is a kind of spontaneous divination of good and evil, is in one sense a confession of philosophical defeat. This spectral moral sense, which Hutcheson himself calls 'an occult quality', and which Imman-uel Kant bluntly deemed 'unphilosophical', is simply a kind of locum tenens for some more solid kind of ethical grounding, a mysterious X marking an empty place in the argument. To posit this sense, a kind of spectral shadowing of our grosser organs of perception, as the source of moral judgement is in one sense tantamount to claiming that such judge-ments cannot be justified at all. It is as question-begging as Molière's 'dormitive power'. It seems that we can deny the reality of this sense no more than we can deny the taste of potatoes; but it is just as perplexing to say what the former consists in as it is to analyse the latter. Moral sense is a kind of *je ne sais quoi*, akin to the aesthetic faculty, as irrefutable as it is undemonstrable. Reason for Hume and Hutcheson must inform our moral sense, but it cannot found it. And this is scarcely surprising, given that reason loses much of its credence when it is defined by an Age of Reason in instrumental terms. If the moral sense is prior to reason, it is partly because reason is now largely in the hands of those for whom it can have no truck with moral ends. All this, then, amounts to admitting that though love, generosity and mutual cooperation are indeed the most resplendent of human virtues, it is impossible any longer to say why.[26] Yet why should we need to do so in the first place? Is this not simply a sign that our spade has hit rock bottom and need sink no further?

Even so, as the eighteenth-century rationalists recognised, there is cause to be alarmed. It is true that to ground moral imperatives in felt experience

---

[26]   Some excellent historical reasons why it is impossible to say why are provided by MacIntyre, *After Virtue*.

is in one sense to lend them the most unimpeachable of foundations. Only those claims which engage our pieties and affections have a hope of being persuasive, as Edmund Burke, the eighteenth century's most eminent philosopher of hegemony, understood in the political sphere. The most loyal subject of power is a sentimental one, in the eighteenth-century sense of the term. Yet to anchor such claims in the subject is also to risk surrendering them to the vagaries of chance, caprice, habit, fancy and prejudice. How does our aversion to torture differ from our aversion to sprouts? What is specifically moral about such disgust? If we do not dignify a distaste for sprouts with the status of a universal law, why should we do so in the case of torture? So it is that Sir John Hawkins, in a flight of sardonic admiration, can accuse the sentimentalists of subjectivising morality away: 'Their generous notions supersede all obligation; they are a law to themselves, and having *good hearts* and abounding in the *milk of human kindness* are above those considerations that bind men to that rule of conduct which is founded in a sense of duty [original emphasis].'[27] Hawkins is rattled by the moral sense merchants in much the same way that modern deontologists find something rather too laid-back about virtue ethics. Søren Kierkegaard was later to register the same opinion: 'let us not speak aesthetically [about morality]', he writes in his *Journals*, 'as if the ethical were a happy geniality'.[28]

Coleridge was equally disconcerted, complaining in his *Aids to Reflection* that Sterne and the sentimentalists had perpetrated far more mischief than Hobbes and the materialists. Oliver Goldsmith, himself a connoisseur of pity and *tendresse*, accused his compatriot Edmund Burke of 'found(ing) his philosophy on his own particular feelings'.[29] The move to entrench moral values in the human subject is just what risks undermining them. Besides, in democratising morality (since anyone can feel spontaneous sympathy), you also court the Pelagian danger of making virtue look far too easy and instinctive, more like a sigh than a struggle. Such easy goodness is a patrician response to the unlovely ethics of the lower-middle-class puritans, with their high-minded insistence on self-discipline and endeavour. A gentleman does not wrestle with his conscience any more than he

---

[27] Quoted by Ann Jessie Van Sant, *Eighteenth-Century Sensibility and the Novel* (Cambridge, 1993), p. 6.

[28] Alexander Dru (ed.), *The Journals of Søren Kierkegaard: A Selection* (London, 1938), p. 385.

[29] See Arthur Friedman (ed.), *Collected Works of Oliver Goldsmith* (Oxford, 1966), vol. 1, p. 28.

wrestles with his valet. But the Protestant middle class is not pleased by such moral facility. As the eighteenth-century writer Elizabeth Carter tartly observes: 'Merely to be struck by a sudden impulse of compassion at the view of an object in distress is no more benevolence than is a fit of gout.'[30]

Carter and Kierkegaard undoubtedly have a point – one which (as we shall see later) Shakespeare's Shylock might well have taken. Morality is too vital a question to be left to the capricious big-heartedness of those who can afford to be affable. The vulnerable need a material bond or code of obligations to cover their backs, a precise piece of wording they can brandish when their superiors turn sour. A rule-bound ethics may sound less agreeable than a genial impulse, but its point is that you should behave humanely to others whatever you happen to be feeling. Its point is also that morality is a matter of what you do, not what you feel. Compassion unaccompanied by a warm glow does not cease to be compassion. Only moral dualists claim that they had love in their heart when they skewered the baby on a spit.

The imaginary ethics of the eighteenth-century 'moral sense' school are dogged by the hoary old suspicion that altruism might simply be a devious form of egoism. Rather as it is hard to tell in the imaginary order which sensations are mine and which are yours, so it is difficult, perhaps finally impossible, to know whether my pleasure in your pleasure is other- or self-regarding. A creaturely ethics for which sympathy with others is a well-nigh sensual kind of gratification must ask itself whether its true goal is the selfless sympathy or the selfish gratification. What if I am as delighted by my own benevolence, as a kind of idealised version of myself, as the small child is charmed by his deceptively coherent mirror image? One thinks of those ghastly Dickensian do-gooders from Brownlow to Boffin whose gruff exteriors conceal a weeping heart, and whose soppy-sternness occasions in them a well-nigh erotic *frisson*. Richard Steele compares the compassionate soul who dissolves in pity for another to the amorous man who is 'melted' by beauty. In Laurence Sterne's sentimentalist praise of 'the glorious lust of doing good', does the emphasis fall on 'lust' or 'good'?

---

[30]   Quoted by Arthur Hill Cash, *Sterne's Comedy of Moral Sentiments* (Pittsburgh, 1966), p. 55.

For the philosopher C. S. Peirce, this is really a pseudo-problem. To say that we act for the sake of pleasure is in his view to say no more than we desire to do what we do.[31] With characteristic cynicism, Thomas Hobbes sees pity for others in purely egoistic style, as 'the imagination or fiction of future calamity to ourselves, proceeding from the sense of another man's calamity'.[32] It is a reminder to the Romantically inclined that the imagination is by no means an entirely beneficent faculty. A far less cynical commentator, Amartya Sen, writes that 'it can be argued that behaviour based on sympathy is in an important sense egoistic, for one is oneself pleased at others' pleasures and pained at others' pain, and the pursuit of one's own utility may thus be helped by sympathetic action'.[33] An imaginary eighteenth-century ethics, as we shall see, is about altruism; but for Lacan the category of the imaginary lies at the very source of the ego.

Perhaps a distinction between benevolence and sentimentalism may prove useful here, hazy though the difference is. Roughly speaking, benevolence in the eighteenth century is a case of selflessness, while sentimentalism is a more self-regarding affair. Benevolence is centrifugal, whereas sentimentalism is centripetal. Benevolentists like Goldsmith, Hutcheson, Smith and Burke are oriented to the other, while sentimentalists like Steele and Sterne are self-conscious consumers of tender feelings, chewing the cud of their own congenial emotions.[34] The benevolentist does benevolent things, but not for the sake of doing so, whereas the sentimentalist's motive is self-satisfaction. What one feels in the latter case is less the other's felicity or misfortune than one's own 'melting' affinity with it. Steele's letters to his wife are full of impeccably polite bleatings and swoonings: she is his 'Dear Creature', 'Dear Ruler', 'Dearest Being on Earth'; he swears that 'I dye for thee I languish' even when he has not the slightest intention of abandoning a dinner with some bigwig.[35] It is now mannerly to be unmanned. Sentimentalism is feeling in excess of its occasion, passing through its object like Freudian desire so as to curve back upon itself and rejoin the subject; benevolence, by contrast, is feeling in proportion to its object. Hutcheson makes this point when he argues in his *Inquiry Concerning the Original of Our Ideas of Virtue and Moral Good* that we do not love

---

[31]   C. S. Peirce, *Collected Papers* (Cambridge, MA, 1931–58), vol. 7, p. 329.
[32]   Thomas Hobbes, *English Works* (London, 1890), vol. 4, p. 44.
[33]   Amartya Sen, 'Rational Fools: A Critique of the Behavioural Foundations of Economic Theory', *Philosophy and Public Affairs*, 6, 1977.
[34]   Sterne, however, is an ambiguous case, as a satirist of sentimentalism as well as a probable champion of it.
[35]   See Raze Blanchard (ed.), *The Correspondence of Richard Steele* (Oxford, 1941).

because it is pleasant or advantageous for us to do so; rather, our feeling arises from its 'proper object'.

Joshua Reynolds congratulated Oliver Goldsmith on 'feeling with exactness', and it is true that Goldsmith himself – a benevolentist rather than a sentimentalist – found something offensively theoreticist about the cult of feeling by which he was surrounded. Only a man who has drawn his ideas from books, he thought, 'comes into the world with a heart melting at every fictitious distress'.[36] As an Irish émigré himself, Goldsmith habitually sees sentimentalism as a kind of 'colonial' oppressiveness: there is something covertly domineering about whimsical largesse, which is a crafty way of putting others in one's debt. As he perceives, it is really a devious form of egoism, in which what you appear to bestow on another is secretly conferred on yourself. Prodigality, pressed to an extreme, treats others simply as convenient objects, as *Timon of Athens* illustrates. It plunders others of their emotional booty to feed its own voracious appetite. As a stout Tory, Goldsmith regarded superfluity as a question of foreign imports which debilitated the native economy. Similarly, England should not ruin its emotional economy by importing sentimental goods from the likes of the French. Tory though he was, however, his theory of the historical origins of surplus has remarkable affinities to historical materialism.[37]

In an essay entitled 'Justice and Generosity', Goldsmith insists that true generosity is not a matter of capricious good feeling, but a duty which carries with it all the severity of a law. It is a rule imposed upon us by reason, 'which should be the sovereign law of a rational being'.[38] The Kantian language is revealing. Goldsmith wants to dismantle the opposition between love and law by converting the former into an obligation; and in this he is true to the New Testament, for which love is a command rather than an option. Love for the Judaeo-Christian tradition has precious little to do with fellow-feeling. If you rely on your affections you are likely to

---

[36]   Friedman, *Collected Works of Oliver Goldsmith*, vol. 1, p. 408.

[37]   Goldsmith argues in *The Citizen of the World* that for science to flourish, a country must first become populous, developing its productive forces by what Marx will later term the division of labour. 'The inhabitant', he writes, 'must go through the different stages of hunter, shepherd, and husbandman, then when property becomes valuable, and consequently gives cause for injustice; then when laws are appointed to repress injury, and secure possession, when men by the sanction of these laws, become possessed of superfluity, when luxury is thus introduced and demands its continual supply, then it is that the sciences becomes necessary and useful; the state then cannot subsist without them . . .' (Friedman, *Collected Works of Oliver Goldsmith*, vol. 2, p. 338).

[38]   Ibid., p. 406.

end up acting compassionately only in the case of those you happen to care for anyway, or only when you feel like it. It is in this sense, as we shall see, that Judaeo-Christian ethics, for which the exemplary love-object is a stranger or an enemy, are not of an imaginary kind. The New Testament's deep-seated antagonism to the family belongs with its anti-imaginary bias. This is no doubt one reason for the extraordinary success of Dan Brown's *The Da Vinci Code*, an execrably written potboiler in which Jesus marries Mary Magdalene and fathers a child. The New Testament's intensely relaxed view of sexuality, in contrast to the views of most of its pious adherents down the ages, is evidently scandalous to a postmodern age obsessed by the erotic. A steamy sexual narrative must accordingly be read into the text, if it is to retain the mildest degree of contemporary interest.

The benevolentist hopes to stop having to feel the discomfort of pity by coming to the aid of the victim who occasions it; the sentimentalist is rather less eager to see off his agreeably sadomasochistic sensations by binding the other's wounds. Shaftesbury notes that excessive pity may actually prevent us from helping another.[39] It is possible, he thinks, to be overfond, too zealously affectionate, a notion that Richard Steele would no doubt have found churlish. The Scottish philosopher David Fordyce writes of the sentimentalist as finding 'a sort of pleasing anguish' in human misery, one which culminates in 'self-approving joy'.[40] Rather as desire for psychoanalytic theory wishes simply to carry on desiring, so what the sentimentalist feels most keenly is the need to feel. Some philanthropists of the day considered that poverty, wretchedness, class distinction and the like were heaven-sent opportunities for the exercise of charity. Pity and commiseration are always *post hoc* responses, indicative of the fact that the catastrophe has already happened. This, no doubt, is the political force of William Blake's savagely *faux*-sentimentalist line 'Weeping tear on infant's tear' in his *Songs of Experience*. The world is given, and our freedom lies solely in a passive response to its immutable forms. In the case of the moral-sense philosophers, for whom sympathy is involuntary, even our response to human misery is not free.

By and large, benevolence is a matter of laughter, while sentimentalism is a question of weeping. Sentimentalism is really a sympathy with one's own act of sympathising, a self-devouring affair in which the world is

[39] Shaftesbury, *An Inquiry Concerning Virtue or Merit*, in Selby-Bigge, *British Moralists*, p. 11.
[40] See Markman Ellis, *The Politics of Sensibility*, p. 6.

reduced to so much raw material for one's lust for sensation, or to so many occasions for exhibiting one's moral munificence. You can thus exchange the objects of your affections from moment to moment, with scant regard for their use-value. It is the mode of feeling appropriate to those who are not much practised in emotion in everyday life, and who can thus manage only a theatrical, over-the-top version of it on the rare occasions when they are called upon to display it. This is no doubt one reason why US politicians sob so helplessly in public. The sentimentalist flaunts his dainty feelings like so many commodities, since like his annuity or landed estate they are part of what secures his *entrée* to polite society. 'The intensity of a special experience of feeling', John Mullan remarks astutely, 'was a substitute (in the eighteenth century) for common and prevailing sympathies.'[41]

Rather as the child in the mirror phase is cajoled by an idealised reflection of itself, so the sentimentalist misrecognises an exalted image of himself in the act of coming to another's help. The other is simply a mirror for his own self-delight. The Yorick of Sterne's *A Sentimental Journey*, to adopt Byron's phrase about Keats, is forever frigging his imagination, dreaming up scenes of distress in order to relish the orgasmic pleasures of pity. Whereas benevolentists see only the object of their compassion, sentimentalists act with one coy eye on the admiring response of others. They are men of substantial emotional property, investing their fine feelings with a stockbroker's hope of a lucrative return.[42] In this sense, they resemble those modern-day narcissists, mostly to be found in the United States, who treat their own bodies with all the wary vigilance of one who carries around with her some indescribably precious, sickening, fragile antique. One is reminded of Dickens's hypocritical Mr Pecksniff, who warms his hands at the fire as benevolently as if they were someone else's. Narcissism, like the imaginary, involves treating myself as an other, as well as treating another as myself.

---

[41]   Mullan, *Sentiment and Sociability*, p. 146.
[42]   Sterne's *A Sentimental Journey* consciously uses balance-of-payments imagery about emotions.

2

Francis Hutcheson and
David Hume

In most standard accounts of eighteenth-century philosophy, Francis Hutcheson figures as no more than a footnote to the mighty David Hume.[1] Yet this extraordinary Ulsterman, the father of Scottish philosophy, taught Hume much of what he knew, as well as deeply influencing the pre-critical writings of Immanuel Kant. His economic doctrine was inherited by his pupil Adam Smith, thus helping to lay the foundations of the modern world. As a full-blooded Harringtonian republican who took a radical Whig line on the right of the oppressed to overthrow an unjust sovereignty, he was a seminal influence on Thomas Jefferson, and thus became a leading intellectual actor in the American Revolution. His *Short Introduction to Moral Philosophy* was regularly imported into America on the eve of the revolution, and an American edition of the text was published in 1788.

Hutcheson's ideas were re-imported to his native Ireland in the insurrectionary doctrines of the United Irishmen. Edmund Burke may also have absorbed some of his writings, which makes him a remote precursor of Romantic nationalism. Yet he was also one of the great luminaries of the Ulster Enlightenment, the richest radical culture which Ireland has ever witnessed, with its heady blend of Lockeian rationalism, classical republicanism, radical Presbyterianism and political libertarianism. As a dogged antagonist of Thomas Hobbes, Hutcheson argued that the state of nature was one of liberty rather than anarchy, and preached the natural equality of human beings. He was a civic humanist of a traditional stamp, convinced that the public good is the highest moral end; yet one of his most innovative achievements was to translate the language of classical republicanism, with its talk

---

[1] The philosopher David Wiggins argues in an account of Hume's ethics that what Hume *could* have said is that '*x* is good/right/beautiful if and only if *x* is such as to make a certain sentiment of approbation *appropriate*' (*Needs, Values, Truth*, Oxford, 1987, p. 187). What Wiggins *could* have said is that this is more or less what Francis Hutcheson *does* say.

of duty, public spirit and political responsibility, into the very different discourse of eighteenth-century ethics and psychology. He championed the rights of women, children, servants, slaves and animals, spoke up for marriage as an equal partnership, and observed that 'the powers vested in husbands by the civil laws of many nations are monstrous'.[2] The moral sense, he stresses in his *System of Moral Philosophy*, is a democratic faculty, common to adults and children, the unlettered and the refined. There is a community of moral sensibility which cuts across social distinctions. He also revealed a remarkably enlightened attitude to non-Western cultures, searching as he did 'for traces of affection, decency and moral sense among natives . . . previously identified as savages'.[3] Despite all this, the three-hundredth anniversary of his birth some years ago passed almost unmarked.

Hutcheson was born in County Down in 1694, the grandson of a Scot. A liberal or New Light Presbyterian, he was educated in Belfast and Glasgow and taught for a while in a Dissenting academy in Dublin, where he became one of the clutch of progressive intellectuals gathered around the Irish Whig peer, merchant and diplomat Robert Molesworth, a protégé of John Locke. Molesworth's religious liberalism had brought him to the attention of the Earl of Shaftesbury, whose moral and aesthetic writings were to mould Hutcheson's own inquiries. Hutcheson finally returned to Glasgow to take up the Chair of Moral Philosophy. He was also a minister of religion for a brief spell in County Armagh, though his strait-laced Presbyterian congregation found his theology rather too liberal for their taste. One such disgruntled parishioner, cheated of his weekly dose of hell-fire and smarting under the deprivation, complained that Hutcheson was a 'silly loon' who had 'babbled' to them for an hour about a good and benevolent God, without a word about the old 'comfortable' doctrines of election, reprobation, original sin and death.[4] The loon in question was twice prosecuted while teaching in his Dublin academy, where he worked alongside the son

---

[2]   Francis Hutcheson, *A System of Moral Philosophy* (London, 1755), Book 3, p. 165. For studies of Hutcheson's writings, see William T. Blackstone, *Francis Hutcheson and Contemporary Ethical Theory* (Athens, GA, 1965); Henning Jensen, *Motivation and the Moral Sense in Francis Hutcheson's Ethical Theory* (The Hague, 1971); W. K. Frankena, 'Hutcheson's Moral Sense Theory', *Journal of the History of Ideas*, vol. 16, no. 3, June, 1955; Peter Kivy, *The Seventh Sense: A Study of Francis Hutcheson's Aesthetics* (New York, 1976); W. R. Scott, *Francis Hutcheson* (Cambridge, 1900); V. M. Hope, *Virtue by Consensus* (Oxford, 1989); and Alasdair MacIntyre, *Whose Justice? Which Rationality?* (London, 1988), Ch. XIV.
[3]   Daniel Carey, 'Travel Literature and the Problem of Human Nature in Locke, Shaftesbury and Hutcheson', unpublished D.Phil. thesis, Oxford University, 1994, p. 200.
[4]   Scott, *Francis Hutcheson*, pp. 20–1.

of William Drennan, one of the founders of the United Irishmen. He was also tried for heresy while teaching in Glasgow.

It was from Shaftesbury, who broke with the rationalism of much seventeenth-century moral thought, that Hutcheson inherited the idea of a moral sense – though what comes through as an emphasis in the former becomes a full-blown philosophical case in the latter. It was also Shaftesbury who had rescued the notion of pleasure for sociability rather than self-interest. Nothing is more delightful to us, he argues, than the condition of the mind 'under a lively affection of love, gratitude, bounty, generosity, pity, succour, or whatever else is of a social or friendly sort'.[5] Shaftesbury's case represents a last-ditch aristocratic resistance to the ethics of bourgeois self-love, as well as a neo-Platonic critique of empiricism. Even a debauch, he claims with a faint touch of desperation, bears some reference to fellowship. Being a debauchee is thus preferable to being a sot, since the former at least drinks himself insensible in company.

Virtue for Shaftesbury is a dialogical affair, a matter of the mutual reflection of actions. We enjoy goodness by 'receiving it, as it were by reflection, or by way of participation in the good of others'.[6] Mimesis is a reciprocal or dialectical matter: our own bountiful acts are the cause of approbation in others, whose esteem for them then deepens our own delight. In fact, our conduct is almost always directed to the other, which is how it accrues its reality: ' 'Tis to this soothing hope and expectation of friendship that almost all our actions have some reference.'[7] The most precious kind of friendship, however, is not that of the other but the Other. 'What trust can there be to a mere casual inclination or capricious liking?', he inquires. 'Who can depend on such a friendship as is founded on no moral rule, but fantastically assign'd to some single person, or small part of mankind, exclusive of Society and the *Whole*?'[8] A sentimental ethics is more than a matter of fleeting fancy or private caprice. In the end, the recognition we seek is not from any single individual, but from the Other or social order as a whole.

The whole of Hutcheson's writing is a broadside against philosophical egoism. Hobbes, he protests in his *Reflections upon Laughter*, 'has overlooked everything which is generous or kind in mankind; and represents

5   L. A. Selby-Bigge (ed.), *British Moralists*, vol. 1 (New York, 1965), p. 35.
6   Ibid., pp. 38–9.
7   Ibid., p. 40.
8   Ibid., pp. 41–2.

men in that light in which a thorow [*sic*] knave or coward beholds them, suspecting all friendship, love, or social affections, of hypocrisy, or selfish design or fear'.[9] The work itself, with its Bakhtinian title, is meant to counter Hobbes's own view of laughter as a sign of superiority. Treatises on laughter have not been the most prolific of genres among Ulster Presbyterians. It is equally hard to imagine Descartes or Frege producing such a study. Virtue for Hutcheson is not a question of calculating one's own advantage, since it is not a question of calculation at all. Instead, there is a special faculty within us – the moral sense – which spontaneously approves selfless actions and condemns callous ones, without the slightest reference to our own interest or advantage. There is, he remarks, 'some instinct, antecedent to all reason from interest, which influences us to the love of others'.[10] The moral sense – that swift, keen, selfless pleasure we reap from the sight of a virtuous act – thus operates as a kind of Heideggerian pre-understanding. It is what we find to be already in place as soon as we come to reason – that which as moral agents we can never get back behind, since it defines what counts for us as a moral response in the first place. There have been some recent attempts to revive the idea, placing it on an apparently more scientific basis.[11]

'By the very power of nature', Hutcheson argues, 'previous to any reasoning or meditation, we rejoice in the prosperity of others, and sorrow with them in their fortunes . . . without any consideration of our own interest'.[12] Dr Primrose, the hero of Goldsmith's *The Vicar of Wakefield*, is just such an appreciative connoisseur of the free-handed gestures of others. Or again:

> As soon as any action is represented to us as flowing from love, humanity, gratitude, compassion, a study of the good of others, and a delight in their happiness, although it were in the most distant part of the world, or in some past age, we feel joy within us, admire the lovely action, and praise its author. And on the contrary, every action as flowing from hatred, delight in the misery of others, or ingratitude, raises abhorrence and aversion.[13]

---

[9]   Francis Hutcheson, *Reflections on Laughter, and Remarks upon the Fable of the Bees* (Glasgow, 1750), p. 6. The book contains one or two excellent jokes.

[10]   Francis Hutcheson, *An Inquiry Concerning Moral Good and Evil*, in L. A. Selby-Bigge (ed.), *British Moralists*, vol. 1, p. 94.

[11]   See for example Marc D. Hauser, *Moral Minds: How Nature Designed Our Universal Sense of Right and Wrong* (New York, 2007).

[12]   Francis Hutcheson, *A Short Introduction to Moral Philosophy* (Glasgow, 1747), p. 14.

[13]   Ibid., p. 75.

There is a kind of mirroring effect in such ethics, as our own sense of dis-interested pain or pleasure reflects that of the agent we are observing. Dis-interestedness in another gives rise to a doubling of it in ourselves, raising it, so to speak, to the second power. Our own glow of satisfaction in regis-tering another's act of kindliness is a symptom of the very benignity it observes. There is a kind of natural mimicry or magnetism between selves, one which is as pre-rational as the imaginary realm itself. Without such a response, an act for Hutcheson does not qualify as moral at all. It is what we feel about a piece of conduct which helps to determine whether it is virtuous or not, rather as an observer may help to constitute certain events in the world of quantum physics. Perhaps, like a tree falling soundlessly in a deserted forest, an unobserved act would not count as virtuous. What makes an action of moral relevance, rather than just a piece of physical behaviour, is its relation to the passions and affections. As with some other eighteenth-century moralists, this is a spectatorial ethics as well as a specu-lar one: Hutcheson thinks of virtue and vice in terms of our responses to others' behaviour, rather than in the first place in terms of one's own. The moral question for him is less 'What should I do?' than 'How do I feel about what you do?'

Men and women naturally desire happiness; and since in Hutcheson's view the pleasures of public virtue represent the greatest happiness of which we are capable, there can be no Kantian-style distinction between personal desire and social obligation. Instead, the moral sense yokes these two spheres together, since it is just those forms of conduct which are socially fruitful which occasion our most intense personal delight. Yet it is not in the name of selfish enjoyment that we act: 'Our sense of pleasure', Hutcheson writes, 'is antecedent to advantage or interest, and is the foun-dation of it.'[14] The concept of pleasure is thus appropriated from the ego-istic hedonists: the good is not simply what gratifies me, even though a sense of gratification is intrinsic to it.

Hutcheson, then, is the finest kind of moralist, one who understands like Aristotle or Aquinas that ethical discourse is an inquiry into how to live most enjoyably and abundantly, realising those desires which are most authentically our own. One of his key differences with Aristotle is his belief that virtue is a disposition of the heart, rather than a disposition to action; yet what Jacques Lacan remarks of Aristotelian pleasure – that it is 'an activity that is compared to the bloom given off by youthful activity – it is,

---

[14] Selby-Bigge, *British Moralists*, vol. 1, p. 70.

if you like, a radiance'[15] – might well be claimed of Hutcheson too. Virtue for this liberal-minded Presbyterian is a matter of gusto, geniality and robust well-being, so that its nearest analogy would be the experience of a supremely successful dinner party. One savours the delectable good-heartedness of another as one might smack one's lips over a succulent dish of prawns. As with Sterne, moral excellence is a kind of comedy, a festive spirit which inoculates you against a surly Puritanism. Comedy is both a foretaste of a more convivial world to come, and a kind of therapy for attaining it. Some eighteenth-century thinkers seem to hold cheerfulness in at least as high regard as charity, and certainly discern an affinity between the two. Laughter for Hutcheson, as for Mikhail Bakhtin, is a mode of human solidarity, as we 'delight to raise mirth in others . . . while we enjoy pleasant conversation, enliven'd by moderate laughter'.[16] It is a model of virtue not least because it occurs for its own sake. Conversational sallies are a case of the contagiousness of virtue, and high-spirited sociality is a pleasure in its own right; whereas the cynical Mandeville holds that people love company for their own self-promotion and selfish amusement.

This, perhaps, is what Hutcheson finds so offensive about Hobbes's theory of laughter – not only that it is unpleasantly sadistic, as we jeer at those less fortunate than ourselves, but that it is in the service of power rather than an end in itself. 'It is a great pity', he writes sardonically in his riposte to Hobbes, 'that we had not an infirmary or lazar-house to retire to in the cloudy weather, to get an afternoon of laughter at these inferior objects . . .'.[17] Given their arguments, he inquires, why don't the Hobbesians collect inferior creatures like owls, snails and oysters 'to be merry upon'? Hutcheson, one might claim, responds to Hobbes as a modern-day humanist might feel about Freud's joke book. In his republican fashion, he also sees laughter as a form of debunkery, a deflation of false grandeur or carnivalesque lurching from high to low. For him, as for a venerable lineage of Irish writers from Swift to Beckett, the comic is above all the bathetic. But a shared jest or sudden shaft of wit is also a sign of the imaginary – of that dimension of human life in which communion with others is instant and intuitive, with none of the laborious conceptual unpacking which is the burden of reason. Humour is an earthly echo of the kingdom of God.

[15]　Jacques Lacan, *The Ethics of Psychoanalysis* (London, 1999), p. 27.

[16]　Francis Hutcheson, *Inquiry Concerning the Original of our Ideas of Beauty and Virtue* (London, 1726), p. 257.

[17]　Hutcheson, *Reflections on Laughter*, p. 12.

The benevolentist is a kind of spiritual *bon viveur*, so that charity and clubbability become hard to distinguish. There is a blithe Hellenism about this ethics, one which is both restrictive and seductive. It is easy to share another's sentiments when you both frequent the same coffee house. Yet Hutcheson is far more than a complacent clubman. To those who accuse sentimentalist ethics of being no more than a kind of moral whimsy, he insists that what makes for a virtuous character is not 'some few accidental motions of compassion' but 'a fix't humanity, or desire for the public good of all'.[18] If the mysterious moral sense lies close to the aesthetic faculty, it is not because virtue is a matter of taste; it is rather that, like art, it is precious in itself rather than a question of sanctions, benefits, obligations, self-advantage or divine ukase. In fact, the comparison can be pressed further – for virtue and art both involve a faculty which lies beyond the purely rational, and both are matters of pleasurable self-fulfilment. The two activities both deal in sensation and perception (the original meaning of the word 'aesthetic'); and both invoke the disinterested or empathetic imagination.

'Men', Hutcheson writes, 'approve deeply that beneficence which they deem gratuitous and disinterested'.[19] If you are really out for enjoyment, he suggests, forget about your own gratification and melt into imaginative unity with the affective life of others. The result will be a more intense delight than you would otherwise have savoured, as long as it is understood that sympathising with others purely for the sake of reaping the bliss it affords us is counter-productive. It would be like drinking whisky simply to get drunk, which is likely in the long run to diminish your pleasure in the stuff. Virtue, in a word, is profitless, self-fulfilling, autotelic, beyond reason and the sworn enemy of self-interest; and as such it stands as a critique of a social order for which the *utile* trumps the *dulce*, reason is a calculative affair, pleasure is almost certainly sinful, self-interest reigns supreme, and next to nothing is done for its own sake. Such a society has failed to appreciate that, as Oscar Wilde might have remarked, uselessness is next to godliness. One should add, however, that if virtue is indeed its own reward then this is a mightily convenient as well as morally creditable doctrine, since it is likely to reap precious other recompense in the kind of world we have created. It is the rogues who end up as the cabinet ministers. The righteous receiving their just deserts and the wicked their comeuppance

---

[18]   Selby-Bigge, *British Moralists*, vol. 1, p. 146.
[19]   Hutcheson, *Inquiry Concerning the Original of our Ideas of Beauty and Virtue*, p. 253.

is now a spectacle increasingly confined to the novel. And even the novel tends to be suitably ironic about it. It is also true that the theory that virtue should be profitable struck a certain kind of genteel eighteenth-century mind as incorrigibly vulgar.

Disinterestedness, that bogeyman of the contemporary cultural left, is in Hutcheson's hands a form of resistance to the marketplace. Possessive individualism can never account for 'the principal actions of human life such as the offices of friendship, gratitude, natural affections, generosity, public spirit, compassion'.[20] In a joint venture among merchants, he points out, there is a conjunction of interests but no necessary affection; one merchant is concerned for the others' conduct only because his own interests are at stake. With parents and children, by contrast, there is affection but no conjunction of interests, since parents do not attend to their children's thirst in order to assuage their own. Disinterestedness is not some bogus impartiality, but a question of projecting oneself by the power of the sympathetic imagination into the needs and interests of others. As both an ethical and epistemic affair,[21] it means an indifference to one's own concerns, not to those of others. As with the omniscient narrator of literary fiction, it involves a delightful decentring of ourselves into the apparently sealed subjective spheres of those around us. It is thus, in the Lacanian sense, an imaginary faculty. Morality, like artistic mimesis, involves a ghosting or enacting of the internal states of others. As a selfless desire for their flourishing, it also signifies a kind of love. And to approve of a disinterested agent is to love those who love. 'The word (*sic*) MORAL GOODNESS', Hutcheson writes in his *Inquiry*, 'denotes our idea of some quality apprehended in actions, which procures approbation, and love toward the actor, from those who receive no advantage by the action'.[22] The first phrase of this sentence is intended as a riposte to subjectivism: Hutcheson is not claiming in emotivist fashion that nothing is good or bad but feeling makes it so.

It is the kindly innocence of Hutcheson's moral vision which we recall, yet his view of humanity was by no means entirely Panglossian. He spoke, as a good Presbyterian should, of a 'depraved and corrupt' humankind for whom 'sensuality and mean selfish pursuits are the most universal';[23] yet there is enough in his writings to suggest that he regarded human nature

---

[20]   Bernard Peach (ed.), *Illustrations of the Moral Sense* (Cambridge, MA, 1971), p. 106.

[21]   See Charles L Griswold, *Adam Smith and the Virtues of Enlightenment* (Cambridge, 1999), p. 78.

[22]   Selby-Bigge, *British Moralists*, vol. 1, p. 69.

[23]   Hutcheson, *A Short Introduction to Moral Philosophy*, pp. 34–5.

as essentially benign. It was a bold act for a Presbyterian to place the name of a notorious deist and cosmic optimist like Shaftesbury on the title page of one of his books. 'Our minds', he writes, show a strong bias 'toward a universal goodness, tenderness, humanity, generosity, and contempt of private goods . . .'[24] In his *Essay on the Nature and Conduct of the Passions and Affections*, vice would seem simply immoderacy: 'every passion in its moderate degree is innocent, many are directly amiable, and morally good'.[25] Or if not immoderacy, then nothing more heinous than a surplus of self-love: 'Let the obstacles from self-love be only remov'd', he insists, 'and Nature itself will incline us to benevolence'.[26] This is perilously Pelagian stuff for a Presbyterian, even one on the liberal wing of the church. Hutcheson's moral sense is among other things a secularised version of the Evangelical appeal to inner feeling, but the differences are more obvious than the affinities.[27] With mildly ludicrous naivety, he believes that children do not torture animals out of malice, merely out of an ignorance of their pain and a curiosity to watch the contortions of their bodies. He is the kind of tender-minded liberal who would turn today's tabloids apoplectic. The popularity of gladiatorial combat in ancient Rome he ascribes not only to the crowd's admiration for courage and heroism, but to the opportunity for compassion such spectacles afford. His mentor Shaftesbury, a touch more realistically, allows that there are those who take a 'savage pleasure' in blood, calamity and distress; but even he cannot accept that any human being could wholly lack sympathy for his own kind.

In his pained acknowledgment of such 'savage pleasure', a phrase which one might take as his own version of Slavoj Žižek's translation of Lacan's *jouissance* as 'obscene enjoyment', Shaftesbury touches for a disconcerting moment on what we might call the Real – on the desire, as he writes, 'to feed, as it were, on death, and be entertained with dying agonys [*sic*]'.[28] It is one of the limits of an imaginary ethics that the masochism of *Thanatos* or the death drive, along with the notion of a purely unmotivated malevolence, is well-nigh inconceivable, except in that gentrified version of these things we know as tragedy. The Sades and Iagos of this world are strangers to the imaginary sphere. Such morbid pleasures, Shaftesbury is eager to

---

24 Hutcheson, *Inquiry Concerning the Original of our Ideas of Beauty and Virtue*, p. 275.
25 Francis Hutcheson, *An Essay on the Nature and Conduct of the Passions and Affections* (Glasgow, 1769), p. 79.
26 Selby-Bigge, *British Moralists*, vol. 1, p. 155.
27 See MacIntyre, *Whose Justice? Which Rationality?*, p. 278.
28 Selby-Bigge, *British Moralists*, vol. 1, p. 165.

point out, have no place where 'civility and affable manners' reign; and those who indulge in them are miserable in the highest degree. Hutcheson, too, holds that human nature is scarcely capable of 'malicious disinterested hatred', and cannot imagine that anyone could relish the wretchedness of others with no profit to themselves. Friedrich Nietzsche is not quite such a sentimentalist: 'To witness suffering', he writes in *The Genealogy of Morals*, 'is pleasant, to inflict it even more so . . . Even in punishment there is something so very *festive!*'.[29]

Hutcheson's disbelief in motiveless malignancy is echoed by David Hume, who maintains that 'absolute, unprovoked, disinterested malice has never, perhaps, a place in any human breast'.[30] That 'perhaps' is an interesting wobble. The same view is taken by Joseph Butler, who preaches in his *Sermons* that nobody does mischief to another purely for its own sake. Butler does, however, issue a timely reminder to the Hutchesonians of this world that disinterestedness is by no means always commendable. 'The utmost possible depravity which we can in imagination conceive', he writes, 'is that of disinterested cruelty'.[31] Yet Butler is right to recognise that evil is in its own way as disinterested as virtue.[32] The truly vicious are as much enemies of utility as the angels. It is no accident that the devil himself is a fallen angel. The Nazis did not reckon the cost to their war effort of the concentration camps. But an imaginary ethics must approach the Real with a certain caution. It threatens to shatter the symmetries of a realm in which one subject's anguish or jubilation, as in a play of mirror upon mirror, obediently reflects another's. To reap pleasure from another's torment is the reverse of the ethical imaginary.

The sanguine view of human nature of much 'moral sense' philosophy reflects an early middle-class optimism, which was later, as we shall see, to sour into a far less bright-eyed vision. Yet if Hutcheson needs to build the moral sense into our very constitution, it is partly because this is the only way in which virtue might withstand the onslaughts of a rapacious society. As with Henry Fielding, who held much the same theory of virtue as Hutcheson, the moral domain cannot be abandoned to anything as fragile and precarious as culture. An aversion to vice and an inclination to virtue, Hutcheson asserts, are established deep in our natures, 'such that no education, false principles, or depraved habits can entirely root this out'.[33]

[29]   Friedrich Nietzsche, *The Genealogy of Morals* (New York, 1954), p. 31.
[30]   David Hume, *An Enquiry Concerning the Principles of Morals* (Oxford, 1998), p. 43.
[31]   Joseph Butler, *Sermons*, in Selby-Bigge, *British Moralists*, vol. 1, p. 194.
[32]   See Terry Eagleton, *Sweet Violence: The Idea of the Tragic* (Oxford, 2003), Ch. 9.
[33]   Hutcheson, *A Short Introduction to Moral Philosophy*, p. 46.

Fielding's Tom Jones is carefully given just the same upbringing as the odious Blifil to make this anti-culturalist point – though in Fielding's case this is also a Tory smack at the utopian progressivists who champion nurture over nature.

If this is in its way a materialist ethics, it is because moral responses, as we have seen already, are anchored in the body – a body which will force its instinctive aversions and approbations upon our social conduct, and which can therefore act as a utopian judgement on it. 'The body . . . is wiser (than the mind) in its own plain way', comments Burke, who was an aesthetician in the original sense of a phenomenologist, one concerned with mapping the sensory life of the body.[34] Before we have even begun to reason, there is already that faculty within us which makes us feel the sufferings of others as keenly as a wound, and spurs us to luxuriate in someone else's joy without the faintest hint of *Schadenfreude*. Yet to embed the moral sense in our species being, to use Marx's term, is to fortify it only at the cost of diminishing it. If our feelings of aversion and approval really are as involuntary as the reflex by which we snatch our finger from a flame, then they are hardly a question of personal merit. They are, to be sure, responses to the voluntary acts of others; but there is a sense in which 'moral sense' philosophy renders our compassion less commendable in the very process of making it more natural. It would seem that we can no more help commiserating with the afflicted than we can fail to remark an elephant in our field of vision.

One point of this doctrine is to make fellow-feeling rather more plausible and pervasive than it might be if it involved the will; but if this is so, why are there so many villains around? It is what one might call the Fielding paradox: goodness is natural, but for so natural a commodity it is in curiously short supply. And if goodness is both a natural instinct and relatively hard to come by, then the virtuous, as in Fielding's fiction, will find themselves a minority under constant siege without being furnished with the cunning and vigilance they need to cope with the onslaughts of the vicious.[35] This is why they are comic as well as admirable. Yet they are also dangerous, since they are likely to be a cause of vice in others. If they do look sharp for themselves, however, it is hard to reconcile this canniness with their innocence. The more you are forced to defend your good nature, the less of it you have. Yet John Milton would have insisted that an untested innocence is not really virtuous at all.

---

[34]   Edmund Burke, *A Vindication of Natural Society* (London, 1903), p. 26.
[35]   See Terry Eagleton, *The English Novel: An Introduction* (Oxford, 2005), Ch. 3.

The point can be put in more political terms. When the middle classes are feeling reasonably content with themselves, virtue seems as plentifully available as claret; yet they have only to glance round at the monstrously egoistic civilisation they have created to recognise that this cannot really be the case. Ideologically speaking, love and affection must be fundamental; empirically speaking, they are clearly nothing of the kind. To say that the moral sense is both as self-evident as a smack in the face and as hard to pinpoint as the odour of coffee is another way of registering this contradiction. As a good empiricist, it would seem that Hutcheson ought to agree with Adam Smith that the senses 'never did, and never can, carry us beyond our own person, and it is by the imagination alone that we can form any conception of what are (the other's) sensations'.[36] What closes us off from the consciousness of others is our bodies; so that it is only by virtue of the imaginary – by a miming or reduplicating within ourselves of what we surmise others to be feeling – that human sympathy is fostered. Hutcheson's moral sense is not far from Smith's imagination; yet by arguing for a moral *sense*, to be added to the familiar five, he remains within the ambit of empiricism while turning the theory against itself. To speak of a moral sense is to supplement the five senses of empiricism with a ghostly shadow of themselves, which can then lend moral notions the apodictic certainty of touch or taste. A discourse of the senses rides to the rescue of moral value. But it is also because of the unreliability of the senses that one must fall back on this sort of sensory intuition. In an empiricist world, language, perception and rationality can always go awry, as *Tristram Shandy* hilariously demonstrates; and it is partly to compensate for this deficiency that the moral sense is imported. Just at the point where the human subject is in danger of being locked solipsistically within its own sensations, Hutcheson will discover precisely in these senses the very key to sociability, finding in a special faculty the passage which opens us up to the world of others.

Yet it is only because the sentimentalists have a defective idea of the body that they need to supplement it with these imaginary appendages. The eighteenth century was familiar with a way of reaching beyond the senses – indeed, of shattering them to pieces – known as the sublime; but it was not so well-versed in that reaching beyond the body which is the body itself. It did not tend to conceive of the body as a self-transcending project; instead, it regarded it as an object along the lines of sofas and

---

[36]   Adam Smith, *The Theory of Moral Sentiments*, in Selby-Bigge, *British Moralists*, vol. 1, p. 258.

escritoires, differing from them only in secreting an animating principle known as the soul. But the silence of a human body is not the silence of a writing desk. Even when you do no more than look at me, you are not present to me in the same way that the teapot is. The empiricists fail to grasp the point that soul talk is simply a reifying way of trying to define what is distinctive about animate, self-organising bodies such as wasps or senior civil servants, as opposed to pieces of furniture. The effect of this failure may be one reason why, when we hear the word 'body', we tend to think of a corpse. The senses for Locke and Hume are passive receptacles, not ways of being in and acting upon the world. The body for Smith and his ilk is in the first place a material object rather than a form of praxis, a centre from which a world is organised. They do not see it as that 'outside' of ourselves which we can never quite get a fix on, yet in whose expressive activity we are present rather as the meaning is present in a word.

Given this version of the body, other selves can be granted reality only on analogy with oneself. This, more or less, is the case argued by Edmund Husserl, for whom other selves are essentially concealed from me, yet who manifest in their conduct what I can identify as part of my own inward experience. The other is never fully present to me, but is knowable as a reflection of myself. In his *Cartesian Meditations*, Husserl sees each ego in imaginary terms as a monad reflecting and containing all other egos, with the consequent possibility of harmony, empathy, communion and reciprocity between them. As Maurice Merleau-Ponty portrays the case: 'I see a certain use made by other men of the implements which surround me, (and) I interpret their behaviour by analogy with my own, and through my inner experience, which teaches me the significance and intention of perceived gestures'.[37] To this extent, I grasp other selves on the model of the 'I' – in terms, that is, of exactly what distinguishes me from them – and can thus never succeed in giving myself the slip. On this theory, Merleau-Ponty argues, 'the body of another, like my own, is not inhabited, but is an object standing before the consciousness which thinks about or constitutes it . . . There are two modes of being, and two only: being in itself, which is that of objects arrayed in space, and being for itself, which is that of consciousness'.[38]

Yet it is precisely the body – that amphibious phenomenon which is neither simply 'in itself' nor transparently 'for itself' – which dismantles this Sartrean polarity. The body of another is present to me, pre-reflectively,

---

[37] Maurice Merleau-Ponty, *The Phenomenology of Perception* (London, 1962), p. 348.
[38] Ibid., p. 349.

as an 'in itself' or object on my horizon which is intrinsically expressive of a 'for itself' – an intentional project which constitutes a movement towards the world rather than rests as an inert piece of matter within its bounds. I perceive your intentionality in your bodily movements, not as some invisible process lurking behind them. Equally, my own body 'makes me other without alienation', as Emmanuel Levinas puts it.[39] There is, Merleau-Ponty considers, an 'internal relation' between my body and yours, just as there is between my body and my 'consciousness'. Or, one might add, between a series of sounds and a set of meanings. Because my own body can never be present to me simply in the way that my wrist watch is, neither can yours be. In viewing things from my own unique perspective, part of what I perceive is that the same objects are present to your body from a different perspective – that our projects are mutually interwoven, and that this shared space forms the common terrain on which what we call objectivity can be established. The fact that I can never fully 'objectify' your body, given the ambiguous entity that it is, is bound up with the fact that your body is the source of a world which intersects with my own.

The form of that common ground is language. Too much discussion of 'other selves' has assumed that such entities do not speak or listen. In the experience of discourse, Merleau-Ponty argues, 'there is constituted between the other person and myself a common ground; my thought and his are interwoven into a single fabric . . . and they are inserted into a shared operation of which neither of us is the creator. We have here a dual being, where the other is for me no longer a mere bit of behaviour in my transcendental field, nor I in his; we are collaborators for each other in consummate reciprocity'.[40] That final phrase smacks a little of what we have been loosely calling the imaginary. Indeed, Merleau-Ponty goes on to speak of the quasi-magical process in which each partner in such a dialogue anticipates the other's thoughts, or 'lends' the other her own. 'The perception of other people and the intersubjective world', he writes, 'are problematical only for adults. The child lives in a world which he unhesitatingly believes to be accessible to all around him'.[41] The small child, so he argues, has no knowledge of a reality articulated into points of view, or an awareness that the subject must be restricted to a single one of them. As in the imaginary, the child can occupy all positions simultane-

[39]   Emmanuel Levinas, *Otherwise than Being* (The Hague, 1991), p. 77.
[40]   Ibid., p. 354.
[41]   Ibid., p. 355.

ously, freed from the constrictions of the symbolic order. And just as the Lacanian infant makes no distinction between inner and outer, so that feelings themselves take on a tangible, quasi-concrete existence, so human gazes for Merleau-Ponty's small child 'have an almost material existence, so much so that the child wonders how these gazes avoid being broken as they meet'.[42]

Hutcheson is closer to a phenomenological sense of the body than Adam Smith. He is much taken with the idea of a speaking or signifying human countenance to which we respond pre-reflectively, without having to 'infer' or 'deduce' the kind of emotion which animates it. It is the inherent expressiveness of the flesh – the fact that the human body is itself a sign – which promises a solution of sorts to Smith's rather desperate dualism. If Smith assumes that we can have access to others only by some special faculty, it is because he imagines that others' states of mind are naturally inaccessible to us, concealed as they are by the fleshly encasements of their bodies. My rage is hidden away inside me, and what bits and pieces you can actually glimpse of it – the fact that I have just set fire to my own hair in frustrated fury, for example – are simply the outward signs of an inherently private condition. What you see is not what you get. My words, likewise, are simply the outward signs of meanings which, because they are images in my head, are just as essentially private as my emotions. It is therefore hard, perhaps impossible, to know whether we are ever really feeling or meaning the same thing, a chronic state of cross-purposes which *Tristram Shandy* milks for its rich comic value. Adam Smith confesses in his *Theory of Moral Sentiments* that we can never know exactly what another is feeling, as though we would necessarily feel for them more profoundly if only we could. If others are inaccessible to us, then it is hard to find a conscious basis for social harmony; so the temptation is strong to posit some elusive faculty – empathy, intuition, imagination, moral sense – which will do in its stead.

The case that we have to imagine what others are feeling is, needless to say, no more plausible than the idea that we need to imagine what they are meaning. Elaine Scarry is surely mistaken to claim that imagination is central to human sympathy.[43] Understanding is not a matter of projecting ourselves empathetically into the spiritual innards of others, the contents of which are assumed to be inherently private. Others, to be sure, can hide

---

[42]   Ibid., p. 355.
[43]   Elaine Scarry, 'The Difficulty of Imagining Other People', in Martha Nussbaum, *For Love of Country: Debating the Limits of Patriotism* (Boston, 1996).

their feelings from us or deliberately garble their meanings; but for them
to do so requires some fairly sophisticated techniques, and such techniques
are always picked up in the public arena. We have access to ourselves in
much the way that we have access to others. Sheer introspection will not
serve here. It cannot be by simple introspection that I become aware that
I am envious or afraid.

'The possibility of another person's being self-evident', Merleau-Ponty
writes, 'is owed to the fact that I am not transparent for myself, and that
my subjectivity draws its body in its wake . . . The other person is never
quite a personal being, if I myself am totally one, and if I grasp myself as
apodeictically self-evident'.[44] Others are bound to appear opaque if we are
deluded enough to believe that we are wholly transparent to ourselves.

David Hume did not share Francis Hutcheson's trust in the innate generosity of the human heart. He was, after all, a Tory sceptic rather than a
republican Whig, one who regarded self-love as the central driving force
in human affairs. If justice is necessary at all, he thought, it was as a counterweight to our inordinate pursuit of gain and self-interest. Yet he also
held that though most people love themselves more than they love others,
their humane affections taken together outweigh their selfishness. In his
blend of genteel affability and worldly hard-headedness, Hume is urbane
in both senses of the term. He is neither as crabbed as Hobbes nor as sanguine as Shaftesbury. He writes at a point when a newly emergent, pre-
industrial middle class is still sufficiently impressed by the glamour of
aristocracy to seek a reconciliation between commerce and civility. It is a
harmony which will become harder to achieve in later, industrial-capitalist
times.

'Custom and relation', Hume writes in his *Treatise of Human Nature*,
'make us enter deeply into the sentiments of others; and whatever fortune
we suppose to attend them, is render'd present to us by the imagination,
and operates as if originally our own'.[45] It is hard to tell whether this is
selfless or self-interested, at least where the more agreeable passions are
concerned. In general, however, Hume is a stout believer in the reality of
benevolence, claiming in Hutchesonian vein that this 'appetite, which

---

[44]   Ibid., p. 352.
[45]   David Hume, *A Treatise of Human Nature* (London, 1969), p. 457. Subsequent page
references to this work will be given parenthetically after quotations.

attends love, is a desire for the happiness of the person belov'd, and an aversion to his misery' (430). He allows generous space for human sympathies, which like Hutcheson he casts in what we might broadly call an imaginary mould. It is true that another's pleasure causes us pain as we contrast it with our own wretchedness, just as someone else's misery leads us to rejoice by throwing our own well-being into relief. Yet in both cases, egoism is mingled with authentic fellow-feeling. If there is something of the rivalry of the imaginary here, there is also something of its empathy. As rivalry and mimesis are indissociable in the imaginary, so are they in Hume's moral thought: we feel pleasure at the pleasure of another, but at the same time know some competitive disquiet.

The liveliest of all objects, Hume remarks in his *A Treatise of Human Nature*, is 'a rational and thinking being like ourselves, who communicates to us all the actions of his mind; makes us privy to his inmost sentiments and affections; and lets us see, in the very instant of their production, all the emotions, which are caus'd by any object' (402). What counts in this communion of spirit is the immediacy with which the inside becomes the outside – the way another's sentiments are not buried inside his body but legibly inscribed on its surface. 'Whatever is related to us', Hume writes, 'is conceiv'd in a lively manner by the easy transition from ourselves to the related object' (402), and this transition happens by resemblance and correspondence: 'men of gay tempers naturally love the gay; as the serious bear an affection to the serious . . . men naturally, without reflection, approve of that character which is most like their own' (403, 654). Or as Freud might put it less agreeably, our object choices tend to be narcissistic. The gentleman's club, like the domain of the imaginary, is a world of magical contagions and resemblances. It is largely bereft of difference. If lightness of spirit and ease of manner count among the social values worth cultivating, then it is easier to practise them with kindred spirits and alter egos than it is with strangers, in whose presence we may have to work at being affable. The company of strangers, Hume considers, is agreeable to us only for brief periods of time.

'In order to produce a perfect relation betwixt two objects', Hume writes, '''tis requisite, not only that the imagination be convey'd from one to the other by resemblance, contiguity or causation, but also that it returns back from the second to the first with the same ease and facility' (405). We are still in the sphere of the imaginary, where, as with the small child and his reflection, there is a closed circuit or two-way traffic between the objects in question. 'The double motion is a kind of a double tie', Hume adds, 'and binds the objects together in the closest and most intimate manner' (405). In what one might call the social imaginary, I find myself reflected in you at the same time as I see you mirrored in myself; and this mutuality may deepen to the point where the two subjects finally cease to be distinguishable, and what is reflected is nothing more than the two-way act of mirroring itself. For Hume as for Lacan, this fascination with doubles, resemblances and comparisons remains an element of all our more mature experience. We are so little governed by reason, Hume considers, that we 'always judge more of objects by comparison than from their intrinsic worth and value' (420).

This symmetry is disrupted, however, the moment a third term trespasses on the scene: 'For supposing', Hume continues, 'the second object, beside its reciprocal relation to the first, to have also a strong relation to a third object; in that case the thought, passing from the first object to the second, returns not back with the same facility, tho' the relation continues the same; but is readily carry'd on to the third object . . . This new relation, therefore, weakens the tie between the first and second objects' (405). It is not hard to interpret Hume's point in Oedipal terms, as the dyadic or imaginary *rapport* between mother and child is triangulated by the entry of the father upon the scene. What Hume is sketching here, in a word, is the movement from the imaginary to the symbolic. Three subjects are a good deal more than two.

Lest this be thought a perverse over-reading of a passage which really concerns the association of ideas, it is worth noting that the *Treatise* instantly goes on to speak of mothers, fathers and children:

> The second marriage of a mother breaks not the relation of child and parent; and that relation suffices to convey my imagination from myself to her with the greatest ease and facility. But after the imagination is arriv'd at this point of view, it finds its object to be surrounded with so many other relations, which challenge its regard, that it knows not which to prefer, and is at a loss what new object to pitch upon. The ties of interest and duty bind her to another family, and prevent that return of the fancy from her to myself, which is necessary to support the union. The thought has no longer the vibration, requisite to set it perfectly at ease, and indulge its inclination to change. It goes with facility, but returns with difficulty; and by that interruption finds the relation much weaken'd from what it wou'd be were the passage open and easy on both sides (405).

Hume, who places himself here in the position of the child, is pitched into a troubled relation with the mother by virtue of her relationship with the (second) father. The bond between child and mother is now asymmetrical, robust on one side only; and this is because the mother is perceived as caught up in the symbolic order, affiliated through her second husband to a set of kinsfolk far removed from the child himself. The point of the second-husband example is to write large the way in which family relations, for all their 'imaginary' closure, shade off into affiliations with strangers, or those who are not blood relations – affiliations which then react back on the primary bond between mother and child with a fatally loosening effect. It is this which seems to cause the child to grope and hesitate (he is 'at a loss what new object to pitch upon'), in what one might well read as a kind of Oedipal crisis. Claiming that it is now more difficult to trace the chain of associations back from mother to child than vice versa looks like a camouflaged way of complaining that she no longer loves him as much as he loves her. Oedipality is displaced into epistemology.

For Althusser, the imaginary sphere of ideology cannot sensibly be spoken of as either true or false. It is simply not an arena to which such judgements are relevant, since ideology is not primarily a question of propositions.[46] How one 'lives' one's envy, contumacy, submissiveness and so on is not a question of cognitive accuracy. There is a chasm for Althusser between theory (the sphere of truth) and ideology (the zone of experience); and those fortunate few who are privy to the scientific knowledge of society, since they remain at the same time common-or-garden citizens, live in divided and distinguished worlds, those of the symbolic and the imaginary. In a parallel way, there is an epistemological break or 'total opposition' for Hume between reason and passion. The passions 'can never be an object of our reason', and ''tis impossible that they can be pronounced either true or false'(510). It would be nonsense for Hume to speak of a reasonable or unreasonable passion, as it would not be for Aquinas or Spinoza. There is no point in asking whether we ought to be feeling the way we do. A passion for Hume is an 'original existence', rather as it is for Friedrich Nietzsche. ('Granted nothing is "given" as real other than the world of our passions and drives . . .', Nietzsche hypothesises in *Beyond Good and Evil*). In Hume's view, emotions are not only beyond reason, but refuse to be confined to any one individual. 'The passions', Hume comments, 'are so contagious, that they pass with the greatest facility from one person to another, and produce correspondent movements in all human breasts' (655). There is something magical about this affective contagion, as though your fright or jealousy might literally infect my own innards, pass like some emotional

[46] See on this subject Terry Eagleton, *Ideology: An Introduction* (London, 1991), p. 142f.

virus from your body to mine. A small child might easily imagine as much.

Sympathy for Hume is not only the chief source of virtue, but a kind of magnetic principle animating the whole of animal creation, a semi-tangible force or mercurial medium for the 'easy communication of sentiments from one thinking being to another' (412). It is the great switchboard of human psyches, and lies at the heart of every passion we can conceive of. It is also what makes life worth living: 'Let all the powers and elements of nature conspire to serve and obey one man: Let the sun rise and set at his command: The sea and rivers roll as he pleases, and the earth furnish spontaneously whatever may be useful or agreeable to him: He will still be miserable, till you give him some one person with whom he may share his happiness, and whose esteem and friendship he may enjoy'(412). In this imaginary fantasy, the world is spontaneously given over to us, as miraculously pliable to our command as the infant's mirror-reflection is to his motions. Yet it is with a co-subject that this communion must be finally consummated.

'The minds of men', Hume comments, 'are mirrors to one another'(414). In a dialectical motion, 'the pleasure, which a rich man receives from his possessions, being thrown upon the beholder, causes a pleasure and esteem; which sentiments again, being perceiv'd and sympathised with, encrease the pleasure of the possessor; and being once more reflected, become a new foundation for pleasure and esteem in the beholder'. The imaginary, with its flashing of mirror upon mirror, is a sort of mutual admiration society, in which in a kind of *mise-en-abyme* each act of reflection gives birth to another, and that to another. This revolving circuit of affections displays the cyclical time of the imaginary rather than the linear evolution of the symbolic order. It is the kind of deepening mutuality one finds in the imaginary dimension of Wordsworth's relation to Nature, in which, in a potentially infinite feedback, the poet's love for the natural objects around him is enriched by the sensations he has invested in them in the past, and those sensations are in turn transformed by the long perspective of the present.

'Ideas', Hume writes, 'never admit of a total union, but are endowed with a kind of impenetrability, by which they exclude each other . . . On the other hand, impressions and passions are susceptible of an entire union; and like colours, may be blended so perfectly together, that each of them may lose itself, and contribute only to vary that uniform impression, which arises from the whole'(414–5). 'Some of the most curious phaenomena (*sic*) of the human mind', he adds, are derived from this condition. In the pre-reflective order of the imaginary, what counts is less 'ideas' than the tangible immediacy of sensations; so that here there can be a mutual coalescence of elements unknown to the symbolic order of thought or language, which functions by reflection, distinction and exclusion. Even causality for Hume constitutes a kind of imaginary sphere, in which the imagination coaxes us into positing a mutuality or internal bond between cause and effect, bonds which reason itself knows to be groundless. Much the same is true of private property, the very lynchpin of the bourgeois symbolic order: here, too, custom and imagination persuade us to perceive a necessary bond between property and its possessor for which, once again, there is no rational foundation. Rather as for Spinoza and Althusser there is an epistemological break between how we 'live' the world and how philosophy knows the world to be, so Hume is aware that from the viewpoint of reason, many of our spontaneous assumptions are simply baseless. It is a truth he finds distinctly unnerving, given his clubman's belief that philosophy should be continuous with common forms rather than prove subversive of them. Moral inquiry should be the pursuit of civilised minds, not of hairy prophets howling in the wilderness.

We have seen that for Lacan, the imaginary does not perish with our infancy. For Hume, it survives into adult life in the sense that 'no object is presented to the senses, nor image form'd in the fancy, but what is accompany'd with some emotion or movement of spirit proportion'd to it'(421). In the pre-reflective world of the imaginary, it is as though we relate to things directly by our sensations – as though our very flesh and feelings become a subtle medium of communication, without the blundering interposition of language or reflection. Without such sentiments and impressions, Hume claims, 'every thing in nature is perfectly indifferent to us'(547–8) – an indifference which, as we shall see later, is an aspect of the symbolic order. Custom, however, causes us to forget that our thought is steeped in these emotional tints and feeling-tones, rather as for Heidegger reason comes to be oblivious of the *Stimmung* or mood that always suffuses it. This legacy of the imaginary fades from view as rationality hits its stride, bleaching our thought into an apparently neutral faculty. Yet for Hume such affections and sensations persist even so, as a kind of phenomenological current running beneath all of our more dispassionate reflections.

It is not hard to imagine the duped infant before the looking glass regarding his image as an object in the world autonomous of himself, unaware that it is simply a projection of his own body. This, in Hume's view, is how most unreflective citizens approach the question of morality, convinced as they are that moral values are part of the furniture of the material world. They do not recognise that such values are in fact imaginary, in the sense of subject-created. Moral good and evil 'belong only to the action of the mind'(516); like the child and his mirror-image, they concern relations between subjects and objects, not (as the realist or rationalist considers) relations between objects themselves. Only in the symbolic order do things come to be considered as given entities caught up in objective interrelations, as the constitutive subject is 'decentred' or banished from the scene. Moral terminology, Hume insists, is not applicable to 'external objects, when placed in opposition to other external objects . . . morality consists not in any relations, that are objects of science'(516, 520). For this emotivist ethics, murder is wicked not in itself, but because of the disapproving sentiment it evokes in us: ''tis the object of feeling, not of reason', and moral value 'lies in yourself, not in the object'(520). 'Morality, therefore, is more properly felt than judg'd of' (522). Francis Hutcheson's moral sense, however quirkily intuitive, is at least a response to the inherent qualities of actions; but Hume presses this case one stage further, claiming as Hutcheson would not that 'to have the sense of virtue, is nothing but to *feel* a satisfaction of a particular kind from the contemplation of a character'(523). As Shaftesbury puts the point: 'If there be no *real* amiableness or deformity in moral acts, there is at least *an imaginary one* of full force'.[47]

We feel human sympathy, Hume argues, on 'the contemplation of a character' who merits it; but how literally is this phrase to be taken? Must those with whom we sympathise be physically before our eyes? This is a more momentous question than it may seem, since it broaches the issue of whether an imaginary ethics can be a universal one. Francis Hutcheson thought it natural for us to love those closest to us more deeply than those at a distance; but he was also, as we have seen, eager to foster comradeship with cultures alien to our own, and even writes rather quaintly of extending benevolence to rational beings on other planets, if any happen to exist. 'Our good wishes would still attend them', he remarks in the emollient tones of a UN ambassador, 'and we should delight in their happiness'.[48] Hutcheson may be in some sense a philosopher of the imaginary, but there is nothing parochial about his vision. Unlike his compatriot Edmund Burke, he was not a Romantic particularist but an Enlightenment universalist, one whose purview was the well-being of all humanity. Indeed, it

---

[47]   Shaftesbury, *Characteristics*, in Selby-Bigge, *British Moralists*, vol. 1, p. 120 (original emphasis).
[48]   Selby-Bigge, *British Moralists*, vol. 1, p. 97.

was he who coined the Utilitarian slogan 'The greatest happiness for the greatest numbers'.[49] In blending this universalism with a theory of sentiment, his thought represents a fruitful point of convergence between Enlightenment and Romanticism. Hutcheson conceded that distant attachments were weaker than intimate ones; like gravity, the force of benevolence diminishes over long distances, 'and is strongest when bodies come to touch each other'.[50] Even so, he believed that one could speak of 'weaker degrees of love', and of a benevolence 'extended beyond neighbourhoods or acquaintances'.[51]

Unsurprisingly for an eighteenth-century Irish liberal, Hutcheson points to the love of country as exemplary of this extended affection. The nation is not only, in Benedict Anderson's celebrated phrase, an imagined community, but an imaginary one as well, in which, as in some sealed, atemporal space, each loyal citizen finds himself harmoniously reflected in the comradely gaze of his compatriots, while each of them is at the same time uniquely acknowledged by that august transcendental signifier, the Nation itself. This, by and large, is the political dream of Jean-Jacques Rousseau: the nation constitutes an imaginary space in which every citizen, in submitting to laws which he has freely fashioned along with his fellow countrymen, surrenders himself to the collective will of the latter only to receive his selfhood back again, enriched a thousand-fold by its harmony with their own. Each citizen contemplates his own visage in the sovereignty which mediates his compatriots to him. The Irish republican Thomas Kettle speaks of nationalism as the elevation of private sentiment into political principle, and proposes the novel form as an analogue of this public rehabilitation of feeling.[52] Like the time of the imaginary, the narrative of the nation knows no origin or end. Moreover, from the eighteenth century onward, the spiritual principle of the nation comes to fuse itself to the political concept of the state, bringing to birth a quite new configuration of imaginary and symbolic. As an imaginary community, the nation acknowledges no internal differences or divisions, as every member finds herself mirrored in every other; but to come into its own on the global stage, this Platonic entity must stoop to being incarnated in profane history, articulating itself in the symbolic structures of law, ethical ideologies, political institutions and the like. Indeed, if the nation-state has been such a

---

[49] Ibid., 107. The phrase is commonly misquoted.
[50] Ibid., p. 130.
[51] Ibid., pp. 96–7.
[52] Thomas Kettle, *The Day's Burden* (Dublin, 1937), p. 10.

supremely successful invention of modernity, it is not least because it harnesses the most tenaciously 'imaginary' sentiments, in the name of which men and women will readily surrender their lives, to the impersonal symbolic order of law, commerce, justice and citizenship.

All the same, an ethics based on the mutuality of selves and the swift contagions of feeling clearly has a problem with less face-to-face relationships. Nature, Hutcheson comments, has so determined us as to love those closest to hand, and this for him is a providential kind of emotional thrift. It prevents us from squandering our affections on far-flung multitudes whose true interests we are bound to be ignorant of, and who are too remote for us to help. Yet there remains 'a universal determination to benevolence in mankind, even towards the most distant parts of the species'.[53] It is also, he believes, possible to formulate rules and maxims which might help to promote the universal good, a task which was part of his legacy to the Benthamites. Those like Hutcheson who base their ethics largely on feeling are wary of drifting too far into the symbolic, for which morality is a matter of universal laws and absolute obligations. The mere mention of such abstract duties is an affront to the spontaneous impulses of the heart. Yet if you are really to go global, it is hard to see how you can avoid speaking of such precepts, and thus find yourself encroaching upon Kantian or Benthamite terrain. Something more than feeling is needed to frame a universal community of moral subjects. Caught between Shaftesbury and Bentham, Hutcheson wants to cling to the idea of spontaneous good nature, while recognising that the universal ethics he commends must be a rule-governed one.

David Hume is far less persuaded than Hutcheson of the truth of universal benevolence. It is true that in his *Enquiry Concerning the Principles of Morals*, he writes of 'some internal sense or feeling (of good and bad), which nature has made universal in the whole species', and speaks of benevolence as promoting the interests of humanity as a whole.[54] Yet if the institutions of justice are indispensable, it is because human beings are not 'so replete with friendship and generosity, that every man has the utmost tenderness for every man, and feels no more concern for his own interests than for that of his fellows'.[55] Hume's view of justice seems roughly that of Marx: it is a necessary virtue in conditions of limited abundance, where we need to argue the toss over what is due to whom; but it is irrelevant in

---

[53]   Ibid., p. 127.
[54]   Hume, *Enquiry Concerning the Principles of Morals*, pp. 5, 12.
[55]   Ibid., p. 12.

conditions of extreme necessity, where men and women will simply grab what they can get. For Marx, it is equally irrelevant in a society of material superabundance, where there will be no call for justice because no need for a regulated distribution of goods. Hume, needless to say, remains soberly unseduced by such utopianism.

In the *Treatise*, Hume specifically rejects the idea of universal love. 'In general', he writes in Swiftian vein, 'it may be affirm'd that there is no such passion in human minds as the love of mankind, merely as such, independent of personal qualities, of services, or of relation to oneself' (231). It is the limits of human generosity – what he calls 'confin'd benevolence' – which Hume seeks to highlight here. In his opinion, such sympathy seldom stretches beyond one's family and friends. 'We love our country-men, our neighbours, those of the same trade, profession, and even name with ourselves'(401); and we cannot help preferring even the less congenial of our friends to the company of strangers. It is the ethics of the coffee house. Freud was in hearty agreement with this prudential sentiment: for him, there simply wasn't that much libido to go around. Striving to love everyone, he argues in *Civilisation and Its Discontents*, is a species of injustice, since it squanders on the undeserving the affection I should reserve 'for my own people'. Strangers, he goes on, have more claim to our hatred and hostility than our kindliness. For Freud, the neighbour is secretly an enemy, which is true in a different sense for Christianity as well. This is why the test-case of loving one's neighbour is loving one's enemy. Anyone can love a friend. If one's neighbour is a source of trauma, as Freud recognised, it is partly because (as Freud did not quite appreciate) few human activities are more unpleasant, exacting, thankless and ultimately lethal than love. *Civilisation and Its Discontents* preaches an outright conflict between sexuality and society: the ideal number for the former is two, since a third, the austerely non-troilistic Freud proclaims, can only be disruptive or *de trop*; whereas society as a whole involves us with a large number of individuals, thus spreading our affections perilously thin. In characteristically modern fashion, Freud confuses love as *eros* with love as *agape* or charity.

For Hume, such emotional provincialism belongs to our nature. There is a well-patrolled frontier between friends and strangers, one which corresponds to some degree to class divisions (since one's friends are for the most part as genteel as oneself), as well as to the distinction between the imaginary and the symbolic. Society for Hume is composed of ever-expanding concentric circles of what Hutcheson calls 'weak love', and the affective air grows thinner the further we move from our blood relations: 'A man naturally loves his children better than his nephews, his nephews better than his cousins, his cousins better than strangers . . .'(535). As though tracing some finely gradated ascent from the troposphere to the ionosphere, Hume claims that our affections for those closest to us are 'much fainter' than our self-love, while our sympathies for those remote from us are 'much fainter' still. It does not seem to strike him that a man might love a political leader he has never encountered in the flesh far more fervently than he loves his wife.

There are ways of compensating for the parochial bent of our sympathies. We can make moral adjustments, so to speak, for our natural indifference to strangers, just as we can know by taking thought that a distant object is not actually as diminished as it appears. Besides, 'we every day meet with persons, who are in a different situation from ourselves, and who could never converse with us on any reasonable terms, were we to remain constantly in that situation and point of view, which is peculiar to us'(653). By modifying our perspective in this way, we come to form more objective estimates of our fellows than we would if we remained ensconced in our allotted social niche. One might call it the argument from slumming. Yet an empiricism for which reality, roughly speaking, is what can be seized by the senses is likely to have trouble with anonymous social relations, and therefore with politics. 'Pity', writes Slavoj Žižek, 'is the failure of the power of abstraction',[56] and for Hume law and politics are the fruit of a failure of the imagination. Since the interests of those remote from us are hard to keep vividly in mind, they must be delegated to such impersonal mechanisms as the institutions of justice.

Hume believes, to be sure, that all human beings are related to each other by resemblance, so that our common nature provides a counterweight to self-love. We can feel pity for strangers, 'and such as are perfectly indifferent to us', even upon hearing a bare mention of their afflictions. Yet he also considers that compassion 'depends, in a great measure, on the contiguity, and even sight of the object'(418), which is one reason why he turns in the same passage to the subject of tragedy. For the point of tragic art is to offer us palpable representations of pitiable figures whom we do not know, which is why the death of Cordelia can move us as deeply as the death of a friend. Sympathy for Hume depends largely on representation. The only strangers we can relate to are those we hear about.

---

[56] Slavoj Žižek, 'Neighbors and Other Monsters: A Plea for Ethical Violence', in Slavoj Žižek, Eric L. Santer and Kenneth Reinhard, *The Neighbor: Three Inquiries in Political Theology* (Chicago and London, 2005), p. 185.

Ethics and epistemology are bound up in at least this sense, that without the image-making mind our sympathetic passions would remain sluggish and inert.

Hume speaks elsewhere in the *Treatise* of coming to the aid of a perfect stranger who is about to be trampled underfoot by horses; but the point is that the stranger in question is physically present, which in Hume's view is a far keener goad to compassion than some nebulous conception of universal benevolence. There is indeed such global fellow-feeling, he considers, in the sense that in principle anyone whatsoever can move us to compassion; but our sympathies, like the juices of a guard dog, only really flow freely if the other is tangible, represented, borne near to hand either by the imagination or material circumstance. 'There is no human, and indeed no sensible, creature', Hume writes, 'whose happiness or misery does not, in some measure, affect us when brought near to us'(533); but it is the final phrase which distinguishes his case from a love of humankind in general, a doctrine which Hume (despite the cosmopolitanism of his cultural interests) here specifically disowns.

At another place in the *Treatise*, he speaks in similar terms of feeling sympathy for 'any person, who is present to us'(432); while in the *Enquiry* he argues that 'we enter, to be sure, more readily into sentiments, which resemble those we feel every day: But no passion, when well represented, can be entirely indifferent to us . . .'[57] Once again, the emphasis falls upon vivacious representation, as in the theatre. Other people must seize our imaginations if they are to provoke our good will; and the imagination, in Hume's pre-Romantic sense of the term, is considerably more susceptible to the near than the far. There is a moral particularism about such empiricist ethics, one which reflects the emotional parochialism of the Tory clubman. It is as though a certain ethics follows on a certain epistemology: a shyness of conceptual abstraction, an insistence on what can be felt on the pulses, can end up persuading us that strangers are not truly neighbours. Things contiguous to us in space and time, Hume believes, have 'a peculiar force and vivacity' which outdoes every other influence (474). It is surprising, then, that eighteenth-century Britain appears to have cared so passionately about its empire – that so remote a set of nations could have engaged its imaginative sympathies as deeply as they did.

The turn to Romanticism is among other things an attempt to correct this moral myopia. Whereas for the eighteenth century the imagination

---

[57] Hume, *Enquiry Concerning the Principles of Morals*, p. 40.

can mean the faculty which generates graphic images of what lies before our eyes, the task of the Romantic imagination is largely to bring home to us what is temporally or spatially absent, and thus to spin a web of universal sympathies as animated and enduring as local ones. Once the imagination itself becomes a universal faculty, as it does with Romanticism, the empiricist case is no longer so plausible.

There are distinct merits to what I have been calling, somewhat oxymoronically, an imaginary ethics. (Oxymoronically, because the Lacanian imaginary is in fact pre-moral). Such a morality is in some ways a secular version of the harmony, affinity and correspondence which were previously, so to speak, laid up in heaven, in the cosmologies of the medieval schoolmen or the symphonic universe of the neo-Platonists. By Hutcheson's time, such grandiose visions have fallen increasingly into disrepute; yet because a disruptive individualism is now on the rampage, there is a move to reinvent them in suitably sublunary form. Human bonds must be smuggled back into a world almost bereft of them. In a culture of soulless contracts and legalistic obligations, the benevolentists' insistence on love, compassion and generosity has an agreeable warm-heartedness about it. It discredits the case, to be expounded later by Kant, that the only alternative to moral obligation is to act for your own selfish pleasure. Indeed, it retrieves the whole category of pleasure from the hatchet-faced puritans and restores it to its central position in ethical thought. It was the mark of a virtuous person, David Hume considered, to reap enjoyment from being merciful and humane. The benevolent philosophers recognise in their own way that, in Bernard Williams's words, 'the line between self-concern and other-concern in no way corresponds to a line between desire and obligation'.[58]

There is a grace and beauty about this imaginary vision, beside which the symbolic ethics we shall be examining shortly can appear anaemic and unlovely. The moralists we have glanced at are right to see that morality is about human fulfilment, and right too about the values which really count, however deluded they may be about how they are to be grounded. In contrast to Aristotle, whose virtuous human being sounds at times like a magnificently successful media baron, and is certainly a supercilious prig, it does not see men and women as self-sufficient, but as in constant need of tenderness and support. Unlike a venerable Western lineage of moral voluntarism, it also grants due weight to the passive moment of

[58]   Bernard Williams, *Ethics and the Limits of Philosophy* (Cambridge, MA, 1985), p. 50.

morality – to the sense of being moved, constrained, impelled, stirred spontaneously into action. It is true that it sees individuals as too little self-determining, too eager to imitate and conform, too anxiously in thrall to the opinions of their colleagues. This is among other things a reflection of the social context of these theorists, who as members of a fairly homogeneous social class shared the same responses without having to think much about it. They were also much preoccupied with their public reputations, which is one reason why the gaze of the other counts for so much with them.

If the sphere of the imaginary has eventually to be prised open, it is because men and woman achieve their autonomy, meagre as it is, only in the symbolic order – and then only at an enormous price. Even so, the positive aspect of this social conformity is the humane sociability of an imaginary ethics, one which refuses to divorce moral values from the grain and texture of everyday existence. It is this respect for everyday life, one also manifest in realist fiction, which marks such egregiously influential eighteenth-century journals as the *Tatler* and the *Spectator*.

All the same, this ethics appears too cliquish and insulated for comfort. Love and compassion are extended in an abstract sort of way to humanity as a whole, but the true neighbour is the cousin or colleague, not the unknown Samaritan. For such a somatically-based ethics, social existence beyond friends and kinsfolk ceases to be an extension of our bodies, and is therefore in danger of slipping below our moral horizon. The concentric circles of fellow-feeling ripple out in a series of fine gradations from the domestic hearth to the nameless hordes languishing in the outer darkness.

It is true that social manners are designed as a kind of mediation or half-way house between friends and strangers – a way of conducting oneself which is affable without intimacy and courteous without familiarity. Bertolt Brecht believed that some such intermediate zone, between the erotic or domestic on the one hand and the anonymous bureaucratic on the other, would be an essential protocol of a socialist culture. The term 'comrade', so to speak, mediates between 'darling' and 'Madam'. Theodor Adorno writes in *Minima Moralia* of 'tact' as such a mediation in early middle-class society, a faculty which, so he fears, has long since atrophied. 'Free and solitary', he writes, '[the bourgeois subject] answers for himself, while the forms of hierarchical respect and consideration developed by absolutism, divested of their economic basis and their menacing power, are still just sufficiently present to make living together within privileged groups bearable.'[59] Yet an imaginary ethics fears that to enter the sphere of universal laws and duties is to abandon local pieties and affections; and to read Kant's ethical writings is to take the point. On the other hand, this vein of moral thought seems to the devotees of august principles, sovereign laws or the terrors of the Real altogether too cosy and clubbish, as well as too vulgarly captivated by such holiday-camp concepts as happiness. Pity and compassion are simply the lachrymose visage which a two-faced capitalism turns to its victims. And happiness, which in Britain today is the responsibility of a government official, is the wonder drug which will keep them working.

Perhaps, however, the choice between love and law is an illusory one. What the moral sentimentalists fail on the whole to grasp is that the only authentic moral law is a law of love – but not at all the species of love which can be couched in terms of sensibility. The only kind of love which counts is one which is 'lawful' rather than affective. In its ruthlessly inhuman refusal to privilege this individual's needs over that one's, it is more like an edict than an instinct. Such a genre of love has the stony indifference to particular persons of the symbolic order; it is just that this indifference is also in the service of an 'imaginary' attentiveness to the uniquely specific needs of anyone whatsoever. It is not a question of universal benevolence – of 'loving everybody' in some dewy-eyed surge of philanthropy, which would be rather like loving the concept of magenta or the idea of the single transferable vote. Hume is wise to dismiss this fantasy. The notion of universal love should be treated rather like the democratic conception of the People. Taken literally, it is a mythical phenomenon. What it signifies, however, is that anyone at all can be a social agent equal in merit to anyone else.

In this sense, genuine love conforms to the Lacanian logic of the 'not-all'. It is a matter not of 'I must love everyone', a vacuous proposition if ever there was one, but 'There is nobody whom I must not love'. Universal love is a question of global politics, not of fuzzy vibrations of cosmic togetherness. As far as individuals go, it means loving everybody in the sense of loving anybody who happens along. As such, it rejects the distinction between friend and stranger – not because it is calloused to personal affections, but because it does not regard love as being chiefly concerned with such things. One need not feel in the least affectionate in order to be able to love.

---

[59] Theodor Adorno, *Minima Moralia* (London, 1974), p. 36.

In the gospels of Mark and Matthew, 'neighbour' means simply the other person, whether friend, acquaintance, enemy or stranger. This was not, needless to say, a doctrine hatched by Christianity: for the ancient Stoics, all men were citizens of the world, and all fellow humans were neighbours. Luke, loyal to an Old Testament tradition for which 'neighbour' signifies those obscure, socially inferior fellow Jews in particular need of protection, sees the love of one's neighbour as realised most characteristically in a concern for the needy and destitute. The neighbour is the first one you encounter who is in distress. For the Wisdom writers and prophets, similarly, 'neighbour' means above all the poor. The Jews of the Diaspora universalised the term to include all human beings.[60]

Hume and Hutcheson are right that it is natural to love our children more than we love our bank manager; but they are thinking of love in the personal or affective sense, which is not its most fundamental meaning. A good deal of trouble has arisen in the Western philosophical tradition from confounding love in the affective or erotic sense with love as *agape* or universal charity. We have seen that Freud is guilty at times of just such an error. This confusion springs in part from the gradual withering of a sense of the political, which then makes the idea of political love sound embarrassingly self-contradictory. When it comes to a choice between slaying my child and shooting my bank manager, however, only a symbolic rather than an imaginary ethics will serve. Love in the sense of what I feel for my child will not serve as a criterion for deciding on the moral thing to do. In fact, there would be no moral thing to do, since the bank manager's life has just as much claim on me as that of my child. The fact that I detest my bank manager, and have tried to strangle him once or twice myself, makes no difference to this elementary fact. I must treat my bank manager as myself, which is not to say that I break out in hot flushes when I encounter him on the street, or that I feel for him the tender warmth that I do for my daughter, or that I would not hesitate to rob his bank under certain pressing material circumstances, or that I would not be delighted to see him grilling burgers when the banks are taken into common ownership. Kwame Anthony Appiah reminds us that 'to say that we have obligations to strangers isn't to say that they have the same grip on our sympathies as our nearest and dearest'.[61] It is not simply a matter of treating strangers as

---

[60] See Edward Schillebeeckx, *Jesus: An Experiment in Christology* (New York, 1989), p. 250.
[61] Kwame Anthony Appiah, *Cosmopolitanism: Ethics in a World of Strangers* (London, 2006), p. 158.

neighbours but of treating oneself as strange – of recognising at the core of one's being an implacable demand which is ultimately inscrutable, and which is the true ground, beyond the mirror, on which human subjects can effect an encounter. It is this which Hegel knew as *Geist*, psychoanalysis knows as the Real, and the Judaeo-Christian tradition as the love of God. For all the admirable tender-heartedness of an imaginary ethics, it is a horror and a splendour which lies beyond its limited comprehension.

One sign of this myopia is the inability of men like David Hume to see the ascetic virtues as anything but monkish and life-denying, in a misreading of Christianity which is fashionable to this day. The Hume of the *Enquiry* rejects celibacy, self-denial, penance and mortification as so much self-repressive perversity. Such self-punitive practices, he considers, stupefy the understanding, harden the heart and sour the temper. In this respect, the comfortable eighteenth-century clubman is at one with the life-affirming liberals of our own age. There is, to be sure, no reason why an eighteenth-century advocate of Enlightenment should regard such values as anything but barbarous. Hume was not a modern guerrilla fighter, who might appreciate the need to be unencumbered with domestic ties, free of property and inured to personal hardship for the ultimate benefit of others. Nor was he a monk, witnessing to the preciousness of sexuality and the life of material abundance by provisionally renouncing such riches in the name of a future domain of truth and justice. Only here, so the religious celibate considers, will this opulence be available to all. Such celibacy involves sacrifice – which is to say, it regards sexuality and prosperity as values to be cherished.

We would not expect an affable bourgeois like David Hume to defend a conception of selfless sacrifice – one which involves the more austere, traumatic, death-dealing virtues, but which exists in the name of a more copious life all round. He is an avatar of the imaginary, not a champion of the Real. He does not see that we must sometimes do what we ought to do in order to be able to do what we want to do. All this strikes him as morbid and masochistic, as it does the conventional liberal wisdom of our own time. It is true that the good life is all about grace, ease and well-being, as these Enlightenment thinkers grasped in their own way as clearly as Aristotle or Aquinas. What they could not see from their historical vantage-point was that to achieve such a condition requires from time to time the sombre revolutionary virtues of sacrifice and self-discipline. That it does so is a tragic fact, though an ineluctable one. This would not have come as news to John Milton; but the revolution which brought to power those for whom David Hume is so superb a spokesman had now receded over the historical horizon sufficiently for him to forget that the ascetic virtues, though they are indeed unlovely and far from a cameo of the good life, are regrettably essential. They are essential both for the practical attainment of virtue and justice, and (as with the religious celibate) as a way of witnessing to their enduring possibility by a strategic refusal of the consolations of the present. Only those who derive their comfort from the enforced sacrifices of others can afford to overlook this fact.

3

Edmund Burke and Adam Smith

What if local feeling and global principle were not the only options on offer? What if there could be a politics of sympathy? Edmund Burke, one of the eighteenth century's most eloquent spokesmen for the preciousness of local allegiances, tipped his hat to universal precepts, but was scarcely enthused by them. In his view, the political could work by imaginative sympathy as much as the personal; indeed, unless it did so with some urgency, one was likely to have on one's hands more calamities like the loss of America, the insurrection in Ireland, the Jacobin terror in Paris and the depredations of the East India Company. To avert such disasters, there must in Burke's view be 'a community of interests, and a sympathy of feelings and desires between those who act in the name of any description of the people, and the people in whose name they act'.[1]

Power in Burke's view must be rooted in love – a doctrine to which we nowadays give the name of hegemony.[2] 'Power and authority', he declares in *Conciliation with the Colonies*, 'are sometimes bought by kindness; but they can never be begged as alms by an impoverished and defeated violence.'[3] The political order for Burke rests on an imaginary foundation of mutuality and affinity: 'Men', he proclaims in his *First Letter on a Regicide Peace*, 'are not tied to one another by paper and seals. They are led to associate by resemblances, by conformities, by sympathies. Nothing is so strong a tie of amity between nation and nation as correspondence in laws, customs, manners, and habits of life. They have more than the force of treaties in themselves. They are obligations written in the heart.'[4]

---

[1] R. B. McDowell (ed.), *The Writings and Speeches of Edmund Burke* (Oxford, 1991), vol. 9, p. 247.

[2] See Terry Eagleton, *Heathcliff and the Great Hunger* (London, 1995), Ch. 2.

[3] F. W. Rafferty (ed.), *The Works of the Right Honourable Edmund Burke* (London, n.d.), p. 184.

[4] Ibid., p. 247.

For Burke, then, it is not a question of contrasting sturdy domestic affections with anaemic political ones, as it is for Hume. Nor is it a matter of inclining one moment to 'imaginary' mimesis and the next to universal benevolence, as it is for Hutcheson. Burke's desire is rather to refashion political society itself along domestic lines. In the pre-modern Ireland from which he hailed, with its local chieftainships and traditional tribal bonds, the border between the two was never exact. His aim is 'to bring the dispositions that are lovely in private life into the service and conduct of the commonwealth'.[5] He would thus have presumably demurred from Gopal Balakrishnan's claim that both religions and nations 'are premised on conceptions of membership which cancel the raw fatalities of birth, kinship, and race'.[6] As 'that tribunal of conscience which exists independently of edicts and decrees',[7] the family offers a persuasive model of obligations without laws. It is an example of hegemonic rather than coercive power. Burke's compatriot Richard Steele penned a pamphlet entitled *A Nation a Family*, which draws parallels between framing an economic policy for the nation and making provision for one's children.[8] In France, Burke warns, sentimentalism is 'subvert(ing) those principles of domestic truth and fidelity, which form the discipline of social life'.[9] In a curious paradox, an exorbitant cult of emotion is playing havoc not with reason, but with feeling in its truest sense – feeling as those tried, taken-for-granted bonds of loyalty and affection of which the family is the supreme model, and which provide the soundest model of social existence itself. Feeling is a traditional practice rather than a theatrical performance.

All the same, Burke is far from extending such social sympathies to the species as a whole. In this, he resembles the Hume of the *Treatise* more than he does his fellow-Irishman Francis Hutcheson. The boundaries of the imaginary can be stretched to encompass a national culture; but you cannot really exchange identities or sympathetic vibrations with those who belong to a quite different form of life. Strangers, so to speak, begin at Calais – while in Calais and Paris the distinction between aliens and

---

[5] Edmund Burke, 'Thought on the Present Discontents', in Paul Langford (ed.), *The Writings and Speeches of Edmund Burke* (Oxford, 1981), vol. 2, p. 84.

[6] Gopal Balakhrishnan, 'The National Imagination', *New Left Review*, 211 (May/June 1995), p. 56.

[7] Edmund Burke, *A Letter to a Member of the National Assembly* (Oxford and New York, 1990), p. 44.

[8] Richard Steele, *A Nation A Family*, in Rae Blanchard (ed.), *Tracts and Pamphlets by Richard Steele* (Baltimore, MD, 1944).

[9] Ibid., p. 43.

intimates is being denied even as Burke writes, much to his anti-philan-thropic fury. He has a virulent contempt for the brand of Godwinian benevolence which would place love of kinsfolk and love of strangers on an equal footing. (Burke's compatriot Swift, who shared his distaste for universal benignity, has the crazed Gulliver go one step further, spurning his kinsfolk and falling in love with a breed of alien quadrupeds.)

Like Hume, Burke thinks it natural to love those nearest to us, and rejects the doctrine of global sympathy as bogus. There is a direct path from universal philanthropy to revolutionary tyranny. Rousseau, who like Hutcheson regards pity as an instinct prior to all reflection, is the chief target of his withering contempt. A lover of his kind but a hater of his kindred, is how the Irishman famously lampoons the Frenchman. 'Benevo-lence to the whole species', Burke protests, 'and want of feeling for every individual with whom these professors come in contact, form the character of the new philosophy.'[10] Burke is at one with Rousseau that sentiments are a more compelling force than reason. Both men hold that if we were to rely on anything as fragile and cumbersome as rationality to prod us into humane behaviour, the human species would probably have stumbled to a halt long ago. Like Thomas Aquinas, Burke also believes that friendship may serve as a prolegomenon to less personal kinds of relationship. But those who seek to stretch such sentiments beyond their natural limits succeed only in tearing them from their roots in a cherished locale and starving them of nourishment. Feelings are turned into luxury goods to be privately consumed, and so can no longer act as a cohesive social force. Sensibility ceases to be political.

Even so, Burke practised his own brand of universal benevolence. Those who recall his celebrated remark that the first principle of affection is to love the 'little platoon' of our friends and kinsfolk generally suppress the phrase 'first principle'. Burke goes on to claim that such local allegiances form the first link in a chain which culminates in a love of country and mankind. He is not, after all, the short-sighted particularist he might appear. Arraigning Warren Hastings before the House of Commons, he insists that Hastings's shabby conduct in India should be judged by just the same moral standards which hold sway at home. No allowance should be made, as the accused himself sophistically pleaded, for differences of cultural context. Moral criteria for Burke do not bend to shifts of geo-graphical locale. The same yardsticks of justice and liberty must prevail

---

[10]   Ibid., p. 35. The notion that Rousseau preached universal benevolence, however, is argu-ably a misinterpretation of his work.

about the Indian people as among the British. 'There are some fundamental points', he writes in *Remarks on the Policy of the Allies*, 'in which (human) nature never changes – but they are few and obvious, and belong rather to morals than to politics.'[11] Burke did not believe that the bonds of affection could expand much further than one's own little platoon; but the principles by which he condemned colonial pillage in Ireland or India were nonetheless universal ones. An ethic of sympathy could bear you beyond the domestic hearth to political society; but it could not take you all the way to humanity as a whole. For this, you needed a more universally framed morality; and though Burke implicitly adopted just such a code in his championship of raped Indian women, tortured Irish rebels and American insurrectionists, he did so with all the chariness of its philosophical implications of a moralist who held that charity begins at home and rarely travels far from it.

What binds society together in Burke's view is mimesis. 'It is by imitation, far more than by precept', he writes, 'that we learn everything; and what we learn thus, we acquire not only more effectually, but more pleasantly. This forms our manners, our opinions, our lives. It is one of the strongest links of society; it is a species of mutual compliance, which all men yield to each other without constraint to themselves, and which is extremely flattering to all.'[12] Theodor Adorno was later to write of how 'the human is indissolubly linked with imitation: a human being only becomes human at all by imitating other human beings'. A certain enabling inauthenticity lies in his view at the root of identity.[13] Mutual imitation is pleasurable not only because we take an instinctive delight in doublings, but because we assume the colour of others spontaneously, unlaboriously, simply by sharing their form of life, which then lends imitation something of the easy pre-reflectiveness of the imaginary. As Burke himself phrases it, we are dealing here with a sphere of 'mutual compliance', in which each subject seems to sway sympathetically from the inside, so to speak, to the motions of another. Society is a kind of rhyming. 'One easily forgets', writes Bertolt Brecht, 'that human education proceeds along highly theatrical lines. In a quite theatrical manner the child is taught how to behave; logical arguments only come later . . . The human being copies gestures, miming,

---

[11] L. G. Mitchell (ed.), *The Writings and Speeches of Edmund Burke* (Oxford, 1989), vol. 8, p. 498.
[12] Edmund Burke, *A Philosophical Inquiry into the Origin of our Ideas of the Sublime and the Beautiful* (London, 1906), vol. 1, p. 101.
[13] Theodor Adorno, *Minima Moralia* (London, 1974), p. 154.

tones of voice.'[14] Precepts belong to the symbolic world of duty, reflection and universal values; but picking up civilised manners is a question of modelling ourselves on the conduct of others, who do much the same themselves. All this, then, is what Burke calls 'beauty', by which he means a sphere of mutual sympathies: 'when men and women . . . give us a sense of joy and pleasure in beholding them', he writes, '(and there are many that do so), they inspire us with sentiments of tenderness and affection towards their persons; we like to have them near us, and we enter willingly into a kind of relation with them . . .'.[15] Beauty is Burke's name for the imaginary affinities which make for social cohesion.

Where, though, does this wilderness of mirrors end? Social existence for Burke would seem to be a potentially endless chain of representations of representations, one without ground or origin. There is an unsettlingly self-enclosed quality about this specular process, which if left unchecked would spell the death of history, difference, conflict and competition. 'Although imitation is one of the great instruments used by Providence in bringing our nature towards its perfection', Burke writes, 'yet if men gave themselves up to imitation entirely, and each followed the other, and so on in an eternal circle, it is easy to see that there could never be any improvement amongst them.'[16] The very conditions which guarantee social harmony also threaten to paralyse human enterprise. Or – to couch the issue in classical Marxist terms – the base of economic dynamism, and the superstructure of social forms, are perilously askew to one another. Sunk in this narcissistic enclosure, sympathies become cloying and incestuous, and men of affairs grow effete and enervated. What is needed to disrupt this inertia is a touch of danger, rivalry and strenuous endeavour, a whiff of death and infinity – all of which, as we shall see later, bears a relation to what the Lacanians call the Real. It is just this stimulus which Burke discovers in the gentrified terrors of the sublime. The vulgar Marxist, drearily obsessed with social class, might also find in this an effort to reconcile a patrician culture of grace and civility with the more anarchic, free-booting energies of an emergent middle class.

---

[14]   Quoted in John Willett (ed.), *Brecht on Theatre: The Development of an Aesthetic* (London, 1964), p. 106.

[15]   Ibid., p. 95.

[16]   Ibid., p.102. I have discussed these ideas in *The Ideology of the Aesthetic* (Oxford, 1990), Ch. 2, a discussion which some of the material here rehearses in rather different form.

We have seen that the imaginary sphere is a matter of imitation and rivalry together; but in Burke's political aesthetics, these registers are split off respectively into the beautiful and the sublime. The sublime, with its virile values of enterprise, ambition, rivalry and daring, breaks violently into the enclosure of the social imaginary, but does so only to regenerate it. It is a kind of phallic 'swelling', in Burke's own term – a negation of settled order without which any such order would wither and die. In turning us from the cloying mimesis of beauty to the more capacious sphere of energy and ambition, it orients us to the symbolic order; yet there is also, as we have suggested, a smack of the Real about the traumatic, death-dealing abyss of the sublime, which like the Real rebuffs all attempts to be caught in the net of language. Like the Real, the sublime lies beyond representation. It is beauty's point of inner fracture, the anti-social condition of all sociality.

Sublimity, then, is the lawless masculine force which goads us beyond the complacent mutual mirrorings of civil society, and in doing so pitches us into a region of mortal danger, where we dice with death in the hope of regeneration. It is not hard to discern in this transition from beauty to sublimity a passage from the imaginary to the symbolic, just as it can clearly enough be read as one from feminine to masculine. But it is also possible to trace here a shift from one classical tragic emotion, pity, to another, fear. Pity is what binds us to others, whereas fear is inspired by the danger of the dissolution of the social bond.[17] If pity is imaginary, fear is Real. Yet it is an emotion equally characteristic of the symbolic order, as clashing autonomous subjects threaten to annihilate one another; and there is also a fear proper to the imaginary, which concerns the more paranoid or competitive aspects of that condition. The terror of tragedy springs among other things from imagining that we ourselves might be afflicted like the tragic hero, and thus has a touch of Hobbesian self-interest about it. The line between the two emotions, as Aristotle acknowledges in the *Rhetoric*, is notably thin – as thin, one might claim, as that between sympathy and rivalry in the imaginary. Pity, Aristotle comments, turns into fear when its object, the tragic protagonist, is so intimate with us that his suffering seems to be our own. It is another case of that confusion between self and other which we have seen as a mark of the imaginary.

---

[17] See Philippe Lacoue-Labarthe, 'On the Sublime', in *Postmodernism: ICA Documents 4* (London, 1986), p. 9.

Like Burke, Adam Smith frames parts of his moral theory in gendered terms. Rather as Burke holds that women are beautiful whereas men are sublime, Smith proposes that women are humane while men are generous-spirited. Humanity in his view is a matter of kindliness and delicate fellow-feeling, one which (the theme is now more than familiar) permits us to enter into the sentiments of others as though they were our own. Women display this empathetic virtue, but they are not remarkable for their generosity: 'That women rarely make considerable donations, is an observation of the civil law.'[18] This is because generosity involves the virile virtues of self-sacrifice, self-command and self-denial, abstemious notions which would scarcely find their way into the frivolous little heads of the ladies. The soldier who throws away his own life to defend his officer's may serve as an instance of such magnanimity. Great-hearted, public-spirited actions are the monopoly of men. Like Burke, Smith sees the need to temper the sweetness of sympathy with a dash of testosterone. The feminine values are all very well in their place, but one needs to know where to draw the line between soft-heartedness and emasculation.

Adam Smith was not exactly a 'moral sense' philosopher.[19] He dismissed the Hutchesonian notion of a special moral faculty, but agreed with Shaftesbury, Hutcheson and Hume that we take a selfless interest in the fortunes of others and find their happiness essential to our own. Such pleasure, as with the pain of feeling another's grief, is so immediate that there is scarcely time enough for self-interest to get off the ground. In the presence of a fellow being, whether friend or stranger, 'we enter as it were into his body, and become in some measure the same person with him' (258). 'In some measure', as we shall see in a moment, positively bristles with problems. Once again, morality is really mimesis: confronted with a suffering friend or stranger, we 'chang(e) places in fancy with the sufferer' (258), in a kind of moral equivalent of transitivism.

Conversely, 'nothing pleases us more than to observe in other men a fellow-feeling with all the emotions of our own breast' (264). Genuine moral sentiment requires something like the imaginative resources of the novelist: we must seek to re-create in our own minds the condition of the one we encounter, right down to the most trifling details. The sympathetic

---

[18]   Adam Smith, *The Theory of Moral Sentiments*, in L. A. Selby-Bigge (ed.), *British Moralists*, vol. 1 (New York, 1965), pp. 315–16. Further references to this work will be provided in parentheses in the text.

[19]   For a recent study of his moral thought, see Jerry Evensky, *Adam Smith's Moral Philosophy* (Cambridge, 2005), especially Ch. 2.

character, Smith writes, 'must adopt the whole case of his companion with all its minutest incidents; and strive to render as perfect as possible that imaginary change of situation upon which his sympathy is founded' (275). For this moralist-cum-political economist, emotional exchange is as much a source of flourishing as the exchange of commodities. It is true that Smith the political economist famously maintains that it is self-love, not benevolence, which impels the butcher, brewer and baker to provide our dinner; yet the market in his view is a civilising influence. There is no essential conflict at this early stage of bourgeois life between commerce and compassion, as there is for, say, Dickens and Ruskin.

Even so, this 'imaginary change of situation' is ultimately something of a mug's game. Given that we are excluded from access to others' emotional innards by the stout walls of their bodies, a sympathetic re-creation of their state of mind can only be approximate. In the common run of things, we can have no very graphic conception of what other people are feeling, and can form no idea of how they are affected by their situations, which is why imaginary transposition is essential. However generous-hearted it may sound, then, such empathy is really a way of compensating for our natural estrangement from one another. Such identification, Smith holds, can never be complete, though there is enough sympathy abroad to ensure social harmony: 'Though there will never be unisons, there may be concords, and this is all that is wanted or required' (276).

Even so, Smith and his colleagues still need to prevent the pleasure we feel at the sight of another's felicity from appearing too shamelessly self-interested. It is equally vital to face down the egoistic case that we bandage the spiritual wounds of others simply to avert the discomfort we may feel at the sight of them. Or, indeed, because our imagination paints a lurid portrait of the pain we ourselves would suffer in the same situation. For these pre-Romantic thinkers, the imagination can be harnessed to the cause of self-interest as easily as it can serve the ideal of altruism. Self and other, egoism and altruism, my pleasure *and* pain in your pleasure, your pleasure and pain in my pain: all this partakes of the intimacies and alienations of the imaginary.

Smith argues the by now familiar case that compassion must spring from imagining one's way into someone else's situation. He also considers, as we have just noted, that this process can never be perfect. The project of a total transposition of selves founders on the rock of self-love: I am bound to feel your rapture or remorse less ardently than you do, simply because I am me. If we feel the emotions of a friend less intensely than she does, then there is clearly an even greater problem in empathising with strangers. If a man were set to lose his little finger tomorrow, Smith observes, he will not sleep tonight; but he will snore contentedly after news of an earthquake which has swallowed up the whole of China and destroyed countless millions of his fellow humans. Or at least he will snore, Smith insists, provided he never claps eyes on the event. As with Hume, it is lively images of distant phenomena which make the difference. Morality is ultimately dependent on the senses. It is really a question of representation.

Smith seeks to sidestep the charge that pleasure in another's pleasure is covertly self-interested by coming up with a rather curious theory of empathy. When we put ourselves imaginatively in another's position, what we feel is not, so to speak, *in propria persona*, but a question of feeling *as* the other. This emotional virtuality or imaginary change of situation 'is not supposed to happen to me in my own person and character, but in that of the person with whom I sympathise' (323). Rousseau writes similarly in *Émile* of 'transporting ourselves outside ourselves, and identifying with the suffering animal, leaving our being, so to speak, in order to take his . . .'.[20] For the Swiss philosopher as for the British sentimentalists, morality is grounded in a pre-social, pre-rational disposition to pity and compassion. It is a sentient rather than a cerebral affair. It is not, Smith goes on to argue, that I consider what I would feel in your place, a case which courts the risk of egoism, but that I am now so wholly ensconced in your place, 'having 'change(d) persons and characters' with you, that my experience is wholly a question of your experience. 'My grief, therefore, is entirely upon your account, and not in the least upon my own. It is not, therefore, in the least selfish' (323). Perhaps this is what is meant by empathy rather than sympathy, though the distinction is far from clear.

It is hard to see how this account can be coherent, however, since if I transpose myself entirely into you, there is no 'I' left over to feel whatever you are feeling. My grief cannot be entirely on your account, since I have no grief of my own left over. Swapping identities with you will not yield me access to your experience. If I am wholly you, it makes no sense to claim that I am feeling what you are feeling. We might postulate some condition in which two egos are linked together, so that each has exactly the other's sensations. One thinks of Wittgenstein's sardonic fantasy of wiring two people up to a machine so that they can both experience the same pain. (But in what sense would it be the same?) Smith's move, however, is more ambitious than this, since if one completely assumes

---

[20]   Jean-Jacques Rousseau, *Émile, ou de l'éducation* (Paris, 1961), vol. 4, p. 261.

another's personality, one can no longer speak of two distinct subjects, however closely allied. Pressed to an extreme, the whole concept of fellow-feeling collapses. It is a conundrum staged in Keats's 'Ode to a Nightingale', in which the distinction between two living beings is negated by an empathy so intense that it prefigures the seductive indifference of death.

The logical strain of Smith's case is betrayed by the essay's manifold inconsistencies. 'Though sympathy is very properly said to arise from an imaginary change of situations with the person principally concerned', he writes, 'yet this imaginary change is not supposed to happen to me in my own person and character, but in that of the person with whom I sympathise' (323). But how can one become another person without suffering the dramatic change that is self-liquidation? Undeterred by this difficulty, Smith goes on to insist that 'in order to enter into your grief I do not consider what I, a person of such a character and profession, should suffer, if I had a son, and if that son was unfortunately to die: but I consider what I should suffer if I were really you . . .' (323). So there is still a separate 'I' to be spoken of here; yet it no sooner surfaces than it submerges again: 'I not only change circumstances with you, but I change persons and characters' (323). Contemplating what I should suffer if I were you is scarcely the same as inhabiting your personality. And what has become of the caveat that any perfect identification with another is beyond our power?

There is a paradoxical quality to the idea of sympathy, since it involves entering into another's experience while retaining enough rational capacity of one's own to assess what one finds there. The cognitive distance which such judgements require cuts against the grain of an imaginary ethics. Sympathy cannot be entirely spontaneous, since it needs to weigh the merits of its object. It would seem to involve splitting the self in two, as one part enters into the other while the other part remains behind to evaluate the results. This, however, is far too half-hearted a proposal for Smith, who as we have seen envisages some more radical form of self-relinquishment. He recognises that reason and judgement play a vital part in the whole emotional transaction, since without them we would be unable to identify the other in the first place, let alone give a name to what he or she was feeling. But this seems incompatible with his dream of total empathy, in which our own mental facilities would appear to be simply erased. Hume, who thought the whole idea of imaginative self-projection into someone else was idle, is far more astute than Smith on the point. Even if such a self-projection were possible, he remarks, 'no celerity of imagination could immediately transport us back, into ourselves, and make us love and esteem the person, as different from us'.[21]

Reason must also be at work from the outset in the sense that true sympathy requires some knowledge of context. When we say 'I know how you're feeling', we usually mean rather more than 'I recognise this emotion of yours as festering resentment.' We also imply that we know something of the circumstances which occasioned the feeling in the first place, and perhaps suggest that it is justified. Confronted with a fellow creature in distress, Smith comments, we 'enter into his abhorrence and aversion for whatever has given occasion to it' (288). Later, however, he insists that we have no fellow-feeling with a murderer on the scaffold. It is not true, as the sentimentalists tend to assume, that the bliss of others always yields us satisfaction, or that we invariably find their affliction a source of distress. And this is not just a question of *Schadenfreude*. It is also a matter of the circumstances – a point to which Smith is rather more sensitive than some of his colleagues. We may think someone's wretchedness serves them right, or that their good fortune is outrageously undeserved, or that their grief is shamelessly exhibitionist. Moral judgments are as much about refusing to reinforce others' emotional states as rushing to confirm them. Sympathy has no value in itself. There are no prizes for those who empathise with the joy of mercenaries high on a killing spree. Hume and Hutcheson would not have imagined that there were; for them, it is beneficent acts which rouse our exultant approval. But there is a prejudice in favour of spontaneous responses in this benevolistic ethics, which is, in the modern sense of the word, sentimental. We cannot approve or condemn states of mind until we know their cause and context; and for this we need more than a built-in instinct.

Smith places enormous store by the gaze of the other. He is fascinated by the way I see others seeing me, which one might technically term the ego ideal. Just as others seek to look at us through our own eyes, so their eyes become mirrors which reflect back to us our own sentiments. This mutual exchange of glances is a property of what Walter Benjamin calls the aura, which involves among other things the sensation of objects returning our gaze. It contrasts in this sense with the era of mechanical reproduction, in which our look is typically not returned: 'What was inevitably felt to be inhuman, one might even say deadly, in daguerreotypy', he writes, 'was the (prolonged) looking into the camera, since the camera records our likeness without returning our gaze. But looking at someone

---

[21]   David Hume, *An Enquiry Concerning the Principles of Morals* (Oxford, 1998), p. 47.

carries the implicit expectation that our look will be returned by the object of our gaze. When this expectation is met . . . there is an experience of the aura to the fullest extent.'[22] Auratic objects, like the roses of T. S. Eliot's *Four Quartets*, have the look of things that are looked at. Maurice Merleau-Ponty finds the most profound meaning of narcissism in the painter's sense of being looked at by the things he is portraying.[23] The philosopher Fichte was haunted all his life by the idea of a look which sees itself. 'The things I see, see me just as much as I see them', writes Paul Valéry of dream perceptions.[24]

This is also true for Benjamin of the commodity, which lovingly returns the gaze of every potential customer while secretly maintaining a frosty indifference to them all. Like all auratic objects, it reveals an interplay of otherness and intimacy, combining the allure of the untouchable Madonna with the instant availability of the whore. 'The deeper the remoteness which a glance has to overcome', Benjamin comments, 'the stronger will be the spell that is apt to emanate from the gaze.'[25] Bertolt Brecht, who refused all truck with such fancy notions, found this line of speculation deeply distasteful. 'Benjamin is here', he writes in his working diary, '. . . he says: when you feel a gaze directed at you, even behind your back, you return it (!) . . . it is mysticism mysticism, in a posture opposed to mysticism, it is in such a form that the materialistic concept of history is adopted! it is rather ghastly.'[26] Benjamin, Brecht no doubt considered, had either been too long in the company of his Kabbalistic friend Gershom Scholem, or had been carrying his experiments with hashish a little too far.

For Jacques Lacan, the imaginary enclosure of glances is fractured by a lack: the fact that I can never look at her from the place where she sees me.[27] The gaze thus becomes an interplay of light and opacity, in which the translucent imaginary is stained by the intrusion of the symbolic, with its non-reciprocities and anonymous relations. It betrays the ambiguity of Baudelaire's urban crowd, in which, as Benjamin comments, 'no one is either quite transparent or quite opaque to all the others'.[28] In Baudelaire's

[22]   Walter Benjamin, *Charles Baudelaire: A Lyric Poet in the Era of High Capitalism* (London, 1973), p. 147. I discuss this idea more fully in my *Walter Benjamin, Or Towards a Revolutionary Criticism* (London, 1981).

[23]   Maurice Merleau-Ponty, *The Visible and the Invisible* (Evanston, IL, 1968), p. 139.

[24]   Quoted in ibid., p. 149.

[25]   Ibid., p. 150.

[26]   Bertolt Brecht, *Arbeitsjournal* (Frankfurt-am-Main, 1973), vol. 1, p. 16.

[27]   Jacques Lacan, *The Four Fundamental Concepts of Psychoanalysis* (London, 1977), Ch. 6.

[28]   Benjamin, *Charles Baudelaire*, p. 49.

poetry, Benjamin remarks, 'the expectation roused by the look of the human eye is not fulfilled' – which is to say that the gaze, reorganised around a constitutive lack, passes all the way through the object of vision in that doomed hunt for a lost plenitude which is desire. In Lacanian parlance, our desire is not for the other but for the Other. As Benjamin remarks in Lacanian spirit: 'the painting we look at reflects back to us that of which our eyes will never have their fill'.[29]

The exchange of gazes which fascinates Adam Smith is of an imaginary kind; yet it also displays a certain failure of symmetry. Since others, as we have seen, are likely to be less devastated or enraptured by our feelings than we are, their reflected glance can temper our own passions, insinuating a kind of calmness into them. As in the imaginary, we view ourselves simultaneously from the inside and the outside, though these two visions are not exactly commensurate. We judge ourselves through the eyes of others or ego ideal, so that our conduct always manifests some admixture of otherness. This, indeed, lies at the very source of morality: an entirely solitary human being, Smith suggests, would have no moral feelings at all, since he could no more view his own qualities from the outside than he could see his own face. (He is presumably speaking of a 'savage', not of a hermit furnished with a pocket mirror.) 'Bring him into society', however, 'and he is immediately provided with the mirror which he wanted before' (298). It is just this, by contrast, that Jean-Jacques Rousseau finds so dismaying. In Rousseau's view, 'savages' are admirably self-sufficient, while civilised beings are despicably dependent on others. It is the fact that our desire is the desire of the Other – that we live only in the gaze of our fellows – that for Rousseau is so debilitating. For him, sociability is a sign of our weakness. Morality is the tiresome consequence of not being on our own. Like Sartre's hell, ethics is other people.

'Every faculty in one man', Smith writes, 'is the measure by which he judges the like faculty in another . . .', so that we measure 'the propriety or impropriety of others' sentiments by their correspondence or disagreement with our own' (271). There would thus seem to be a disturbingly circular quality about moral judgement, as I judge you by myself, and you judge her by judging me. Each subject would seem in sophistical style to be the measure of all things. To halt this relativist rot, Smith argues that 'our continual observations upon the conduct of others, insensibly lead us to form to ourselves certain general rules concerning what is fit and proper either to be done or to be avoided' (303). So general rules are assigned a

---

[29]   Ibid., pp.146–7.

place, as long as they are inductions from our customary conduct rather than, in rationalist fashion, *a priori* principles from which vicious or virtuous behaviour can be deduced. Such rules are really no more than a distillation of 'the concurring sentiments of mankind' (305), yet they exert a potent force over us even so. They act as a kind of impartial Other, an ideal judge of our behaviour of which we are always conscious.

For Smith as for Lacan, then, our actions are always at some level a message directed to the Other. It is just that in Lacan's view this dialogue can never be reduced to the imaginary reciprocities of a Smith, for whom each of us thrives under the benignant eye of a collective other. For how do we recognise that we are recognised? This is scarcely a problem for an imaginary ethics, for which recognition is as instant and intuitive as the taste of apricots. In the symbolic order, however, the primary medium of our relations with others is language; and for Lacan language insinuates the possibility of misinterpretation into those mutual encounters. The medium which brings us together also wedges us apart. The signifiers in which we recognise each other's demand for recognition can never be as unequivocal as we might wish. Neither, for that matter, are the physical gestures of the pre-linguistic imaginary, like the wordless communings of Sterne's Walter and Toby, which aim for a mutuality less treacherous than one founded on the word. For gestures, too, need to be interpreted, and thus fail to elude the mark of the signifier. You do not avoid the slipperiness of the signifier by bunching a fist or shaking a stick.

The advocates of the imaginary dream of a single luminous signifier, a magical mark which would encapsulate one's essence and convey it whole and entire to another in the twinkling of an eye. This all-privileged sign has sometimes passed under the name of the Romantic symbol, though Lacanians prefer to dub it the phallus. But because the symbolic order is an order of meaning, and because meaning has a tendency to miss its mark, the possibility of mutual misrecognition is built into it from the outset. It is because the phallus does not exist that there can be tragedy, but also that there can be history. Besides, if my identity is caught up with yours, and yours with another's, and so on in a perpetually spawning web of affiliations, how can I ever know that your approving glance is *your* glance, rather than the effect of an unreadable palimpsest of selves? The specular ethics of the imaginary thus finds itself disrupted by the opacity of the Other. Imaginary mutuality gives way to symbolic non-reciprocity. And just as there is no outside to the imaginary, which curves back upon itself rather like cosmic space, so there is no exterior to the symbolic either. In Lacanian jargon, there is no Other of the Other – no meta-language which would allow us to investigate our intersubjective meanings from a vantage-point beyond them, since this language would in turn need to be interpreted by another one. To claim that we are the effects of the signifier is to suggest that there is no external prop to our shared discourse, rather as for Adam Smith there is no ground to our world beyond 'the concurring sentiments of mankind'. The symbolic order must necessarily lack a foundation.

The *Oxford English Dictionary* defines empathy as the power of 'identifying oneself mentally with (and so fully comprehending) a person or object of contemplation'. But identification and comprehension are not necessarily on such intimate terms with each other as this might suggest. I cannot understand Napoleon by 'becoming' him – not only, as we have seen, because there would then be nobody left to do the comprehending, but because this would seem to assume that Napoleon understood himself, which assumes in him an impossible self-transparency. Understanding may indeed be a matter of gaining access to someone else's head, but it is a mode of breaking and entering known as language. To comprehend is not a question of magically merging with the other's body. Even if I accomplished this feat, how would I recognise what I found there? Only because I had language in the first place, which might have saved me the trouble of such a phantasmal invasion. Sympathy and understanding do not require mental images of others' emotional states. For one thing, such states are not in principle hidden. For another thing, you can commiserate with my mislaying of the priceless medieval manuscript without any particular image of the document leaping to mind, and without struggling to replicate what is going on in my emotional guts.

It is of course possible to sympathise with experiences which you have not only not had, but which you could not possibly have. Smith's example is a man's compassion for a woman in childbirth. It is even possible to feel someone else's joy or trouble more acutely than they do themselves, which represents one kind of flaw in the dream of perfect reciprocity. Besides, to feel for someone's pain is not necessarily to feel it. There is a difference between feeling sorry for you and feeling your sorrow. I can also be numbed by your grief without feeling any particular moral response to it, just as I can feel outraged without reflecting on whether I am justified to be so.

Those who rush to the aid of casualties in a road accident are usually too preoccupied to have mental images of the victims' putative sensations. Conversely, we can entertain animated images of other people's sensations without feeling the least inclination to come to their assistance. 'It is perfectly meaningful to say: "I can quite visualise your feelings, but I have no pity for you"', writes the phenomenologist Max Scheler.[30] Sadists like to experience what their victims are going through; as Nietzsche points out, cruelty needs a degree of sensibility, while brutality does not. Masochists may be reluctant to assist those in pain because they derive exquisite pleasure from identifying with their agonies. They may object on the same grounds to having their own miseries relieved by others. The mere capacity to feel what someone else is feeling is no more a moral affair than the gift of flawlessly imitating their accent. There is also a difference between sympathy in the sense of compassion, and sympathy in the sense of sharing someone else's emotional state. If we can claim some credit for the former, we can sometimes claim little enough for the latter. Plenty of people are both ultra-sensitive and monstrous egoists.

With the exception of Shaftesbury, none of the moralists we have been examining was English. In fact, the English are in as short supply among this group as they are in the ranks of so-called English literary modernism. Almost all of the thinkers we have been discussing stemmed from the Gaelic margins of the metropolitan nation, a fact that may not be insignificant. Gaels like Burke, Hume, Hutcheson, Smith, Fordyce and Ferguson, along with figures like Goldsmith, Steele, Brooke and Sterne who were born in Ireland or of part-Gaelic provenance, were no doubt more inclined to the cult of sentiment and benevolence than their Anglo-Saxon counterparts. This is not because Gaels are genetically more genial than the English, but because Scotland and Ireland both had powerful traditions of clan- or community-based allegiances.

It is true that kinship structures, binding customs, unwritten obligations and so-called moral economy had long been under siege in both nations from a colonially imposed system of contractual relations and possessive individualism. But aspects of this traditional way of life survived precariously alongside more modern institutions, and in the political militancy of small tenants, crofters and labourers could offer such modernity some ferocious resistance throughout the Age of Reason. In her study of the Scottish Enlightenment, Gladys Bryson notes that 'much of the sentiment and loyalty of the older *Gemeinschaft* carries over (in their work) into the *Gesellschaft* . . . we find in all their writings great attention to communica-

---

[30]   Max Scheler, *The Nature of Sympathy* (London, 1954), p. 9.

tion, sympathy, imitation, habit and convention . . .'.[31] A contemporary instance of such Gaelic-style preoccupations is to be found in the work of Alasdair MacIntyre, a philosopher who in pursuit of such values has moved in his time from Christianity to Marxism, and from Marxism to Catholicism and communitarianism. MacIntyre's critique of Enlightenment universalism belongs to a legacy of what one might dub national particularism in both Scotland and Ireland – an insistence by national intellectuals on the historical peculiarities of such cultures, their resistance to a certain place-blind rationalism and refusal to conform to some supposed universal (but often simply metropolitan) norm.[32] MacIntyre's scepticism of Enlightenment universals, along with his habit of restoring moral and social concepts to their historical contexts, have, one might venture, a certain Gaelic flavour.

John Dwyer argues that the Scottish drive to an advanced economy, of which luminaries like Hume and Smith were such articulate apologists, was nonetheless eager to preserve a degree of national integrity and preserved a traditionalist suspicion of unbridled commercialism. 'Sociability, not individualism', he writes, 'was the critical ingredient in the Scottish definition of sensibility, as the whole notion of sensibility becomes an alternative to a self-interested social order.'[33] Thomas Bartlett observes that 'one notable feature of Irish rural life from the 1770s onwards had been the emergence of the phenomenon of sociability, the growing pressure to associate for various purposes'.[34] The politics of sentiment known as nationalism played a key part in such rural solidarity, as militant underground dissenters harnessed pub, wake, pattern, shebeen, fair, market and crossroads to their subversive ends.

Benevolence and moral sense, one might claim, represent a kind of *Gemeinschaft* of the spirit still flourishing within the *Gesellschaft* of everyday commercial life. In any case, life in far-flung Kerry or Aberdeenshire was a somewhat less rationalised, anonymously administered affair than it was in the English capital. Alasdair MacIntyre suggests that the Scottish Enlightenment's belief in a stock of self-evident first principles has its

---

[31]   Gladys Bryson, *Man and Society: The Scottish Inquiry of the Eighteenth Century* (Princeton, NJ, 1945), pp. 146–7. I have discussed this question more fully in my *Crazy John and the Bishop* (Cork, 1998), Ch. 3.

[32]   I have explored this question further in my *Scholars and Rebels in Nineteenth-Century Ireland* (Oxford, 1999).

[33]   John Dwyer, *Virtuous Discourse: Sensibility and Community in Late Eighteenth-Century Scotland* (Edinburgh, 1987), p. 39.

[34]   Thomas Bartlett, *The Fall and Rise of the Irish Nation* (Dublin, 1992), p. 311.

source in the common fund of taken-for-granted beliefs of pre-modern social orders.[35] For the Scottish *Aufklärer*, human society is natural to individuals. It is best seen as an extension of domestic kinship – a belief plausible enough in communities for which personal, sexual, social and economic relations were less easily distinguishable than they are in the modern suburbs. Marriage and sexuality, for example, are still bound up in such conditions with property, labour-power, dowries, religious faith, inheritance, emigration and social welfare. Perhaps it was because the family in Ireland was not yet an entirely privatised outfit that figures like Burke, who as a child had attended a hedge school in County Cork, could propose it as an image of national unity to an England aghast at the prospect of revolution. In this sense, Gaelic *Gemeinschaft* came to serve metropolitan ends.

It is not surprising, then, that the culture of sensibility should seep into the colonialist nation largely from its less modernised margins. The English, as in their extraordinary fervour for the saccharine lyrics of Thomas Moore, imported wistful, exotic or melancholic feeling from their colonial peripheries, where there was indeed much to be melancholic about. The idea of unwritten obligations might be a way of characterising, say, tenants' rights in eighteenth-century Ireland; but it also serves to portray the ethics of the sentimentalist school, for which laws are implicit in manners and styles of feeling, and do not need to be vulgarly spelt out. Much the same is true for Shaftesbury, who as a neo-Platonic aristocrat is at war with the mean-spiritedness of bourgeois Man. In his liaison with Hutcheson, English patrician and Gaelic outsider link hands in a common front against the ideologies of unfeeling reason, rather as Oscar Wilde was both English dandy and Gaelic outsider in the same body.

The greatest of eighteenth-century Irish philosophers, Bishop Berkeley, was Anglo-Irish rather than Gaelic-Irish; yet his thought is almost certainly indebted to the world of early Celtic mythology, with its vision of the universe as a kind of mighty spiritual discourse, a set of powers or epiphanies in which God communicates himself freely through sign and image to his creatures. 'The phaenomena of Nature', Berkeley writes, '. . . do form not only a magnificent spectacle, but also a most coherent, entertaining and instructive discourse. . . .'[36] In discovering the relations between causes and effects, for example, we are learning to master the grammar of Nature. The

---

[35] Alasdair MacIntyre, *Whose Justice? Which Rationality?* (London, 1988), p. 223.
[36] Alexander Campbell Fraser (ed.), *The Works of George Berkeley DD* (Oxford, 1871), vol. 1, p. 460.

whole cosmos is a kind of divine semiosis. In Berkeley's view, things are signifiers of God, and like any language they live only in the perceptions of a human subject. In an imaginary mode, they are at one with their presence to their perceivers. In his eyes, res and *signum* are identical, rather as there is a coalescence between signifier and signified in the imaginary sphere.

It is significant in this respect that when Fredric Jameson comes to describe the Lacanian imaginary, he slips spontaneously into Berkeleyan language, speaking of 'the indifferentiation of (an object's) *esse* from a *percipi* which does not know a *percipiens*'.[37] In Berkeley's anthropocentric universe, things exist only in so far as they are (in the Heideggerian phrase) 'to hand', given over to us, centred benignly upon human subjects. In an off-duty essay entitled 'Pleasures, Natural and Fantastical', he indulges in the playful fantasy that the world was fashioned for him personally: 'The various objects that compose the world were by nature formed to delight our senses ... Hence it is usual with me to consider myself as having a natural property in every object that administers pleasure to me ... I have a property in the gay part of all the gilt chariots I meet, which I regard as amusements designed to delight my eyes ....'[38] In a kind of ludic parody of his own epistemology, all things have their substance in his own sensuous relishing of them, as one imagines they may do for the infant at the breast.

Like a number of eighteenth-century Irish divines, Berkeley is out to counter the theological implications of empiricist scepticism – a scepticism which threatened to undermine the doctrine of the Church of Ireland of which he himself was so illustrious a prelate, and hence the authority of the Anglo-Irish colonialist Ascendancy of which he was also a member. His philosophical response to this menace is a flamboyant version of the idealism which from John Scottus Eriugena to W. B. Yeats had constituted the main current of Irish philosophy. English rationalism and empiricism never took more than shallow root in the neighbouring island, not least on account of its scholastic legacy. If Locke's empiricism opens a gap between thing and concept down which true knowledge is at risk of disappearing, Berkeley seeks to seal this rift by redefining phenomena themselves as nothing but complexes of sense-data. The point of his idealism is thus not to abolish objects but to yield us untrammelled access to them. In doing

---

[37]   Fredric Jameson, 'Imaginary and Symbolic in Lacan', *Yale French Studies*, 55/56 (New Haven, CT, 1977), p. 355.
[38]   Campbell Fraser, *Works of George Berkeley DD*, vol. 3, pp. 160–1.

so, he presses the logic of the empiricists to an extreme limit at which it implodes – for these English philosophers, while claiming that we can know the substances of things, assert in the same breath that all knowledge is a matter of sense-data, and sense-data are a sign of substances rather than the things themselves.

The great secret that Berkeley triumphantly lays bare, in the manner of the child artlessly announcing the nakedness of the Emperor, is that what the appearances of things are concealing is the fact that there is nothing behind them; that they are consequently not appearances at all; and that this hard core we call 'substance' is as flimsy as a fantasy. If God lies at the heart of all things; and if (for Berkeley as much as for Eriugena) he is no kind of entity at all but a sublime abyss of pure nothingness; then what sustains phenomena is a sort of *néant* or abyssal void. As for St Augustine, the world is shot through with non-being from end to end. To say that things lack substance is to say they are the eloquent discourse of the divine. God – sheer nothingness – is of their essence. The elusive *objet petit a* known as substance is simply a fantasy object filling out the void of the Real – which is to say, for Berkeley, the unbearable presence of the Almighty. And since God would have no tangible presence on earth without that ceaseless deciphering of his discourse which is human perception, our own existence is necessary in the manner of the imaginary, not contingent in the style of the symbolic. We and the world are leashed together, and it is in our direct sensory experience, rather as with the small infant, that this link is forged. In this sense, Berkeley's vision is a broadly imaginary one. It is therefore not surprising, given what we have said already of such a register, that he emerges in his work *A New Theory of Vision* as a kind of phenomenologist *avant la lettre*, much preoccupied like his compatriot Burke with the body, sensory intuition and the ratio between one organ of sensation and another. In both thinkers' aversion to abstract notions, some commentators have detected a peculiarly Gaelic penchant for the concrete.

Eighteenth-century benevolence did not really survive the advent of Jeremy Bentham. As the domain of sentiment was taken progressively into private ownership, it could provide less and less of a model for the public sphere. Instead, benevolence abandoned moral philosophy and took up residence in that form of moral inquiry we know as realist fiction. It would not be too fanciful to claim that the great inheritor of Shaftesbury and Hutcheson was Charles Dickens. It is now the novel which constitutes the most potent antidote to human egoism, and this as much in its multi-voiced form as in its humanistic content. Industrial capitalist England is a good deal more tangled and opaque than a Whitehall club, but the novel is an incomparably sensitive instrument for exploring submerged relations and mystified connections. Or, as George Eliot puts it in her essay 'The Natural History of German Life', for amplifying our experience and extending our contact with our fellow humans beyond the bounds of our personal lot. It is thus an antidote to the imaginary as well as to self-interest. It is in the novel above all that we can lend an imaginative shape to those buried regions of social life which stretch beyond our own experience, and in doing so evoke a sense of affinity with a myriad faceless others. The twin enemies of the genre are egoism and anonymity. There are pressing political reasons as well as admirably humanitarian ones for this enriching of sympathies – for a society which can no longer conceive of itself as a community of feeling is perilously vulnerable to conflict and division.

Yet as sentiment is increasingly driven from the public domain, thrust back into the private sphere to take up its home among a set of twinkly-eyed eccentrics and amiable freaks, it begins to grow sickly and self-consuming. It is no accident that the cult of sentiment reaches its apogee among the dark Satanic mills of the Victorians. The trek from the generous-hearted Brownlow in *Oliver Twist* to the dandyish Harold Skimpole in *Bleak House* is one from an impassioned apologia for feeling to a disenchanted sense that it can be part of the problem quite as much as the solution.

PART II

THE SOVEREIGNTY OF
THE SYMBOLIC

Introduction: The Symbolic Order

The passage from the imaginary to the symbolic is one from the closed sphere of the ego and its objects to the open field of intersubjectivity.[1] It is to the latter that Lacan gives the name of the Other. The human subject, severed from its symbiosis with the other/Mother by the advent of difference in the form of the Name-of-the-Father, must renounce its enjoyment of the mother's body under pain of castration. It must thrust this *jouissance* underground, in order to assume its place in the structure of roles and relations which Lacan calls the symbolic order. One might say that the function of the symbolic order, rather like that of the Christian Eucharist, is to convert flesh and blood to sign. The subject is now supposed to be identical with its signifying place within a pre-given web of social relations.

Yet since the object of its gratification is now forbidden to it, the subject is hollowed by this prohibition into the perpetual non-being or *manque d'être* we know as desire. In its search for fulfilment, the subject is fractured and dispersed, stumbling from one sign or object to another in doomed pursuit of an eternally elusive totality of being – a totality for which each of these signs or objects is a mere stand-in or place-holder. Since there is no transcendental signifier – no word which in some miraculous epiphany would give voice to the subject's being as a whole – the subject slips through the gaps between these various signifiers. It can seize on this or that specific meaning, but only at the price of suffering a calamitous loss of being. It

---

[1] Some central features of Lacan's thoughts on the symbolic order can be found in his *Écrits* (Paris, 1966), especially in the essay 'Subversion du sujet et dialectique du désir dans l'inconscient freudien'. See also Jacques Lacan, *Le Seminaire Livre 1: Les Écrits Techniques de Freud* (Paris, 1975).

can 'mean' – but only at the cost of disappearing as a 'full' subject from its own speech. There is no signifier which can adequately represent the subject who is deploying signifiers, or the place from which he or she is doing so.

So the subject is both excluded from and represented in the signifying chain. Because it cannot be wholly present to itself, it can be no more directly known than Kant's infamous *noumenon*; instead, its presence can be detected only negatively, in the lack which stirs at the heart of language. In this sense, the subject's entry into the symbolic order is a kind of *felix culpa* or fortunate Fall. It cannot achieve its identity otherwise; yet like Oedipus, the price it must pay for this precious gift disfigures it for life. It must now look for its identity not in the mirror of itself, but in a play of difference – in the fact that each location in the symbolic order (father, grandmother, sibling and so on) is constituted by its relations to the others, rather as a word is no more than its place in a chain of difference. This is not to say that the world of the imaginary is simply abandoned. On the contrary, the subject is now split between the *moi* or ego, with its narcissistic object-relations, and that truth about itself as a signifying being which it receives from making itself over to the Other, or the field of language as a whole. It must accept that its truth lies in the keeping of the Other, not in what it deludedly affirms of itself. And since the Other is never wholly accessible to it, neither is the truth of its own identity. It can have no certainty that what it is for itself coincides with what it is for the Other. It is in this slippage or ambiguity that the unconscious is born. What I am will always exceed my grasp.

None of this takes place without a struggle. To be a subject is also to question one's place within the order of the Other, to find ourselves out of joint within it, to refuse to be fobbed off with the cryptic, disturbingly Kafkaesque messages it returns to our insistent queries ('Who am I?' 'What am I to do?' 'What is it you want of me?'). We are never entirely at home in this blankly anonymous order, and the 'excess' in us which the Other fails to assimilate forms the very core of our subjectivity. The order which constitutes the subject also alienates it, so that what we encounter when we emerge into ourselves is a kind of self-estrangement. Yet if the core of the self is deeply strange and illegible, it is precisely here that it finds itself at one with the similarly indecipherable order of the Other.

The symbolic order is a matter not only of difference, but of exclusion and prohibition. You cannot, for example, be daughter and wife to the same man. It is a realm of regulation and legality, unlike the polymorphous nature of the imaginary. The face-to-face bonds of the imaginary give way to the impersonal force of universal laws, while intuitive knowledge yields ground to that knowledge-without-a-subject which is science or theory. For the Oedipal child, 'content' – the body of the mother – must take second place to 'form' – to a paternal law which consists in nothing but an empty prohibition. Yet only by submitting to this castrating law or super-ego can one assume a signifying place in the system of kinship, and thus enter into subjecthood. The Oedipal crisis is rewritten in semiotic terms. Only by laying violent hands upon itself, repressing its illicit desire and guiltily renouncing its *jouissance*, can the subject come into its own as a speaking, acting, apparently autonomous being. *Jouissance*, or the enjoy-ment of the mother's body, so Lacan remarks, is forbidden to him who speaks. The subject is divided, then, between law and desire – though at the heart of the symbolic order, as we shall see later, lurks a stalled dialectic between the two known as the Real.

To enter the symbolic order is to submit to a kind of exile. Our relation to the world no longer has the (spurious) immediacy of the imaginary, but is now mediated through and through by the signifier. And this involves a certain haemorrhaging of reality – for the signifier is a form of castration, a cutting edge severing us from the real. Rather than fantasise about closing our fist over actual things, we must settle instead for those second-hand significations of them known as language. The symbol, Lacan remarks, is the death of the thing – rather as the sovereignty of the signifier spells the 'fading' of the full subject. To speak – to be no more than an empty move-ment from one signifier to another – is in this sense to anticipate one's death, as the non-being of the subject yields it a foretaste of its final self-loss. Perhaps this is one meaning of St Paul's remark that we die every moment. Signifiers themselves are inherently lacking: since meaning is a product of difference, it takes at least two signifiers to produce one. And since these two signifiers implicate countless others, the whole process is as tangled and untotalisable as desire itself.

Besides, these are not marks or sounds we invent ourselves. In order to mean, the subject must draw on the great stockpile or repository of codes, rules and signifiers which Lacan calls the Other; so that it only ever makes sense at long range and second-hand, by deploying signifiers which are scored through with the intentions of countless anonymous others. Every signifier is a palimpsest. My demand to be recognised as uniquely myself is thus caught up in a medium over which none of us has proprietorship; which has its own logic quite independent of our will; and which 'speaks' me far more than I speak it. It is the signifier which gives birth to Man, not vice versa. The delusion of mastery of the mirror-stage infant, along with its bogus self-identity, is accordingly deflated. The Other from which I borrow my speech tells me not only what I may say, but what I may desire; so that the most intimate core of my being is constituted by my relations to what I am not.

We are fated, then, to express ourselves in a tongue which is forever foreign. Even if I can articulate my desire, I must do so in a medium – the Other, or whole field of intersubjectivity – which cannot itself be articulated. There is no other to the Other, no perspective from which this terrain might be surveyed as a whole, since this surveying would need to be signified within it, and would thus fail to transcend it. What Lacan calls the phallus, as we have seen, is the magical signifier which would enable one to grasp the full meaning of one's own speech, while dissolving the indeterminacy of the other's; but the phallus is an imposture. This elusiveness of the signifiers I am constrained to use, the way their ambiguous effects persistently outrun my intentions, is known as the unconscious. The subject is divided between the ego and the unconscious – which is to say, between its speech, and the location and significance of that speech within the Other or whole network of signifiers, of which it cannot be properly aware. The unconscious is thus a performance, not a place. The human subject is like the messenger-slave of ancient times 'who carries under his hair the codicil that condemns him to death (yet) knows neither the meaning of the text, nor in what language it is written, nor even that it had been tattooed on his shaven scalp as he slept'.[2] For Lacan, the impersonality of the symbolic order has much to do with the anonymity of death.

If Lacan labels his order 'symbolic', it is because what is at stake here above all are signifying positions, not flesh-and-blood individuals. We become 'real' subjects only by assuming one or other of these symbolic locations, rather as we become persons only by learning to speak. This is not so of the imaginary, where symbolisation has yet to take place. The subject of the symbolic, as Fredric Jameson puts it, 'is transformed into a representation of itself'.[3] We are dealing, then, with a purely formal structure, within which individuals are distributed and locked into place by a supervening law which applies indifferently to them all. What matters are relations, which a role such as 'father' signifies, rather than the empirical individuals between whom these relations hold. I behave towards my second cousin in the superiorly joking way I do because he is my second

[2]   Jacques Lacan, *Écrits* (London, 1977), p. 307.
[3]   Fredric Jameson, 'Imaginary and Symbolic in Lacan', *Yale French Studies*, 55/56 (New Haven, CT, 1977), p. 363.

cousin, not because he is particularly risible as a person. To venerate one's father because he is clever, Kierkegaard comments, is a form of impiety. Pascal's *Pensées* contrasts the sceptic who sees through authority, and the credulous populace who revere it as sacred, with a third, more acceptable group: those who respect authority, but not because it is precious in itself. The symbolic order is thus a kind of fiction: we know, for example, that our political rulers are every bit as morally shabby as we are, but to regard them as rulers in the first place is to suspend this debilitating insight. The places within the system, then, are notional or symbolic, and as such may be combined or exchanged according to certain rigorous rules. Or rather, the law permits certain permutations while ruling out others (incest, for example).

There is a distinction here between 'imaginary' and 'symbolic' exchange. The mutualities of the imaginary, as we have seen, involve a blurring of the boundaries between self and others, so that bodies seem to merge seamlessly into one another, living each other's lives and clothing themselves with each another's flesh. This, then, is as literal an exchange of selves as one could imagine. Symbolic exchange, by contrast, rests upon abstraction: one item may replace or stand in for another, since what matters is not its specific nature but its ordained location within the system. Like a commodity, it exists not in itself but in its traffic with others of its kind. One might claim in Marxian terms that the symbolic order is a question of exchange-value, whereas the imaginary, in which we relish the tangible qualities of the other purely for their own sake, is a case of use-value. As Kierkegaard remarks of the former species of order in *The Sickness Unto Death*: each individual 'is ground as smooth as a pebble, as exchangeable as a coin of the realm'.[4]

If you and I relate to each another through a medium (the Other) which transcends us both, this fact has consequences for our chances of mutual intelligibility. The Other, as the mythical place where countless, anonymously entangled meanings have been sedimented, is opaque and ambiguous; and since it is from here that you and I borrow the speech in which we communicate, we become opaque to one another as well. Or, in Lacan's cryptic typography, the other becomes the Other. (A case in point: a friend of mine, mishearing the subject of this study as Essex rather than ethics, inquired whether I was dealing with Colchester. I spent an anxious few days wondering if Colchester was a moral philosopher whom I ought to have heard of.) But the point runs deeper than mere verbal equivocation.

---

[4]   Søren Kierkegaard, *The Sickness Unto Death* (London, 1989), p. 64.

Does this breast signify love, one can imagine the small infant wondering, or just the averting of hunger? Is it a response to its need for recognition, or simply to its need? One can imagine the small child being bombarded with equivocal messages from the Other, traumatised by the enigma of what it is that this Other desires of it. To this extent, the child is in much the same situation as the fearful Protestant, unable to decipher the insistent but inaudible messages of a deity shrouded in darkness. The Other is a hidden God, whose commands are sibylline yet binding.

So there can be no untrammelled access to others, lying as they do, like ourselves, behind the wall of language. What allows you to acknowledge me is also what shuts you off from me. There is no longer a sharp contrast, as there was for David Hume, between those who are familiar and those who are remote. Now, on this remarkably pessimistic theory of communication, even the most intimate are necessarily alien. All neighbours are strangers. Even pillow talk is impersonal. The idea of a social order in which self-determining subjects set up transparent, symmetrical exchanges with other equally luminous subjects is unmasked as a myth. Indeed, one might claim that it is *the* myth of middle-class society.

There is a tragic quality to this vision, which has been noted often enough. In a disconcerting paradox, it is just when the world appears most thoroughly humanised– when it is woven through from end to end by the signifier – that we find ourselves most profoundly estranged. The signifier may be a way of possessing one another more deeply than wordless creatures can, but it also marks an irreparable loss. We receive our humanity from that which is entirely inhuman – marks, traces, sounds, imprints, incisions. Scooped out by the lack which language insinuates into it like a virus, the subject can now cling to the sublime object of its desire only in the form of a fragmentary substitute for it, a stray bit of waste or leftover which Lacan terms the *objet petit a*. The imaginary relation between the self and its world is ruptured, leaving in its wake that festering psychic wound known as subjectivity.

Reality turns its back upon us, like a former lover who now stiffly refuses to acknowledge our existence. In Copernican or Darwinian fashion, the human subject is dislodged from its imaginary centrality. The world no longer owes it a living, and will certainly not expire like some emotionally dependent spouse on the day of its own demise. We must now think in terms of a universe of distinct subjects who exist, in Emmanuel Levinas's phrase, side by side rather than face to face, all of them replaceable elements of a structure which is centred upon nothing, least of all itself. If the space of the imaginary is womblike, that of the symbolic is a flat but differentiated field. It is this space which we encounter in the major varieties of symbolic ethics: Kantianism, liberalism and Utilitarianism. One might contrast the self-enclosure of imaginary space with the eternally open field of the Other; yet there is an equivalent kind of self-enclosure about the symbolic order, which receives back no echo of its own discourse from the world beyond. Any such echo would need to pass through the duplicitous signifier, and thus would constitute no sort of 'outside' at all. The symbolic order is a realm of pure contingency without foundation. Any ground to language would have to be expressible in language, and thus would be part of the problem rather than the solution. There is no transcendental signifier.

Is this, then, what so-called maturity and enlightenment signify – that we are deprived of comfort and consolation from beyond our own resources, cut off from reality by the very medium (language) which is supposed to throw it open to us? It would seem that our emancipation is at the same time our self-estrangement. Our autonomy thrives on a repression of our dependency. We have exchanged a reliance on Nature for an addiction to desire. The gash in our being caused by being torn from our pre-reflective unity with the world will never heal; yet without this original sin there could be no history, no identity, no alterity, no love.

For the cultural left of a previous era, the idea of the symbolic order posed something of a problem. It seemed in some ways a glamorously avant-garde notion, with its hymning of lack, desire, difference, otherness, detotalisation, the fragility of identity and the sovereignty of the signifier. In contrast to the imaginary, with its infantile fantasies and narcissistic investments, the symbolic had a smack of mature realism about it, however wistful and defeatist. Yet seen from another angle, what it seemed to represent was nothing less than the political status quo. If it was about lack and desire, it was also about law, symmetry and regulation. Was one, then, launching a critique of the 'imaginary' of ideology from the very belly of the beast?

Theorists thus stood in need of some notion or other which promised to transcend both imaginary and symbolic registers simultaneously. Jacques Derrida came up with a limitless play of difference, Julia Kristeva with the 'semiotic', Michel Foucault with the idea of power, and the early Jean-François Lyotard with a vision of libidinal intensities. The kind of desire triumphantly celebrated by Gilles Deleuze and Félix Guattari refuses to submit to anything as straitjacketing as the symbolic order, or endure anything as humiliating as lack and castration. For all these thinkers, the symbolic order is to be undone – but not by a regression to the imaginary. In fact, as we shall see, Lacan had his own way of accomplishing this end, known as the Real. By virtue of this abstruse category, it was now possible to outflank and 'outleft' both imaginary and symbolic simultaneously.

4

Spinoza and the Death of Desire

Copernicus paid a price for dislodging Man from the centre of the universe, and so did his philosophical counterpart Benedictus de Spinoza. The son of a Portuguese Sephardic Jew who migrated to the Netherlands in flight from religious persecution, Spinoza was expelled from his Amsterdam synagogue for heresy, fellow-travelled with dissenting Christians, and saw his magnificent plea for religious and political tolerance, the *Tractatus Theologico-Politicus*, denounced as a work 'spawned in hell by a renegade Jew and a Devil'. The book is also a historical and scientific critique of the Bible, with the aim of demolishing the superstitions on which despotism thrives.

This great exponent of rationalist disenchantment was in his own way a champion of what one might call a symbolic ethics. It is not, to be sure, of the fully-fledged kind we shall find in the writings of Immanuel Kant. He believes, as Kant does not, that the symbolic order of society has the support of Nature – that Nature and humanity are not only bound up indissolubly with one another, but that they are facets of a single system, governed by the laws of a totality to which the *Ethics* sometimes gives the name of God. The forces which ordain the fall of a leaf are also those which mould our passions. Yet Nature has no regard for us humans, and is quite void of purpose. In order to encounter each other in the imaginary, subjects must stand over against each other, even if they do so only to slip inside each other's skins. In Spinoza, however, we are no longer invited to view the world from inside the glowing interior of the subject. Instead, men and women are viewed naturalistically from the outside, as dispassionately as an entomologist might view earwigs. They are elements of a systemic order, one whose laws are for the most part as impenetrable to them as the deep structure of a myth is concealed from Lévi-Strauss's tribespeople. Spinoza, who believes that all true thought aspires to the condition of geometry, acknowledges that it will seem strange to his readers that he should 'treat on the vices and failings of men in a geometrical manner, and should wish to demonstrate with sure reasoning those things which they cry out against as opposed to reason, as vain, absurd and disgusting' (82). Even so, this geometrical spirit is ultimately in the name of love and forgiveness, and in Spinoza's eyes more dependably so than any short-lived spasm of warm-heartedness.

Nor are men and women for Spinoza autonomous agents, as they are for Kant and the 'symbolic' thinkers – Habermas, Rawls – who champion that current of ethics in our own time. On the contrary, they are as much the helpless victims of causality as a cancer patient. Yet for Lacan, at least in his most 'structuralist' phase, this autonomy is in any case mostly illusory: the ego's belief that it is the master of its own house masks its dependency on the law of the signifier. Or, in Spinoza's view, on the laws of Nature. For the common people, as opposed to the cognoscenti who brood upon their behaviour, freedom is the ignorance of necessity. It is because we are oblivious of the causes of our actions that we can entertain that agreeable fantasy known as liberty. In one of the most cited passages of English criticism, T. S. Eliot illustrates his notoriously passive conception of the creative imagination by writing of how the poetic mind spontaneously associates such sensations as falling in love, hearing the sound of the typewriter, smelling the dinner cooking and reading Spinoza. What the first three experiences have in common is their independence of the will, unless the smelling in question is a sniffing; so it is fitting that the philosopher whose name comes to Eliot's mind had no faith in such a faculty. If Spinoza's name came to Eliot involuntarily, the passage may be an example of what it illustrates.

Even Spinoza's God, who does not love us but does not hate us either, is not free to do whatever takes his fancy. He is free in so far as he is self-determining, moved by the necessity of his divine nature; but he could not *not* be like this and still be God. This in its context is a politically radical view: God is not some whimsical absolute monarch who rules by arbitrary fiat, as pampered and capricious as a rock star. We must take the greatest care, Spinoza admonishes us in the *Ethics*, not to confuse the power of God with the power of kings. Unlike tyrants, God must respect the way the world is – indeed the way the world is *is* what we mean by God, who is immanent in Nature rather than transcendent of it. The world, in brief, is God's body; and if it were to be other than it is, God would no more be God than I would be myself if I had a different body altogether. Since all the Almighty's actions are a question of necessity, he could not have created the world other than the way he did, a reflection which in Spinoza's view is a powerful incentive to stoicism. The wise will look upon the pratfalls and catastrophes of human existence rather as the English look on their weather: these things are not agreeable, but there is a perverse kind of consolation in the thought that they could not be otherwise. Besides, there is always the possibility that we, too, can become Godlike, acting purely by the necessity of our own natures without external compulsion. It is this which Spinoza, anticipating Kant, knows as freedom. Freedom is not the absence of determination, but the arduous project of self-determination.

The fact that nothing could be other than it is is not of course the conventional wisdom of the populace. Louis Althusser, who professed a peculiarly Spinozist kind of Marxism, sees both necessity and freedom as features of ideology: necessity, because under the sway of ideology we imagine that our individual existence is somehow essential to society as a whole, that we are leashed to the world as an infant is bound to its parent; freedom, because the ideological imaginary, by 'centring' us in this fashion, furnishes us with enough coherence and sense of autonomy to act as purposive agents. The bleaker domain of theory is conscious that our existence as individuals is purely contingent – that the symbolic order is a matter of given locations, and that who actually gets to fill them is a strictly secondary matter. Yet theory is also aware that there is a necessity to our everyday existence, as 'bearers' of the laws of class-history, to which we are mostly blind. For Spinoza, the popular mind assumes that things in the realm of ideology – which is to say, in the incurably mystified world of everyday experience – are free, contingent, swayed by chance and effort, while philosophy is conscious that they are carved in stone. If the Lacanian subject is split between imaginary and symbolic, something of the same is true for Spinoza of human society itself, divided as it is between the deluded rabble and the purveyors of true knowledge. Spinoza's ethics are in this sense as class-based as Aristotle's.

Spinoza, then, belongs to a philosophical lineage from Plato, Schopenhauer and Marx to Nietzsche, Freud and Lévi-Strauss, for which experience itself is the homeland of delusion. The contrast with the stoutly commonsensical world of Hutcheson and Smith, men with a buoyant faith in what they can touch and feel, could not be greater. For this sceptical heritage, the sources of our subjectivity are opaque to us, and (for most of these thinkers) necessarily so. Only by repressing, forgetting or mystifying the true determinants of our being can we become the subjects we are. We are fluent in the discourse of the world, but its grammar is indecipherable to us.

In Spinoza's view, popular consciousness is spontaneously anthropocentric. The ideology into which we all lapse at birth is a kind of spontaneous humanism. Men and women are instinctively 'imaginary' or subject-centred, regarding reality as delivered over to them and fashioned for their purposes. They fail to grasp that, as with the Lacanian symbolic, things exist purely in relation to each other, with no subjective centre to converge upon. Spinoza's own thought is resolutely anti-teleological; but the masses assume that the world has a point, and that this purpose reaches its apogee in their own welfare. Each individual trusts that God 'made all things for man', and 'that God may love him above the rest and direct the whole of nature for the gratification of his blind cupidity and insatiable avarice'.[1] The gullible masses also believe that storms, diseases, natural catastrophes and the like are sent to punish them. False consciousness is the inability to decentre one's own delusory sovereignty into the cheerless truth of reality. Though they would be surprised to hear it, the common people are really ethical utilitarians, convinced that the good is whatever is conducive to the gratification of their desires, and the bad whatever impedes it. 'Good' for them means 'This is useful/pleasurable to me or to us' – which is to say that the populace, unknown to themselves, are devotees of David Hume. The upshot of this anthropocentrism is relativism, as each judges 'according to the disposition of his own brain' (36).

An imaginary ethics, then, is the upshot of the mob's obtuse self-centredness. For Spinoza himself, all created things are an end in themselves, and their sole *raison d'être* is to maintain themselves in being; for the populace, things are the conveniently provided means to their own flourishing. There must, they assume, be 'some governor or governors, endowed with human freedom, who have taken care of all things for them and have made all things for their use' (32). Ordinary men and women 'think all things were made for them, and call their natures good or bad, healthy, or rotten and corrupt, according as they are affected by them' (36). The masses are thus unable to see themselves in the light of the symbolic. They cannot contemplate their lives from Nature's own dispassionate viewpoint, as one set of causally determined phenomena in a world where materiality and subjectivity are no more than alternative aspects of the mind of God. They do not understand that 'all final causes are merely fabrications of men' (33). Instead, they take refuge in appeals to the will of God – 'that is, the asylum of ignorance' (34). Like present-

---

[1]   Spinoza, *Ethics* (London, 2000), pp 31, 32. All subsequent references to this work will be provided parenthetically after quotations.

day enemies of Darwin, they imagine that the human body is too astonishingly intricate a phenomenon to have sprung from anything but a supernatural art. Humanity is thus 'compelled by passion, opinion and imagination to deny its own nature'.[2]

In all these ways, the common people 'mistake their imagination for intellect' (35), a distinction which Louis Althusser would later rewrite as one between ideology and theory. Popular knowledge tells us nothing about reality, but a great deal about the structure of the common *imaginaire*. Ordinary people believe, for example, that the world is well-ordered – but this in Spinoza's view means only that 'when things are so disposed that when they are represented to us through our senses we can easily imagine and consequently easily remember them, we call them well-ordered' (35). And things which we can easily imagine we find pleasurable. In Spinoza's own view, order in Nature is nothing 'save in respect to our imagination' (35), a case which David Hume would have readily endorsed.

The coordinates of popular knowledge, then, are those of the imaginary: pleasure, passions, the senses, representation, the imagination, self-centredness, fantasies of coherence. It is not that the imagination is false, any more than ideology is for Althusser. We really do perceive the sun as closer to us than it actually is; but sensory 'knowledge' of this sort is utterly unreliable and stands under the absolute judgement of Reason. 'The perfection of things', writes Spinoza *contra* the 'vulgar', 'is to be estimated solely from their nature and power; nor are things more or less perfect according as they delight or disgust human senses, or according as they are useful or repugnant to human nature' (37). Eudaemonism and utilitarianism are thus sent packing by a brand of rationalism for which the ethics of the populace is really a kind of monstrous collective egoism. The vulgar cannot rise to the challenge of looking at the world as though they were not looking at it. Strictly speaking, then, moral discourse rests on a mistake. It arises from misrecognising the true causes and natures of things. It passes judgement on isolated acts, for example, rather than grasping them as integral parts of a totality; and to this extent it has much in common with what Marxism knows as moralism.[3] Marxist theory is not hostile to ethical discourse, of which it is itself a prime example, but to that myopic form of moral judgement which plucks the object under evaluation from its

---

[2] Roger Scruton, *Spinoza* (Oxford, 1986), p. 33.
[3] For an excellent account of Marxist ethics, see R. G. Peffer, *Marxism, Morality, and Justice* (Princeton, NJ, 1990).

historical context. It is not surprising that Plekhanov hailed Spinoza as an ancestor of atheistic materialism.

As Stuart Hampshire comments, 'exhortations and appeals to emotion and desire are as useless and irrelevant (for Spinoza) in moral as in natural philosophy'.[4] The whole of 'moral sense' theory is dismissed *en avance*: emotive terms like 'joy', 'disapprobation' and so on simply lend a specious uniformity to a vast diversity of responses. We might as well praise or blame others for their tastes and allergies as for their 'moral' acts. 'Whatever (someone) thinks to be a nuisance or bad', Spinoza writes, 'and whatever, moreover, seems to him impious, horrible, unjust or disgraceful, arises from the fact that he conceives these things in a disturbed, mutilated and confused manner' (187). It is just the same with reading scripture: the ignorant take literally such emotive phrases as 'God was angry', rather than grasping these utterances as metaphors of eternal truths. 'Moral problems', as Hampshire puts it, 'are essentially clinical problems.'[5]

Coming as it does from the pen of a hounded Jewish heretic, this view of morality is as admirable as it is perverse. Spinoza would not have considered anger or resentment to be appropriate responses to his persecution, as he did not consider morality to be an emotive matter in the first place. Human appetites and aversions spring from our *conatus* or built-in striving for self-preservation, and as such lie no more within our mastery than the Freudian unconscious or the capitalist mode of production. We must adopt a hermeneutic of suspicion in our judgements, steadfastly purge all reference to the subject, and take a speaker's own account of her feelings and motives as (in the Freudian sense) symptomatic, or (in the Freudo-Marxist sense) a rationalisation. The truth is necessarily eccentric to one's experience: it resides in the physical and material causes underlying such states of consciousness, and can never be captured within them. To be a subject is to misinterpret.

The revolutionary force of this view is hard to underestimate. Louis Althusser saw Spinoza as having 'introduced an unprecedented theoretical revolution in the history of philosophy, probably the greatest philosophical revolution of all time'.[6] These profoundly subversive doctrines, launched by an obscure lens grinder widely honoured as a saint among philosophers, undermine entire moral orthodoxies and sabotage whole reaches of human prejudice. Everyday experience – the very homeland of morality for Locke,

4   Stuart Hampshire, *Spinoza* (Harmondsworth, 1951), p. 121.
5   Ibid., p. 142.
6   Louis Althusser, *Reading Capital* (London, 1970), p. 102.

Hutcheson and Hume – is confused, irrational, pre-scientific and sponta-neously self-interested; words like 'vicious' and 'virtuous', rather like aes-thetic judgements for Kant, indicate not objective properties of things but a speaker's attitudes to them; moral terminology cannot apply to human beings, since they are no more free agents than goldfish; and the self is never so thoroughly a slave to causality than when it imagines itself to be at liberty. Men and women are causally determined natural objects, and in learning and embracing this hardest of truths lie the paths to sanctity and salvation.

Only those who can rise above interest and desire can embrace this doctrine of wise disenchantment; and by 'disinterested' Spinoza means something rather different from the eighteenth-century sentimentalists. For them, as we have seen, to be disinterested is not to practise some bland *apatheia*, but to feel sympathy for another when there is nothing in it for you. In Spinoza's philosophy, however, this feeling for another's body from the inside is no adequate sort of knowledge, since our knowledge of objects which affect us through our bodies, which includes knowledge of other people, is of a 'confused and mutilated' kind. Neither can we attain ade-quate knowledge of our own bodies, which also throws a spanner into the sentimentalist works. Emotions are a warped form of cognition, and the intellect must gain ascendancy over them. (Even so, strangely enough, Spinoza remarks *en passant* that there can never be too much merriment.) Everyday language is just as slippery as our emotional life, governed as it is by the imagination rather than by clear and distinct ideas. We move in a world of smudged meanings and ambiguous objects, from which only the combined efforts of philosophy, mathematics and theology can hope to redeem us.

What the benevolentists saw as the very wellspring of morality – feeling – is thus for Spinoza a fount of false consciousness. He agrees with them that all feeling is founded in imaginary representations; it is just that he refuses to regard this as a source of genuine knowledge.[7] This is because true cognition of things is possible only 'in God'. It is knowledge *sub specie aeternatis*, rather as theory for Althusser is without a history. To see the world properly is to see it, so to speak, from its own standpoint; and this involves a shift from the imaginary, in which knowledge is refracted by desire, to the moral maturity of the symbolic. We must cease, in St Paul's words, to see through a glass darkly, and instead adopt a God's-eye view

[7] See Genevieve Lloyd, *Spinoza and the 'Ethics'* (London, 1996), p. 76.

of ourselves, serene in the knowledge that neither ourselves nor anything else in the cosmos could have been other than what they are.

It is this for Spinoza which constitutes true wisdom and virtue. Indeed, he practised such austere detachment in his own life, holding (unlike his great but ambitious contemporary, Leibniz) that philosophy should be untrammelled by self-advancement and state power. It was for this reason that he turned down the Elector Palatine's offer of a Chair at Heidelberg, preferring to live as a humble manual worker. Desire, he believes in psychoanalytic style, is 'the very essence of man' (125) – and by desire he means 'any of a man's endeavours, impulses, appetites and volitions, which vary according to the varied constitution of the said man, and are often opposed one to the other as the man is drawn in different directions and knows not whither to turn' (126).

In this volatile zone of being, human love is of an imaginary, mimetic kind. 'He who imagines that which he loves to be affected by pleasure or pain', Spinoza remarks, 'will also be affected by pleasure or pain . . . If we imagine anything to affect with pleasure what we love, we are affected with love towards it . . .' (98). As we have seen, it is the kind of emotional contagiousness that eighteenth-century moral philosophy will regard as a powerful source of social bonding. In Spinoza's eyes, however, it represents a degenerate kind of affection in contrast with that 'intellectual love of God' which for him represents the highest human good. Indeed, he believes pity to be a reprehensible, 'effeminate' sort of sentiment, and feels much the same about compassion. As with Kant, we must act under the ordinance of reason, not under the spell of some passing emotional stimulus.

In an act of self-transcendence which finds echoes all the way from the Buddha to the Stoics and Schopenhauer, the truly free individual suspends his desire to attain an unclouded kind of contentment. The free individual will refuse to blame others or the universe for the injuries they inflict upon us, since such apparent blemishes – rape, torture, massacres and the like – are simply divine necessities misunderstood as deficiencies. It is an edifying sort of reflection – for if others, given a deterministic world, cannot help cheating, lying or cutting us into a thousand small pieces, our awareness of this compulsion can bear fruit in the virtues of tolerance, mildness, forgiveness, forbearance, patience and equanimity, along with a blessed relief from envy, hatred and contempt. The virtuous return love for hatred, and think little of death. Determinism is thus conducive to saintliness, not cynicism or despair. Reason, objectivity and disinterestedness are on the side of love and mercy, not power and prejudice. It is the world's necessity which renders it non-tragic: if nothing is fortuitous, there is no point in lamenting or resisting it. Those who insist that if we do not resist the inevitable we will never know how inevitable the inevitable was in the first place, can rest assured that it was ineluctable from all eternity and consequently save their efforts.

It would certainly seem to take either a saint or a fleshless rationalist to think in this fashion. Yet Spinoza does not simply abjure the flesh; like Hegel, Schiller and Marx, he trusts rather in its re-education. 'To make use of things and take delight in them as much as possible', he observes, '. . . is the part of a wise man' (170). The point is not to shun the passions but to bring reason to bear upon them, dredging to light the invisible determinants of our being in the manner of the analyst. Spinoza is a democrat and republican who wishes to enlighten the masses, not to conceal from them the appalling truth of the world in the strategic manner of a Leo Strauss. In any case, he holds *contra* Hobbes that their desires are malleable enough to be moulded. Philosophy is a critique of desire, rather than (like some postmodern thought) an affirmation of it. It thus has an activist political and ethical agenda: the masses can be persuaded into virtue, and so, being creatures of habit rather than reflection, can come to do good spontaneously. In which case, they will require less discipline and repression – a fact which will render them less rancorous, and therefore more ready to submit to their superiors. Like Burke and Schiller, Spinoza is an early theorist of what Gramsci would later call hegemony.

The aim of the virtuous individual is therefore to become self-determining, allowing herself to be swayed by nothing as trivially extraneous as emotion. The case prefigures the thought of Immanuel Kant, and there are other such anticipations in the Dutch philosopher's writings. Reasonable men and women, he suggests, desire nothing for themselves which they do not also seek for the rest of humankind. To act according to reason is nothing less than to follow our nature considered as an end in itself, and to accomplish this is to be free. We must love ourselves; but in pursuing what is best for ourselves we also create the conditions for a true commonwealth, a society characterised by peace, friendship and social harmony. In such a republic, there would be no censorship of speech or writing. This is among other things because such freedom is in Spinoza's view necessary for the exercise of reason, and therefore for the disclosure of truth. Yet part of what that truth teaches us is that there is no such thing as freedom, at least as commonly conceived. All the same, this truth about non-freedom will itself set us free.

For all his stringent fidelity to the symbolic, Spinoza's view of the world culminates in a curious kind of imaginary vision. His conception of the just society, one which reaches beyond the liberal doctrine of which he was so magnificent a champion, is one which 'composes the minds of all as it were into one mind, and the bodies of all as it were into one body . . .' (153). This mutuality goes hand in hand with a unity between the mind and Nature, in which each harmoniously mirrors the other. In the highest state of wisdom, the ideas which constitute the mind are identical with those which go to make up the mind of God. There is a kind of 'higher' imaginary at stake in this semi-mystical aspect of Spinozist thought, one which points forward to the final self-realisation of Hegel's *Geist*. After its wanderings through the symbolic domain of loss, negativity, difference and alienation, the World Spirit for Hegel finally comes into its own in a sublime version of the imaginary. It is the aim of knowledge, Hegel remarks, 'to divest the objective world of its strangeness, and, as the phrase is, to find ourselves at home in it; which means no more than to trace the objective world to the notion – to our innermost self'.[8] Spirit finds its own blessed visage reflected in the history and Nature it has fashioned, rather as the Father recognises himself in the beloved Son in whom he is eternally well-pleased.

---

[8]   *The Logic of Hegel* (Oxford, 1968), p. 335.

5

Kant and the Moral Law

We have seen that the eighteenth-century benevolentists were advocates of love, but with a keen sense of its limitations. Like memory, the affections fade the further away from their object they move. In any case, in social orders where self-interest reigns sovereign, sympathy is in chronically short supply. This is not to say that such sympathies are not potentially universal. Richard Sennett has pointed to the paradox that in eighteenth-century England, private affections were regarded as natural, in contrast to the artifice of public culture, and were therefore viewed as universal. 'The public', Sennett writes, 'was a human creation; the private was the human condition.'[1] It was the most private of institutions – the family – which was also 'the seat of nature', representing as it did a kind of democracy of the heart. And it is here, so Sennett argues, that one finds *in nuce* what will later become known as natural rights.

In this sense, the private could pass judgement on the public. 'By identifying certain psychic processes as inexpressible in public terms', Sennett writes, 'as transcendent, quasi-religious phenomena which could never be violated or destroyed by the arrangements of convention, [eighteenth-century citizens] crystallised for themselves one way, and not the only way, surely, but a tangible way, in which natural rights could transcend the entitlements of any particular society.'[2] We are not abandoned to a culturalism or conventionalism for which the sources of radical social critique must logically remain obscure. Instead, as with the moral sense theorists, we have a sure judgement-seat in Nature itself. Yet these emotions, 'inexpressible in public terms' as they are, are as elusive as they are intense.

[1] Richard Sennett, *The Fall of Public Man* (London, 2002), p. 98.
[2] Ibid., p. 90.

There is another problem to compound this particular one, which we have glanced at already. For though natural sympathies are inherently universal, they are, as we have seen, only locally activated. And this makes for trouble with strangers – with those, as Sennett argues, of that 'gathering of strangers' which is the eighteenth-century metropolis, who are perilously difficult to decipher from their outward semiotic marks. The eighteenth century, Sennett claims, 'was a place in which people made great efforts to colour and define their relations with strangers; the point is, they had to make an effort'.[3] The modern idea of a faceless mass of others is still resisted; yet it is also steadily encroaching on the knowable community. One could greet a stranger on the street, as long as this was understood not to signify some importunate claim on his person. Such greetings are no more 'sincerely' meant than the words of an actor; yet this is not to say that, as with the theatre, one is not emotionally bound up in the situation to hand. Flowery figures of speech were deployed in greeting others, but of a scrupulously indiscriminate kind, implying no acquaintance with the other's life-history or material circumstances. Social class provided what one might call an impersonal intimacy, as it sometimes does today: gentlemen recognise each other for what they are even at a distance. Yet as the ranks of the middle class became swollen in the new urban metropolises, the problem of anonymity grew accordingly more acute.

There is a need, then, to compensate for the deficiencies of natural feeling, and one name for this compensation is law. Law, or more generally the symbolic order it underpins, is one major way in which we conduct ourselves towards those we do not know. Like the market, it is a mechanism for regulating the way we treat countless anonymous others, ensuring (and here the market analogy begins to unravel) that if we cannot find them personable or erotically appealing, we can at least behave towards them with justice. It is, to be sure, a less agreeable motive to virtue than geniality; but it is also a more equitable and dependable one. Hegel writes scornfully in his *Philosophy of Right* of those Romantic theories which 'would banish thought and have recourse instead to feeling, enthusiasm, the heart and the breast'.[4] The law in modern times, as the tribunal before which we are all on an equal footing, is the enemy of privilege, a word which means 'private law'. Moreover, because law, reason and the symbolic order transcend individual interests and appetites, it is possible for them to provide

---

[3]   Ibid., p. 60.
[4]   T. M. Knox (ed.), *Hegel's Philosophy of Right* (Oxford, 1942), para. 21.

a critique of them, which is not the case with the imaginary. We can ask, for example, whether a particular desire is reasonable – a question which would have seemed no more legitimate to Hobbes or Hume than it would to Gilles Deleuze.

Because it has to mediate between so many individuals, each of them furnished with his or her peculiar interests and desires, the law must cultivate the virtue of reticence, aiming to say as little as possible. Those who seek to conform to it are consequently plunged into neurotic anxiety about whether they are obeying it or not, how they would know this in any case, and whether this conception even makes sense. The law, so to speak, is stretched so tight across such a multitude of men and women that it dwindles to an extreme thinness. The less definitive content it has, the more effectively it can accomplish its role. In this sense, moral laws resemble physical ones, which are simply mathematical relationships expressible with very little information.[5] If it is to provide a ground for human unity, the law must do so by systematically overlooking our differences. For the Aristotelians and Thomists, we have a rational nature in common; for the benevolentists, this nature has dwindled to a set of feelings we share, shorn of a rational basis; with the Kantians, human communality has shrunk even further to a set of shared formal procedures; for some modernists and postmodernists, there is only difference.

If there is to be a community of subjects in a fractured society, the law must abstract from everything that is specific and peculiar to those under its sway. The advantage of such an operation is that the law is properly deaf to those who seek to pull rank; the danger is that it ends up creating a commonwealth of ciphers. It is as though human beings must be flattened and cloned if equality and universality are truly to be realised. Each individual is now cherished as unique and autonomous; yet because all of them are to be indifferently prized in this way, this value is constantly on the brink of negating itself. Everyone is equal – but only, it would appear, because they have been reduced to straw men with the stuffing knocked out of them.

Even so, this conception of law is an ingenious way of achieving universality at a time when more traditional ways of doing so – the notion of a common human nature, for example – are floundering, not least on account of travellers hotfoot from their voyages with news of human diversity. It means, however, that we now need reflection and calculation in

5   See Paul Davies, *The Goldilocks Enigma* (London, 2006), p. 263.

order to take others into account. A certain early bourgeois spontaneity or *sprezzatura* has been irrevocably lost. As the bourgeois class in Europe enters upon the accumulation of industrial capital, with its anonymous labourers, faceless competitors and ferocious class struggles, the gentleman's club yields ground to the court of law or political arena as a paradigm of moral discourse.

Such is the celebrated moral law of Immanuel Kant, to which all human beings are subject in the same kind of way, and which has all the absolute force of a divine edict while remaining quite sublunary. Like God, this law is simply given: it cannot be reduced to any more fundamental principle, and is not susceptible of rational demonstration. For Lacan, as we have seen, we are constituted as subjects only under the sway of a law which articulates our being with that of others. Whereas in the imaginary we face inwards, so to speak, each of us now faces outwards towards an authority which links us anonymously together. For Kant, one becomes an authentic human subject – free, rational and autonomous – only by bowing to the sovereignty of a law which regulates and harmonises one's ends in accordance with the ends of all other such free, rational beings. The difference between the two philosophers on this score is that Kant locates this freedom underground, in a noumenal sphere inaccessible to the conscious mind, whereas for Lacan it is in just this underground or unconscious domain that we are least at liberty. Whatever the difference, however, we have now ventured into a territory which is instantly recognisable as modern: a culture of contractual relations, enlightened self-interest, moral rules, equitable laws, the maximisation of utility, respect for the autonomy of others, consensual norms and rational procedures. It is an order very far from the fleshly immediacies of the imaginary; but it is also, as we shall see later, everything that the advocates of an ethics of the Real find most unpalatable.

Early in his career, Kant expressed his admiration for the method of moral inquiry of Shaftesbury, Hutcheson and Hume, finding in this view of ethics what he called a 'beautiful discovery of our age'. What struck him about such moralists (ironically enough, given his own later rejection of an anthropological ethics) was their preoccupation with what happens rather than with what ought to happen – the fact that they proceeded not from abstract premises but from the nature of humanity.[6] In the *Critique of Pure Reason*, by contrast, Kant warns that nothing is more reprehensible than to seek to derive the laws prescribing what ought to be done from

[6]   See Ernst Cassirer, *Kant's Life and Thought* (New Haven, CT, 1981), p. 235.

what actually is done. In a social order characterised by selfish individualism, this is no doubt a prudent enough *caveat*. Kant's nervousness of the
empirical is among other things an implicit comment on his social surroundings. If one did try to derive values from facts in such a context, one
might well end up with all the least savoury kinds of value. Far from being
a simple expression of the way the world is, values must be insulated from
it – partly (for society in general, if not for Kant in particular) so that they
can serve to legitimate it.

Kant was not, to be sure, to build on the marshy terrain of British moral
theory himself, even though he was greatly influenced by Shaftesbury's
case that fundamental moral principles cannot be matters of subjective
preference but must be universally binding. Like Shaftesbury, Kant holds
that morality involves the feelings – in his case, respect, anger, indignation, prudence, esteem, remorse and the like. We have the capacity to feel
delight in the fulfilment of our moral duty – indeed, such a sense of satisfaction is both legitimate and desirable. But such sentiments cannot
provide the motive for our actions. Hegel thought much the same. Desire
cannot be a factor in right action. On the contrary, what we feel above all
in such circumstances is pain – for the moral law sets its face sternly
against our natural inclinations, and this is one way in which we become
aware of its exalted presence. Kant also makes room in his ethical thought
for happiness; but though happiness is the reward for virtue, in the after-
life if not for the most part in this mundane one, it cannot be its guiding
impulse. Happiness is merely an empirical notion, not an ideal of reason.
Eudaemonism is an unprincipled affair. One must strive for universal
contentment – but a contentment which is combined and in conformity
with the purest moral principle. He does not believe that moral principles
can be founded upon sensation, emotion or the pursuit of well-being. The
senses allow us no access to our true selves or to things in themselves,
whatever the benevolentists may claim of the intuitive communion of two
kindred souls. Sensation is no basis for self-knowledge. The moral subject
belongs to the realm of the intelligible, not of the sensible. We must take
no account of the principle of happiness where our duty is concerned. A
sense of virtue must surely be more than a *frisson* of satisfaction. One must
act on principle, not on what Kant scornfully dubs 'melting sympathy'. In
this, he is at odds with Theodor Adorno, who writes that 'the true basis
of morality is to be found in bodily feeling, in identification with unbearable pain'.[7]

---

[7] Theodor Adorno, *Metaphysics: Concepts and Problems* (Cambridge, 2001), p. 116.

In fact, Kant comes to dismiss this British strain of moral thought as a doomed attempt to derive the concept of virtue from experience. For him as for Spinoza, experience is far too shifting, contingent a basis for moral judgement, just as it is too frail a foundation in itself for establishing the objectivity of truth. It is, Kant remarks, an 'ambiguous monstrosity' which resists all orderly formulation. Sensibility is a grossly unreliable guide. Morality is above nature, and cannot be rooted in the body or its empirical circumstances. Feelings, propensities and inclinations can yield us no objective principles. With Hutcheson in mind, Kant refers slightingly in his *Groundwork of the Metaphysics of Morals* to 'an implanted sense' or 'supposed special sense', scoffing that 'those who cannot *think* believe they can help themselves out by feeling'.[8] With the same ethics in mind, he insists that imitation has no place at all in questions of morality.

He does, however, concede that moral sense theory, however misguided, pays a certain proper homage to the dignity of the moral life. It is as though these generous-hearted if wrong-headed philosophers feel in the presence of others the delight and esteem which for Kant should be reserved for the moral law in general. Their sentiments, then, are less inappropriate than misplaced. There are those souls, he acknowledges, 'so sympathetically attuned that, without any other motive of vanity or self-interest they find an inner satisfaction in spreading joy around them and can take delight in the satisfaction of others so far as it is their own work'.[9] Yet in Kant's eyes such fellow-feeling is no more a moral affair than hankering after a tot of rum. Only acts performed for the sake of the law can be classified as moral. One must be benevolent out of duty, not out of sympathy. You must not do things only because you want to. Needs and inclinations, he tells us, have a 'market price', while that which is precious in itself is priceless.

It is true that in the mid-eighteenth century Alexander Baumgarten had launched a curious new science called aesthetics, whose purpose was to clarify and regulate our sensory life, reducing our somatic world to some sort of quasi-lawful order. The senses, rudely ejected by certain strains of Enlightenment reason, were to be smuggled in again by the back door in the guise of a science of perception. But this disciplined inquiry into our sensory life can yield us no access to the moral realm. Warm-heartedness is no more of an ethical category than the concept of triangulation. 'It is a

[8]   Immanuel Kant, *Groundwork of the Metaphysics of Morals* (Cambridge, 1997), p. 49.
[9]   Ibid., p. 1.

very beautiful thing', Kant writes in his *Critique of Practical Reason*, 'to do good to men from love to them and from sympathetic good will, or to be just from love of order, but this is not the true moral maxim.'[10] Pity and tender-hearted compassion are all very fine; but if they, rather than the idea of duty, constitute the cause of our action, then in Kant's own words they become a burden on the right-thinking, who accordingly wish to be rid of them and to be subject to the law of reason alone. Such emotions are examples of what he brands 'pathological love'. Jacques Lacan, speaking up for the Real rather than the symbolic, also insists that 'as guides to the real, feelings are deceptive'.[11] If you eliminate all sentiments from morality, he claims, we would end up with the vision of a Kant – or, for that matter, of a Sade. Kant does not see that the acts of renunciation and idealisation themselves can be sources of covert libidinal pleasure. It is not without a certain grudging affection that we confront those who would deprive us of our gratification.

The British argument has a certain aesthetic allure, then, but it is far too soft an option. Benevolence, Kant considers, is a mere inclination. He has a Protestant wariness of values which one can purchase on the cheap, without some heroic inner drama of struggle and self-conquest. Kant admires the angst of the high-minded bourgeois wrestling with his conscience, not the breezy spontaneity of the patrician. He is no admirer of that fine, haughty, look-no-hands nonchalance which the Renaissance knew as *sprezzatura*. What is precious is what you sweat for; so that to be born with a compassionate nature is a genetic fact about people, not a moral one. Whereas Aristotle considers that those who reap no satisfaction from acting virtuously are actually defective in virtue, and David Hume insists that such pleasure is the very mark of the virtuous, Kant holds that those who are cold in temperament but manage despite this to do good rank highest of all in the moral stakes. The more we combat our spontaneous inclinations, the more morally commendable we become. Pleasure is a lowly sort of motive in his censorious eyes, as it is not for Shaftesbury and Hutcheson. Since such sudden surges of sympathy do not involve acts of will, they do not count as moral responses at all. Sensibility is largely the enemy of the ethical, and what is not inspired by duty must be done purely for pleasure. It is the playing-fields-of-Eton view of life: if it doesn't hurt, it can't be doing you good. As with cigars, it is better on the whole not to find virtuous conduct too delectable.

---

[10] Immanuel Kant, *Critique of Practical Reason* (London, 1879), p. 249.

[11] Jacques Lacan, *The Ethics of Psychoanalysis* (London, 1999), p. 30.

A good deal of middle ground is squeezed out by the Kantian antithesis between inclination and obligation. What is excluded among other things is the Aristotelian notion of a moral disposition, which is a question neither of abstract duty nor sentient urge, blind habit or strenuous act of will. Dispositions involve emotions; but they are emotions bound up with judgements and geared to potential action, not inner flutters and twinges to be nurtured à la sentimentalism for their own sake. To act really well, we must have certain appropriate judgements, feelings and attitudes; but what matters in the end is to act well. To this extent, Kant's purely rational moral agent is as defective an image of virtue as the benevolentists' wholly intuitive one, which seems to leave scant space for rational assessment. Dispositions are not blind outbursts of spontaneous feeling, but states which must be strenuously cultivated, disciplined, exercised and reflected upon, until the actions to which they incline us become easy and habitual. Mercy, compassion, the desire for justice: these are not just questions of conceptual calculation, but neither are they to be modelled on a stab of hunger or sudden access of envy. They involve both reason and passion, reflection and emotion. Nor can these faculties be respectively assigned to our dealings with those we do not know and those we do; for we are stirred by the mishaps of strangers, and brood on our intimacy with those around us. Kant is right to see that the benevolentists risk secluding themselves from universal fellowship; but he is mistaken to imagine that only an abstract reasoning can take us beyond the motions of the heart.

Good will, remarks Aristotle in the *Nicomachean Ethics*, resembles friendship but is not identical with it, since you can have it for those you do not know. For Kant, in search of some principle of communality beyond the personal affinities of his British predecessors, the notion of a good will should play a supremely pivotal role. Yet it is risky to rely overmuch in ethical matters on questions of motive and will. Since a good deed can be dubiously motivated, Kant is mistaken to suppose that the will reigns supreme in moral affairs. What counts most in such matters is what you do, not what you will or intend. Throwing small change to vagrants in order to salve your conscience is a great deal preferable to passing them by. Besides, Kant's hypostasised idea of the will seems far from plausible, compared, say, to the concept of will we find in Thomas Aquinas. For Aquinas, the will is not some unconditioned mental impulse. It is a kind of primary orientation of our existence, a built-in inclination to the good or natural bent towards well-being. Given the kind of bodies we are, we have an appetite for goodness which is not itself optional. Questions of choice, Aquinas considered, depended in the end on the make-up of our material bodies. It is a concept of the will which has a rather more plausible ring than most of its modern counterparts.[12]

Throughout his ethical writings, Kant makes the cardinal error of assuming that the moral difference that counts is one between inclination and obligation. So, as we shall see later, do some present-day exponents of an ethics of the Real, who remain in this sense closet Kantians. If you are not a rational agent, then you must be a hedonistic egoist. Kant would not accept that desiring to do something, providing it is not injurious, is a perfectly good reason for doing it. In any case, even non-human animals can act out of more than sheer hedonism from time to time, even if they may have difficulty in wrapping their heads around the categorical imperative. It was Kant above all who set ethical thought on the path which led to the spurious equation of morality with duty, a conflation of which we shall find traces as late as Emmanuel Levinas and Jacques Derrida. (Yet there is, so Bernard Williams reminds us, no ancient Greek term for 'duty'.)[13] Kant assumes that morality involves some unconditional value, rather as (so we shall see) the Lacanian moralists do as well. Otherwise, in Kant's view if not in Lacan's, we are likely to be plunged into the maelstrom of moral relativism. Those who press this case seem not to recognise that the relativist is usually the flip side of the authoritarian, the Oedipally rebellious son of the metaphysical father. To those for whom moral value must be absolute or nothing, whatever falls short of absolute status is bound to look like some frightful chaos. They do not see that reason and chaos entail one another, chaos being for the most part whatever a rational order excludes.

The astonishingly radical upshot of Kant's argument is hard to overstate. To spend your life like, say, Nelson Mandela, inspired by outrage and compassion to transform the lot of untold millions, is all very fine; but it is by no means so fine a thing as ensuring that when you refrain from pilfering a peach, you do so not because you live in fear of the greengrocer, but because you conform your action to a law which can be prescribed for all other potential pilferers as well. It is in this, not in giving a crust of bread to a beggar out of pity, that true moral beauty lies – or as Kant might say (since the moral law, like God, lies beyond representation), true sublimity. The case is as breathtaking as it is brutal. At an extreme, it warrants the dryly amusing judgement which Bernard Williams passes on the ultra-

---

[12] I discuss this point further in *Holy Terror* (Oxford, 2005), Ch. 4.
[13] Bernard Williams, *Ethics and the Limits of Philosophy* (Cambridge, MA, 1985), p. 16.

rationalist William Godwin, 'with his ferociously rational refusal to respect any consideration that an ordinary human being would find compelling'.[14]

How strange to imagine, as Kant does, that to be prompted by love or compassion is to be unfree! One might claim that his view of humanity is at once too high and too low – or, in Milan Kundera's terms, at once too angelic and too demonic.[15] The two are generally to be found nestling cheek-by-jowl: when social existence is 'demonic', governed by appetite and self-interest, a correspondingly 'angelic' ideology will generally be required to legitimate this fact. Moral value will need to have as little truck as possible with empirical fact. This is one reason why the United States, one of the world's most rampantly materialist societies, is also possessed of a comically earnest, moralistic, high-toned public discourse. A somewhat less high-minded view than Kant's, mixing conscience with emotion, is advanced by the English philosopher Joseph Butler, for whom spontaneous affection is commendable, but becomes even more worthy when it sediments into a settled principle.

Kant's own view, however, is more uncompromising than this. No genuine universal law can be plucked from the common desire for happiness, since each person desires happiness in his or her own idiosyncratic way, and ethical reason remains consequently immured in blind particularity. There must be a more absolute, unconditional ground to morality than this, a sort of secular version of the unconditional Almighty, which like all such absolutes bears its credentials entirely within itself. Rather as God is his own eternal *raison d'être*, so too for Kant is the moral law, which is necessarily an end for everyone because it is an end in itself. It is what all men and women are capable of willing, quite apart from their personal yearnings and proclivities, and which they can therefore also will for one another. Hence the celebrated categorical imperative: act only according to that maxim which you can propose as a universal law. If to be human is to be rational, then for me to act rationally is inevitably to prescribe my form of action for all others of my kind. To be free is to disentangle oneself from all contingent objects and desires, all so-called 'pathological' interests, in order to act only in accordance with a law which one can establish for oneself – a law luminous with the aura of being entirely an end in itself, with no regard to the distinctive nature of this or that individual, and thus of universal application. Because we bestow this law on ourselves, it

14   Ibid., p. 107.
15   See Terry Eagleton, *Sweet Violence: The Idea of the Tragic* (Oxford, 2003), pp. 258–9.

constitutes the very ground of our freedom, since freedom is tantamount to self-determination. Later generations will be rather more sceptical of this claim, suspecting that the laws we impose on ourselves are generally the most brutally coercive of all. There is, as Theodor Adorno perceives, something compulsive about Kant's supposedly non-pathological freedom under law, to which Freud will give the name of the superego.

This, indeed, is the unpalatable underside of Kant's enlightened ethics. Because we can never be justified before the law, it breeds in us a perpetual disquiet or out-of-placeness which is nothing less than the state of being a subject. The moral law is a cruel God. At its most brutally sadistic, it reduces us by its senseless terrorism to non-beings, superfluous entities, meaningless bits of matter. The correlative of the exalted moral law is the human being as left-over, excremental, pure negativity. Confronted with this traumatic lack of sense (for the law is entirely empty of substance), the subject suffers a crisis or breakdown of meaning, one which is a permanent state of emergency rather than a momentary outbreak of panic. In this sense, the symbolic law harbours at its heart what Lacan will call the Real – that condition in which we are destitute, out-of-joint, pitched into the abyss of non-meaning, crushed by a traumatic core of meaninglessness which is closer to us than breathing.

There is a tension at the heart of ethical thought between the universal and the particular. Moral behaviour is a material affair, bound up with the needs and desires of mortal animals, part of their expressive or symbolic communication and so ineluctably local; but it is also supposed to stretch beyond this specificity into some more universal domain. It would seem strange to claim that torture is permissible for me but not for you, or to rank statements like 'Eye-gouging is forbidden' with expressions of personal taste like 'sprouts are disgusting'. Like language, ethics is both grandly general and irreducibly specific. It involves thick concepts as well as thin ones. J. M. Bernstein distinguishes between 'morality', meaning what he calls 'centralist', top-down general principles, and those thick, descriptive or evaluative 'ethical' concepts which are logically prior to such pale if indispensable universals.[16] What was briefly known in the 1960s as 'situation ethics', a vein of ethical anti-universalism much favoured by certain liberal-minded Christians, ran aground on the problem that no human situation can ever be exactly circumscribed, and that every such situation involves features which are far from peculiar to it. Besides, if the meaning of words like 'love' and 'justice' can be grasped only in mutually incompa-

---

[16]   J. M. Bernstein, *Adorno: Disenchantment and Ethics* (Cambridge, 2001), pp. 60–1.

rable situations, such terms are emptied of all general application to leave us adrift in a sea of ethical nominalism. If there is no necessary relation between the idea of justice and a pattern of conduct which is consistent across different situations, then any pattern of conduct, including decapitating all those over the age of sixty, could be claimed to conform to it. On the other hand, an ethics which appears to set aside specific contexts altogether seems scarcely worthy of the name. We shall be looking at this dilemma again in a moment, when we come to examine Shakespeare's views of it.

In Kant's view, ethics is both an individual and universal affair, and to this extent resembles aesthetic judgements. An ethical act is one which is purely and wholly mine; yet where I am most peerlessly myself is at the same time where I become no more than the bearer of a universal law. It is of the essence of the individual subject to be a universal animal, and we are at our finest when we act in this fashion. Something inhuman or impersonal lies at the core of the self, making it what it is – though whereas for Augustine and Aquinas the name of this sublimely unfathomable power is God, and for Freudians it is known as desire, Kant calls it the moral law. There is thus a direct passage for him from the individual to the universal – though it is one we can steer only at the expense of concrete particularity.

So abstract universalism and irreducible specificity are sides of the same coin. Individual subjects are the driving force of this civilisation, yet they are divested of what they are by the abstract powers they let loose. Freedom means endorsing no principle which one does not legislate for oneself; yet this very self-determination threatens to reduce the subject to a pointless tautology. It is up to men and women to confer value on themselves, rather than, in the manner of the imaginary, finding their value underwritten by the world or the other. The symbolic order into which Kant ushers us is entirely self-supporting: it has no ground either in Nature or the supernatural. Even divine decrees must be run past human rationality to screen out logical flaws. It is as though we now take our stand on nothing but ourselves; and if this is a feature of our ethical coming of age, as we slough off our imaginary infantile dependence on others and the universe, it is also the measure of our estrangement from a Nature which, having been diminished to so much raw fact, can have no truck with anything as exalted as value. The exultant boast of the modern – 'I take value from myself alone!' – is thus only ever a hair's breadth away from the hollow cry of anguish 'I am so lonely in this universe!'

To act morally, then, is to be guided purely by reason, and by the duty which reason proposes, rather than by the mixed bunch of motives (pleasure, desire, happiness, utility, well-being and the rest) which we receive from others, from the world around us or from our own creaturely appetites, and which are therefore unworthy of rational animals whose end lies wholly in themselves. The truly moral act is independent of what it accomplishes – a curious ethical assumption, sure enough. In a sublime tautology, we should be moral because it is moral to be so. What makes an action moral, rather as what makes a material object a commodity, is something it manifests over and above any distinctive property it possesses, namely its willed conformity to a law which is capable of being universalised. Humanity has no access to such portentous metaphysical entities as the Supreme Good, which are as barred to it as the Lacanian Other; so that the only possible substitute for this lost Thing, given that it must be something entirely unconditional, is the unconditional form of the moral law. The law, then, emerges to fill a void – the lack of the Supreme Good or maternal body – with its paternal injunctions; and in this sense we are speaking of a transition from the imaginary to the symbolic.

Like the work of art, morality or practical reason is autonomous and self-grounding. It contains its ends in itself, spurns all utility, disdains all consequence, and brooks no argument. As with Spinoza, the key terms of eighteenth-century benevolentism and sentimentalism – pleasure, emotion, intuition, sensation, fulfilment, imagination, representation – are relegated for the most part to the degenerate domain of the amoral. (We may note that these terms, too, belong to the language of aesthetics.) We are speaking, then, of an ethics beyond the pleasure principle. Moral action has nothing to do with offering lively representations to the imagination. The Humean case that we require such animated images to stir our torpid moral imaginations is rejected out of hand. On the contrary, Kant regards such 'images and childish devices' not only as unworthy of rational creatures like ourselves, but as actually tempering the sublime majesty of the moral law, and thus diminishing its formidable force. There can be no graven image of human reason or freedom: the sheer inscrutability of freedom, so the iconoclastic Kant maintains in the *Critique of Judgement*, precludes all positive presentation. It is a purely noumenal phenomenon, which can be known only practically, not captured in a sensory image. We know we are free because we catch ourselves acting that way out of the corner of our eye; but like the spectral other who walks beside you in *The Waste Land*, this elusive entity vanishes like a wraith if you try to look at it straight.

This, to be sure, poses something of a problem for a middle-class social order of which liberty is the very linchpin. The most inestimable value of all now slips clean through the net of representation, leaving it a kind of suggestive cipher or mere trace of transcendence. The subject, the founding principle of the whole enterprise, gives the slip to our categories and comes to figure within them as no more than a mute epiphany or pregnant silence, a presence which laps soundlessly up against the boundaries of our thought. It can be felt only as a kind of empty excess or transcendence of any particular. At the very peak of his powers, then, bourgeois Man is self-blinded, since his freedom – the very essence of his selfhood – is by definition indeterminable. All we can claim of subjectivity, that strange vacuity we are made out of, is that whatever it may be it is nothing at all like an object, and thus baffles cognition. Knower and known no longer share the same terrain. The enterprise of science is eminently possible, but the scientist as a subject falls outside the realm he or she investigates. Even the things she deals with she can know only in their phenomenal appearances. Only a negative theology of Man, so to speak, is therefore feasible.

It is, then, as though the subject is squeezed out of the very system it pins together, as at once source and supplement. It is both the ground of the entire system and a dark hole at its centre. Its unfathomable power is at the same time sheer negativity. Trying to lend this spectre a determinate shape is like trying to leap on our own shadows. It cannot be *in* the world, any more than the eye is part of the field of vision. For Kant, the subject is not a phenomenon in reality but a transcendental viewpoint upon it. It is through the subject that, in his celebrated Copernican revolution, he will seek to restore to us the objective world; but in the process of doing so the subject 'in itself' slides over the rim of knowledge and disappears into that crypt of entombed entities known as the noumenal, about which nothing whatsoever can be said. The subject is simply not a feasible object of cognition, any more than guardian angels or square triangles. At the high point of its power, the bourgeois class finds itself expropriated by the very social order it has fashioned, wedged between an impenetrable subject on the one hand and an unknowable object on the other.

Strictly determined from the outside yet self-determining on the inside, the human subject is everywhere free and everywhere in chains. For Spinoza, these two aspects of its existence are at one: freedom lies in the knowledge that one is enchained, and is the fruit of one's consequent striving to become self-determining. It means coming to view oneself not as an isolated being but as part of a system of necessity. Kant subscribes to this Spinozist determinism, shorn of its metaphysical underpinnings, but adds to the iron causalities of Nature a transcendent domain of spirit. In doing so, he salvages freedom at the expense of its intelligibility. In Spinoza's eyes, it is an imaginary or mythical affair; in Kant's view it is a necessary hypothesis. Wisdom for the Dutch philosopher consists in reflecting upon our identity with Nature; for his German counterpart, it is a question of establishing our autonomy of it.

So it is that, in an audacious move, Kant shifts the whole business of morality from the imaginary to the symbolic – which is also to say from content to form, or from the substantive to the procedural. This involves a transition from being able to back up your morality with something beyond it – God, Nature, History – to the mixed benefits of being eternally cut adrift from any such foundation. Moral philosophy, Kant declares in his *Groundwork of the Metaphysics of Morals*, must be purged of all empirical and anthropological content. Since any act of will motivated by an empirical object or inclination is 'pathological', it follows that the only supreme good is the pure act of willing the good itself. And to will the good is to will not any specific thing, but the pure fact that one acts in accordance with the moral law. This law therefore has absolutely nothing to say other than to promulgate itself. As Kafka wrote to his friend Gershom Scholem, it has 'validity but no significance'. The medium, so to speak, is the message. Its command is unconditional, yet it does not instruct us in what to do. Like a liberal-minded school principal who seeks to foster personal initiative among his or her pupils, it advises us what general form our actions should take, but is deliberately tight-lipped about their content. Enlightened persons do not need to be handed a list of moral injunctions from on high. Indeed, those who require such injunctions would be for that very reason ill-equipped to see them through, as one would hesitate to accept food from a chef who required detailed instructions on how to recognise a cauliflower.

In its empty or tautological quality, the Kantian law would seem to differ from the unconditional demands of the God whose shoes it fills – a deity who spells out his decrees in rather more uncomfortably precise terms. In another sense, however, it differs from him scarcely at all – for the so-called Ten Commandments are simply Yahweh's style of stating 'This is how I am to be loved.' God's fundamental demand is not that one should refrain from theft or adultery, but that we should allow him to love us, so that by the power of this grace we may be able to love him in return. The tautology of the symbolic law – 'You must obey, since the law, after all, is the law, and duty is duty' – becomes the tautology of a pointless love, the vacuity of absolute transcendence. If the law had a specific content, then it might always be possible to bargain with it, sweet-talk it, exchange a spot of dutiful submission for a sizeable reward. But because the Mosaic law is the law of love, its content must always go beyond its form. What frustrates the Pharisees of this world is the silence of those eternal spaces.

The divine imperative, like Kant's categorical imperative, is therefore quite empty of substance. It is St Augustine's 'Love, and do what you will.' It hints in its taciturn quality at God's transcendence of the human. It belongs to this transcendence that he does not place crippling demands upon his creatures, in the manner of the sadistic, crazedly unrealistic super-ego, since he has no need of them. His love, in a word, is free of desire. It is this, rather than the Kantian moral law, which is the true form of uncon-ditionality. Divine love means not counting on a return – which is why we share in it most deeply when we ourselves manage to love thanklessly or unilaterally. If Yahweh in Judaeo-Christian doctrine is not some superegoic autocrat who fastens monstrously oppressive burdens to our backs, it is among other things because he is free of the world – which is to say that he created it gratuitously, out of love rather than need. The Creation was the original *acte gratuit*. It is a question of *jouissance* – which is to say, of a delight which is in Lacanian phrase 'good for nothing'. Being is gift, not fate. There was no necessity for God to bring about even the most minute particle of matter, and on mature reflection he may well bitterly regret having done so. If the Lacanian Other is itself desirous, the Judaeo-Christian God is not. Since he is accordingly free of neurotic need, he demands not that we cajole him by burnt offerings, dietary regulations or morally impec-cable behaviour, but that we should put aside such shoddy haggling and accept the intolerable truth that he has always already forgiven us. We need not be plunged into Protestant angst in an effort to unscramble what he demands of us, since he demands nothing of us beyond love. Because love is practical and particular, it must be capable of being legally encoded; yet those who identify it with such formulations are as much in error as those who dematerialise it.

Moral value, for Kant as much as for Spinoza, springs not from con-templating each other in imaginary terms, peering at others from within the heated interior of one's own subjectivity. It depends rather upon regarding oneself from the outside, from the dispassionate vantage-point of the moral law itself – which is to say, regarding oneself as a universal subject, and thus treating oneself as one treats all others. For Kant, there is no hard-and-fast distinction between aliens and intimates. If I deal with others as though they were myself, I also relate to myself as a kind of stranger. Ethically speaking, we are most authentically ourselves when we behave as though we were anybody or everybody. It is only when I split myself in two and look upon myself from the standpoint of the symbolic order itself, scrutinising myself with the impartial gaze of a stranger, that I can be truly self-identical. Nothing could be further from the amicable, affective ethics of a Hume or Smith, though both camps are utopianists in their different ways. If the benevolentists glimpse a kind of paradise in the throb and glow of sympathy, which like some splendid feast figures as a foretaste of utopia, some of their more disenchanted successors, now faced with the unlovely spectacle of an atomised, distinctly non-clubbable social order, are obliged to thrust their utopia ever more deeply underground, into that shadowy noumenal region which is the ideal republic of rational, self-determining subjects, and the harmonious totality of their ends.

Indeed, it is secreted even deeper than this. If Kant, who is by and large a pessimist about humanity, has need of the idea of God, it is not least because virtue and happiness are far more likely to coincide in the next world than in this one, unless one is thinking of the newly emergent novel. The gap between the ideal and the actual is evident in his comment that the categorical imperative would still be binding even if nobody had ever succeeded in acting in accordance with it. Indeed, whether anyone actually could succeed in conforming to it remains an open question. How could we ever be sure that we had acted without the slightest taint of 'pathological' motivation? Are we ever without sin before the Almighty? The moral law, as Kant is aware, is an impossibility – a quality which, as we shall see, it shares with the Lacanian Real.

In the writings of Hutcheson and Hume, pleasure and moral value, self-love and sympathy, the empirical and the ideal, are closely interwoven. With Kant, utopia has to be pushed further and further off from a degraded sensory world, so that how it becomes incarnate there – how the noumenal takes on phenomenal existence – is bound to remain something of a mystery. It is as though absolute value must be preserved from the ravages of the real by being permanently entombed. It is ironic, then, that moral law, which looks upon men and women as abstractly exchangeable with each other, is modelled in large measure on empirical reality – on the very market society of which it is also a powerful critique. The truly ethical act, like the commodity, is a model of exchange; yet in the ethical sphere this means treating both oneself and others as ends in themselves, a doctrine which is quite at odds with the logic of the marketplace. Against the self-interestedness of commercial dealings, the British benevolentists pit sentiment and affection. The German philosopher, by contrast, turns the logic of the marketplace against itself.

Kant's unfleshly ethics, for all their daunting austerity, are in some ways closer to the Christian conception of love than is the congenial world of Shaftesbury and Hutcheson. To be beneficent where one can, he insists, is a duty, not an option. He is right to see that love is not chiefly a matter of sentiment – that if we rely on such fortuitous promptings we are likely to restrict our charity to a fairly tight circle. Instead, with the New Testament in mind, he speaks of 'the love that can be commanded', contrasting it with that debased species of loving which is spontaneous and 'pathological'. Søren Kierkegaard likewise dismisses a love based on the contingencies of tenderness for one with the eternal consistency of a law. 'Only when it is a duty to love', he writes, 'only then is love eternally secured against every change. . . .'[17] St Paul contrasts the law with grace, to the detriment of the former; but he also contrasts grace as the law of God, in which he takes delight, with the law of sin. Mark's gospel draws on the general Jewish understanding of the law of God as being consummated in the love of one's fellows. For Matthew, composing with Mark at his elbow, all commandments are grounded in the love of one's neighbour. For John, writing in the Wisdom tradition, neighbourly love is the whole of the law. The Provost in Shakespeare's *Measure for Measure*, a text we shall be investigating shortly, reveals a traditional biblical understanding of the relations between law and love when he speaks of being 'bound by my charity'.

As far as love-as-law goes, Kant provides the right, most radical answer to the question which troubles the British benevolentists – how are we to treat those anonymous millions beyond the range of our affections? – by denying that affection is what is at stake here in the first place. The categorical imperative, as we have seen, makes no distinction between strangers and neighbours. The fact that, when it comes to morality, it doesn't matter a toss to Kant who you happen to be is in one sense a flaw of his abstract brand of reasoning, and in another sense a formidable strength. For Christianity, similarly, it is not local bonds or cultural identity which count for most: religious faith is not a question of kinship, parochial customs, peculiar dietary arrangements, household gods, national heritages or traditional identities. The Christian gospel is a critique of identity politics *avant la lettre*.

---

[17]   Søren Kierkegaard, *Works of Love* (Princeton, NJ, 1995), p. 29.

This is not to deny that the New Testament occasionally assigns a special privilege to the love of the Christian 'brethren' for one another. But since this can only strengthen their universal mission, it is not to be contrasted too sharply with the love of strangers. The line between them is blurred – rather as it is by the masks worn in carnival, which as Barbara Ehrenreich argues, 'dissolve the difference between stranger and neighbour, making the neighbour temporarily strange and the stranger no more foreign than anyone else'.[18] In a similar way, radical political groups whose members manage to maintain comradely relations with one another and with other such outfits, a rare enough achievement in the fissiparous annals of the left, have a greater chance of political effectiveness than those which do not. Aristotle maintained that you could be friends only with those you knew, and considered it more reprehensible to defraud a friend rather than a stranger. Failing to help a brother was a more serious defect in his eyes than failing to help some anonymous fellow-human. Yet he also discerned a continuity between friendship and political relations, speaking in the *Ethics* of fellow citizens as friends. In the various associations and communities which constitute the *polis*, public duties and personal affections are closely interwoven. Political states whose citizens have achieved a degree of mutual concord represent a public version of personal friendship.

Kant, by contrast, sets a low value on friendship. Nobody can attend to their own happiness better than themselves; and a complete reciprocity of selves, in which one's desire for the other's good is the ground of his or her wish for yours, is not only improbable, but likely to harden our hearts against those outside this charmed circle.[19] In moral affairs, Kant maintains, we must 'abstract from the personal differences of rational beings'.[20] What he fails to grasp is that genuine universality means not disregarding the distinctiveness of others, but attending to the peculiar needs of anyone who happens to come along. It is in this sense that identity and difference may finally be reconciled. It is not a matter of loving everybody, but of loving any old body. This is the point of the Good Samaritan parable, Samaritans being regarded by most orthodox Jews of the time as a particularly low form of life, as it is, more generally, of the Christian notion of universality. As such, it represents an authentic conjunction of the individual and the universal. Kierkegaard,

---

[18]   Barbara Ehrenreich, *Dancing in the Streets* (New York, 2007), p. 253.
[19]   I have drawn here on Mark Vernon, *The Philosophy of Friendship* (London, 2005).
[20]   Kant, *Groundwork of the Metaphysics of Morals*, p. 41.

who considered in puritanical fashion that loving one's friends was self-indulgent, regarded one's neighbour as whoever you bumped into when you walked out of the door.

In this sense, Kant is further from the Christian conception of love than Hegel, in whose secular vision of redemption men and women are gathered into the universality of *Geist* in all their sensuous particularity. He also differs from the Christian concept of love in assuming that the kind of sacrifice which really counts is the sacrifice of oneself to the law, rather than to the selfless service of others. Kant also diverges from the New Testament in failing to see that love for Christian belief is a question of excess, superfluity, overriding the measure, rather than of the gentrified symmetries of exchange value.[21] It is a form of useless expenditure – one which refuses to seek a return on its investment not least because, the world being the way it is, it is exceedingly unlikely to receive one. The New Testament is among other things a polemic against accountancy. Love disrupts the precisely calibrated equivalences of the symbolic order with its carnivalesque refusal to calculate, reckon the cost, return like for like.

We shall see later that the Lacanian Real has something of the same effect. Jacques Derrida remarks that Abraham is 'in a position of non-exchange with respect to God',[22] a status which is not only true of Abraham. Careless of calculability, the so-called New Testament recommends that if someone smacks you on the cheek, you should proffer the other one; that if you are asked to walk one mile, you should walk two; that if your coat is required, you should surrender your cloak as well. Like William Blake's *Proverbs of Hell*, these are deliberately exorbitant, over-the-top admonitions aimed at scandalising the anally-fixated petty bourgeois of every epoch. Yet these starkly eschatological injunctions, which seek to unhinge Christians from the logic of the *status quo* in the light of its imminent conflagration, are not to be taken as making nonsense of the claims of justice. Derrida himself sidesteps this problem by making justice, too, a matter of infinite obligation, rather than a granting of what is due. For Christianity, the surplus or gratuitous expenditure which is love is reflected most obviously in the virtues of mercy and forgiveness, which throw the predictable tit-for-tat of justice out of kilter. To love one's enemies is an affront to exchange value.

---

[21]   See Terry Eagleton, *The New Left Church* (London, 1966), Ch. 1.

[22]   Jacques Derrida, *The Gift of Death* (Chicago and London, 1996), p. 96.

All this, in Pauline phrase, is folly to the Gentiles – to those, in short, who seek like Kant to maintain a well-managed moral or symbolic economy. There is, to be sure, a dark underside to this creative recklessness known as revenge, which can be excessive and disruptive in all the wrong ways. This is why the tit-for-tat of justice, along with the symbolic order to which it belongs, cannot be simply laid aside, as some apologists for the Real would prefer. The Old Testament instructs us to demand an eye for an eye – an enlightened enough injunction in its context. This is not (as popular wisdom would have it) *carte blanche* for some atrocious reprisal, but an attempt to limit such retribution to a penalty proportionate to the offence. We are to demand an eye for an eye, not the whole body. Overriding the measure is not always to be recommended. It is this which an ethics of the Real largely fails to recognise, as we shall see later.

Kant is not a legalist because of his devotion to legality. Only anarchists and aristocrats refuse the law such inherent recognition. He is a legalist because he believes that the law should be loved and respected for its own sake, rather than for the sake of what it enjoins. Moral action must not only conform to the law, but must be done for the sake of it. Indeed, the law for Kant enjoins nothing at all, other than that our actions should manifest a certain form. It is more like a teacher of deportment than a preacher of dogma. St Paul, by contrast, regards the law as a discipline appropriate for children or moral probationers, neophytes who need to be reared in its precepts before they are mature enough to grasp their true meaning. They are like children who must endure the tedious business of learning their tables by rote if they are to end up as eminent mathematicians. The law is propaedeutic rather than an end in itself. It is, to be sure, an essential prototype of the good life; but is not for those who have arrived at moral maturity – which is to say, none of us whatsoever. Those who need the law as the equivalent of a mechanic's manual are still in their moral infancy, as only a tenderfoot speaker of Arabic needs to keep consulting the dictionary. Only when they are able to cast away this crutch of the law will they see the world aright. But since moral infancy is a chronic human condition, the law, unluckily for us, is as persistent a presence as the poor.

Paul regards virtue as the spontaneous habit of goodness which results from the law being inscribed on the heart rather than codified on tablets of stone. He seems to regard the moral law, rather like the scapegoat or *pharmakos*, as both blessed and cursed – partly because it alerts us unwittingly to the possibility of sin, like a tabloid sex *exposé* which wraps its lasciviousness in a thin tissue of moral indignation, but also because it orients us to the good without constituting a good in itself. In setting us on the right path, then, it can always intervene between us and what it advocates, becoming itself the fantasy object of our desire; and it is this which makes the law so morally two-faced. We can always fall for the law rather than for what it decrees, rather as we can find ourselves infatuated with the coach rather than enthusiasts of the game. Among those who fall in love with the law for its own sake, missing the content for the form, are those fetishists or Pharisees who find the sublime negativity of God insupportable, and seek to plug this intolerable abyss of Otherness with a determinate image of him. It is this fetishism which is forbidden in the iconoclasm of the first commandment, since the only authentic image of Yahweh is human flesh and blood.

The commandment, in other words, is directed against the realm of the imaginary – against those who pride themselves as being on first-name terms with the Almighty, and who see him not as the violent terrorist of love that he is, but as a civilised creature agreeably akin to themselves. As Lacan remarks with characteristic lucidity, 'man as image is interesting for the hollow the image leaves empty – by reason of the fact that one doesn't see in the image, beyond the capture of the image, the emptiness of God to be discovered. It is perhaps man's plenitude, but it is also there that God leaves him with emptiness.'[23] To say that men and women are fashioned in God's image is to say among other things that they are shot through from end to end with non-being, since God is not to be seen as any sort of entity. This is why it is in the void of the Real rather than in the plenitude of the imaginary, in the desolation of Calvary rather than the consolations of idolatry, that he stages his disgracefully belated appearance amongst them.

The way to rid oneself of the law's oppressive power is not to internalise it, which will only deepen its pathological compulsion. To be free of this ambiguously cursed and blessed command is not to install it inside ourselves in the shape of the despotic superego, so that we may come to obey its edicts with a spontaneity which superficially resembles the habit of virtue. This, roughly speaking, is the Schillerian response to Kant: the law remains sovereign, but its rigours must be softened by implanting it securely in the senses.[24] As with Burke, we will only truly obey it when it has been aestheticised. It is, so to speak, a move from absolute monarchy

---

[23]   Lacan, *Ethics of Psychoanalysis*, p. 196.
[24]   See Terry Eagleton, *The Ideology of the Aesthetic* (Blackwell, 1990), Ch. 4.

to a species of hegemony. Nor do we topple the law's sovereignty, in the manner of Gilles Deleuze, by ditching this whole burdensome apparatus in a surge of defiant libertarianism, opting instead for the intrinsically revolutionary dynamic of 'desire'. We are set free from the moral law only when we come to recognise that what it commends is good in itself, not good simply because it is commended. Kant therefore remains its prisoner, since in his opinion, as we have seen already, the law commends nothing but itself. It is true that he is in one sense an iconoclast rather than a fetishist where the law is concerned, insisting on its sublime unrepresentability; yet in his belief that an act is ethical only by virtue of manifesting a certain law-like form, he is at risk, so to speak, of falling for the coach. He is also in danger of an excess of radical Protestantism. Mainstream Christianity teaches that things are good not because God commands them, which would make the Almighty just the kind of capricious autocrat Spinoza is out to discredit. Rather, God wills what is good in itself, and to come to acknowledge this is a sign of moral maturity. It is an easy step from claiming that the good is whatever a whimsical law chooses to ordain, to holding like Kant that the good is to be found in the very form of the law itself.

Above all, we are liberated from the law when we come to recognise it as the law of justice and mercy, rather than some forbiddingly imperious edict. This, indeed, is the lesson of Calvary, as the death of Jesus overturns the Satanic or Pharisaical image of Yahweh as Nobodaddy, superego or bloodthirsty despot to unmask the law itself as a demand for love and justice – a demand which is likely to bring those who adhere to it to their death at the hands of the political state. It is because Jesus is at one with this liberatory law of the Father – is, as they say, the 'Son' of the Father – that he is tortured and murdered. It is the law itself which is transgressive.

Even so, the Kantian moral law is radical precisely in its anonymity. If it partakes of the logic of the commodity form, it does so in an enlightened as well as oppressive spirit. For Marx, for whom history progresses by its bad side, even the commodity has its affirmative aspect. As a universal language, it helps to override forms of 'bad' particularity, overturn the barriers erected by the *ancien régime*, draw men and women into potentially universal communication with one another, and thus lay the foundations for international socialism. 'This formalism (of the Kantian law)', Theodor Adorno writes, 'humanely prevents the abuse of the qualitative differences of things in favour of privilege and ideology. It stipulates the universal legal norm, and thus, despite and because of its abstractness, there survives in it something of substance: the egalitarian ideal.'[25]

It is thus that Kant, the most magnificent champion of liberal Enlightenment, progresses, so to speak, by his bad side. You are now entitled to freedom, respect and equal rights with your fellows not because your father is a lord or landgrave, but because you are a member of the human species. The baldness of the claim is stunning. Such, *pace* the postmodernists, is the revolutionary force of abstraction and universality. Moreover, once this doctrine is established, bourgeois society is able to take the measure of how far short it must inevitably fall of its own profoundly admirable ideals. A symbolic ethics may be an alienated, atomistic one; but it also heralds the coming of age of the self-determining subject. As such, it points a way beyond the less palatable aspects of what Hegel calls *Sittlichkeit*: cultural conformism, unreflective custom, the blind coerciveness of tradition. But since it impels you at the same time beyond the more positive aspects of *Sittlichkeit* – kinship, community, habitual virtue, local affections – this turns out to be both its glory and its calamity.

Kant is not the kind of liberal who is content to leave others to their own devices so long as they stay off his patch. On the contrary, he sails as near as a liberal can to the notion of a communal good and a mutuality of selves. It is not enough simply to coexist with others in a pact of civilised non-interference. Instead, to seek the just society is actively to promote the moral ends of others as well as our own. Alan Wood speaks of Kant's moral vision as one of 'reciprocally supportive' ends.[26] Yet just as there is a distinction between the Kantian moral law and the Christian conception of love, so there is a related difference between Kant's liberalism and the politics of Hegel and Marx. The British advocates of benevolence, as we have seen, promote a mutuality of subjects; but this two-way traffic of selves remains snared in the toils of the imaginary, confined largely to face-to-face relationships with those of one's own kind. By and large, the doctrine commits the familiar error of mistaking global humanity for an English gentleman.

It follows, as we have suggested already, that moralists of this ilk have something of a problem with aliens and antitypes, who can be less readily commended by the imagination to their affections. Kant, by contrast, welcomes the stranger through the medium of the moral law, but in doing so demotes friendship and sentient fellow-feeling. Since they must strive to

---

[25]   Theodor Adorno, *Negative Dialectics* (London, 1973), p. 236, translation amended.
[26]   Alan Wood, *Kant's Ethical Thought* (Cambridge, 1999), p. 166.

further each other's ends, men and women in Kant's eyes are far from being solitary monads; yet in so far as these ends are posited by each autonomous individual for himself, rather than being mutually constituted through common practice, he remains within the confines of liberal doctrine. For to love is to find one's ends in the other, not simply to promote the ends she proposes to herself. Unsurprisingly, he also fails to see that for individuals to promote each other's ends on a grand scale is possible only in a social order which is not structurally divided.

What both imaginary and symbolic theories are in need of here is a concept of the institutional. To Hume, Hutcheson and their colleagues, the only institutions which seem to count are the family and the club. Law and property, to be sure, are questions which engage Hume intensely; yet for the most part he deals with them in disembodied guise, as concepts rather than social realities. For Kant and his disciples, the moral law is certainly an institution in the broad sense; yet their primary moral datum is the individual, one treated for the most part as shorn of a social context. Could there, then, be a form of human reciprocity which was not simply a face-to-face affair – which was, in a word, symbolic rather than imaginary? Hegel and Marx respond to this query in the affirmative, as Rousseau had done earlier. In his view, the state must be so fashioned as to translate our instinctive concern for the needs of others into a conscious regard for the common good.

For Hegel, Kant's focus on freedom and universality is essential but one-sided. He has bought his radical autonomy at the cost of a certain social and political nullity. Only when this freedom is practised in the context of *Sittlichkeit*, through the subject's participation in a concrete form of social life, can it truly blossom. The formal abstraction of Kantian morality, which obdurately refuses all appeal to the way the world is, must be returned to the empirical realm of social relations. The law must be made flesh in our dispositions and workaday culture. One might see this as representing, roughly speaking, a fusion of the imaginary and the symbolic – of a social context in which we find ourselves reflected back by our familiars, and the universal realm of moral law. For Hegel, as for the Aristotle to whom he is indebted, ethical existence is a question of politics – above all of the state, which for Hegel both incarnates a specific form of life and embodies the spirit of universal Reason. To this extent, individual and universal, freedom and community, abstract right and concrete virtue, can be united. Unlike Kant, both Hegel and Marx acknowledge that the subject and its ends are constituted by its relations with others. For them, it is not simply a question of separately constituted individuals proceeding in Kantian fashion to harmonise their diverse ends, seeking to render such ends mutually consistent while promoting one another's capacity to achieve them. What enables Hegel and Marx to think in this style is the concept of institutionality. It is Hegel, above all, who recognises that morality must be a question of social organisation, not simply of isolated individual wills. Institutions are how others can be constitutive of the self even when they are unknown to us. They are a way of roping complete strangers into one and the same project. To this extent, they represent a solution of sorts to the problem of the imaginary and symbolic – the former reciprocal but restrictive, the latter universal but atomistic.

Take, for example, the idea of a self-governing cooperative, of the kind Marx envisaged flourishing under socialism. The members of such an enterprise do not promote one another's ends by an act of will; instead, a form of reciprocity is built into the structure of the institution itself. It is one which works just as well when the cooperative's members are strangers to each other as when they happen not to be. By contributing her own distinctive efforts to the set-up, the institution ensures that an individual member is at the same time engaged in promoting the development of her colleagues. The impersonality of the symbolic is harnessed to a mutuality of selves, one which has a mild flavouring of the imaginary. It is this, rather than Kant's joint-stock company notion of moral virtue, which is the ethical foundation of socialism. The fulfilment of each becomes the condition for the fulfilment of all. It is hard to think of a more precious form of ethics.

Even the austerely self-denying Kant cannot abjure the seductions of the imaginary altogether. The world is not against us; but neither, as far as we can judge, is it on our side. One does not get the sense that reality is exactly cheering us on. Even so, there is a way in which Reason and Nature can be harmonised, and this is the sphere of the aesthetic. Though we can never answer such abstruse metaphysical questions as what reality is like in itself, we can nevertheless allow ourselves to imagine that it is governed by purposive ends, regulated by a kind of lawfulness, and thus of the same nature as ourselves. It is this sort of heuristic fiction which we posit when we pass aesthetic judgements on Nature – when we are struck by the sense that its forms seem to conform to some kind of law, even though we are quite unable to say what that law might be. For Kant, the aesthetic object does not involve an act of cognition; yet it seems to address itself to what we might call our capacity for cognition in general, revealing to us in a kind of Heideggerian 'pre-understanding' that the world is the kind of place we can in principle comprehend, wonderfully adapted as it is to our minds even before any specific act of knowledge has taken place.

Part of the pleasure of the aesthetic, then, springs from a sense that we are at home in the world in a way which seems contrary to the findings of reason. In the act of aesthetic judgement, we perceive the object as though it were a kind of subject, exhibiting the kind of unity, purposiveness and self-determination that we display ourselves. In this way, we sense a delightful conformity of the world to our own imaginative and intellectual faculties, almost as though the place were mysteriously designed to suit our ends. The object is lifted out of the web of practical functions in which it is routinely enmeshed, and endowed instead with something of the freedom and autonomy of a fellow human. By virtue of this crypto-subjectivity, the thing seems to speak meaningfully to those who perceive it, stirring in them the pious hope that Nature is not entirely indifferent to their ends.

If reason and the moral law lift us out of the imaginary, then, the aesthetic plunges us back into it. Self and other turn their faces affably towards each other, and reality seems spontaneously given over to us, like an object which insinuates itself into our palms as though designed with our prehensile powers miraculously in mind. In the aesthetic, we are able to stand apart a little from our own vantage point, turn round upon ourselves, and marvel at the seemingly tight fit between our cognitive capacities and the world itself. We thus find ourselves in the company of those present-day physicists who find it astonishing that our minds, products of blind evolution, are able to decipher the underlying structures of the universe, and to no apparent practical benefit. An object of beauty, Kant considers, has a unique yet universal status; it appears wholly given over to the subject and addressed to its faculties; it 'relieves a want' and seems miraculously self-identical; and though it brings us a keen sense of repletion, it evokes from us no libidinal response. It is perhaps not too fanciful to find in this idealised material form, one from which all desire and sensuality have been stripped, a memory of the maternal body as it is perceived in the imaginary.

In such a context, Nature seems to conform to the human understanding; and for Kant it is no great step from this to fostering the fantasy that it was designed for our understanding as well. Sustained in this way by what surrounds us, we can dream that we are not as negligible in the eyes of the universe as we fear – that the cosmos itself saw us coming and shares something of our purposes. As one of Kant's commentators, H. J. Paton, writes:

> It is a great stimulus to moral effort and a strong support to the human spirit if men can believe that the moral life is something more than a mortal enterprise in which he can join with his fellow men against a background of a blind and indifferent universe until he and the human race are blotted out forever. Man cannot be indifferent to the possibility that his puny efforts towards moral perfection may, in spite of appearances, be in accord with the purpose of the universe. . . .[27]

It is as though Thomas Hardy, with his hard-headed refusal of a benignly complicit universe, were finally to throw in his hand with the Vatican. In the end, the vision of a world stonily bereft of meaning proves too ideologically unnerving for Kant, and certainly for H. J. Paton, whose comments are published in the wake of the Second World War. That there may be some purposive collusion between ourselves and the cosmos, some pre-arranged harmony between subject and object, remains a mere hypothesis; yet it is one which is likely, in Paton's Baden-Powellish idiom, to furnish us with 'a great stimulus to moral effort'. Men and women find it hard to accept that their moral values are grounded in nothing but themselves, and may well suffer a panic-stricken collapse into nihilism as a result of this recognition. What reason, or the symbolic, tells us is not exactly what ideology, or the imaginary, would like to hear. The aesthetic is a fading memory of organic unity in a rationalistic age, a faint trace of religious transcendence. Harmony is more than ever essential in an individualist society; but it is to be found in a community of sensibility or shared structure of feeling, rather than in political or economic institutions.

When the small infant of the mirror stage contemplates its own body, it imputes a coherence to itself which actually belongs to the representation. This, indeed, is the source of its delight. When Kant's observer encounters a thing of beauty, he finds in it a unity and harmony which are actually the effect of his own mental faculties. In both cases, an imaginary misrecognition takes place, though with a certain reversal of subject and object from the one theory to the other. The Kantian subject of aesthetic judgement is among other things Lacan's jubilant, narcissistic infant.[28] In

---

[27] H. J. Paton, *The Categorical Imperative* (London, 1947), p. 256.
[28] I have written more fully on this topic in *The Ideology of the Aesthetic* (Oxford, 1990), Ch. 3.

case we become too smugly ensconced in our self-love, however, the Kantian sublime is on hand to prod us out of our inertia. It is there to remind us of our homelessness, of the unfathomable infinity which is our only true resting-place. As with Burke, we must be chastised and cajoled by turns, exposed in turn to beauty and sublimity, consensus and conflict, feminine and masculine. The world must appear hospitable to us if we are to act purposefully within it; but we must also submit to being terrorised by it from time to time, dislodged from a too complacently centred selfhood, if we are to strive to the limit of our powers.

6

Law and Desire in *Measure for Measure*

With his usual precognitive power, Shakespeare weighs up the pros and cons of Kantian ethics in *Measure for Measure*.[1] The play, as its title suggests, is all about tit for tat or exchange value; but it also examines the problems into which this logic of equivalence can run. When the drama opens, the law is in poor shape: Vienna's excessively liberal ruler, Duke Vincentio, has allowed it to fall into disrepute, and appoints the austere Angelo to restore authority. The Duke has 'Lent him our terror, dress'd him with our love' (1.1.20) – which is to say, invested his deputy with what Burke would regard as both the sublime and beautiful aspects of the law, its power to coerce and cajole by turn.

The 'precise' Angelo, a man 'of stricture and firm abstinence', 'whose blood is very snow-broth', and whose urine is said to consist of congealed ice, adheres to a strict separation between flesh-and-blood individuals and the symbolic order. This is why he is able to step into the Duke's shoes with apparent ease, since what is at stake is a symbolic substitution rather than an empirical one. In fact, there would appear to be no hiatus between Angelo as an individual and his symbolic location, between private inclination and public action. 'Look, what I will not, that I cannot do', he tells Isabella (2.2.52). He regards himself from the Olympian standpoint of the symbolic order itself, as no more than an impersonal bearer of its impartial authority. 'It is the law, not I, condemns your brother,' he informs the stricken Isabella, when her brother Claudio is condemned to death for fornication. 'Were he my kinsman, brother, or my son, / It should be thus with him' (2.2.80–2).

There is something necessarily inhuman about a perfectly just law, heedless as it must be of partisanship and particularity. Its apparently glacial quality is the mark of its humanity. Angelo, so to speak, is a good Kantian

---

[1] See Terry Eagleton, *William Shakespeare* (Oxford, 1986), Ch. 3.

universalist, properly disdaining that prejudice in favour of friends and kinsfolk which distinguishes a David Hume. If it is not to become the property of a corrupt ruling-class cabal, the law must be scrupulously even-handed in its treatment of strangers and neighbours. The good-hearted Provost, who has nothing of Angelo's *froideur*, remarks that he would not pity a murderer even if he were his brother. Angelo argues cogently that in acting without favouritism and refusing to allow exceptions, he is showing compassion for those whom such gestures would rightly offend. He also points out that by executing a criminal he is protecting other potential victims from harm. Justice is not the enemy of compassion, but a precondition for its richer flourishing. There is no true contradiction between the symbolic and the affective. If the law were to compromise itself for the sake of flesh and blood, it would jeopardise the security of all the flesh and blood which seeks its protection.

Pleading with this severe viceroy for her brother's life, Isabella declares that 'If he had been as you, and you as he, You would have slipp'd like him . . .' (2.2.64–5). This is hardly a knockdown argument. All it establishes is that if Angelo had been Claudio he would have behaved like Claudio. If this view is pressed too far, each individual becomes his or her own criterion – a situation which is just as absolutist in its own way as Angelo's unbending justice. Being a law unto oneself parallels the crashing malapropisms ('respected' for 'suspected', and so on) of the minor comic character Elbow. Malapropisms are a kind of private language in which you yourself decide what you mean – just as privilege literally means 'private law', an anarchic condition in which each individual becomes his own measure.

Isabella herself maintains in her absolutist way that 'truth is truth to the end of reckoning' (5.1.45–6); indeed, this is only one of her ironic points of resemblance to the Angelo whose judgement on her brother she abhors. But she is forced in the heat of argument into a more contextual view of justice, which she illustrates with a linguistic example: 'That in the captain's but a choleric word / Which in the soldier is flat blasphemy' (2.2.130–1). The law, she means, should be as responsive to shifting contexts as language is. Perhaps it should; but the danger with such a case is that, pressed to an extreme, we might all end up as Elbows, privately legislating Humpty-Dumpty-wise the meaning of our own words. For Shakespeare himself, the relation between two different uses of the same term is more like the relation of simultaneous identity and non-identity which holds between the Duke and his surrogate Angelo. It is not simply a question of pure difference, as Isabella sophistically argues. Some of the play's most throwaway imagery, tucked away in casual comments and minor metaphors, turns on the notion of a constancy or consistency which can nevertheless be distinguished from rigid self-identity.

The case for which Isabella is fumbling is that we are all in some sense interchangeable because of our shared moral infirmity – that there is an equality of flesh and blood or pure humanity, as well as one of abstract law. If everyone condemns everyone else in a perpetual circle, why not cancel this pointless mutual arraignment through an act of forgiveness, breaking the circuit and inaugurating a new kind of moral regime? Angelo, however, parries this move with something of its own logic. If he were a sinner like Claudio, he tells Isabella, he would expect to be judged just as severely:

> You may not so extenuate his offence
> For I have had such faults; but rather tell me,
> When I, that censure him, do so offend,
> Let mine own judgement pattern out my death,
> And nothing come impartial.
>
> (2.1.27–31)

It is the corollary of treating others as you would have them treat you. The fact that I am morally spineless is no bar to my judging moral turpitude in others, just as the fact that I cannot sing a note does not mean that I cannot recognise a world-class tenor when I hear one.

In Angelo's eyes, mercy, like sentimentalism, is dangerously abstract. It overlooks the inherent merits or demerits of actions, sacrificing such judgements to a purely subjective impulse. In this sense, ironically, mercy has something of the indifference to the specific of the very law that it seeks to temper. Yet Angelo is mistaken to imagine that mercy is a kind of cognitive blind spot. 'Use every man after his desert, and who shall 'scape whipping?', as Hamlet upbraids Polonius, does not mean that one should not register faults, simply that one should forgive them. Isabella makes this mistake as well, demanding rhetorically of Angelo, 'How would you be / If He, which is the top of judgement, should / But judge you as you are?' (2.2.75–7). But the point is that God does indeed see men and women as they are. He sees them in all their fearfulness and fragility, which is precisely why he finds it so easy to forgive them. Love and knowledge, as the Duke implies, make a natural pairing. Genuine love, as Lacan argues, is love of the other in so far as she is lacking. Mercy and realism are intimately allied.

Similarly, a just law does not simply abstract from the concrete situations on which it hands down judgement, cavalierly laying aside what is distinctive about them. Instead, it applies its general norms to these situations with a degree of tact, or (as Aristotle would say) *phronesis*, sensitive to their peculiar shape and texture. As such, legal judgements are like verbal utterances – irreducibly specific applications of certain highly general conventions. If the law did not abstract and equalise, we would end up with as many laws as there are situations; and each of these situations would then be autonomous (literally, a law unto itself) and thus absolute. There is no arguing with the self-identical. That which is purely itself cannot be weighed and measured, which is one reason why *Measure for Measure* is so taken with tautologies. Such legal nominalism, for all its warm-hearted passion for the particular, would spell the death of justice. Yet for all its conjuring of identity from difference, the law, like language, lives only in specific human contexts, which can never be simply read off from its formal tenets. What mediates between general and particular in the case of both law and language is an act of interpretation. When the Duke visits a prison, he asks 'to make me know / The nature of their crimes, that I may minister / To them accordingly' (2.3.6–8). Charity is indiscriminate, refusing unlike Victorian Evangelicalism to distinguish between those who are deserving of it and those who are not; but it is meticulous all the same in discriminating between different kinds of need. Like any effective law, it is both universal and *ad hominem.*

The problem, however, is how to be just or merciful without lapsing into the hard-boiled indifference of Lucio, whose streetwise cockiness threatens to subvert the idea of value as such. If Angelo, as his name suggests, is angelic, Lucio is demonic. Whereas the angelic, as Milan Kundera argues, are notable for their peculiarly 'shitless' discourse, all vapid rhetoric and edifying sentiment, the demonic see nothing around them but shit. Parsons and politicians are angelic, whereas tabloid journalists are demonic. The demonic are not evil, since to be evil entails believing in value if only to negate it. Milton's Satan is not demonic, but the devil of Thomas Mann's *Doctor Faustus* is. Lucio is an ethical naturalist for whom only desire is real, and for whom 'flesh and blood' is a descriptive rather than normative category. His nonchalant attitude to the law is captured in his friend Pompey's *faux*-respectful response to the news that brothels are to be banned in Vienna: 'Does your worship mean to geld and splay all the youth of the city?' (2.1.136). 'A little more lenity to lechery' (3.2.53) is the alternative policy Lucio self-interestedly recommends to Angelo. His broad-mindedness is really a form of cynicism: the only absolute he acknowledges is biological appetite. Laws, titles, values and emblems are just so much flashy cultural window-dressing.

The cynic is one who believes only in the Real of enjoyment, regarding the Other or symbolic order as so much empty make-believe to be exploited for his own ends. In this sense, cynicism is a savage parody of comedy – a genre which trusts in moral value but which also views it ironically, debunkingly, in the light of our ineluctable failure to live up to it. In refusing to demand too much from us, it is a therapy for those under the pitiless sway of the superego. Comedy celebrates human value in a wry awareness of the arbitrariness of our conventions and the groundlessness of our being. It is in this sense, not simply as a foretaste of a harmonious future, that it is a utopian mode. Its brio and exuberance offer a momentary transcendence of the charnel house of history.

Lucio can no more speak the discourse of moral value than a snail could be expert in algebraic topology. His urbane tolerance of vice is a parody of genuine forgiveness, not least because it costs him nothing. It is valueless because it is bought on the cheap. In this sense, just as there can be a wild kind of justice (revenge), so there can be a worthless kind of mercy. As the Duke observes, 'When vice makes mercy, mercy's so extended / That for the fault's love is th'offender friended' (4.2.88–9). Isabella distinguishes between what she calls 'lawful mercy' and a 'devilish mercy' which forgives for all the wrong reasons, or simply out of moral indolence. The quality of mercy is not (con)strained, as Portia immortally declares in *The Merchant of Venice*, but it is not sheer licence or gratuitousness either. It must not be allowed to make a mockery of justice, or of the inherent use-values of things. You can be too precise, like Angelo; but you can also overflow the measure in a way which undercuts exact discriminations and merges all human situations promiscuously into one. *King Lear* is another Shakespearian drama much preoccupied with the perilously thin line between too much and too little, something and nothing, lethal and life-giving forms of surplus.[2]

Lucio's moral *apatheia* is paralleled in *Measure for Measure* by the astonishing spiritual inertia of the criminal Barnardine, a Musil-like psychopath so careless of life and death that he objects to being executed only because it will interfere with his sleep. In a sense, Barnardine is dead already: he has anticipated and thus disarmed his impending demise, living it out in the form of a pathological moral torpor. Sunk in this spiritual sluggishness, he exists already at that end point where all odds are struck even. Death seems to confirm what both he and Lucio suspect, that all values are ulti-

---

[2] There are parallels here with Nietzsche's treatment of mercy in *The Genealogy of Morals*.

mately on a level. They do not see that there is a less cynical way of striking the odds even, which is the act of forgiveness. Forgiveness is a gratuitous rupture of the circuit of exact equivalences, of tit for tat and measure for measure, and thus a foretaste of death within the regulated symmetries of the present.

Having vanquished death in this fashion, Barnardine is enviably invulnerable. Those who consciously embrace their own destiny transcend it in that very act, transforming it into a kind of freedom. It is this ambiguity which classically distinguishes the tragic hero. Claudio declares that 'If I must die, / I will encounter darkness as a bride, / And hug it in mine arms' (3.1.91–3). In this coupling of fate and free decision, the tragic act provides a solution of sorts to the conflict between the gratuitous and the given, liberty and bondage, lawlessness and constraint, on which the play meditates. The state must defer Barnardine's dying until he has been brought willingly to accept it: unless he somehow 'performs' his death, converts it into an authentic act of his own, it will fail to constitute an event in his life and so will discredit the authority which has inflicted it upon him. His death must be a conscious piece of practice rather than a mere biological occurrence. At the most intolerably real moment of our existence, on the very brink of extinction, we must prove ourselves to be accomplished actors. 'Persuade this rude wretch willingly to die', the Duke instructs the Provost (4.3.49). There are few more effective ways of resisting power than genuinely not caring about it. This monstrous representative of the living dead understands in his own way that power exists only in the response it exacts from those who are subject to it. So, as it happens, did David Hume, who remarked that when it comes to sovereignty, the governed always have the upper hand.

As it turns out, anarchy and autocracy in the play are by no means the opposites they appear. For one thing, libertinism breeds repression: if, like the Duke, you permit the law to fall into disrepute, you are only paving the way for an Angelo-like authoritarianism in the future. The play is well-stocked with images of self-thwarting strategies and counterproductive acts. 'As surfeit is the father of much fast,' comments Claudio, 'So every scope by the immoderate use / Turns to restraint' (1.2.76–8). As a man who is carried off to prison for illicit sexual intercourse, he is presumably in a position to know. For another thing, it is the law, as in the Oedipal prohibition, which breeds desire in the first place. So it is that Angelo, confronted with the chaste, untouchable Isabella, falls prey to an ungovernable lust, offering to pardon her brother if she will have sex with him. In representing an abstract principle to Angelo in person, Isabella discovers to her dismay that she has seduced him by her person rather than by the principle. The governor's virtue turns out to be like Lucio's description of the bones of a prostitute's pox-ridden client: 'as sound as things that are hollow' (1.2.57). If Angelo incarnates the moral law, he also represents its obscene underside. A law or form of reason which like Angelo's 'never feels / the wanton stings and motions of the sense' (1.4.58–9) is a stranger to the body, and so is likely to be caught napping by a sudden insurgency of desire.

Angelo, in short, has failed to absorb the lesson which Schiller sets out to teach Kant in his *On the Aesthetic Education of Man* – that if reason wishes to secure its sovereignty over desire, it must first of all infiltrate the senses as a kind of fifth columnist, informing them from within rather than remaining icily aloof from appetite. Much the same applies to the question of political sovereignty over the masses. Hence the fairy-tale motif of the king who moves incognito among the common people, of whom the Duke of *Measure for Measure* is merely one Shakespearian example. Effective political power is neither despotic not slackly indulgent, but hegemonic. The problem for the law is what one might call the Prince-Hal-and-Falstaff dilemma: how is it to be on familiar enough terms with human frailty to understand it from the inside, while putting sufficient daylight between it and oneself to pass impartial judgement on it? The Duke Vincentios of this world must go to school with the Lucios without simply becoming their dupe. The law must accomplish the difficult trick of being at once immanent and transcendent – rather as, in the Christian subtext of *Measure for Measure*, the transcendent Father who forgives sin is also the incarnate Son who was done to death by it. Yet if mercy springs from an inward sympathy with sin, then to be both merciful and virtuous begins to sound mildly self-contradictory. At what point does sympathy become complicity?

Angelo's interview with Isabella is by no means his first encounter with the shattering force of desire, whatever he may suppose himself. On the contrary, the snake was curled up in the garden from the outset. Its deadly venom has infected him already in the form of his pathological will to dominion, within which Freud would doubtless detect the shadow of the death drive. Angelo represents a pure cult of the superego, with its lethally aggressive rage for order, its neurotic fear that without fine definitions and unimpeachable grounds the world will collapse into chaos. Because they are secretly fuelled by the death drive, the very powers which set out to subdue chaos are secretly in love with it. The urge to order is itself latently anarchic. It is prepared to subjugate the world into sheer nothingness. The superego, as Freud taught, borrows its terrifyingly vindictive force from the unruly id.

This is why Angelo can keel over with scarcely a struggle from ascetic authoritarian to libidinal transgressor. The same goes for the law, or indeed for any system of symbolic exchange. Because such symbolic economies are precisely regulated, they tend to stability; but because the rules which regulate them can permutate any one item with another, indifferent to their specific nature, they can breed an anarchic condition in which every element blurs indiscriminately into every other, and the system appears to be engaging in transactions purely for their own sake. There is something in the very structure of stability which threatens to subvert it. This is most obviously so in the case of the symbolic order, which in order to work effectively must allow flexible permutations between its various roles, and thus cannot avoid generating the permanent possibility of incest. Without this monstrous horror at its heart, the system would not be able to operate.

Measure for Measure is full of acts of symbolic substitution, as bodies circulate ceaselessly. Angelo stands in for the Duke, Isabella represents Claudio's pleas for mercy to him, while the Duke substitutes for himself in moving among his people in disguise. Angelo wants Isabella's body in return for Claudio's, but ends up making love to Mariana, who takes Isabella's place in his bed. Barnardine's decapitated head is meant to stand in for Claudio's, but since Barnardine is too indolent to be executed it is exchanged at the last minute for Ragozine's. Angelo uses Claudio as an example to other potential miscreants, thus turning him into a general representative who, like Christ, is 'made sin' for the sake of others.

The final distribution of bodies to their appropriate places is the event of marriage, with which the play, as befits a comedy, comes to a close. Bodies are a kind of language, which can either falsify (as in the bed trick with Mariana) or serve, like words, as fluent forms of communication. The play is concerned with both truth of speech and truth of the body. The proper consorting of bodies in marriage parallels the harmonious liaison of words and things. Angelo is in this sense an appallingly shoddy translation of the Duke, while Elbow shows up the misalliance between signifiers and signifieds which language opens up. Rather as we feel the power of the law through its violation, so there could be no truth without the perpetual possibility of lying or misspeaking. To represent another involves a kind of exchange value, and thus implicates both difference and identity; indeed, the play is rife with imagery of one individual minting, imprinting, figuring or impregnating another. Yet just as justice must be modulated by mercy, so there is always some slippage or hiatus between the act of representing and what is represented. In what one might call his prelapsarian state, Angelo, as we have seen, comes near to closing this gap, regarding his own person as no more than a bearer of the law. But the subsequent slippage between man and role is in his case severe. The only perfect identity between representation and represented would be to represent oneself, the political equivalent of which would be democracy.

This is another reason why *Measure for Measure* is so fascinated by tautologies ('grace is grace', 'truth is truth', and so on), since they give the slip to exchange value, albeit in a worthless kind of way. It is this dislocation or residue of difference between the elements of an exchange which makes room for mercy. Whereas Angelo is at first wholly identical with his public role, the Duke is aware that subjectivity is never at one with its signification. There is a gap between the symbolic role of judge and the individual who is the bearer of it, a creative non-identity which allows the rigours of the law to be mitigated by compassion. That there is no true identity in exchange is obvious enough in the play's notoriously factitious conclusion, in which the distribution of body to body in marriage leaves much to be desired. Shakespeare even marries off Isabella to the Duke, in what seems more authorial fantasy than dramatic logic.

It is part of Lacanian doctrine that the registers of imaginary, symbolic and Real overlap and interpenetrate. Some versions of the mirror stage, for example, see symbolic difference as already encroaching on imaginary identity in the shape of the mother, whom the child beholds in the looking-glass beside him. Moreover, we have seen already that at the core of the symbolic lies a traumatic horror, which is not simply incest but the shadowy presence of the Real. It is not surprising, then, that Kant, exponent *par excellence* of a symbolic ethics, should also have been claimed as a moralist of the Real, as we shall see in the next part of the argument.

PART III

THE REIGN OF THE REAL

Introduction: Pure Desire

In the 1970s and 1980s, at least in British cultural theory, the Real was by far the most underprivileged member of the Lacanian Trinity, and certainly the least understood. It is only in recent decades, not least through the work of Lacan's representative on earth, Slavoj Žižek, that its growing centrality to the former's thought has become apparent.[1] Indeed, just as the Real itself is said always to return to its place, so it does in Žižek's voluminous writings, which for all their flamboyant, faintly manic versatility return again and again in self-parodic, compulsively repetitive fashion to this elusive entity, circling constantly around an absence to which they hope but fail to lend a tongue. Žižek's books, as in Freud's notion of the uncanny, are both familiar and unfamiliar, breathtakingly innovative yet *déjà lu*, full of arresting new insights yet perpetual recyclings of one another. If he reads Lacan as a succession of attempts to seize upon the same persistent traumatic kernel, much the same can be said of his own work, which continually bursts out anew with Schelling or Hitchcock or race riots or computer games, but never shifts its gaze from the same fearful, fascinating scene.[2]

The fact that this devoted disciple of Lacan hails from the former Communist world is probably not irrelevant in this respect. It is hardly surprising that Žižek and his fellow Ljubljana Lacanians should have found themselves attracted during the neo-Stalinist era to a theory which subverts

---

[1] Most of Žižek's numerous works contain some discussion of the Real, but see in particular *The Sublime Object of Ideology* (London, 1989), *For They Know Not What They Do* (London, 1991) and *The Indivisible Remainder* (London, 1996).

[2] I draw here upon some previous comments of my own on Žižek, in *Figures of Dissent* (London, 2003), pp. 196–206.

the bogus authority of the so-called Master Signifier. No doubt they were equally enthused by an insistence on the opacity of the human subject and the precariousness of its identity, in a social order where both a sham transparency and a cult of essentialistic selfhood were the order of the day. At the same time, the actual lack of transparency of the Yugoslav system, its Byzantine mystifications, would seem to have played its part in rendering Lacan's thought relevant. Moreover, in the nationalistic, ethnically divided Balkans, a terrain which has long represented one of Europe's minatory Others, psychoanalysis – the science of how human subjectivity comes to be constructed – can assume a political resonance which is rather less obvious in Rome or New York. Scapegoating, fetishism, splitting, foreclosure, disavowal, projection, idealisation: if these are familiar enough psychic mechanisms, they are also the stuff of ethnic strife and military conflicts.

The Lacan of Žižek and his colleagues is less the modish Parisian post-structuralist for whom the world is dissoluble into discourse ('spaghetti structuralism', as Žižek scornfully dubs it) than the later champion of the intransigent Real; and this proclivity makes a degree of sense in their political conditions. It is little wonder that those who write with murderous feuds raging on their doorstep should be rather more sensitive to that which resists symbolisation than most of their counterparts in Cornell or Christ Church. It is the discrepancy between their own professional patch – roughly speaking, language – and what surpasses it which is likely to strike intellectuals in politically turbulent situations. Nor is it a matter for astonishment that the Real should bulk so large for those with a political interest in what defeats totality, not to speak of how an autocratic authority sadistically enjoins its victims to hug their chains. All this can surely be read against the background of that mass blockage of desire which was bureaucratic Communism.

There is a parallel here with that other Eastern European heretic, Milan Kundera. We have seen already that Kundera deploys the terms 'angelic' and 'demonic' in ways which are relevant to ethics; but they are equally applicable to politics. In *The Unbearable Lightness of Being*, he sees totalitarian states as 'angelic' – as fearful of obscurity, determined that no particle of human conduct shall escape sense-making, dragging everything into luminous significance and instant legibility. In a wry anecdote, the novel recounts how a drunken Czech being sick in the centre of Prague in the neo-Stalinist period is approached by a compatriot who shakes his head and murmurs 'I know exactly what you mean.' In this paranoid world of express intelligibility, even throwing up must assume some portentous significance. What Kundera calls the 'demonic', by contrast, is marked by a cynical cackle which revolts against the tidy schemas of tyranny and revels in the obscene meaninglessness of things. It is not hard to spot Lacan's symbolic order in the former state of affairs and his Real in the latter – or, for that matter, to grasp why the sheer raw contingency of the Real, its habit of fissuring closed symbolic economies with a residue of ungratified desire, should have had a certain wistful appeal to Eastern European intellectuals of the Cold War era. What we shall shortly see as Lacan's ethical imperative – the injunction not to give up on one's desire, however impossible it may appear – sounds rather like the manifesto of Polish Solidarity in its darkest hour.

Indeed, the psychoanalytical cure from a Lacanian viewpoint is not dissimilar to the achievement of political independence, which may be another reason why the Balkans should have proved so fertile a seedbed for psychoanalysis. The patient who emerges 'successfully' from Lacanian analysis is one who has learned to be eternally dissatisfied – to acknowledge that his desire has no support in the Other, that it is entirely self-grounding, and thus is every bit as absolute and transcendent as the Almighty was once rumoured to be. If desire were transitive – if it had a specific object in its sights – then we could investigate the contexts which breed such longings, and desire would consequently cease to be foundational. It is the fact that it has no real target beyond itself which makes it a ground beneath which it is impossible to delve. Rather as the Holy Spirit represents the Father's eternal delight in the image of himself which is the Son, so desire never ceases to contemplate its own visage and chase its own tail, contemptuous of the flashy bagatelles which are held out here and there for its instant gratification. Since desire, like the Almighty, is an abyssal kind of ground, and therefore in a sense no ground at all, the subject of psychoanalysis must actively assume the contingency of her own being, relinquishing the futile quest to find it authenticated by an Other whose existence is in any case a mirage. If this has a mild resemblance to the business of getting out from under a political oppressor, it also has more than a smack of the saint. No doubt this is one reason why psychoanalytic treatment is generally such a protracted affair – one lengthy enough, in fact, for a whole galaxy of small nations to achieve their autonomy in the meantime.

Despite Žižek's admirably lucid expositions, the Real remains an enigmatic concept, as well as (in Aquinas's sense) an analogous one, working at several different levels simultaneously. It is a sign of its elusiveness that even as finely intelligent a critic as Fredric Jameson mistakes it for material history, which is the very last thing it is. 'It is not terribly difficult to say what is meant by the Real in Lacan', Jameson writes. 'It is simply History itself. . . .'[3] To which one can only riposte that it is indeed remarkably difficult, and that the Real, whatever else it may be, is in Lacan's view utterly unhistorical, always returning to precisely the same place, as indissoluble as a stone in a stream. This is one reason why the whole concept is something of a scandal to those postmodernists who prefer their reality to be rather more malleable and soft-centred.

Not only is the Real not synonymous with common-or-garden reality, but it is almost the opposite of it.[4] It is true that in Lacan's earlier writings, the term could sometimes be taken to signify the recalcitrance of the material world, or the unrepresentable bodily drives, or a *jouissance* which lies beyond the phallic order, or the non-verbal residue of desire which escapes the symbolic order. In his later work, it is an equally versatile concept: it can allude to the supposed impossibility of the sexual relationship, or to that unconditional fidelity to the law of one's own being, however inscrutable to reason this law may be, which is the foundation of all true ethics. In the latter case, we are speaking of what Lacan calls an ethics of the drive rather than one of desire – one which has traversed the fantasies which sustain desire, to emerge in some less mystified place on the other side. Alternatively, the Real is what Milan Kundera calls in his novel *Immortality* the unique 'theme' of an individual's identity – that irreducible morbidity of desire which is peculiar to each human subject. If *Eros* and *Thanatos* are universals, they nevertheless leave a unique imprint on each individual.

Even so – to return to Jameson – to equate the Real with historical reality *tout court* is surely a misreading. Reality for Lacan is just a low-grade place of fantasy whose function is to shelter us from the abyss of the Real, a kind of Soho of the psyche. Fantasy is what plugs the void in our being so that the set of shop-soiled fictions we know as reality are able to emerge. It is in dream, not in that meretricious place called reality, that for Lacan we approach the Real of our desire. The Real is what disrupts these agreeable fabrications, skewing the subject out of shape and bending the symbolic order out of true. It is the subject's point of failure and impasse, the way

---

[3]   See Fredric Jameson, 'Imaginary and Symbolic in Lacan', *Yale French Studies*, 55/56, p. 384.

[4]   A point which Anika Lemaire fails to appreciate in her *Jacques Lacan* (London, 1977), a study which equates the concept with reality or lived experience.

it fails to be at one with itself, the primordial wound we incurred by our expulsion from the pre-Oedipal Eden. It is the gash in our being where we were torn loose from the maternal body, and from which desire flows unstaunchably.

It is this originary trauma – the terrifying paternal prohibition, the castrating edge of the law, the anguish of separation, the eternally lost object of desire, the obscene super-egoic imperative to wallow in our guilt – which persists as a kind of horrific hard core within the subject. In the deathly cat-and-mouse game between law and desire, we are driven to practise the morbid, compulsive self-tormenting of the living dead. Rather as Schopenhauer regarded us as all permanently pregnant with monsters, constituted as human by the malignant power he called the Will, so the Real is a kind of foreign body lodged inside us. It is that in the subject which is more than the subject, a lethal virus which invades our flesh yet which, as Aquinas says of the Almighty, is closer to us than we are to ourselves.

Desire is nothing personal. As Jean Racine recognised, it is an affliction that was lying in wait for us from the outset, a tragic scenario which we inherit from our elders, a disfiguring medium into which we are plunged at birth. It is the 'object in the subject' which makes us what we are, an alien wedge at the core of our being. Yet it is also, as we shall see a little later, a potential means to redemption. The Real is both what is most permanently awry with us, and what is most truly of our essence; and in this ambiguous status it figures as a kind of *felix culpa* or fortunate Fall, the flaw or lack of self-identity which ensures that we never quite add up, yet without which we would be incapable of being ourselves. Like the sublime, of which it is a modern-day version, it is seductive and repugnant at the same time – a source of unspeakable horror, yet (as we shall see in a moment) that unsearchable source of our being with which we must at all costs keep faith.

The Real is traumatic, impenetrable, cruel, obscene, vacuous, meaningless and horrifically enjoyable. In its impenetrability, it is a version of Kant's unknowable thing in itself; and what is ultimately beyond our knowledge is humanity itself. To adapt Wittgenstein's remark about ethics, the Real involves running our heads up against the limits of language; and the bruises we receive in the process are the livid signs of our mortality. We can grasp this alien phenomenon only by constructing it backwards, so to speak, from its effects – from how it acts as a drag on our discourse, as astronomers can sometimes identify a celestial body only because of its warping effect on the space around it. For the Real to take on tangible shape, for it to put in an appearance in reality itself, is the fate of the psychotic, whose capacity to symbolise has broken down. The Real is the McGuffin, the joker in the pack, the pure meta-sign or empty element in any semiotic system whose function is to indicate the truth that it cannot be totalised. From one perspective, this cipher is the human subject itself, the void at the heart of the symbolic order. This void is the precondition for the order's effective functioning, but can never fully be represented there.

As the symbolic order's point of inner fracture, the Real is what resists being symbolised, a kind of surplus or leftover which remains when reality has been thoroughly formalised. It is the point at which our sign-making trails off into incoherence and our meanings begin to unravel at the edges; and as such it registers itself not directly, but as the outer limit of our discourse or the silence inscribed within it. It represents a hard kernel or gaping void at the core of our symbolic schemata (the contradictory metaphors are appropriate), which in preventing them from ever being quite at one with themselves is the ruin of all totality and the sabotaging of all sense-making. It is the rumble of sheer meaninglessness which echoes within our articulate speech, the kink in our being which no amount of spiritual hard labour will straighten out. At the root of meaning, as of poetry, there is always a sustaining residue of non-sense.

It is this shadow of the Real which the painter Lily Briscoe senses towards the end of Virginia Woolf's novel *To the Lighthouse*, as she tries to finish a painting and at the same time make sense of a world bereft of its radiant centrepiece, her beloved Mrs Ramsay. With the abrupt withdrawal of this sheltering maternal body, Lily feels 'as if the link that usually bound things together had been cut, and they floated up here, down there, off, anyhow. How aimless it was, how chaotic, how unreal it was, she thought, looking at her empty coffee cup.' As the bereaved Mr Ramsay mumbles his disjointed, death-ridden cries ('Alone', 'Perished'), Lily has the sense that if she could only put these stricken signifiers together, 'write them out in some sentence, then she would have got at the truth of things . . . what she wished to get hold of was that very jar on the nerves, the thing itself before it had been made anything'. Modernism in general is marked by this passion for an eyeball-to-eyeball encounter with the Real, only to find to its chagrin that it has already been mediated by the signifier; and this, one might claim, is both its triumph and its despondency. But the Real in Woolf's novel is also what snags and skews: the human apparatus for painting, as for feeling, 'always broke down at the critical moment; heroically, one must force it on'. Lily is hunting for words to express the vacancy of the death she bears in her body, the sense of some 'centre of complete emptiness' which seems to find its source not so much in the dead Mrs Ramsay as in the sheer act of longing in itself, the pure, untrammelled essence of desire. If Lily cannot complete her canvas, it is not least because each time that gaunt harbinger of death, Mr Ramsay, bears down upon her with his noisy hankering for sympathy, 'ruin approached, chaos approached', in this 'house full of unrelated passions'.

For all his infantile self-pity, however, Ramsay finally proves capable of passing beyond the imaginary sphere of pity and sympathy into 'some other region . . . out of one's range', as he finally lands triumphantly at the lighthouse like a hero whose damaged manhood has been miraculously restored. 'What was it he sought', Lily asks herself, 'so fixedly, so intently, so silently?' Meanwhile, as Ramsay travels to the limit of his own desire in encountering the solitary lighthouse, Lily feels herself 'drawn out of gossip, out of living, out of community with people into the presence of this formidable ancient enemy of hers – this other thing, this truth, this reality, which suddenly laid hands on her, emerged stark at the back of appearances and commanded her attention. She was half unwilling, half reluctant. Why always be drawn out and hauled away?'

Yet this momentous summons of the Real is also a sense of the inherent disproportion of things, the way they go minutely awry or appear suddenly estranged, like a sudden grimace or shadow on a beautiful countenance: 'One forgot the little agitations; the flush, the pallor, some queer distortion, some light or shadow, which made the face unrecognisable for a moment and yet added a quality one saw for ever after.' There is terror as well as ecstasy in this feeling of extreme risk and exposure, beyond the protective habits of the symbolic order: 'Was there no safety? No learning by heart of the ways of the world? No guide, no shelter, but all was miracle, and leaping from the pinnacle of a tower into the air? Could it be, even for elderly people, that this was life? – startling, unexpected, unknown?' We shall see later how this contrast between the habitual and the miraculous informs the work of some contemporary ethicists of the Real.

As 'outer things' begin to blur into unreality, Lily's unfinished painting is haunted by the sense of a presence at once 'so light that it could not ruffle your breath; and a thing you could not dislodge with a team of horses'. Still meditating upon the dead, she continues to 'encounter some obstacle in her design', until it flashes upon her that she might move a stroke representing a tree to the middle of the canvas, and knows in that moment an enormous exultation. Like Mr Ramsay, she too has now crossed an invisible frontier, leaping beyond the loving yet oppressive Law of the flesh which Mrs Ramsay symbolises for her, and recognising in a delirious surge of freedom that she need never bow to that Law through marriage herself. Mr Ramsay, too, has been transformed into the bachelor he once was, setting foot lightly like a young man on the lighthouse 'as if he were leaping into space', looking 'for all the world . . . as if he were saying "There is no God."' If he becomes a confirmed atheist in this luminous, opaque moment of revelation, it is because the Real of his desire is shown to be self-grounded, borrowing no support from beyond itself. At the same time Lily, driven by the perilous adventure of her painting to the extreme limit of her own resources, draws a line suddenly in the centre of the canvas, as the novel ends with a quotation from Christ on the cross: 'It was done; it was finished.' In the light of this artistic portrait of the Real, it is not surprising that Woolf's other masterpiece, *Mrs Dalloway*, should have death, psychosis and the disintegration of meaning at its centre.

In one sense, the Real is the stain of senseless material contingency which the symbolic order can never fully assimilate, the force which blocks Lily Briscoe's artistic drive for order. In another sense, it is a register closely allied with the bodily drives, which in their pure or actual state are as opaque to us as the Kantian *noumenon*, and which must pass through the defiles of the signifier in order to enter human consciousness. As if all this were not enough, the Real may also be identified, as in *To the Lighthouse*, with the forever misplaced Thing – with that barred, impossible object of our desire which is the maternal body, the feverish pursuit of which is familiar to psychoanalysis as the course of human history. If this lost paradise were ever to be recovered, history – which is no more than our continually rehearsed failure to attain it – would stumble to a halt. In so far as it involves the maternal body, the Real is the home of a lost *jouissance* – of that ecstatic enjoyment of the Other beside which the gentrified pleasures of the symbolic appear poor indeed.

Yet this *jouissance* or orgasmic delirium also bears the minatory imprint of the superego – of the law which commands us to grovel pleasurably in our own humiliation, plucking a kind of febrile life from the grisly business of doing ourselves to death.[5] It is a terrifying, rapacious form of enjoyment, in which we reap gratification from the way that the law or superego unleashes its demented sadism upon us. It is a law as devoid of meaning

---

[5]   I have discussed this more fully, particularly in relation to the idea of evil, in *Sweet Violence: The Idea of the Tragic* (Oxford, 2003), especially Ch. 9.

as the American waiter's perfunctory, intransitive injunction: 'Enjoy!' In the presence of the Real we are always in the shadow of death – more precisely, of what Freud taught us to see as the death drive, by whose sadistic decree we lust for our own annihilation. It is above all in this fateful deadlock between law and desire, in the stalled dialectic by which each reinforces the death-dealing potency of the other, that the presence of the Real can be sensed.

Yet there is a redemptive face to the Real as well as a destructive one. What is most real about us, from a psychoanalytic viewpoint, is desire; and to be true to our desire is therefore to be loyal to ourselves. Yet this must inevitably be a fidelity to failure, since desire is unstaunchable by nature. Those who have the courage to embrace this fact are the true heroes, rather as the classical tragic protagonist is one who snatches victory from the jaws of defeat. The very courage which allows him to submit to his destiny is also a power which transcends it. The literary figures we shall be examining in the next chapter, who would rather march proudly to their deaths than back down on their absolute demand for honour, justice, chastity or recognition, are those for whom a particular human claim has become metonymic of desire as such – of that within them that surpasses all articulable demands. It is for this reason that they invest the objects of their longing with such cruel intensity.

For Lacan, then, morality lies beyond the good, useful, virtuous and pleasurable, in the rigorously lawful domain of desire. Those altruists who earnestly seek to be of service to others, fulfilling their needs and enhancing their well-being, do so only because the true form of enjoyment which is *jouissance* – a pleasure which is 'good for nothing' – has lamentably failed them. The utilitarian or political reformer is he who is incapable of enjoyment without an end in view. Those who prate of the good, so ethicists of the Real suspect, suppose in implicitly autocratic style that they know just what good others need; whereas the love of the analyst for his or her patient never falls prey to such presuppositions.

A politics of the good accordingly involves a kind of bureaucratic paternalism – one which defines the good in partisan style, defends it from certain powerful competitors in the moral marketplace, and determines its distribution and regulation. To which one might riposte that the genuine lover is not she who instructs another in the nature of his good, but she who is herself the ground of it. It is just this kind of mutuality which a Realist like John Rajchman is keen to deny, writing as he does that psychoanalysis 'raises the question of an erotic bond which would not be based in communality, reciprocity, or equality, but in the singular "bearings" each of us has to the Real'.[6] Psychoanalysis, in brief, is just as much a form of depoliticisation as the vulgar Marxists darkly suspected it to be, only now for considerably more sophisticated reasons. The question of communal or reciprocal bonds which are themselves based in the Real is simply put aside. As we shall see, it is a question which theology, for which the only imperishable community is one founded upon violent, sacrificial love, seeks to raise – though Rajchman, having noted in his splendid study that Christianity is one influence on Lacan's writing, fails, in the most glaringly symptomatic of silences, to raise the subject ever again.

Desire, then, as the one and only ethical universal, is to be contrasted in Lacanian eyes with the good; whereas for a thinker like Aquinas, for whom the good is what we cannot help desiring, the two are not at all opposites. Desire in Thomist terms is simply the inscription of the sovereign good within us, the way it is built into our material bodies and seizes upon us independently of the abstract will. In his *Summa Theologiae*, Aquinas anticipates Lacan in his belief that it is desire which makes us what we are; and this desire, which acts as the organising principle of all our actions, is the yearning for what he calls *beatitudo* or happiness. It is natural for us to desire happiness, but also natural for us not to attain it, as self-divided, time-torn creatures who are incapable of coinciding with ourselves. Desire for Aquinas is infinite, just as it is for his psychoanalytic successors. Dissatisfaction is our normal condition, and the perfection we seek would signal the death of our humanity. The Thomist view of the human condition is remarkably similar to the Lacanian one, though shorn of its tragic dimension. For the desire which depletes us into non-being is in Aquinas's view consummated in the love of God, who is both cause and object of it.[7]

In Lacan's more jaundiced view, the good is a screen which defends us against our own deathly *jouissance*, and thus figures as a vestige of the paternal prohibition. Psychoanalysis, the science of that which fails to find satisfaction, of our perverse resistance to the very possibility of happiness, thus inaugurates in Lacan's view a revolutionary break with all previous ethical thought. It is because there is that in our libido which is fundamentally askew to our well-being (the Freudian version of original sin, so to speak) that we can no longer rest content with an ethics of virtue or hap-

---

[6]   John Rajchman, *Truth and Eros: Foucault, Lacan, and the Question of Ethics* (New York and London, 1991), p. 70.

[7]   See Stephen Wang, 'Aquinas on Human Happiness and the Natural Desire for God', *New Blackfriars*, 88: 1015 (May 2007).

piness, one more fit for politicians and social workers than those select rebels of the human spirit like Lacan himself. 'For Freud', as Rajchman pithily frames it, 'our *eros* is at odds with our *ethos*.'[8] There is the law of justice and the supreme good of the *polis*, incarnate in Sophocles's *Antigone* in the person of Creon; and there is another law altogether made manifest in the dissident Antigone herself – an unwritten, unknowable edict which in its deathly intransigence lies beyond both the pleasure principle and the reality principle, and which is implacably indifferent to the petty-bourgeois *mores* of the city.

If Lacan can take his stand so unflinchingly on this latter imperative, it is among other things because he is hardly enraptured by the political vision of the just city. Freud himself, so he considers, placed no faith in social progress or revolutionary politics, and was perfectly right to refuse such anodyne delusions. Lacanian thought belongs in this sense to a post-revolutionary epoch, one notably unenthused by communal energies or political panaceas. It is to be read among other things in the light of the corruption of socialism and the rise of fascism. Yet the Sophocles whom Lacan so admires is scarcely at one with his own political scepticism. To turn from *Antigone* or *Oedipus the King* to *Philoctetes* and *Oedipus at Colonus* is to encounter a very different species of politics – one in which the adamancy of an Antigone is finally overcome, as the sacred powers of the obdurate self-exile are harnessed to the task of repairing the *polis*. *Thanatos*, in Freud's own parlance, is yoked in sublimated form to the life-yielding project of *Eros*, as it is at the conclusion of Aeschylus's *Oresteia*. By embracing the symbols of death, disease and disorder, whether in the form of the avenging Furies, the pus-ridden Philoctetes or the cursed Oedipus, the city opens its eyes by an act of grace to the monstrosity which lurks at its own heart, and in this terrible encounter with the Real unleashes the sublime power to protect and refashion itself.[9] It is not, after all, a matter of the sullenly anti-social rebel versus the inertly consensual city, however such a Camusian contrast may appeal to a politically defeatist age. Creon may prove deaf to Antigone's desire, but the same is not true of the Theseus who graciously welcomes within his walls the fearfully corrupted protagonist of *Oedipus at Colonus*. Pentheus, ruler of Thebes in Euripides's *The Bacchae*, may treat Dionysus and his crew with Creon-like repressiveness; but there is no necessity for him to behave with such fearful impiety to these death-loving, anarchic figures, symbolic as they are of the obscene

---

[8]   Ibid., p. 47.
[9]   See Terry Eagleton, *Holy Terror* (Oxford, 2005), Ch. 1.

enjoyment of the Real. Indeed, he is urgently counselled not to do so. Politics and desire need not be eternally at loggerheads. William Blake was wiser in this respect than Jacques Lacan. For the latter, the two cannot effect that vital encounter which is known as the political re-education of desire, a project which the Realists seem able to imagine only in the form of some insidious castration.

Lacan's claim to ethical novelty is surely precarious. Christianity, as we have just seen, places desire (the human longing for God) at the focus of its moral reflection, and so do its elder brothers and sisters, the Jews. Equally uncertain is the case that desire and well-being are necessarily at odds – a case which rings plausibly only if one erases the mediation between the two known as love. For the Christian gospel, desire, in the shape of the love or yearning which is both faith and hope, is less the opposite of the supreme good than the obscure signifier of it in actuality. It is only because God's love lies at the core of the self, sustaining it in being, that we are able to seek that good in the form of a desire for it. In this sense, one negativity – that of the abyssal, unspeakable, unimaginable God – is overlaid by another, that of our perpetual longing for him. It is a desire for the Real which seizes the self violently by its roots and shatters its foundations. Moreover, this good which is God has for Christian belief all the enigma of the Real, not the translucency of some contemptible rational ideal. If God is the supreme instance of the Lacanian *sujet-supposé-à-savoir*, possessed of a fathomless knowledge, it is not by drawing upon such omniscience that we can repair our moral condition. It is by faith, not knowledge, that we recognise the law of our own being. For both Christianity and psychoanalysis, redemption is a practical, relational affair, not a set of theoretical propositions.

Equally unfounded is Lacan's rather brash assertion that all previous moral thought has been centred upon pleasure. Not all moralists before Freud were unabashed hedonists – though it is true that any ethics of self-realisation, whether Aristotelian, Hegelian or Marxist, must come to terms with that botching, backfiring, stymieing excess or missing-of-the-mark which is the effect of desire. In Lacan's rather misty-eyed view, however, Freud is an absolute pioneer in this regard. His avant-garde gesture is to situate the moral law not in relation to the symbolic order, but to that perpetually missing object of our yearning, what Lacan himself theatrically calls the Thing, and which he occasionally translates as the maternal body. The desire to which psychoanalysis lends a tongue is that of the Real, the turbulent power which transgresses the confines of the symbolic order; and it is in this that it is ethically original.

In one sense, to be sure, this desire conforms to the universal nature of the symbolic order, since it is the same for everyone. Yet it assumes a different form in everyone, too, appearing to them 'in its intimate specificity with the character of an imperious *Wunsch* (wish)'.[10] It is the law of one's own utterly peculiar being, and thus the most irreducibly specific of edicts – even if this is a specificity to be found in us all. Desire has the elusive uniqueness of the 'law' of the work of art, rather than the abstract uniformity of the moral law. It is more like Kant's aesthetic judgement than his practical reason. Unlike the law of the symbolic order, this overbearing desire, 'preserved in the depths of the subject in an irreducible form' (24), is quite incommensurable with any other, and cannot be judged from the outside. Despite Lacan's notable indifference to Nietzsche, there is an echo here of the German's vision of a law peculiar to each individual.

In Lacan's eyes, the conventional notion of a sovereign good – the philosopher's stone of much traditional moral theory – can only be a species of false idealism, and thus a stumbling block to a genuine ethics. As an ethical avant-gardist, he seems to regard all previous moral discourse – virtue, duty, utility and the like – as little more than a specious idealising of our chronic discontent. It is as though there was no truly materialist morality – no Hobbes, Marx or Nietzsche, for example – until Freud and his Parisian avatar arrived on the scene. In contrast to such spurious sublimations, his own ethics, in the words of John Rajchman, 'would rather be an ethic or teaching of the difficulty we have with what is ideal in us, with what we suppose is our Good, and thus with our passionate relations with ourselves and one another'.[11] Both the pursuit of the good life and the question of moral duty must be relocated in relation to the problem of desire. We shall see a little later that there is more than a dash of exalted idealism in the Lacanian alternative to the good, useful and dutiful, namely the heroism of desire; but meanwhile we may note that even if there is a sovereign good, it must for Freudian theory be a prohibited one. Rather as those who fall in love with the law find it blocking their path to the good, so to desire the forbidden Thing – to aim directly at some absolute good – is to provoke the law's censorious cutting edge, thus landing ourselves with that perpetual tail-chasing of law, desire, aggression, guilt, murderous self-loathing and self-lacerating *jouissance* which is, so to speak, our state of original sin.

---

[10] Jacques Lacan, *The Ethics of Psychoanalysis* (London, 1999), p. 24. Further references to this text in this section will be given parenthetically after quotations.

[11] Rajchman, *Truth and Eros*, p. 17.

As Lacan himself puts it, our desire flares up only in relation to a law which is ultimately the law of death. There is that in life which prefers death; and it is here, as Lacan rightly comments, that we border upon that eternal embarrassment of the *bien-pensant* liberal or leftist, the problem of evil.[12] The Real in its more positive sense, however, as an eternal fidelity to the law of our own being, lies on some outlandish terrain beyond this symbolic law, which is why it has the power to cut the deadly knot of yearning and prohibition which is the dark secret of the symbolic order. Precisely because the desire of the Real is, so to speak, pure desire, desire in its rawest state, desire in and for itself rather than for this or that supreme or contingent good, it can give the slip to the law which intervenes to punish all such craving for particular objects, since in its paranoid way the law discerns in any such innocent longing an impious hunger for the forbidden Thing. The patron saint of a Lacanian ethics, then – the psychoanalytic counterpart of St Teresa, so to speak – is Sophocles's Antigone, driven as she is by a good which is beyond all goods, which is beyond morality itself as the parson or prime minister understands the term, and which is therefore difficult for the self-respecting moralists of this world to distinguish from evil.

All of Sophocles's mighty protagonists, so Lacan points out, have strayed beyond the protective shell of the symbolic order into some trackless territory of the spirit, thrust by some implacable demand or preternatural purity of being outside the stockade of civic decency to a place of extreme solitude and self-exposure in which they are set apart in the manner of the sacred. The sacred signifies those ambiguously cursed and blessed objects which are earmarked for death, and which in being thus marked with the livid signs of their own mortality can unleash a formidable power for transformation. These acolytes of the Real are all liminal creatures, pure incarnations of *Thanatos*, at once animate and inanimate, men and women who are dead but won't lie down. They are characters lingering in the departure lounge of life, individuals who like the protagonists of high tragedy sightlessly move among the ranks of the living dead, and in whose dumb agony death can already be felt stealthily trespassing upon the terrain of the living. As such, they are exemplars of the truth that, in Lacan's own phrase, 'all that is lives only in the lack of being' (294). Desire in the end is desire for nothing. It is no more than the living relation of men and women to their own lack of being, the *néant* which keeps them on the move. Psychoanalysis is the resurgence in secular, scientific guise of the

---

[12]   For the relations between evil and the death drive, see Eagleton, *Sweet Violence*.

tragic sense of life. In Lacan's hands, it becomes an atheistic style of religion, clinging like Beckett's tramps to a redemption which will never arrive. The keystone of religion – God – is placed under censure, but the whole elaborate edifice remains remarkably intact. What is the desire of the Real but what Augustine and Kierkegaard knew as faith?

So there is no sovereign good, it would seem, beyond clinging intractably to one's longing for it. To replicate something of Lacan's own baroque wordplay, an ethics of the Real can be summarised in the imperative: Lack on! I shall be casting some doubt on this case later on; but in the meantime it is important to understand that to have realised one's desire 'in the end' is not to have achieved its object, since in the end it has no object other than itself. Like Goethe's Faust, the Lacanian moral hero 'will only encounter that (sovereign) good if at every moment he eliminates from his wishes the false goods, if he exhausts not only the vanity of his demands, given that they are all no more than regressive demands, but also the vanity of his gifts' (300). As with Kant's moral law, the desire of the Real has no truck with anything as commonplace as human needs, appetites and interests. It is as monkish and self-denying as a Carthusian. Classical morality has its rather humdrum sights set on nothing more exotic than the realm of the possible; an ethics of the Real, by contrast, is concerned with 'nothing less than the impossibility in which we recognise the topology of our desire' (315). We shall be assessing the pros and cons of this ethics of heroic failure in our final chapter.

7

Schopenhauer, Kierkegaard and Nietzsche

It would be possible, no doubt, to cast the three Lacanian registers in the form of an historical narrative, one which in a rather vulgar Marxist allegory would trace the rise and decline of bourgeois civilisation. Hutcheson, Hume and the imaginary would mark an emergent moment of optimism and self-assurance, as a still sanguine, blithe-spirited middle class has yet fully to register the alienating effects of its own activities, delights in its own humane sentiments, and is still able to envisage society as a qualified kind of *Gemeinschaft*. What follows with Kant and Hegel is the more abstract, regulated, impersonal order of the symbolic, one which is paradoxically both thoroughly civilised and profoundly unsociable. It is this which represents the high point of middle-class culture, with its great creeds of liberalism and Utilitarianism, its egalitarian zeal and humanitarian agendas, its courageous promotion of human rights and individual liberties.

As the nineteenth century wears on, with the tragic, sceptical or revolutionary reflections of Schopenhauer, Kierkegaard, Marx and Nietzsche, it is now the motifs of blockage, impasse and contradiction which come gradually to the fore, to culminate, in a *fin-de-siècle* of capitalist crisis and savage imperialist conflict, in the profoundly pessimistic meditations of Sigmund Freud. It is this whole epoch which represents, so to speak, the reign of the Real, as desire itself, once so buoyant and affirmative, now betrays something incurably diseased at its heart, and benign conceptions of authority begin to yield to predatory or sadistic notions of power. With the carnage of the first world war and its turbulent political aftermath, the symbolic order of Europe enters into prolonged crisis – a condition from which fascism hopes to redeem it by pressing the resources of the imaginary (blood, earth, *Volk*, motherhood) into the service of the symbolic. In a lethal fusion of Lacanian registers, the primitivist and archaic are harnessed to the ends of dominion and rationalisation.

Mythology is yoked to the service of a savagely instrumental rationality. And at the heart of this barbarous experiment, in the death camps of central Europe and the fascistic cult of *Thanatos*, lies the horror of a Real which eludes representation.

Like most grand fables, such a narrative is shot through with anomalies. What of the great seventeenth-century rationalists, of Descartes, Leibniz and Spinoza? Is eighteenth-century philosophy uniformly bright-eyed? Is everything that comes after Hegel an unmitigated horror story? All the same, there is surely no doubt that from Schopenhauer to Freud, the great project of Enlightenment runs aground on some recalcitrant Real, some obdurate core of Will or desire, religious faith or material history, which throws it alarmingly out of kilter. What appears as a benevolent Reason in Hegel becomes in Schopenhauer's hands the blind, insatiably hankering Will, which was to influence Freud's own reflections on the unconscious. Indeed, one can read the whole of Schopenhauer's extravagantly gloomy *The World as Will and Representation* as a grisly parody of the thought of his academic colleague Hegel, one in which the universal forms of a number of Hegelian categories (freedom, justice, reason, progress) are preserved, but emptied of their exalted content and filled instead with the degraded materials of everyday middle-class existence: greed, rivalry, appetite, conflict and the like. Philosophy with Schopenhauer is still confident enough in its forms to unify and universalise, but its content is now distinctly unedifying. It is as though the uncouth rapacity of the average bourgeois has been elevated to cosmic status, grasped as the prime metaphysical mover of the entire universe.[1]

The Will for Schopenhauer, like desire for Lacan, is driven by lack: 'All *willing* springs from lack, from deficiency, and thus from suffering'.[2] It is the blindly persistent appetite at the root of all phenomena, the force that builds the very stuff of our blood-stream and intestines, and which can be observed in the surging of the waves or shrivelling of a leaf as much as in some more lofty motion of the human spirit. Whether it includes Schopenhauer's reflections on it is an intriguing question. Unlike Hegelian Reason, however, the Will is an implacably malevolent force, one which lies at the very pith of the human subject but which is nonetheless relentlessly indifferent to its flourishing. This Will which lies at the well-spring

---

[1]   Some of the material on Schopenhauer which follows is adapted from my *The Ideology of the Aesthetic* (Oxford, 1990), Ch. 6.

[2]   Arthur Schopenhauer, *The World as Will and Representation* (New York, 1969), vol. 1, p. 196.

of subjectivity, which I can experience from the inside of my body with incomparably greater immediacy than I can know anything else, is as blankly unfeeling and anonymous as a tornado or a bolt of lightning. Like desire in its psychoanalytic sense, it is entirely without meaning and is glacially indifferent to all the objects in which it invests, which it uses simply for its own fruitless self-reproduction.

Unlike Hegel, Schopenhauer's thought is resolutely anti-teleological, with all the unity and dynamic of a grand narrative but with none of its purposefulness. The Will is a malicious parody of Hegel's Idea. Human beings are simply its ephemeral bearers, to be cast peremptorily aside once they have accomplished its ends; yet its ends lie entirely in its own pointless self-perpetuation, to which there is no closure. We are simply the walking materialisations of our parents' copulatory instincts, which in turn are mere manifestations of the Will. We are, then, in the realm of a Faustian infinity of desire, as the whole world comes to be recast in the image of the marketplace. The virulently misanthropic Schopenhauer speaks with scarcely suppressed disgust of 'this world of constantly needy creatures who continue for a time merely by devouring one another, pass their existence in anxiety and want, and often endure terrible afflictions, until they fall at last into the arms of death'.[3] It is a far cry from Hutcheson's *bonhomie* or Kant's peaceable kingdom. Only some myopic sentimentalism, in Schopenhauer's view, could imagine that the paltry pleasures of human existence, that low burlesque which lacks even the *gravitas* of high tragedy, might compensate for its unrelieved wretchedness.

'Desiring', Schopenhauer observes, 'lasts a long time, its demands and requests go on to infinity; fulfilment is short and meted out sparingly'.[4] Or as Shakespeare puts it rather more unstintingly in *Troilus and Cressida*: 'This is the monstruosity in love, lady, that the will is infinite, and the execution confin'd; that the desire is boundless, and the act a slave to limit'. Once you have entered the domain of desire, the empirical world is instantly devalued. It serves simply to remind you of what it is you do not want. 'Compared with anything the subject seeks out', Lacan remarks, 'that which occurs in the domain of motor discharge always has a diminished character'.[5] He who says desire says bathos. It was Freud who reminded us that whereas the ancients in their wisdom placed their emphasis on the instinct, we moderns have foolishly shifted it to the object.

---

[3]   Ibid., vol. 2, p. 349.
[4]   Ibid., vol. 1, p. 196.
[5]   Jacques Lacan, *The Ethics of Psychoanalysis* (London, 1999), p. 42.

Schopenhauer, however, will reverse these priorities, thus prefiguring Freud himself. Rather as the sole end of the accumulation of capital is to accumulate afresh, so, in a catastrophic collapse of teleology, the Will comes to appear independent of all specific objects of its attention. Desire therefore appears to be invested entirely in itself, brooding upon its own being like some malignly narcissistic spirit. In a social order in which possessive individualism is the order of the day, Schopenhauer is perhaps the first major modern thinker who is empowered by historical circumstance to place at the centre of his work the abstract category of *desire itself*, as opposed to this or that specific form of longing; and it is this formidable abstraction which Freud, who in a curious lapse of intelligence considered Schopenhauer one of the half-dozen greatest individuals who ever lived, will inherit. We shall see in a moment, however, how it is possible to read the moral thought of Kant in something like the same way.

The Will, then, is an unfathomable force, a kind of purposiveness without purpose (to adopt Kant's celebrated comment about art). What is now irreparably flawed is nothing less than the whole category of subjectivity, not simply some repression or estrangement of it. Human subjectivity is itself a form of alienation, as we bear within ourselves an intolerable weight of meaninglessness, living immured in our own bodies like lifers in a prison cell. Subjectivity is what we can least call our own. If we do not receive it *à la* Schopenhauer as a poisoned gift from the Will, there are plenty of alternative donors to hand: the Idea for Hegel, God for Kierkegaard, history for Marx, the Will to Power for Nietzsche, the Other for Lacan.

What distinguishes the work of Schopenhauer from these rival apostles of the Real is the fact that what he pits against the horrors of the Real is nothing less than the imaginary. In an extraordinary reversion to the cult of empathy, we can cheat the devious Will not by action, which is merely another manifestation of its odious force, nor by suicide, which simply allows it to flaunt its own immortality in contrast with our own finitude, but by extinguishing the desire-tormented ego in a moment of pure self-lessness. The intolerable tedium of existence is that we can never burst out of our own skins, as we drag our squalid egos after us like a ball and chain. Desire signifies our incapacity to see things straight, the subjective squint by which we compulsively refer all objects to our own supremely trifling interests. To be a subject is to desire, and to desire is to be deluded. In the domain of the aesthetic, however, desire drops away from us, the Will is momentarily suspended, and for a blessed moment we are able to see the world as it is. The price for this precious epiphany is nothing less than the wholesale dissolution of the subject, that most precious of all bourgeois categories, who in a serene self-immolation is now empathetically at one with its object. The world can be liberated from the ravages of desire only by being converted into an aesthetic spectacle, in the process of which the subject itself dwindles to a vanishing-point of pure disinterestedness. It is as though we take pity upon the various things around us, infected as they are by our longing, and redeem them from this lethal contagion by effacing ourselves from the scene, gazing upon this whole landscape of human carnage with the equanimity of an observer so supremely dispassionate that he is no longer even present.

Nothing is more arduous in Schopenhauer's eyes than this hard-won objectivity, which is the fruit of moral discipline rather than of some naïve objectivism or callow look-and-see. Objectivity, he remarks, is a work of genius. As with the Buddhist thought which marked him so profoundly, it is a 'letting-be' which cannot really be fought for, since such labour could only be that of the ego, and thus part of the problem to which it proposes a solution. Only by somehow piercing the veil of *Maya* or commonplace illusion and recognising the fictional status of the ego can one behave towards others with true indifference – which is to say, make no significant distinction between them and oneself. It is in this sense that the imaginary resurfaces in Schopenhauer's writings. Once the *principium individuationis* is unmasked for the fraud that it is, selves may be empathetically exchanged in an act of loving compassion. The primary source of all ethics, Schopenhauer remarks, is the act of sharing in another's suffering independent of all self-interested motives. To act ethically is not to act from a particular standpoint, but to act from no standpoint at all. The only good subject is a dead one, or at least one in perpetually suspended animation. Since the subject *is* a specific perspective on reality, all that is left behind when it is surmounted is a kind of pure negativity or nirvana. In Schopenhauer's hands, the philosophy of the subject self-destructs, leaving in its wake nothing but a selfless contemplation which can attach itself to nobody in particular.

Yet it is not exactly accurate to claim that the imaginary for Schopenhauer acts as a therapy for the Real. It is rather that the Real is turned ingeniously against itself, entangled in its own strength and thus brought low. This is because the force which dissolves the subject to a selfless cipher, thus allowing it to melt compassionately into others, is itself what Freud will later term the death drive. In regarding the world of human shrieking and howling as so much idle extravaganza, we achieve a detachment from it, and an erasure of subjectivity, which is very like the state of death; yet at the same time we are allowed to indulge a fantasy of immortality, serene in the knowledge that this theatre of cruelty can no longer do us harm. Because we are in a sense dead already, we are as delightfully invulnerable as Shakespeare's Barnardine; and by attaining this Olympian vantage-point we wreak a delicious vengeance on the forces which would hound us to extinction. It is just this condition of indulging a vicarious joy in destruction, while rejoicing in our own cartoon-like unkillability, which distinguishes the eighteenth-century sublime.[6]

Schopenhauer's aestheticising of reality, in which we draw life from the process of our own annihilation, involves a cat-and-mouse game between *Eros* and *Thanatos*, the instinct for life and the lust for death; and to this extent it is a question of the Real. Yet because the form taken by the death of the subject is one of empathy, it is also, as we have seen, a matter of the imaginary. The whole wretched delusion of individuality is relinquished, as we come to feel for the sufferings of others at a level incomparably deeper than the ego. We end up, in effect, with a transcendence without a subject: the place of absolute knowledge is preserved, but there is nobody left to occupy it. Disinterestedness teaches us to shed our disruptive passions and live humbly, ungreedily, with the simplicity of a saint. I suffer with your afflictions because I am aware that your inner stuff, the cruel Will, is also my own. As with Hume and Hutcheson, I know this by virtue of an immediate access to both you and myself, not through the tiresome circumspections of reason. 'Every living thing', Schopenhauer comments in a striking formulation of the imaginary, 'is just as much our own inner being-in-itself as is our own person'.[7] We can meet in sympathetic union, however, not simply as in a mirror but on the ground of the Real, which as the core of the subject is what we have most profoundly in common. To inscribe the imaginary in the Real is to foster a fellowship which goes all the way down. Only by converging on a third terrain, one which is both strange and as close as breathing to us both, will our personal or political relations prove to be durable.

It is thus that Lacan understands the scriptural injunction to love one's neighbour as oneself – a command which is not to be grasped in the imaginary, as the love of an alter ego, but in the far less translucent dimension of the Real. Of the former, Lacan is sardonically dismissive: 'What I want', he writes, 'is the good of others provided that it remains in the image of

---

[6] For a fuller discussion, see Terry Eagleton, *Holy Terror* (Oxford, 2005), Ch. 2.
[7] Schopenhauer, *World as Will and Representation*, vol. 1, p. 231.

my own'.[8] There is, as he points out, 'a big difference between the response of philanthropy and the response of love'.[9] To love another is to recognise that what makes him so horrifically unlovable – what Lacan himself calls his harmful, malignant *jouissance*, or what Freud himself saw as the sheer malice, evil and aggression at his core – also dwells at the heart of oneself. When I turn in fear from this malevolent other, I take flight from the deathly Real within myself, which surges up and threatens to overwhelm me as the neighbour approaches. This, no doubt, is what Lacan intends by his cryptic comment that 'there is no law of the good except in evil and through evil'[10] – or, as Christianity might translate that statement, no resurrection which has not passed through the hellish negativity of suffering and self-loss.

Love is thus situated on the far side of the law, accessible only by our *transitus* through the obscene enjoyment of the Real, the trace of the death drive within us, in the frail hope of emerging somewhere on the other side. Our resistance to the scandalous command to love ourselves is in Lacan's view a resistance to being confronted with our own terrifying *jouissance*, as we sense 'some form of intolerable cruelty' on the horizon. In that sense, Lacan admonishes, 'to love one's neighbour may be the cruellest of choices'.[11] The neighbour is always a stranger, and in Freud's eyes the stranger is always a kind of enemy. The Christian command to love one's enemies is thus scarcely as outrageous as it might appear – for what else are those we encounter but potential enemies? But it is no easy matter to love oneself either, if that is to mean a Real rather than imaginary self-acceptance. One would not like to be loved by some other people in the way that they love themselves. Kenneth Reinhard, in an otherwise illuminating essay, is mistaken to claim that love of oneself is necessarily imaginary – 'the specular reflection on myself that constitutes the narcissistic ego in the mirror stage'.[12] Repentance is the self-acceptance which springs from acknowledging the self's disfigurement, one which involves an authentic self-love rather than a narcissistic one.

If the Real and the imaginary are both at work in Schopenhauer's ethic of empathy, so too is the symbolic, which is exactly what the Schopenhau-

[8]   Lacan, *Ethics of Psychoanalysis*, p. 187.
[9]   Ibid., p. 186.
[10] Ibid., p. 190.
[11] Ibid., p. 194.
[12] Kenneth Reinhard, 'Towards a Political Theology of the Neighbor', in S. Žižek, E. Santner and K. Reinhard (eds), *The Neighbor* (Chicago and London, 2005), p. 71.

erian view from nowhere involves. To see the world as it truly is, quite independent of our own needs and appetites; to register the mind-bending truth that things are eternally what they are, whatever importunate claims we would make on them: this, which Schopenhauer calls the aesthetic or supreme disinterestedness, is also the moment of the symbolic in his writing – that condition in which we renounce the infantile clamour of the ego, reaping a perverse delight from the fact that reality has no need of us whatsoever and is no doubt all the better for it.

There is a parallel between the Lacanian stages of imaginary, symbolic and Real and Søren Kierkegaard's three categories of the aesthetic, ethical and religious. The parallel between the imaginary and the aesthetic is perhaps the least exact. The aesthetic individual for Kierkegaard leads an existence without purpose or direction, shifting restlessly from one mood or persona to another, paralysed by the prospect of a myriad possibilities, too capricious and diffuse to be a self-determining subject. He inhabits a zone of sensuous immediacy which knows no temporal or historical consistency, a sphere in which its actions can only dubiously be called his own. Bereft of a determinate life project, identifying itself with the passing moment or impression, the subject of the aesthetic is all surface and no depth. Appearances are its sole reality. A mere prey to circumstance, it is a self-deceived creature lacking all autonomy or responsibility. Most social existence for the censorious Kierkegaard is no more than a 'higher' version of this sensuous passivity: 'immediacy with the addition of a little dose of self-reflection', as he remarks sardonically in *The Sickness Unto Death*.[13] There is, however, an even higher version of this self-decentring, which goes by the name of religious faith. For the inhabitants of the imaginary or aesthetic, as for Oscar Wilde, truth is simply one's latest mood. For religious believers, it lies beyond the self in God, who turns us inside-out in our pursuit of it.

To this extent, the aesthetic and imaginary share a number of features in common. Where they differ most sharply is that the aesthetic is also for Kierkegaard a kind of Hegelian 'bad infinity' as well as 'bad immediacy', in which the subject, lacking a determined centre of self, is plunged into an abyss of infinite self-reflection, in which self-irony tumbles on the heels

---

[13] Søren Kierkegaard, *Fear and Trembling and The Sickness Unto Death*, ed. Walter Lowrie (New York, 1954), p. 191.

of self-irony in an orgy of unrealised possibilities. Viewed from this angle, the aesthetic subject fills in its own vacuity not by seizing upon the fugitive sensation, but by re-inventing itself *ex nihilo* from one moment to the next, seeking to preserve a sense of unbounded freedom which is in truth sheer self-consuming negativity. Intoxicated by its own empty excess, the aesthetic ironist lives subjunctively rather than indicatively, concealing his nihilism beneath the panache of this flamboyant self-fashioning. Whereas the subject of religious faith holds together the finite and infinite in the unthinkable paradox of the Incarnation, the aesthetic subject lurches from the one to the other. Either it takes flight into sensuous finitude, flattening itself into a craven conformism to the social order; or it is monstrously inflated and volatilised, taking flight from the need to become itself in an unending spiral of self-cancelling ironies.

The Lacanian imaginary already finds itself overshadowed by the symbolic – so that, for example, the alienation it involves provides a foretaste of the rather different alienations of the symbolic; or the presence of the mother in the mirror anticipates the later triangulation of the family set-up; or the rivalry with the imaginary other prefigures the Oedipal conflict. In a similar way, the aesthetic for Kierkegaard is invaded by an ominous form of negativity, to which he gives the name of dread. Dread is the self's encounter with its own nothingness, the *néant* which haunts even the realm of sensuous immediacy. Dread, or anxiety, is a kind of dim premonition of the symbolic order which is still to come, an ominous foretaste of freedom, difference, autonomy and otherness. The very repleteness of the aesthetic state becomes somehow suggestive of lack – though not, to be sure, a lack that could be given a name. All immediacy harbours a dread of nothingness. One might even find in this Kierkegaardian notion a resonance of Julia Kristeva's concept of the 'abject', that originary sense of horror and nausea involved in our first efforts to separate ourselves from the pre-Oedipal mother.[14] The Fall, in short, has always already happened. If Adam were not already prone to sin, how could he have flouted God's edict in the first place? It is Adam's transgression, so Kierkegaard argues, that first opens up the possibility of difference, and thus (in Lacanian terms) inaugurates the symbolic order; yet he could not have fallen unless some obscure sense of the possibility of freedom were already at work in him, some dim, primordial grasp of the possibility of difference before difference had yet occurred. We are speaking not of the emergence of possibility but, so to speak, of the dawning of the possibility of it. In the

---

[14] See Julia Kristeva, *Histoires d'amour* (Paris, 1983), pp. 27–58.

beginning, then, is not innocence, but that structural possibility of transgression which Christianity knows as original sin.

If the fit between Lacan's imaginary and Kierkegaard's aesthetic is hardly seamless, the relation between his ethical sphere and the Lacanian symbolic turns out to be more direct. The ethical, as the Kierkegaard portrays it in *Either/Or*, turns on the autonomous, self-determining individual whose actions, in Kantian fashion, express the universal. Ethical Man is social, self-responsible, *bürgerlich* man, secure in his marriage, profession, property, duty and civic obligations. Unlike the capricious creature of the aesthetic, he is strenuously self-directing, with a Stoic indifference to the vicissitudes of fortune. In his complicity with public norms and standards, his ethical life is a creditable instance of Hegel's *Sittlichkeit*. In contrast to the aesthetic subject, inner and outer worlds are harmoniously balanced in his personality. Kierkegaard's ethical subject is comfortably at home with the ideas of decision, commitment, universality, objectivity, self-reflection, centred identity and temporal consistency.

Yet this subject is not as tediously reputable as he may seem. For one thing, Kierkegaard's belief that the ethical subject must radically 'choose' itself – though in a strong sense of the term, the subject does not properly exist prior to this act of choice – presses beyond Kantian autonomy toward an existentialist notion of authenticity. It also involves a concept of self-fashioning which is closer to Nietzsche than it is to Kant – though Kierkegaard's self-choosing subject, far from embodying some fantasy of free, aesthetic self-invention, must assume its personal reality in all of its hopeless unregeneracy, confronting the self as a form of necessity as well as a form of freedom. The self for Kierkegaard is both a *donnée* to be discovered and a project to be accomplished. Once an ethical decision is taken, as a fundamental option of one's being rather than for this or that particular, it must be ceaselessly re-enacted, in a process which binds together the subject's history into a self-consistent enterprise. We shall find an echo of this doctrine of repetition later in the writings of Alain Badiou. To live in the ethical is to be infinitely interested in existing – existing for Kierkegaard signifying a task rather than a given, something to be achieved rather than received; and in this dimension of infinity the ethical foreshadows the religious, rather as the aesthetic bears within it a prefigurative trace of the ethical.

In so far as the ethical concerns the public, universal and communitarian, the Protestant-individualist Kierkegaard can find little in it worth salvaging. As such, it is no more than collective false consciousness. Yet in so far as it signifies a preoccupation with inwardness, it alludes in some obscure manner to the religious faith which transcends it. Such faith shatters the symmetries of the ethical, subverts the complacently autonomous self, and represents a scandal to all civic virtue. Its intense individual inwardness rebuffs the social and turns its back contemptuously on mass civilisation. As we shall see later with the French advocates of an ethics of the Real, faith can never be gentrified, assimilated to the mores and good sense of a social order. It is permanently askew to consensus and an affront to social orthodoxy. Faith is too much of a matter of perpetual inward crisis to be capable of oiling the wheels of social life, in the manner of some more civic or sociable ethics. It is *kairos* rather than custom, fear and trembling rather than cultural ideology. It can never crystallise into habit, tradition or institution, and is therefore radically anti-historical. The human condition, Kierkegaard remarks in *The Sickness Unto Death*, is always critical.

This ardent subjectivism is obdurately particular, averse as it is to all reason, theory, universality and objectivity. 'Reality cannot be conceived', Kierkegaard writes, and 'the particular cannot be thought.'[15] Existence is radically heterogeneous to thought, in a tradition of reflection of which Theodor Adorno will be the great twentieth-century inheritor. It signifies the anguished separation of subject and object, rather than their harmonious alliance. The philosophical bugbear here is Hegel, who fails to grasp that all grand narratives and rational totalities are shipwrecked on the rock of faith. Such complacent idealism is unable to acknowledge the realities of sin and guilt – the fact that before God we are always in the wrong, that the self bears with it a crippling burden of injury and misery which cannot be blandly sublated. It is also incapable of stomaching the truth that history is sheer contingency. Sin – the sheer ontological awryness of humanity – is the stumbling block on which all purely rational ethics or historical schemas are bound to come a cropper. The crux of Christianity, the Incarnation, is the ruin of all reason – for how can the infinite dwell within the confines of the finite? Truth is not theoretical but passionately subjective. It is 'the venture which chooses an objective uncertainty with the passion of the infinite'.[16] To believe is to be.

'Christianity is spirit', Kierkegaard writes, 'spirit is inwardness, inwardness is subjectivity, subjectivity is essentially passion, and at its maximum an infinite, personal, passionate interest in one's eternal happiness.'[17]

---

[15]   Søren Kierkegaard, *Journals* (London, 1938), p. 151, and *Concluding Unscientific Postscript* (Princeton, NJ, 1941), p. 290.
[16]   Kierkegaard, *Concluding Unscientific Postscript*, p. 182.
[17]   Ibid., p. 33.

Whereas the symbolic or ethical order is marked by the equity and disinterestedness of law, faith is passionately partisan; whereas the symbolic is abstract, universal and egalitarian, faith is existential, absolute and incommensurable. The self of the ethical order, the coherent, self-transparent, luminously legible ego of everyday bourgeois existence, is thus sundered by an impassable gulf from the fraught, unstable, contradictory, self-opaque subject of faith or the Real. The latter will always remain a scandal and an enigma for the former, plagued as it is by conflicts which it can resolve not theoretically but existentially, leashing them provisionally together in the moment-to-moment venture of actual existence rather than resolving them in the tranquillity of the concept. The subject of faith binds contradictions together in the act of living them. Like Lacanian desire, faith is self-founding, self-validating and eternally unachieved. The Real lies on the far side of language, the living mark of the symbolic order, rather as Abraham travels beyond the frontiers of the articulable in his fidelity to God's mad demand that he slaughter his son. It is a form of pure singularity pitched beyond the universal, the triumph of a wise absurdity over a foolish rationality. In the teeth of the ethical, in the face of every human decency, Abraham refuses to give way on the inscrutable desire which is faith.

There is, however, a positive and a negative version of the Real in Kierkegaard, as there is, one might claim, for Lacan. The Real to be affirmed is God, the infinite abyss at the core of the self; but there is a more sinister sort of negativity at the heart of humanity, to which Kierkegaard gives the name of despair in *The Sickness Unto Death*, and which is really a version of the Freudian death drive. More exactly, it is the abyssal sense of nothingness of those who, unable to become the selves they desire to be, wish to be rid of themselves, yet who are stuck fast in the demonic condition of being unable to die. I have argued elsewhere that this realm of the living dead, who can prove to themselves that they are still alive only by the *jouissance* they reap from destroying others, is very close to what is classically known as evil;[18] and although Kierkegaard's despairers are scarcely this, given that what they feed upon is not others but themselves, they manifest what he calls a 'demonic madness', raging spitefully against existence, in love with annihilation, yet perversely keeping themselves on this side of extinction by virtue of this very sullen rancour. This, traditionally, is the state of being known as Satanic. In Lacanian terms, these are men and women trapped helplessly in the deadlock of law and desire, and thus prime victims of the Real. It is a condition which in Kierkegaard's eyes can

---

[18]   See Terry Eagleton, *Sweet Violence: The Idea of the Tragic* (Oxford, 2003), Ch. 9.

be undone only by that life-yielding form of the Real which is the grace of God. For Kierkegaard, only by being afflicted with this despair in some form or other – a despair which constitutes 'the corridor to faith' – can one come through to eternal life. In so far as it demands that one loses one's life in order to save it, his vision is a tragic one. It is close to the Lacanian faith that only by clinging tenaciously to the negativity of the Real can one emerge as a fully ethical being. Like the Lacanian Real, Kierkegaardian faith introduces permanent crisis and disruption into the insipid assurances of the ethical.

Kierkegaard's writings reach back beyond the collective ethical life of Hegel's *Sittlichkeit* to Kant's severely Protestant divorce of duty and happiness. Faith has nothing to do with human well-being or sensuous fulfilment; the true Christian 'calls one away from the physical man's pleasure, life and gladness'.[19] The Real is militantly anti-aesthetic, even if it shares the aesthetic's remoteness from the universal. Nor is faith a matter of sentiment. It 'is not the immediate inclination of the heart but the paradox of existence'.[20] There is no royal road *à la* Shaftesbury or Hutcheson from the heart's affections to ethical absolutes. Yet in reverting in this way to Kant, Kierkegaard does not only reject his gentrifying assimilation of religion to morality. He also dismantles his autonomous, self-determining moral subject, as well as his vision of that subject as harmonised with others in the kingdom of the universal. The self as its own master, he writes in *The Sickness Unto Death*, is like a king without a country. It is really a form of rule over nothing, a resounding tautology. As for dependency, Kierkegaard rightly sees that it is radically prior to autonomy – though in his case the dependency in question is on God, supreme donor of subjectivity, not on other human beings. In classic Protestant fashion, the subject of faith is caught up in an abject dependency on a God whose logic entirely escapes it; and it is on this foundation alone that it can fashion for itself some form of free selfhood. The individual is the subject of a unique calling or vocation, a divine decree addressed to it alone, which cannot be accommodated by such suburban matters as universal principles and civic obligations. We shall be encountering later another version of this unique command, in that inimitable 'law of one's being' which is the desire of the Real.

The Real thus trumps the symbolic, as the self's stance towards the absolute takes precedence over its relation to the universal. Such an ethics, as with its later French apologists, has political implications. There is no

[19]   Kierkegaard, *Journals*, esp. p. 363.
[20]   Kierkegaard, *Concluding Unscientific Postscript*, p. 390.

possibility of what one might call the social imaginary, in which men and women can achieve some communal fulfilment by finding themselves reflected in the mirror of one another. All forms of the communal are now to be convicted of bad faith and false consciousness, as they are, by and large, for Emmanuel Levinas and the later Jacques Derrida. The more one sheds one's social identity, the more one stands naked and trembling as a solitary soul before God. True heroism is to risk being unreservedly oneself – a condition which, as both Levinas and Derrida will later agree, involves what Kierkegaard calls an 'enormous accountability'. Individuals are solitary atoms, illegible to themselves and each other. Particularity can be preserved only at the cost of sociality. 'Finite experience', Kierkegaard writes, 'is homeless'.[21] The reality of another is never a fact for me, only a 'possibility'. There can be no direct communication between irreducibly specific individuals, no imaginary empathy or spontaneous sense of fellow-feeling among them. Such a belief involves the pernicious ideology of identity – the heresy that the subject can be equal to itself or others, rather than radically incommensurable with everything else in the world. The idea of virtue – the spontaneous habit of goodness – is repudiated as a pagan doctrine. It is far too unlaborious for Kierkegaard's severely puritanical taste, even if, as one commentator remarks, 'his whole concern is with self-realisation, the individual's quest for fulfilment'.[22] Imitation, that cornerstone of the imaginary order, is rejected out of hand: no one individual can mime or appropriate the inner reality of another. All men and women are 'incognitos'. At best, society can aspire to the 'negative unity of the mutual reciprocity of individuals', a mutuality which is in no sense constitutive of their being.[23]

Kierkegaard thus emerges as an early exponent of that brand of spiritual aristocratism known as *Kulturkritik*, a legacy we shall be glancing at later. He is a splenetic elitist who rails intemperately against the 'mob', holding as he does that very few men and women are capable of becoming themselves. Democracy is the opposite of authenticity. The demand for human equality is an odious form of levelling which undermines concrete human bonds and annuls the pure difference of the individual. The abstract, universal subject of bourgeois civilisation is to be contemptuously spurned. Social progress, civic order, public opinion and humanitarian reform are

---

[21] Quoted in Mark C. Taylor, *Journeys to Selfhood: Hegel and Kierkegaard* (Berkeley and Los Angeles, 1980), p. 64.

[22] Anthony Rudd, *Kierkegaard and the Limits of the Ethical* (Oxford, 1993), p. 135.

[23] Quoted in Taylor, *Journeys to Selfhood*, p. 57.

menial affairs fit for the subsidiary register of the symbolic, beneath the lofty purview of the knight of faith. Kierkegaard has a disdain for the humanitarian which we shall encounter later in the Lacanians. The 'deep humanity' of the knight of faith, he remarks, 'is worth more than this foolish concern for others' weal and woe which is honoured under the name of sympathy, but which is really nothing but vanity'.[24] The sentiment is pure Lacan.

Modern men and women, unable truly to 'exist', have succumbed without a struggle to the sphere of the anonymous and dehumanising, to bloodless universals and soulless collectivities, in an age which in augmenting knowledge has proportionately diminished spiritual wisdom. It is the bloodless dominion of Heidegger's *das Man*, the triumph of the quantified and generic over the *sui generis* and nonpareil. In an access of *mauvaise foi*, men and women take flight from the troublesome question of personal authenticity to dissipate themselves in one or another dream of totality: the public good, the spirit of the age, the march of history, the progress of humanity. In doing so, they identify themselves in imaginary fashion with a social order to which the subject of faith always stands sceptically askew. History after Hegel is no longer the place where the subject can find either its mirror-image or its fulfilment. On the contrary, men and women must now retrieve their faith from an increasingly reified public reason, withdrawing from a degraded world into their own interior depths. The same destiny will come to afflict art in the era of modernism. Kierkegaard's achievement is to convert the very offence and absurdity of faith in a rationalist epoch into a perverse sort of advertisement for it.

Kierkegaard may not be in general an apostle of the imaginary; but there is one place where he embraces it unreservedly, and this is in the act of writing itself. The reader, as he argues in *My Point of View as an Author*, must not be brashly confronted with an absolute truth, which she would only reject; instead, she must be worked upon indirectly, subjected to a kind of Socratic irony, so that her false consciousness may be undone from the inside rather than tackled head-on. By adopting a succession of partial arguments and pseudonymous personae, the author can launch a series of guerrilla raids on the reader, drawing her through fiction, irony and subterfuge towards a moment of decision which in the end can only be hers alone. As Sartre will argue a century later, writing, to be morally fruitful, must engage the reader's freedom. It is a question, as Kierkegaard puts it,

---

[24] Kierkegaard, *Fear and Trembling*, p. 107.

of 'going along with the other's delusion' – of entering by imaginative empathy into her sphere of value, rather in the manner of a novelist with his or her characters. And this, Kierkegaard confesses, has an inescapable element of deceptiveness about it, just as the imaginary does. Writing is in this sense a dialogical affair, continually overhearing itself in the ears of its recipient and revising itself accordingly. Truth is truth, to be sure; but in the fallen world of human discourse it must work by a serpentine wisdom, as the author sidles up to the *terra incognita* of the reader like a fifth columnist in the enemy camp.

There are complex overlappings between Kierkegaard's three categories, as there are with Lacan's. The religious must stoop to the aesthetic – which is to say that the raw material of the evangelist is the unregenerate stuff of fantasy and appetite. Faith, Kierkegaard observes, must grasp the eternal, but also hold fast to the finite: 'To have one's daily life in the decisive dialectic of the infinite, and yet to continue to live: this is both the art of life and its difficulty'.[25] There is something of this irony – of being in the world but not of it, detached but not indifferent – in the thought of the Lacanians. When Kierkegaard observes in *Fear and Trembling* that 'it is great to give up one's desire, but greater to stick to it after having given it up',[26] he is thinking of Abraham's love for Isaac and hope for his safety, a love and hope he clings fast to even as he renounces them in the name of his faith in Yahweh. Lacan, too, believes in a desire which is impossible, but which should at all costs be adhered to.

There are other relations between the three dimensions. Faith and the aesthetic may be at loggerheads, but they also share an immediacy lacking to the ethical. To choose oneself is the supreme ethical act, foreshadowing the resolute subject of faith; yet since it means opting for oneself in all one's dreary 'aesthetic' degeneracy, it does not leave that sphere behind. Similarly, the religious 'suspends' the ethical rather than liquidating it. Even so, Kierkegaard does not understand the relationship between ethics and the Real in traditional Christian style. For the New Testament, faith is not so much a leap beyond the ethical as the revelation of its ultimate ground. It is the truth that those who love without reserve will be done to death. It is in this sense that Jesus is the consummation of the moral law, disclosing its fearful inner logic, rather than the annihilation of it. Faith is not at odds with ethics because it is faith in the God of justice, freedom, friendship and equality. What distinguishes the humanist commitment to those values

---

[25] Kierkegaard, *Concluding Unscientific Postscript*, pp. 78–80.
[26] Kierkegaard, *Fear and Trembling*, p. 52.

from Christian faith is the fact that the latter holds to the absurd proposi-tion that, all historical appearances notwithstanding, they are bound to win through. And this is because, so this faith even more foolishly maintains, there is a sense in which they already have.

Nietzsche is an astonishingly radical thinker, and his view of morality is no exception. Rather than intervene in ethical debate, weighing this value against that, he is one of the first modern thinkers to challenge the whole conception of morality as such. Another such sceptic is his contemporary, Karl Marx, for whom morality is essentially ideology. So is it for Nietzsche, even if he does not use the term. For both philosophers, morality is not so much a matter of problems as a problem in its own right. Both of them forge arrestingly original connections between ethics and power. If moral discourse in Marx's view belongs to a social superstructure which among other things obstructs the development of the forces of production, its prime function in Nietzsche's view is to block the flourishing of the will to power. Morality as we know it is 'herd' morality, suitable enough for the timorous, spiritually mediocre masses but fatally stymying for those noble, exceptional souls who bear more than a passing resemblance to Nietzsche himself. Morality is a conspiracy against life on the part of those who are fearful of joy, risk, cheerfulness, hardness, solitude, suffering and self-overcoming. It is as chimerical as alchemy. This whole decaying apparatus must now collapse, given that its metaphysical buttresses have been increas-ingly weakened.

If Kierkegaard excoriates the masses, Nietzsche easily surpasses him in sheer venom. Both thinkers see in social mores a craven avoidance of the perilous venture of becoming a person. Morality in Nietzsche's eyes is a matter of tyranny, idiocy, slavish conformism and sadomasochistic resent-ment. It is the herd instinct within each individual, which disciplines him or her to be no more than the function of a faceless collective. Utterly without truth or grounds, sign of the despicable triumph of the communal over the individual, it exists merely for the growth, preservation and pro-tection of communities, rather than for the vital enhancement of life as such. As such, in Nietzsche's resolutely naturalistic view, morality is a func-tion of biology, psychology, physiology, anthropology and the ceaseless struggle for domination. Its roots lie not in the spirit but in the body. It cannot be in Kantian style grasped as a phenomenon in itself, but can be explained only from a viewpoint outside itself, as a function of 'life, nature and history'. Like Marx, Nietzsche is concerned with the natural history or material conditions of morality, of which the thing itself is no more than symptomatic. Moral norms represent nothing more edifying than a mindless obedience to custom, *habitus* and what one might call the social unconscious. Absolute moral values spring from a spineless submission to traditions and sentiments which are entirely contingent. The whole history of moral judgement has been one long error – if, as we shall see in a moment, in some respects a productive one. One must destroy morality if one is to liberate life, Nietzsche insists in *The Will to Power*.

There is, indeed, scarcely a single aspect of conventional ethics which Nietzsche does not haughtily repudiate. Moral values invariably have their roots in a history of suffering, conflict and exploitation: 'how much blood and cruelty lies at the bottom of all "good things"', he comments in Benjaminian fashion in *On the Genealogy of Morals*.[27] Every morality, then, is immoral when judged by its own lofty standards. The victory of a moral idea, Nietzsche remarks in *The Will to Power*, is achieved by just the same means as every other victory: force, lies, slander and injustice. There are no moral facts, motives, intentions, qualities, or indeed specifically moral phenomena of any sort.

If there are no moral or immoral actions, it is because this whole ideology of human behaviour rests on a false conception of the will. There is no such thing as free will, though to claim that the will is unfree would merely be the reverse of the same misconception. The notion of free will is the upshot of a diseased desire to punish and condemn. If only those actions are moral which are performed out of freedom of will, Nietzsche comments wryly in *Dawn*, then there are no moral actions at all. It is a blind spot of 'symbolic' ethics to imagine that men and women are wholly self-moving and self-determining, and so entirely responsible for their own actions. On the contrary, everything about an action which is conscious, knowable, visible and intentional, Nietzsche writes in Freudian style in *Beyond Good and Evil*, belongs merely to its surface and skin. The so-called free human subject is simply one who has internalised a barbaric law, who therefore takes himself in hand as a submissive citizen, and is thus no longer in need of external coercion. Since the law needs somewhere to implant itself, it opens up in us that interior space of guilt, sickness and bad conscience which some like to call subjectivity. It is these aspects of Nietzsche, among others, which will be inherited by Michel Foucault. The inward world thickens and expands, as otherwise healthy,

---

[27]   Walter Kaufmann (ed.), *Basic Writings of Nietzsche* (New York, 1968), p. 498.

outward-directed instincts turn in upon themselves under the law's repressive power to give birth to the 'soul' and conscience, the police agent within us all. Meanwhile, the subject reaps masochistic pleasure from the punitive law or superego installed in its interior. Freedom is a question of hugging one's chains.

This is not to say that Nietzsche is a rank determinist. It is rather that he is out to develop a more subtle psychology than the grossly simplifying dogmas he finds ready to hand, one which will dismantle the whole classical opposition between freedom and necessity. He will do so not least by investigating the process of artistic creativity, which in a sense is his motif from beginning to end, and which is a question neither of acts of willing nor iron necessity. Most men and women, in any case, are not up to such majestic ideals as autonomy and responsibility; they are mere conditioned reflexes of their own natures, so that moral praise or blame are in their case wholly misplaced. The *canaille* can no more be held accountable for the intricate web of invisible forces which mould their characters than can a tiger.

If Nietzsche sets his face against the symbolic order, he gives equally short shrift to the imaginary. Rather as Spinoza claims that the morality of the masses consists in treating the world as a mirror of their own prejudices and predilections, so Nietzsche regards moral judgements as springing from the tendency to feel that whatever harms the self is evil, and whatever benefits it is good. This egocentrism also takes a collective form in society itself. The notion of an intuitive moral faculty strikes him as the height of naivety. When the English imagine that they know intuitively what is good and evil, he scoffs in *Twilight of the Idols*, they are victims of self-deception. Conventional virtue is little more than 'mimicry', he declares in the same text, thus repudiating a whole Burkeian vision of moral mutuality. In fact, one of his rare points of agreement with moralists like Hume is his resolute anti-realism. Moral values are not written into the world, any more than they are for his eighteenth-century predecessor. They are bits of the world's furniture we ourselves manufacture, not bits we find lying around.

He is equally dismissive of sentiment and sensibility. Sentiments are merely the affective symptoms of what we have been schooled to believe. If they seem as natural and spontaneous as they do to Hume and Hutcheson, it is simply because we have successfully internalised a baseless moral law. Behind the high-minded assumption that moral actions are acts of sympathy with others, Nietzsche argues in *Dawn*, lies a primordial dread of the threat which the other poses to us. Love of one's neighbour, he remarks in *Beyond Good and Evil*, is fundamentally inspired by fear of the neighbour.

It is a purely secondary, arbitrary, conventional injunction. Fear is the 'mother of morals', but is habitually disguised as love. The case is not far from Freud's, who inherits a number of Nietzsche's doctrines.

The altruism of the benevolentists is thus rebuffed as entirely mythical. Ideas of sacrifice, selflessness, self-denial and disinterestedness are entirely bogus. The compassionate subject is a castrated one. There is no built-in capacity for benevolence. Human beings are naturally competitive, egoistic animals, and dispositions to benefit others are always derivative of our own interests. If moral actions are to be characterised as those performed purely for the advantage of others, then they do not exist. The value of human pity is grossly overrated. It is a compact with those who are likely to corrupt us. The sentimentalist luxuriates in human suffering, a phenomenon which Nietzsche also regards as of inflated importance. The Overman takes adversity in his stride, finding in it a vital schooling for creative achievement. He may, to be sure, give aid to the unfortunate, but more in the manner of the magnanimously unbending aristocrat than the zealous middle-class humanitarian. It is those spiritual weaklings who are blind to morality as self-mastery and self-overcoming who 'exalt the good, sympathetic, benevolent sentiments of that instinctive morality which has no head, but rather seems simply to be all heart and helping hands'.[28]

For his part, the Nietzsche of *The Genealogy of Morals* would prefer to celebrate 'everything haughty, manly, conquering, domineering'.[29] The will to danger, conquest, pain and 'sublime wickedness' has been insidiously sapped by a gutless moral humanism. Sympathy and compassion as we have them are the diseased virtues of that religion of the rabble, Judaeo-Christianity, symptoms of a self-odium and disgust with life which the lower orders, in their rancorous resentment, have cunningly persuaded their own masters to internalise. By a stroke of perverted genius, the weak have infected the strong with their own festering nihilism, and bestowed on this catastrophic condition the name of morality. In reaction, the Overman must steel himself to the sufferings of others, driving his chariot over the morbid and enfeebled.

If pity and sympathy are strictly for plebeians, so are the ideals of happiness, utility, well-being and the common good. 'And how should there be a "common good"!', Nietzsche scoffs in *Beyond Good and Evil*. 'The term contradicts itself: whatever can be common always has little value.'[30] The

---

[28] Quoted by Richard Schacht, *Nietzsche* (London, 1985), p. 468.
[29] Kaufmann, *Basic Writings of Nietzsche*, p. 265.
[30] Ibid., p. 330.

concept of the general welfare, he remarks in *Beyond Good and Evil*, is less an ideal than an emetic, while the principle of utility reflects no more than the thwarted aspirations of the violated and downtrodden. As for the paltry business of happiness, only the English, he jeers with the Benthamites in his sights, bother their heads with that. Moral codes, like concepts, inherently oversimplify, reducing the ineffably particular to the debased logic of the generic or universal. This militant nominalism is one of many of Nietzsche's positions which have passed into postmodern thought, a current of which, indeed, he is the prime begetter. In his belief that the general is intrinsically flat and falsifying, he shares a good deal with Kierkegaard. Indeed, he surpasses even the rabidly individualist Dane in his belief that consciousness itself is a vulgarisation of the world, thinning the rich thicket of reality to a meagre shadow of itself. There is something necessarily obtuse and obfuscatory about thinking. The body is a richer, clearer, more trustworthy phenomenon.

All the same, Nietzsche is far from simply writing off the symbolic order or the reign of mass morality. For one thing, it is the best that most men and women will ever be able to manage. Evolutionarily speaking, the symbolic order is a sphere admirably adapted to their spiritually troglodytic condition. Human kind cannot bear very much reality, and would perish of the truth were they hapless enough to confront it head-on. So the birth of the humanist subject is not simply to be regretted. In this, Nietzsche differs significantly from many of his less cautious disciples. For another thing, the symbolic order, with its abstract norms and levelling standards, its apotheosis of the mediocre and straitjacketing of the exceptional, has an ultimately productive consequence, one which is certainly absent from Kierkegaard's appalled vision of it. This is because Nietzsche, unlike most of his modern champions, is a full-blooded teleologist for whom morality moves in three historical stages. These are not exactly the imaginary, symbolic and Real; they could be more accurately described as the animal, symbolic and Real.

The animal phase is often falsely regarded as Nietzsche's moral ideal. It is the primitive age of 'free, wild, prowling men', despotic warriors who know no guilt, live out their beautiful, barbaric instincts in splendid unconstraint, and injure and exploit without a care. These are more alluring creatures than Moral Man, but less fascinating and intricate as well. Moral Man emerges when the brutal dominion of these blonde beasts drives the free instincts of those they subjugate underground, thus generating that morbidly self-lacerating state of guilt and bad faith which constitutes the 'slave morality' of conventional society. Caught in this self-destructive collusion between law and desire, conventional moral creatures languish in the grip of the Real, in the negative sense of that term; whereas the Overman, as we shall see, moves in that shadowy region in a far more affirmative sense, one in some ways closer to Lacan's idealised Antigone (though shorn of her sullenness and intractability) than it is to the self-harming acolytes of a castrating Judaeo-Christianity.

Yet the sadomasochistic self-disciplining of the moral animal is also, in its own way, a marvellous creation. There is something beautiful about the bad conscience. Humanity derives erotic stimulation from its self-torture, just as the perverse, malicious Nietzsche does from the vision of it. Moreover, though the steady corruption of the instincts renders human life more vulnerable and precarious, it also opens up fresh possibilities of experiment and adventure. This repression of the drives is the foundation of all great art and civilisation. If our passions are enfeebled, they are also refined and subtilised; and the punitive self-discipline this demands of us then paves the way for the blithe self-mastery of the Overman. Our perilous dependence on calculative reason is at once an insidious softening of fibre and the advent of an incomparably enriched existence. Nietzsche is by no means a simple irrationalist, deep through his hatred of the Enlightenment runs. In this respect at least, he is as dialectical as Marx. The Fall, as in many a teleology, turns out to be a fortunate one. Only when the old savage passions have been tempered and sublimed by the imposition of 'herd' morality is the way open for the grand entrance of the Overman, who will take these propensities in hand and bend them to his autonomous will. The human subject is born in sickness and subjection; but this will prove an essential workshop for the harnessing of otherwise destructive powers.

'Profoundest gratitude for what morality has achieved', Nietzsche writes in *The Will to Power*, 'but now it is only a burden which may become a fatality!'[31] 'Many chains have been placed upon man', he remarks in *The Wanderer and his Shadow*, 'that he might unlearn behaving as an animal: and in point of fact he has become milder, more spiritual, more joyful, and more circumspect than any animal. But now he still suffers from having borne his chains too long. . . .'[32] One is reminded of the Pauline attitude to the Mosaic law, the point of which, like all effective regulations, is to bring one to a place where one no longer has need of it. Like the New Testament, Nietzsche believes in his own atheistic fashion that the law must

---

[31] *The Will to Power* (New York, 1968), p. 404.
[32] Quoted by Schacht, *Nietzsche*, p. 370.

serve an abundance of life rather than serve itself. Once it has accomplished its end, it can be discarded. The sovereign individual, for Nietzsche if not for Kierkegaard, is the product of straitjacketing custom, even if he also transcends it. The blonde beast must be degutted and debilitated in order to be made fit for civilised existence. Without being rendered calculable and abstractly interchangeable, human beings would remain wild animals at the mercy of their instincts, and the ground for the advent of the supremely civilised Overman would never be laid. The symbolic order has its uses after all. Only by being disciplined to internalise a speciously universal law can one attain to the self-government of this splendid new creation, who lives not by some faceless suburban morality but according to the peerless law of his own being. The aristocrat does not share his moral values with his inferiors, any more than he shares his supper with them. Few opinions enrage Nietzsche more than the suggestion that individuals might be in some sense commensurable. In this, he is a true philosophical comrade of Kierkegaard. As a law unto himself, the Overman moves in the dimension of the 'positive' Real – proud, resolute, utterly singular, beyond the reach of collective moral norms, dauntless in the face of death and nothingness; but he can do so only because he has been trained in the hard school of the symbolic. Civilisation is the product of moral barbarism. Only by losing your self can you gain it.

There is, then, a tragic quality to Nietzsche's teleology. In the end, human life can flourish only on the back of an appalling amount of violence, wretchedness and self-loathing. Yet there is nothing in the least tragic about the Overman himself, who radiates an excess of courtesy, serenity, high spirits and what Nietzsche rather quaintly calls 'loftiness of soul'. Far from figuring as some predatory barbarian, he is a virtuoso of cheerfulness, self-discipline and magnanimity, as single-mindedly dedicated to his own flourishing as is an artist to her canvas. Launched upon the endless adventure of self-creation and self-experiment, the Overman or Meta-Man is artist and artefact in the same body. He is, so to speak, clay in his own hands, free to mould himself into whatever magnificent image will pay most homage to life, growth and power. We must be 'poets of our lives' down to the minutest details. There must indeed be morality; but it must be tailor-made for one's inimitable personality, not off-the-peg.

This is not some errant individualism. The Overman refines and enriches his powers not for his own sake, but for the sake of the greater flourishing of the species. He is as much an oblation on this altar as are those organisms which had to perish in the name of evolutionary progress. In this respect, Nietzsche is an eminent Victorian. Altruism, then, returns at a superior level. In one sense, the Overman is as subject to an exacting law as the most meekly conformist of citizens; but this is a law which he fashions for himself, and thus a unique and incomparable version of the universal law to which Kant (a timorous old eunuch in Nietzsche's derisive view) insists that we stoop. It is thus that brutal coercion gives way to self-hegemony. Rather as Nietzsche borrows from Kant the notion of duty, while denying that this can ever mean a duty to everybody, so he purloins from the earlier philosopher the vision of a free appropriation of the law, but in doing so strips that law of its uniformity and universalism. The law of the future is of a curiously antinomian kind, entirely peculiar to each individual. The Overman is an out-and-out decisionist, taking his cue from his own joyful superfluity of powers rather than from some *a priori* principle or general code. Like a work of art, he generates his own laws and norms. What genuine philosophers decree is a plenitude of life, not a specific style of conduct. It is not clear what criteria are to determine what counts as an 'enhancement' of life. Nietzsche cannot appeal to intuition here, any more than he can appeal to current mores. Besides, if the will to power encompasses all phenomena, so that there can be no moral criteria beyond its reach by which to judge it, we cannot know that it is beneficent; in which case what is so admirable about enhancing it?

Nietzsche has little patience with the notion of virtue, which flows from the Aristotelian moral tradition we shall be examining later. He tells us in *Human, All Too Human* that morality begins as compulsion, then becomes custom, then transmutes itself into instinct, and finally links itself with gratification under the title of virtue. Virtue is just a sublimated form of blind compulsion, as it sometimes appears to be for Jacques Lacan. Even so, there are elements of so-called virtue ethics in the life of the Overman. Like Aristotle, the Overman's supreme aim is self-realisation – though Nietzsche, unlike his ancient forebear, is in grave doubt as to whether anything resembling an autonomous self actually exists, and in any case such self-realisation exists in his view not for its own sake, as with Aristotle, but for the augmenting of 'life' as a whole. All the same, there are times when he speaks in terms reminiscent of Aristotle of the 'highest well-being' of the 'whole person', as well as penning phrases like 'the further free development of oneself', which are common enough in the covertly Aristotelian Marx. Like the virtuous individual, the Overman is a creature of habit, one who lives according to instincts which have incorporated into themselves the finest values of culture and civilisation. In this sense, he combines the instinctual energy of the 'animal' phase of humanity with his own idiosyncratic selection of the values of its 'moral' epoch.

There is another point of contact between Nietzsche and virtue ethics. The latter tradition, as we shall see later, is not opposed to moral laws and precepts; it is simply that this, unlike Kantian morality, is not where it begins. It begins rather with certain conceptions of virtue, excellence, well-being, self-realisation and the like, and assesses the function of norms and prescriptions within this broader context. Injunctions and prohibitions are not to be viewed as ends in themselves. Nietzsche follows suit on this point: there will still be laws in the future kingdom of freedom, but they will exist for the greater enrichment of life. If he had thoroughly assimilated Aristotle, however, he might have recognised that even the morality of the degenerate present does not need to be primarily a matter of laws and obligation. This is one of the more affirmative implications of the ancient philosopher's doctrine. Ironically, Nietzsche subscribes to the dubious Kantian proposition that ethics is a question of duties and prescriptions, only to reject this whole super-egoic conception for his own very different vision. He sees morality as first of all a question of prescribing certain courses of action and censuring certain types of action and individual, all of which he naturally rejects. But if he had not defined morality in such impoverished terms in the first place, he might not have needed to disown it so flamboyantly. To this extent, he falls victim to herd morality in the act of denouncing it. There is a similar irony in Marx, who seems at times to reduce morality to moralism, and who thus fails to grasp that his own work constitutes a moral inquiry in the classical, non-moralistic sense of the term.[33]

The Overman is a supremely positive being, overflowing with rude health and *joie de vivre*. Yet he differs most fundamentally from Aristotle's great-souled man in the terrible price he must pay for his eternal yea-saying. It is the price of a fearful confrontation with the Real – a recognition that there is no truth, no essences, no identities, no grounds, no ends or inherent values in the world. The human subject is a fiction, and so are the objects which appear to him so sturdy. To acknowledge all this is to gaze into the unsearchable Dionysian abyss portrayed in *The Birth of Tragedy*, while refusing all anodyne Apollonian illusion. It is to convert even this terrible knowledge of the death drive into finely instinctual habit, dancing without certainties on the brink of the abyss. The Overman is he who

---

[33]   For an excellent discussion of Marx's ethical thought, see R. G. Peffer, *Marxism, Morality, and Social Justice* (Princeton, NJ, 1990).

plucks virtue from dire necessity, converting the groundlessness of reality into an occasion for aesthetic delight and a source of unceasing self-invention. Like Lacan's ethical heroes of the Real, he has passed through and beyond the baptism of fire which is tragedy to a place altogether beyond such joyful affliction. To achieve this enviable condition, however, the human species must buckle itself to the hard lessons of the symbolic order.

There is a sense, then, in which for Nietzsche the authentic human creature progresses from the *felix culpa* of the symbolic order, through a chastening encounter with the Real, to a state of virtue which converts discursive reason to spontaneous instinct. The Overman is bountiful and generous-spirited, but with the fine, carefree nonchalance of the nobleman. In this condition, bodily impulse and affect are paramount, which makes it in some respects a higher version of the imaginary. We shall see later that morality for Jacques Lacan and Alain Badiou consists in a clenched fidelity to the Real, to which one must cling despite the snares and delusions of the symbolic order. The truly ethical act for the Parisian avant-garde is one which spurns the fudges and *longueurs* of the everyday for a sustained commitment to this sublime truth. This is not the case with Nietzsche. It is true that only through a bruising encounter with the Real can one perceive that the world is without moral foundations, that God is not only dead but was never alive in the first place, and that orthodox moralities are for the most part detestable and demeaning. Yet once one has become one's own spiritual master in this way, the result will be a life of virtue in the sense that Edmund Burke might have understood it. In any case, some of Nietzsche's favoured virtues coincide closely enough with conventional ones: courage, cheerfulness, geniality, magnanimity and the like. One criticism of Nietzsche, then, is not that his writings represent the end of civilisation as we know it, but that the Overman bears a disappointing resemblance to a familiar kind of old-style aristocrat. He is less a demoniac figure than a character out of Disraeli.

8

Fictions of the Real

There is a moment in *Measure for Measure* when the Duke seeks to persuade the condemned Claudio to accept his fate:

> Be absolute for death; either death or life
> Shall thereby be the sweeter. Reason thus with life:
> If I do lose thee, I do lose a thing
> That none but fools would keep . . .
> Happy thou art not;
> For what thou hast not, still thou striv'st to get,
> And what thou hast, forget'st . . .
>   (3.1.6–8, 21–3)

Persuaded by this eloquent apologia for death, Claudio assents to the Duke's plea:

> I humbly thank you.
> To sue to live, I find I seek to die,
> And, seeking death, find life. Let it come on.
>   (3.1.41–3)

In being absolute for death, turning his face from the perpetual dissatisfactions of the living, Claudio will discover a deeper, sweeter kind of life. This is not a contrast between death and desire, but a recognition that desire itself, in its mundane guise, is merely a banal succession of *petits morts*, and as such anticipates its own cessation. To be in love with death rather than life – to embrace its darkness as a bridegroom clasps his lover – is not to spurn desire but to opt for it in its purest form. It is to refuse to compromise one's desire, acknowledging its transcendent nature rather than stuffing its aching void with this or that idol or fetish. The law of desire is an iconoclastic one, dismissive of false gods and graven images. Being resolute for death is not some morbid necrophilia, but a loving fidelity to the essence of one's own identity – an essence which exceeds all particular objects of desire and is nothing but a kind of empty surplus over and above them. Unlike the postmodernists, Lacan is indeed a devout essentialist; it is just the essence of humanity – desire – is a kind of nothing. It is those who invest too deeply in living, waylaid by this or that perishable love-object, who are untrue to what is most alive in themselves.

The price one pays for this truthfulness, however, is high. As Slavoj Žižek writes, such men and women, of whom Sophocles's Oedipus is one of the great prototypes, 'have lived "the human condition" to the bitter end, realising its most fundamental possibility; and for that reason, (they are) in a way "no longer human" and turn into inhuman monsters, bound by no human laws or considerations'.[1] In their radical destitution, they incarnate some unspeakable horror – the kind of naked, unadorned humanity on which, like the frightful victims of the Nazi concentration camps, it demands supreme courage to look upon and live. It is where we are most purely human, stripped of all cultural insignia, that we are also most inhuman, most monstrous and disfigured. Those who confront the Real move, as we have seen, in some twilight zone suspended between life and death, in which a human being 'encounters the death drive as the utmost limit of human experience, and pays the price by undergoing a radical "subjective destitution", by being reduced to an excremental remainder'.[2] In Christian terms, we are speaking of Christ's descent into hell, the sign of his solidarity with human torment and despair, without which there could have been no resurrection from the dead.

Like the Kantian sublime, desire rebukes our investments in common-or-garden reality, sternly reminding us that our true home is with infinity. It is not, as it is for Christian faith, an infinity we might finally attain; it is rather, like Goethe's Faust, the infinity of the process of seeking it out. Perpetual desire is the secular version of eternal life. It is an infinity which looms up in negative guise in our persistent failure to be gratified, as though the very fact of such frustration gestures beyond itself to some currently unimaginable fulfilment, and is the most we shall ever know of it. To be loyal to the lack of being which is ourselves is not to seek how to live well (the classical pursuit of ethics), but to learn how to live with our radical disenchantment. It is, in a word, a kind of negative theology, in which we remain faithful to a God who has failed. In this, too, it has a resonance of

---

[1]   Slavoj Žižek, *The Ticklish Subject* (London, 1999), p. 156.
[2]   Ibid., p. 161.

orthodox Christian belief, for which the only good God is a dead one and the only victory one wrested from failure.

Not to give way on one's desire is to live in joyful expectation of a Messiah who will never do anything quite as definitive as arriving, and who is to be all the more passionately anticipated precisely on that account. As obedient devotees of the Real, we remain as bent upon our radical non-fulfilment as St Augustine was besotted with a deity in whom alone all desire came to rest. In its own way, the desire of the Real is a version of St Anselm's perverse 'I believe because it is impossible.' We must strive to be perfected in our incompleteness, perpetually confirmed in the tragic absence of being which we are. It is the intransitivity of desire that we must refuse to jeopardise. To aim for some supreme good – universal benevolence, let us say, or love of our neighbour – would be on this view to short-circuit the potentially infinite chain of significations which is desire, seek to confront the lost and hunted Thing eyeball to eyeball, and thus in Lacan's terms to risk psychosis: that direct, traumatic encounter with the Real of those whose capacity to symbolise has broken down.

It comes as no surprise, then, that Shakespeare's Claudio and Isabella are siblings, since she, like him, is prepared to choose life over death. Faced with a choice between death and honour, she plumps without hesitation for the former:

> Then, Isabel, live chaste, and, brother, die:
> More than our brother is our chastity.
>
> (2.4.184–5)

It is scarcely the most filial of sentiments; indeed Claudio, swiftly recovered from his momentary acceptance of execution, hotly upbraids her for it. Isabella is ready to die for (in Lacanian parlance) that in herself which is more than herself – that 'object in the subject' known as chastity, honour, integrity, authenticity or simply selfhood, about which there is no real choice in the first place, since without it one is in effect already dead and the question of choice is accordingly irrelevant. The one thing to which life must logically be sacrificed is whatever it is that makes it worth living. It is the same with the martyr and her cause. In a sense, she cannot fail to die for it, since she is faced with a kind of Hobson's choice: if she does not die she becomes a meaningless nothing rather than a signifying one. The martyr chooses death because in certain extreme conditions it is the only way to bear witness to a cause that will sustain the living. She rejects the world out of love of the world, which is what distinguishes her from the suicide. The suicide languishes in the grip of the death drive, turning it against his own flesh in a spasm of obscene enjoyment; whereas the martyr finds a way of utilising this drive for the fulfilment of others, pressing *Thanatos* into the service of *Eros* or *agape*.

For the suicide, life has become both worthless and unbearable. One may contrast this condition with that of Sophocles's Antigone, who despite declaring from the outset that 'I am dead and desire death', is allowed at the last moment to regret the fulfilled life of marriage and children that she is passing up, in order to mark her difference from the suicide. No death for which life is valueless can have value. The martyr opts for meaning over being, allowing this signifier to shine forth against the dark backdrop of her own mortality. Being steadfast for death is not a rejection of life but a way of life in itself, one enriched and transfigured by being audaciously plucked from death. Those who act as though they will live forever are a menace to civilised society. The sluggish Barnardine does not care for death, which is why he does not care for life either. Not to see death as momentous is to devalue the living. Only an ethical being, which is the last thing Barnardine is, can conjure something meaningful from its own mortality. The fatal lack of agency which prevents him from personally appropriating his death is also what prevents him from living a life less impoverished than a pig's.

This 'heroism of the lack', as Slavoj Žižek calls it,[3] is, in a word, an ethics of the Real; and for Lacan one of its great progenitors, surprisingly enough, is Kant. In a seminal essay entitled 'Kant avec Sade',[4] Lacan claims that it was the German philosopher who first planted the seed of psychoanalysis in his conception of the moral law, which in Lacan's view is really a portrait of desire in its purest state. It is the kind of desire that goes entirely beyond the pleasure principle, like Sade's pursuit of an impossible, immortal form of *jouissance* beyond all mere empirical enjoyment. As Lacan remarks elsewhere, this species of desire 'culminates in the sacrifice, strictly speaking, of everything that is the object of love in one's human tenderness – I would say, not only in the rejection of the pathological object, but in its sacrifice and murder'.[5] It is a far cry from the empathetic world of a Hutcheson or the affability of a David Hume. Desire, in brief, is the latest form of transcendence – one which with the ascetic vigilance of a Carmelite must

---

[3] Slavoj Žižek, *The Indivisible Remainder* (London, 1996), p. 96.

[4] The essay is included in Jacques Lacan, *Écrits* (Paris, 1966), and translated into English in *October*, 51 (winter 1989).

[5] Jacques Lacan, *The Four Fundamental Principles of Psychoanalysis* (London, 1977), pp. 275–6.

preserve its intransitivity from all 'pathological' objects (which is to say, all objects of love, appetite and affection), resting only in itself and its own lack of a *telos*. This, as it happens, is also how Goethe's Faust can hope to achieve salvation. Since Kant's moral law similarly eschews all specific ends and goods in its rigorous formalism, sacrificing the self and its pleasures to its own sovereignty, and grounding itself only in its own portentously empty imperative, the affinity between the two phenomena becomes clear. Each of them is empty of content; both of them give the slip to the signifier, and are therefore sublime.

Moreover, law and desire both have an iron necessity about them. Our freest actions are those which we cannot help performing if we are still to be ourselves. They are not the product of 'acts of will', but of a yielding to the non-negotiable law of our being, a submission to that within us which is more tenaciously ourselves than any mere act of reflection. With desire as with law, the subject is the mere bearer of a power which will brook no denial. Desire is an absolutist sovereign. It is clear, too, that just as Kant's categorical imperative is in a sense impossible, since one can never be sure that one is acting 'non-pathologically', so too is the Lacanian ethical absolute – the injunction not to give up on one's desire. Only the saint or the martyr could live in this way. It is not an ethic for the riff-raff. What Kant fails to see in Lacan's opinion is that desire, in its disregard for empirical motives, objects and effects, is itself an absolute law, as rigorous and peremptory as any Angelo. The distinction between law and desire accordingly collapses: to fulfil the law of desire which is the essence of one's selfhood is no less than one's binding duty.

To act in accordance with this desire is also to reconcile freedom and dependency. If the subject of the imaginary is excessively dependent, captivated by an image outside itself, the subject of the symbolic is too autonomous. If the imaginary subject lacks a sense of agency, its symbolic counterpart dreams of being purely undetermined. The subject of the Real, however, comes into its own as an agent precisely by hearkening to that in itself which is more than itself. To betray this determining power would be to betray itself. In this sense, as in several others, psychoanalysis is really displaced theology. The subject of the Real takes its cue from the subject of Judaeo-Christianity, whose freedom lies in acknowledging its dependence on that ground of being which is God. This act of acknowledgement is known as faith. For both doctrines, infantile dependency and false autonomy are both to be rejected in the name of a deeper form of determination, one which constitutes the very source of personal freedom.

The moral law may take a lofty attitude to pleasure; but it is tainted itself by that obscene enjoyment which is 'good for nothing', which lies beyond all common-or-garden pleasure in the region of the death drive, and to which Lacan gives the name of *jouissance*. This shadowy underside of the law is the sadistic delight of the superego, which like the moral law is cruelly indifferent to the subject's well-being, and which not only commands it to submit to precepts which are absurdly impossible to obey, but which fosters in it a lethal culture of guilt for failing to perform the impossible. As if all this were not enough, the superego also decrees that the subject reap pleasure from the morbid drama of permitting this guilt to hound it to its death. For an ethics of the Real, however, the act of staying true to one's desire is not one coerced by the superego, since the subject of pure desire, one most eloquently figured for Lacan by Sophocles's Antigone, feels no stain of guilt in fulfilling the obligation of sustaining her desire. True ethics takes us beyond the superego, as the loyal subjects of the Real prove themselves ready to risk death for the sake of a symbolic rebirth. It is the difference in *Measure for Measure* between Angelo and Isabella; but what inspires Isabella to opt for death is also, as we shall see later, what drives one of Shakespeare's most hauntingly enigmatic figures, the Shylock of *The Merchant of Venice*.

To stay faithful to one's desire would seem often enough to involve a kind of preternatural mulishness or monomania, as Lacan's exemplary case of it, Sophocles's Antigone, might suggest – though Lacan himself, reluctant to hear a harsh word of his fictional beloved, rejects out of hand the eminently reasonable view that she is indeed intransigent, and in doing so oversimplifies the intricate ebb and flow of dramatic sympathies. He is similarly partial about Oedipus, whom he sees as going to his death in ethical Realist fashion – 'unyielding right to the end, demanding everything, giving up nothing, absolutely unreconciled'.[6] This sounds rather more like a Parisian philosophical *prima donna*, not perhaps a thousand light years removed from Lacan himself, than the *pharmakos* who in *Oedipus at Colonus* becomes the cornerstone of a new political order. Oedipus's polluted body signifies among other things the monstrous terror at the gates in which, if it is to have a chance of rebirth, the *polis* must

---

[6] Jacques Lacan, *The Ethics of Psychoanalysis* (London, 1999), p. 176.

recognise its own hideous deformity. This profoundly political dimension of the tragedy is given short shrift in Lacan's own meditations.

Yet there is no doubt that the Real and the recalcitrant are closely allied. Take, for example, Heinrich von Kleist's extraordinary tale of political terrorism, *Michael Kohlhaas*. The piece was first published in 1810, one year before Kleist struck a suicide pact with a young woman suffering from incurable cancer, shot her dead and then blew his own brains out. His death was as theatrical and extravagant as his art. The couple had prepared for death by putting up at an inn, drinking several bottles of wine and rum and around sixteen cups of coffee, while singing and praying together. 'The public', one newspaper reported sternly if superfluously, 'are far from admiring, or even of approving, this act of insanity.'[7]

Earlier, Kleist had joined the Napoleonic army in the hope of being killed, but managed to his intense chagrin to remain alive. He was also perhaps the only individual on human record to have been done to death by Immanuel Kant. Kleist interpreted Kant's epistemology to mean that truth is eternally elusive, reason faulty and unfounded, appearance and reality indistinguishable, and the whole of reality bafflingly ambiguous and opaque. Since existence consequently lacks a discernible purpose, blowing one's brains out seemed as valid an act as any, and mildly more gratifying than most.

Michael Kohlhaas is a decent, civic-minded, sixteenth-century Brandenberg horse dealer whose two black horses are mistreated while in the possession of the arrogant Junker von Tronka. Kohlhaas patiently sues for justice from the law for this abuse, enduring one fudge and deferment after another; but his wife Lisbeth is killed by one of the Elector's bodyguards while pleading her husband's cause. It becomes evident that the court is in cahoots with von Tronka, and has suppressed Kohlhaas's petition for his case to be heard. Kohlhaas then gathers an armed band and burns down the Junker's castle, along with various parts of Wittenberg. His hired militia put women and children ruthlessly to the sword. Before long, he has metamorphosed into a Robin Hood figure, spreading military mayhem and waging all-out war on the state – a war which elicits the fervent support of the common people. In a passing fit of megalomania, he declares himself to have formed a new world government, and demands that Tronka be handed over to him for chastisement. He sets fire to Wittenberg three

---

[7]   Quoted in D. Luke and N. Reeves (eds), Heinrich von Kleist, *The Marquise of O – And Other Stories* (London, 1978), p. 8.

times, storms Leipzig, and defeats some formidable military expeditions thrown against him.

Kohlhaas's demand for recompense for his two famished horses now escalates surreally to the point where it pulls in Martin Luther, the Elector of Saxony and the Holy Roman Emperor, the former of whom agrees that the horse dealer has indeed been wronged. On Luther's advice, the Elector issues an amnesty to Kohlhaas and his band of paramilitaries, who accordingly disbands his men and resumes his search for justice by legal means. But the savage actions of a marauding splinter group of Kohlhaas's men play into the hands of the court, which revokes the amnesty on this pretext and puts the horse dealer on trial. He offers no defence of his actions, and is sentenced to be burned and quartered. Through the political intervention of the Elector of Brandenberg, the penalty is altered to beheading, a verdict which Kohlhaas greets serenely on learning that his claims against Junker von Tronka are to be met in full. At the place of execution, his two horses, now sleek and frisky, are presented to him fully restored to health, along with the information that the Junker has been sentenced to two years' imprisonment. The Elector of Brandenberg solemnly delivers to him the neckcloth, florins, bundle of washing and other small items which his groom had been forced to leave behind at the Junker's castle. Kohlhaas declares himself fully satisfied with this resolution, and is ready in his turn to make reparation by his death for having broken the law. The story ends with his beheading.

It is not quite the stuff of social realism. As Kohlhaas's actions become increasingly extravagant and bizarre, and the frantic political intrigues of the state over a couple of knackered horses deepen by the page, the grotesque discrepancy between the horse dealer's obdurate demand for justice and its trifling cause reveals plainly enough that this is a narrative not of realism, but of the Real. As the horse dealer's crimes and the machinations of the state accumulate on an epic scale at a ludicrously rapid pace, it is evident that we are in the presence of a deadpan mixture of tragedy, farce and the grotesque. Indeed, when Kolhaas's wretched animals are first seen in public by a crowd who know what spectacular disruption they have caused, there is a gale of uproarious laughter at the sight of 'the horses on whose account the state has been rocked to its very foundations – a pair of horses already in the hands of the knacker!' There is something bathetic about desire, which with what the narrator calls 'lunatic stubbornness' will kick up the most extraordinary fuss over next to nothing. But this, as we shall see, is because the 'almost nothing' is its occasion rather than its object.

Apart from the fact that he is a brutal mass murderer who sells his own family into poverty to raise funds for his cause, Kohlhaas is really quite a reasonable character. He is widely considered 'a paragon of civil virtues' until the Junker ill-treats his horses, and in a sense remains so throughout the tale. He is, after all, in admirably unswerving pursuit of that exemplary civil virtue known as justice, even if the means he uses to secure it are a trifle unorthodox. In the name of universal justice, he is prepared to become the living incarnation of its exact opposite. By slaying and ruining countless numbers of innocent men, women and children, he succeeds in demonstrating just how absolute a virtue justice is – the only phenomenon, so Jacques Derrida has claimed, which cannot be deconstructed.

Kohlhaas's sense of justice, we are informed by the narrator, 'was as fine as a gold-balance'. His first reaction to the Junker's outrage is entirely rational, indeed well-nigh forgiving; and he pursues the matter through the proper legal channels with exemplary scrupulousness. He does so not primarily for personal motives, but in the name of those of his fellow citizens whom the high-handed Tronka has also oppressed. The horse dealer is not just a private citizen but a self-appointed political reformer who is out to 'chastise . . . the deceitfulness which now engulfs the whole world' and who appeals to the people to join him in establishing a 'better order of things'. He has, in short, succeeded in universalising his personal grievance to a class-based view of the world. It is only when his aspiration for justice through the juridical system is thwarted by state cronyism and corruption that he resorts to arms.

Even then, despite the crazed surfeit of his military actions, he is meticulous in confining his demand for restitution to precisely what he has been illicitly deprived of – a combination of excess and exactness which we shall also be noting in the case of Shakespeare's Shylock. It is perfectly clear, despite the narrator's tendentious mutterings about 'the hellish torment of unsatisfied revenge', that what he is in quest of is not vengeance but justice. We have learnt enough from the terrorism of our own time to know that a thwarted hunt for justice has the power to breed monsters. This 'insane, incomprehensible, terrible man', as Luther calls him, coolly composes a list of the handful of articles which his head groom has left behind with the horses, along with their value; but he refuses to request compensation for the loss of his entire wealth and estate, or even for the cost of his wife's funeral. His sole desire is for the Junker personally to fatten the horses he has allowed to starve and restore them to him. It is only when Tronka haughtily refuses to comply with this wish that Kohlhaas burns down his castle and embarks on his career as a terrorist or guerrilla leader. It is a campaign against the detestable patrician which the common people full-bloodedly support: it is Tronka and not Kohlhaas, they consider, who has brought fire and sword upon them. Even the luckless inhabitants of Wittenberg, burned out of their dwellings by his soldiers no less than three times, remain among his most zealous disciples.

As we shall see in the case of Emily Brontë's Heathcliff, it is only because he has been thrust beyond its frontiers as an outcast that Kohlhaas believes that he has a right to wage war on human society. Indeed, the state itself, desperate to contain his violence, considers relabelling him a 'foreign invading power' rather than an internal rebel. The guerrilla leader treats Luther with the deepest respect, despite the foul insults the cleric hurls at him and the fact that he refuses to hear his confession; and it is Kohlhaas who proposes to Luther the idea of an amnesty, promising to lay down his arms in return for a fair hearing in court. Kohlhaas may be an outlaw, a figure driven beyond the symbolic order; but there is an inordinate violence at the very heart of that order, a strain of vindictiveness and malign excess within the law itself; and it is the horse dealer's political role to expose it for what it is. It is the state officials who are twisters and traitors, not the protagonist; and the narrative insists not only on their knowledge that the charge he has laid against Tronka is perfectly just, but on their embarrassed sense that it is they themselves, by their complicity with oppression, who have put into his hands the sword he is wielding against them. Not many contemporary ruling powers are quite so percipient.

Michael Kohlhaas ends with the protagonist exultantly announcing the fulfilment of his deepest wish on earth, as his horses paw the ground before him in all their former vigour. But it is not, needless to say, the horses as such which are the object of his desire. Nobody would burn down Wittenberg just because someone neglected his nags. The horses are perhaps better seen as an instance of Lacan's *objet petit a* – that modest, contingent scrap of matter which becomes invested with all the formidable power of the Real. If Kohlhaas perishes in tragic joy, plucking victory from his death in the act of bowing an obedient knee to it, it is not because of a welcome addition to his livestock, but because he has managed not to give up on his desire. (In Kleist's drama *Prince Friedrich von Homberg*, the eponymous hero is similarly so absolute for death that, like Abraham on the point of sacrificing Isaac, his very resoluteness wins him the grace of a last-minute reprieve.) It is true that Kohlhaas's immediate demand – for the restitution of his goods – is satisfied; but he has been prepared to live without gratification, and to confront death in the same spirit, as long as this was withheld from him. The horses become that thing in their owner that is more than himself, signifying as they do a demand for justice and recognition that is at once eminently reasonable and insanely exorbitant, and which is crafty enough to press into its service the terrifying frenzy of the death drive. Kohlhaas's passion is as uncompromising as it is because, like the Freudian drive, it is not in the end defined by its object. Justice is absolute, and its denial drives men and women to a well-nigh ungovernable rage; yet though it is true that the denial of justice in a single instance also undermines the claims to justice of all, how can the claims of these others be sacrificed, as in Kohlhaas's case, to one's own clamour for equity – which (as Kohlhaas himself is aware) can never be simply one's own? If mercy and forgiveness are creative forms of superfluity, an unslakeable thirst for justice can prove a self-undoing one. You can be prodigal in your quest for the precise. Yet forgiveness can be excessive as well: as we saw in the case of *Measure for Measure*, it cannot be allowed to override the demands of justice altogether. The wicked must be brought to book, which is not to say that they must not go unforgiven. Kohlhaas himself seems not to grasp this point, begging Luther as he does to be allowed to forgive all the other corrupt figures of authority involved in the case, but to compel the Junker even so to fatten his horses for him. Yet to force his enemy to do this would be no more than justice, not necessarily (as he himself seems to believe) a refusal of forgiveness.

Whenever we stumble in literary works across a desire which starkly isolates a protagonist; renders him or her strange to themselves; expresses an ineluctable inner need; manifests an adamant refusal to compromise; invests itself in an object more precious than life itself; maroons a character between life and death, and finally bears him or her inexorably to the grave, we can be reasonably sure that we are in the presence of the Real. Joseph Conrad's Lord Jim is a case in point, as is more than one Ibsenite protagonist. Kleist's remarkably fine tragic drama *Penthesilea*, a play laced with Dionysian ecstasy or *jouissance*, which one commentary portrays as powered by 'a relentless elemental drive in which tenderness and the lust to destroy and devour are profoundly fused',[8] represents a rather more obvious theatre of *Thanatos*, as the Amazon queen of the play's title speaks of tearing her lovers apart with her teeth. Kohlhaas, too, is seized by this kind of furious passion: he can butcher without conscience, since in the light of the implacable Real every purely sublunary object is radically devalued.

---

[8]   Ibid., p. 1.

There is a sub-plot to Kleist's fable, which treats literary realism even more cavalierly than the main narrative. Some scholars have disregarded it on these grounds, but no dismissal could be more myopic. This fantastic sub-plot, which disdains even to make a perfunctory stab at plausibility, revolves on a scrap of paper which has come into Kohlhaas's possession, and on which is inscribed a prophecy concerning the future destiny of the Elector of Saxony, the man who cheated the horse dealer by offering him an amnesty and then reneging on the promise. The Elector knows of the existence of the scrap of paper, though not what is written on it, and tries frantically to lay his hands on it; it is, he observes, more valuable to him than his life. He is tormented by the idea that all knowledge of its contents will perish with its possessor, who is on the point of being despatched to eternity, and attends Kohlhaas's execution so as to retrieve the paper from his corpse. Kohlhaas, advised in advance of this stratagem, strides up to the eagerly expectant Elector at the very moment of death, gazes steadily at him, takes the paper from the locket around his neck, reads it and swallows it.

It is not hard to see the prophetic message as a version of the instruction which condemns the slave to death but which, tattooed on his skull while he sleeps, remains forever inaccessible to him. Lacan, as we have seen, uses this striking image to illustrate the way in which we are dependent for our identities on a place of signification (the Other) which is necessarily unfathomable to us. From this viewpoint, Kohlhaas himself, a character who has waded through blood in his demand for recognition from the Other, now comes himself to figure as the mysteriously impenetrable Other for the Elector, bearing with him a signifier which represents the secret of the prince's destiny but which will remain forever inaccessible from him. It is as though the condemned man uses his own death to deprive the Elector of a degree of mastery over his. In an extraordinary power-reversal, the oppressed wreaks vengeance on his oppressor by becoming privy to a portentous knowledge, one for which the Elector himself would willingly die. It is the impossible, unpossessable knowledge of how he is seen by the Other – the secret of what he truly is which lies forever beyond his reach. Kohlhaas, however, negates this revelation, destroying the signifier and withdrawing it forever from circulation. It is this, not the recovery of his horses, which represents his true victory. The blank of the horse dealer's death becomes the non-presence of his enemy to himself, blocking his access to the Real of his desire. Kohlhaas, as a German tragic hero should, strides triumphantly to his death; but after the trauma of his final act, the Elector lives on as a broken man. Both figures are in different ways exemplars of the living dead. In the satiric gesture of self-nourishment of a dead man, Kohlhaas absorbs into his own dying body the lethal signifier which represents the key to the other's identity, thus striking the Elector dead for the remainder of his days. It is as though the horse dealer becomes quite literally the embodiment of the Real for his opponent, as he coolly absorbs the *objet petit a* of the prophecy into his own body. He devours the Elector's identity like a cannibal, leaving no shred of him remaining, and in doing so achieves the supreme power of complete nothingness, which not even the most predatory Junker can purloin from him. In writing his narrative, Kleist brings to mind Lacan's observation that 'to have carried through an analysis to its end is nothing other than to have encountered that limit where the entire problematic of desire is posed'.[9]

If a piece of paper represents the *objet petit a* which the Elector prizes more than his life, another kind of written document – Shylock's legal bond – plays a parallel role in *The Merchant of Venice*. In a celebrated tit-for-tat, Shylock strikes a commercial bargain with Antonio in which the latter will render him a pound of his own flesh if he fails to return the money he has loaned him. When Antonio's ships founder, Shylock prosecutes his legal suit against him with ruthless persistence:

> let him look to his bond: he was wont to call me usurer; let him look to his bond: he was wont to lend money for a Christian courtesy; let him look to his bond.
>
> (3.1.50–4)

Later, the repetition of 'bond' becomes even more strangely insistent, tolling for the endangered Antonio like an ominous bell:

> I'll have my bond; speak not against my bond:
> I have sworn an oath that I will have my bond.
> Thou calld'st me dog before thou hadst a cause,
> But, since I am a dog, beware my fangs:
> The Duke shall grant me justice . . .
> I'll have my bond; I will not hear thee speak:
> I'll have my bond; and therefore speak no more.
> I'll not be made a soft and dull-eyed fool,
> To shake the head, relent, and sigh, and yield
> To Christian intercessors. Follow not;
> I'll have no speaking: I will have my bond.
>
> (3.3.4–8, 12–18)

---

[9]   Lacan, *Ethics of Psychoanalysis*, p. 300.

Shylock's bond, like any other legal document, is couched in language; yet whatever it signifies seems to lie beyond words, stopping the mouth ('I'll have no speaking'). In dramatic context, the comment means among other things that the moneylender will have none of the wheedling rhetoric and ideological soft-soap with which Christians who have spat in his face in the past are now begging him to display a mercy in which they themselves have proved notably deficient. It is a signifier of the desire which drives Shylock on – a desire which like Michael Kohlhaas is one for justice ('I stand for judgement; answer; shall I have it?', Shylock cries defiantly to a law court packed with anti-Semitic bigots), but also, like Kleist's hero, a demand from the dispossessed for recognition from an unscrupulous bunch of governors. Shylock, like Kohlhaas, would have his due and no more; yet this exactly calculated exchange is also monstrously disproportionate:

> If every ducat in six thousand ducats
> Were in six parts, and every part a ducat,
> I would not draw them; I would have my bond.
> (4.1.89–91)

The flesh for which Shylock hungers is priceless – both in the sense that it is worthless, nugatory, an unprofitable chunk of raw meat, but also because it is inestimable, uncommodifiable, transcending the common-or-garden circulation of goods. For Shylock, it functions within the symbolic order as a legal bargaining chip or substitute for material wealth; yet this trifling, incalculably dear scrap of tissue also signifies a form of negativity at the heart of that order, a disruption of its scrupulously calibrated exchanges which cannot itself be represented. The ruthless intensity with which this Jew demands his pound of flesh resembles the cruel exactitude with which the Christian court instructs him to take no more than a hair's weight over or below his due; but the two demands belong to quite different orders, the former to the Real and the latter to the symbolic. Shylock's behaviour can be illuminated by a comment of Lacan on the practice of psychoanalysis: 'If analysis has a meaning, desire is nothing other than that which supports an unconscious theme, the very articulation of which roots us in a particular destiny, and that destiny demands insistently that the debt be paid, and desire keeps coming back, keeps returning, and situates us once again in a given track, the track of something that is specifically our business.'[10]

---

[10] Ibid., p. 319.

Shylock refuses gold for flesh, since he rightly perceives that the latter cannot be quantified. Despite Gratiano's typically loutish reference to a 'maid not vendible', bodies and bags of ducats are incommensurable. But the scrapings of a human breastbone are also worse than nothing, as Bassanio remarks of his own debt-ridden condition when Antonio's ship is lost, since other sorts of animal flesh are, as Shylock points out, eminently marketable. What Shylock desires is the Real of the human body as such, which is what his pound of flesh or *objet petit a* signifies. More exactly, he demands an acknowledgement from these well-fed Christian bodies that he too is fashioned of flesh and blood – that even a reviled Jew laughs when he is tickled and bleeds when he is pricked. It is to the shared stuff of the material body, not to cultural affinities, that Shylock appeals in his memorable polemic against anti-Semitism.

Shylock's desire, then, is for human reciprocity, of which his demand for a pound of Christian flesh is a grisly parody. It is as though he tries to convert the symbolic directly into the Real, substituting a mutuality of bodies for an exchange of merchandise. His fleshly bargain with the contemptuous Antonio is a kind of black mass or grotesque travesty of Eucharistic fellowship, in which the only way Shylock can possess Antonio's body is through a sign or metonymic residue of it. The death-dealing conflict between Jew and Christian is a satirical inversion of the true comradeship which one part of Shylock desires. Only in this negative form, driven by a ferocious aggression or death drive of which Antonio is the luckless target, is a genuine reciprocity available to him. In these conditions, love can only express itself as the hatred with which it is so unnervingly allied. Like Kohlhaas in his dying breath, Shylock is a symbolic cannibal, which is what those who take part in the love-feast of the Eucharist are too. But if his action belongs in this sense to the symbolic order, it also aims at an unmediated encounter with the Real of the body and of death; and since what Shylock desires is nothing less than a blending of bodies, it has its imaginary dimension as well. His lethal rivalry with Antonio belongs to this imaginary relation as much as his sense of him as fellow-businessman and alter ego.

So it is a matter of flesh and blood between the two men in every sense. Even Shylock's hatred of the merchant is couched in terms of embracing and assimilating him: 'If I can catch him once upon the hip, / I will feed fat the ancient grudge I bear him' (1.3.47–8). He speaks later of 'feed(ing) upon / The prodigal Christian' (2.5.14–15). To refuse Shylock his pound of flesh is to deny him, and so to deny *his* flesh and blood, his famished demand for recognition. The Real on which Shylock refuses to give up is another man's body – which is to say, the common humanity which Antonio and his ruling-class cronies owe to the untouchable Jew but arrogantly refuse to concede. Shylock claims that he wants to be Antonio's friend and win his love; and though the claim may be partly bogus, no more than a wily baiting of the mantrap, it is not entirely to be discounted.

Shylock claims Antonio's flesh as his own, which in a sense it is in any case; and his bond looms as large as it does in the play because it is the signifier of this fundamental affinity. 'Bond' in the sense of a binding legal agreement is also 'bond' in the sense of human rapport, which is why Shylock invests such a terrifying amount of libidinal energy in his ill-starred lawsuit. The impersonality of juridical language reflects the impersonality of the bonds of our common humanity or species being, which no mere cultural prejudice or subjective whim may set aside. For the Hebrew scriptures in which Shylock trusts, the human body is not in the first place a material object but a principle of unity with others. It is genuine communication with Antonio and his ilk that he is after, as opposed to pragmatic deals, racist insults, specious persuasion and vapid signifiers. Shylock is engaged in a Hegelian life-and-death struggle for recognition from the Venetian governing caste. He wants Antonio so badly that he is prepared to eat him up, venting his lethal violence on him in the act of fusing with his body. If this is the only way he can wrest a glimmer of recognition from his Christian oppressors, so much the worse. Perhaps it is only as an enemy – as a man under threat – that Antonio can be Shylock's friend, in the sense that it is with Shylock that the merchant's fate is irreparably bound up.

It is characteristic of an ethics of the Real that however traumatic its encounter with truth may be, it releases the uncanny power to inaugurate a new human order. Only by passing through a sacrifice or symbolic death, divesting oneself of both imaginary and symbolic identities, can one struggle through to such transformation, for which the New Testament term is *metanoia*. The Christian Eucharist is a celebration of comradeship – of a new way of belonging to each other which provides a foretaste of the just society or kingdom of God of the future; but this revolutionary form of life is possible only by a symbolic sharing in Christ's own bloody passage through death to resurrection. In this sense, the symbolic and the Real are blended in a single action. The bread and wine which constitute the language of solidarity in the Eucharist are also signifiers of a mutilated body, which is present in them rather as the meaning is present in a word. This is why the sacrament (the theological word for 'sign') involves eating and drinking – not only because such things are a customary expression of friendship, but because the nourishment which they afford is inseparable from destruction. If Antonio, Bassanio and their anti-Semitic colleagues were able to grasp the true meaning of Shylock's demand for a pound of Antonio's flesh (which is not to assume that Shylock recognises its true significance himself, let alone that he consciously wants to wolf down a piece of Antonio), this recognition might found a new kind of moral and political regime, one based on peaceable fellowship rather than rivalry and division.

It may be, of course, that the pound of flesh is as much about castration as cannibalism. Shylock, after all, is allowed to carve it from whatever part of Antonio's body he chooses, and may well gesture sportively to the merchant's groin as he utters his demand. If this is so, then Shylock is cast as the punitive, patriarchal law or castrating Name-of-the-Father; but there may be more to the matter than that. Writing of *Hamlet*, Jacques Lacan speaks of the object of desire as whatever it is which fills the place of a primordial loss, one he characterises as 'that self-sacrifice, that pound of flesh, which is mortgaged in (the) relationship to the signifier'.[11] To enter the symbolic order or establish a relationship to the Other is to exchange flesh for sign – to relinquish one's claim on the maternal body as the price for gaining access to language, sexuality and social existence. The utopian promise of the Eucharist, by contrast, lies in the fact that flesh and sign are at one. Only he who abandons the fantasy of incest, Lacan maintains, can speak. Only by virtue of this passage from the imaginary to the symbolic can one accede to the status of a subject, and hence to one's desire. Shylock, then, may be inviting Antonio to make just such a transition – to sacrifice part of his identity, forgo a portion of his bodily *jouissance*, in order to enter into relationship with the Other, which is what Shylock represents for him in more senses than one. The pound of flesh is the 'good object', in Lacan's terms, that one must yield up for the fulfilment of one's desire. It is the signifier, in the form of Shylock's bond, on which Antonio is utterly dependent; but though the letter killeth, it can also yield life. The two Venetians are now yoked to each other through a piece of writing which is both potentially lethal and (in Shylock's phrase) a 'merry sport', a harmless frolic, a ludic parody of a kosher commercial contract. The zany arbitrariness of Shylock's request is as much at odds with the symmetries of the symbolic order as the Real which it invokes.

---

[11] Jacques Lacan, 'Desire and the Interpretation of Desire in *Hamlet*', *Yale French Studies*, 55/56 (New Haven, CT, 1977), p. 28.

In his reflections on the Freudian concept of sublimation, Lacan illustrates this diverting of a base desire on to a higher object with a reference to the *Book of Revelation* (10:9), in which an angel instructs the narrator to consume a scroll of writing. 'Eat this book!' is a lapidary enough summary of the process Freud describes. It is as though Shylock desires to eat Antonio symbolically, at the level of the signifier of his bond. The signs of the bond, in Eucharistic fashion, incarnate a dismembered body. Its script is a semiotic sublimation of Shylock's hunger to eat Antonio's flesh, assimilating his body in an act that suggests both the affinities and aggressions of the imaginary. All three Lacanian registers of being, then, are involved in this complex transaction. In fact, Lacan himself claims that the word used by Sophocles to describe Antigone's stiff-neckedness can also refer to eaters of raw flesh.

Shylock makes out his deal with Antonio to be a friendly one ('this is kind I offer'), an assessment which is not entirely tongue-in-cheek. 'Kind' here means kinship, common humanity, as well as generous-hearted. Astonishingly, the notorious Jewish usurer is setting aside his customary credit-and-debit calculations in the name of a bizarre *acte gratuit* or piece of *comédie noire*, demanding both more and less than he usually would in such matters. It is true that Antonio is being asked to flirt with death, as is generally the case when one runs up against the Real; yet the chances of his being unable to repay his debt are slim enough to make the offer an uncharacteristically bountiful one. Indeed, Antonio thinks so himself, though in his high-handed way he makes a point of agreeing to the bargain as a foe, not as a friend. What for Shylock himself has a smack of the Real, his debtor treats as a purely symbolic or empirical transaction, haughtily refusing the spirit of the bargain as Portia's devious courtroom rhetoric will later refuse the spirit or commonsensical meaning of Shylock's bond.

Portia's case that the bond makes no allusion to the taking of blood is an outrageously opportunistic quibble, a piece of legal shuffling by which the Christians get one of their own kind off the hook while plundering Shylock of his goods under cover of prating about mercy. The bond, to be sure, does not actually state that the moneylender may shed Antonio's blood while carving him up, but this is a reasonable inference from the text, as any actual court would recognise. It is absurd to claim that a document, to be legally valid, must spell out every conceivable circumstance of the situation to which it refers. As Portia herself admits, the bond does not stipulate that a surgeon should be at hand, even though this, as she herself points out, would be a charitable provision. By interpreting Shylock's bond too literally, she is flagrantly false to its meaning. There can be an excessive kind of exactness (Shylock's own tight-fistedness is another illustration of it), just as there can be a lavishness which (as with Timon of Athens's neurotic open-handedness) overrides the measure in a destructive way. Shylock's scrupulousness in confining himself to no more than a pound of his rival's flesh is a superfluous sort of precision, since in taking one pound he will almost certainly take the lot.

Shylock cannot win, since his true demand is for recognition, not revenge. But neither can he entirely lose, since his lawsuit risks forcing the Venetian state to discredit its own authority. In penalising him for his Jewish importunity, it reveals itself to be just as refractory as he is, outdoing his own 'inhuman' legalism. In the end, for daring to pursue a legally binding debt, Shylock has his goods confiscated by the authorities and is forced to turn Christian. His despairing response is to ask the court to take his life instead. In the meantime, however, the Jew has unmasked the justice of the Christians as a sham. To catch them out in a particular piece of legal chicanery is to bring their law in general into disrepute, rather as to lend money *gratis* in the manner of Antonio is to affect the general rate of exchange in the city. Shylock himself is not slow to recognise this fact:

> The pound of flesh which I demand of him
> Is dearly bought, 'tis mine, and I will have it.
> If you deny me, fie upon your law!
> There is no force in the decrees of Venice.
>
> (4.1.99–102)

It is a forceful point, one cogent enough to convince the doomed man himself. Antonio sees that the thing will look bad in the eyes of Venice's trading partners, and might therefore provoke economic disaster. Will power, then, maintain its proper indifference to individuals, chastising one of its own respectable adherents at the behest of an odious outsider? If it does not, it risks dismantling its own protocols, allowing Portia to deploy just the kind of subjective paltering that the law is supposed to spurn. The ultimate consequence of such hermeneutical licence might be political anarchy, two kinds of riot which in Shakespeare's mind are intimately allied.

Shylock's act, by contrast, is not anarchic but deconstructive. As a citizen-outcast, a figure central to the city's economy yet one who is socially unassimilable, he enters the tit-for-tat symmetry of the symbolic order so as to induce it to implode on an absurdity. 'The villainy you teach me', he remarks to one of Antonio's friends, 'I will execute; and it shall go hard but I will better the instruction.' Imitation is the sincerest form of aggression. The Christians, he points out, buy bodies (slaves) with whom they are reluctant to part; why then should he himself relinquish that morsel of Antonio which is now in his legal possession? By pressing the logic of exchange to a self-parodic extreme, he reveals the vacuity of the Real at its core.

This is not to claim that Shylock discredits a symbolic ethics, even though he shakes it to its roots. On the contrary, it is his fanatical fidelity to the symbolic order which brings it close to unravelling. The very bond which marks his participation in that order is excessive of such symbolic economy, signifying among other things the 'Real' of flesh and blood. Shylock lays bare the truth that this particular symbolic order, which like any such regime exists officially to protect flesh and blood, conceals its actual oppression of it; but he does not thereby conclude that law, duty, merit, justice, obligation, desert, strict recompense and the like are so many subsidiary matters or so much ideological window-dressing. He is not one of Jacques Lacan's 'non-dupes', who imagine that they have seen through the symbolic order as no more than an elaborate fiction, and for just this reason are ensnared in the deepest delusion. On the contrary, he cultivates an exactitude which would be by no means to the taste of today's rather more hyperbolic advocates of an ethics of the Real. He does not believe in the manner of Emmanuel Levinas and Jacques Derrida that obligation is infinite. Instead, like Kohlhaas, he demands only his due. The justice which these two characters seek to extract is not excessive of scrupulous calculation; what is excessive is the absoluteness with which they adhere to such exactitude. Shylock and Kohlhaas are far from naive libertarians: both respect the protocols of the symbolic order, and appreciate the point of law and authority. 'I crave the law' is Shylock's cry, at once respectful and rebellious. It is only when the law is at odds with the justice it is supposed to enshrine that these men drive a coach and horses through it. At that point, the demand for justice becomes itself a form of sabotage, a scandal and stumbling block for civilised society. By taking that society's ideological rhetoric altogether too seriously, such a demand succeeds in exposing its covert barbarism. Shylock and Kohlhaas are driven beyond ethics in the name of the ethical.

Derrida and his colleagues, as we shall see a little later, take a somewhat lordly view of a symbolic ethics, or an ethics of equivalence. Calculability, which Derrida can for the most part see only as vulgarly utilitarian, joins

a series of implicitly demonised notions in his lexicon: law, closure, identity, equity, economy, logic, stability, normativity, consensus, theory,
knowledge, orthodoxy, decidability, commensurability, the generic, universality, conceptuality and the like. To pit these terms against their opposites (non-identity, undecidability and the rest) is then to land oneself with
just the kind of binary opposition which the practitioners of deconstruction are generally supposed to undo. Derrida's thought betrays a well-nigh
pathological aversion to the determinate, just as the work of Michel Foucault harbours a well-nigh pathological loathing of subjectivity. Identity,
determinacy and the like, so deconstruction prudently confesses, are
entirely inescapable notions – a recognition which among other things
seeks to protect it from the charge of being no more than a latter-day
Romantic libertarianism. Yet for all these cautious concessions, the deconstructive heart lies undoubtedly with slippage, excess, infinity, indeterminacy and impossibility. It is thus a shamefaced libertarianism rather than
a self-avowed one.

As a member of a reviled group, however, Shylock cannot permit himself
this luxury. It is the Venetian upper-class liberals who regard precise
demands, of the kind inscribed in Shylock's bond, as heartless and inhuman.
To their mind, such rigour is simply another instance of flinty Jewish legalism, the mindset of one who has not read far enough in his bible to have
encountered the virtue of forgiveness. Even the Venetians' clamour for
mercy is anti-Semitic. Shylock, by contrast, understands that the oppressed
require the protection of print. For Portia and her sort, the human is what
eludes the dead letter of the text. It is manifest in the impassioned elo-
quence of her speech in court, rather than by the despotic exactitude of
script. Against the punctiliousness of justice, she offers the lavishness of
mercy. On this view, one like Shylock who spends his life basely haggling
can surely have no notion of the gratuitous – an ironic assumption, to be
sure, given the arbitrariness of his bargain and the strangely unmotivated
tenaciousness with which he pursues it almost to the death.

Shylock, however, needs his piece of parchment because he would be
foolish to rely for his deserts on the big-heartedness of his social superiors.
The symbolic order can work to safeguard the weak as well as exploit them,
which is why only a privileged, cerebral sort of leftism impugns it as such.
Trade unionists would be ill-advised to bank on the whimsical good nature
of their employers for a wage rise. The victimised need an unambiguous
contract, however drearily determinate this may strike the open-minded
intelligentsia, since they can never know when their masters are likely to
be seized by a spontaneous bout of joviality or mean-spiritedness. Writing

is not 'inhuman', but a question of flesh and blood. Indeed, Bassanio
speaks of the letter which brings tidings of the loss of Antonio's goods as
resembling 'the body of my friend, / And every word in it as gaping wound
/ Issuing life-blood' (3.2.267–9). Words, to be sure, should not be confounded with bodies, for all that Shakespeare never ceases to permutate the
two throughout his writing; but an authentic form of signification, not least
of a legal kind, is one which conforms itself to the body, moulded by a
sense of its material needs. If script is impersonal, it is so only in the fashion
of a properly impartial law. Written contracts protect you from the fickle-
ness or treachery of others. Law is not inherently at loggerheads with love
and mercy. The symbolic order of writs and scripts cannot simply be
spurned in the name of an eyeball-to-eyeball encounter with the Real.
Psychoanalytically speaking, the likely consequence of such a short-circuit
is psychosis; politically, it is the infantile disorder of ultra-leftism, a species
of wide-eyed libertarianism.

Portia's celebrated plea for mercy is thus more suspect, not to speak of
more politically self-interested, than the critics have tended to suppose:

> The quality of mercy is not strain'd;
> It droppeth as the gentle rain from heaven
> Upon the place beneath . . .
>
> (4.1.184–6)

Portia means to contrast the unconstrained quality of mercy with compulsion, a word which has just left Shylock's lips. Yet mercy for the Christian
gospel is not as unpredictable as rain. That meteorology is an inexact
science is scarcely to the point here. Portia's seductive imagery seeks to
persuade us that forgiveness is sporadic and spontaneous, as opposed to
the mainstream Christian view that it is more of an obligation than an
option. Use every man after his deserts, as Hamlet inquires, and who shall
escape whipping? To be merciful for Judaeo-Christian doctrine is to share
the life of God; and mercy is not a whimsical affair for him, whatever it
might be for some of his creatures. In a parallel way, the surplus of interest
is an obligatory part of a commercial deal, which is one reason Shylock
offers for detesting a rival who dispenses with it.

What *is* gratuitous in the play is not mercy, which the Christians are
obliged to dispense but don't, but Shylock's terrifying tenacity. In the
course of the drama he offers an extraordinary number of reasons for his
refusal to give way on his desire: that Antonio is an odious Christian; that
he is personally detestable; that he is an anti-Semite; that he lowers the rate

of interest in Venice by doling out free loans; that it is the Christians' own custom to exact revenge, so why shouldn't he do the same?; that Antonio is a dangerous commercial rival to be disposed of; that he won't be made a fool of, and so on. Yet Shylock grasps the true nature of this thing within him that is more than himself no more than his antagonists do. It is, he is forced to concede before the court, as inexplicable a passion as an aversion to pigs or bagpipes. Antonio, for his part, sees from the outset that his rival's obscure object of desire is no more negotiable than the sea or wind, and begs his fellow Christians to abandon their attempt to soften his 'obdurate' heart. Shylock, as one character remarks, is an 'impenetrable' figure, representing as he does an unreadable enigma at the heart of the text. What is at stake in the drama is a hunger for the Real which will brook no compromise, and which skates perilously close to consigning Shylock to his death. He refuses to absolve Antonio not so much because he is in the grip of revulsion as because he is under the sway of necessity.

In the play's sub-plot, Antonio's henchman Bassanio, having improvidently thrown his money around, aims to buy up the well-heeled Portia. His love for her must be put to the test in the celebrated caskets scene, as this mercenary-minded suitor is required to choose between gold, silver and lead containers. The gold casket, which bears the motto 'Who chooseth me shall gain what many men desire' (2.7.5), invites Bassanio to identify his desire with the desire of the other. In doing so, it signifies that sphere of rivalry and mimesis which we know as the imaginary. The silver casket, displaying as it does the motto 'Who chooseth me shall get as much as he deserves' (2.7.7), alludes to the symbolic realm of equivalence and exchange. Silver, Bassanio comments, is the 'pale and common drudge / 'Tween man and man' (3.2.103–4), the universal commodity which links us by the sort of anonymous bonds which seem the very opposite of love. It is certainly the substance on which the play's mercantile, profiteering, wealth-obsessed Venice revolves. The lead casket, by contrast, is fashioned from the stuff with which coffins are lined (it is a casket in the American as well as English sense of the word), and appropriately for such a *memento mori* bears the inscription 'Who chooseth me must give and hazard all he has' (2.7.9). It is in the domain of the Real that one must risk one's life for the sake of one's desire. In opting for the lead casket, then, Bassanio plumps for a kind of nothing, a material as lowly and worthless as Shylock's pound of flesh; yet just as in Shylock's eyes an infinity of meaning is staked on this paltry substance, so Bassanio also manages to convert nothing into everything, alchemising a lump of lead into the prodigious wealth of his newly-won wife. Having described Portia in his first allusion to her as 'richly left' (i.e.

a wealthy heiress), this down-at-heel adventurer is canny enough to win her heart by sanctimoniously spurning the allures of gold and silver. If lead is inestimable in the sense of worthless, love for Romantic types is inestimable in the sense of surpassing all measure. ('There's beggary in the love that can be reckon'd', boasts the improvident Antony in *Antony and Cleopatra*). Bassanio sees love as transcending the degenerate realm of the commodity at the very moment he is buying up a woman. It is thus, in Marx's words, that the 'romantic viewpoint . . . will accompany (the utilitarian viewpoint) as its legitimate antithesis up to its blessed end'.[12] A desire which supposedly beggars all calculation and utility is harnessed to the meticulous calculations of the marriage market, a place in which flesh and sign converge in the form of bodies and the money to buy them with.

It is with an exchange of bodies that *The Merchant of Venice* ends, like most Shakespearian comedies. The final moment in such comedy is to distribute bodies to their appropriate locations in the form of marriage. Yet if marriage is a matter of law, contract and symbolic exchange, it is also a question of desire; and desire has a capriciousness about it which continually threatens to upend such symmetries. The desire that reproduces human society is a hard business to regulate. What sustains the symbolic order is also what threatens to disrupt it, rather as Shylock's stiff-necked fidelity to what he is owed by law throws a spanner in its wheels. Hence the lovers' quarrels with which the play ends, with their suggestion of sexual infidelity. From the standpoint of the symbolic order, marriage is a matter of what is just and fitting; yet since the subversive truth is that anyone can desire anyone else, as the dizzily rotating love intrigues of *A Midsummer Night's Dream* would suggest, there is always a smack of contingency or whiff of the Real about these supposedly symmetrical matchings. The Real is the point at which the best laid symbolic schemes come unstuck. Shylock himself, a widower who loses his daughter to a Christian and his domestic goods to the state in the course of the play, is a kind of sexual as well as a social outcast from the symbolic order.

Throughout his drama, Shakespeare returns again and again to the question of excess versus equity – or, as one might say, of the Real versus the symbolic. Unlike most of today's proselytes of an ethics of the Real, however, he does not allow the excessive and inordinate to devalue the essential business of the symbolic order. He sees well enough that a passion for the Real can be the badge of the monomaniac as much as the martyr, and that the distinction between the two is occasionally undecidable. There

---

[12] Karl Marx, *Grundrisse* (London, 1973), p. 162.

is a difference, sometimes imperceptible to the naked eye, between those who die in the name of an abundance of life and those who perish because they are morbidly in love with death. There is also a distinction between an absolute desire for justice, and a desire which has its absolute end in nothing but itself. There are properly inhuman forms of exact exchange as well as cruelly inhuman ones. There are life-giving forms of recklessness such as forgiveness, as well as injurious ones like revenge. An honourable demand for no more than one is owed can prove to be lethally excessive. The Real, like the sacred or the sublime, is a place of terror as well as transcendence.[13] And an ethics based upon it sees the need for revolutionary transformation only at the risk of courting a brutally elitist extremism. We shall be looking more closely at this elitism later on.

Bassanio scoffs that his friend Gratiano 'speaks an infinite deal of nothing', but so in a different sense does his colleague Antonio. From his first words ('In sooth I know not why I am so sad'), which are also the opening words of the play, the merchant of Venice reveals himself to be languishing in the grip of melancholia – an emotion which Freud describes as 'mourning without an object', and which is thus a kind of much ado about nothing. The critics have accordingly been quick to flesh out the nameless cause of Antonio's emotional condition, speculating that the root of his wretchedness lies in his homosexual love for the doggedly heterosexual Bassanio. Perhaps so; yet it is logical that a merchant should be melancholic – that his desire should lack a determinate object – since this, after all, is how he earns his living. It is the exchange-value of things which interests him, not their specific properties or some imagined end to their accumulation. Melancholy has an instrumental way with objects, plundering them in order to feed itself. Jacques in *As You Like It* can 'suck melancholy out of a song, as a weasel sucks eggs' (2.5.9–11). The more inflated the condition grows, the more its objects appear depleted. In this sense, melancholia is an apt image of desire itself.

Shakespeare is thus alert to the affinities between trade and desire. Both treat things abstractly, as mere occasions for their own self-increase. The same may be said of melancholia. Just as merchants accumulate goods for the sake of further accumulation, so Antonio appears to be despondent for the sake of despondency. It is not financial anxieties which are the cause of his low spirits, as he himself reassures his friends. The drama opens, then, with an infinite deal of nothing – with a vacuity which appears so bereft of a cause or object that Antonio seems at times almost gratified by

13   See Terry Eagleton, *Holy Terror* (Oxford, 2005), Ch. 2.

the prospect of Shylock's knife. He certainly takes remarkably few measures to avert his own death.

The most familiar Shakespearian name for this *Weltschmertz* is not Antonio but Hamlet. If Gratiano speaks an infinite deal of nothing, Hamlet is the incarnation of it. Like Antonio's melancholia, his *ennui* devalues the whole world, reducing it to a shadow of that listless negativity which is the human subject:

> O, that this too too solid flesh would melt,
> Thaw, and resolve itself into a dew!
> Or that the Everlasting had not fix'd
> His canon 'gainst self-slaughter! O God! God!
> How weary, stale, flat, and unprofitable,
> Seem to me all the uses of this world!
> (1.2.129–34)

Hamlet's face is set towards death from the outset, a death prefigured in the vacuity which is himself. Once the imaginary relation between himself and his mother Gertrude has been ruptured by the entry of Claudius, he loiters irresolutely on the brink of the symbolic order, unwilling to assume a determinate location within it. Hamlet, who is pure non-being, refuses to compromise the Real of his desire by investing it in anything as banal as a specific object. He will behave neither as heir to the throne, chivalric lover, respecter of the elderly, docile subject of the king, forgiving son, reconciled stepson or obediently avenging child. His jealously guarded inwardness represents an excess over all of these roles, a pure negativity which refuses the mark of the signifier. As a result, he falls down the cracks between the various public identities on offer to him, none of which, in T. S. Eliot's phrase, can provide an adequate objective correlative of his selfhood. Having 'that within which passeth show', he rebuffs those who would pluck out the heart of his mystery. Like an inept actor who cannot identify with his role, suiting the action to the word and the word to the action, the prince figures as the ruin of all symbolic identity and exchange, spurning the false equivalence of revenge, contemptuously rejecting sexual reproduction and refusing to bow to the desire of the Other. As fluid as his father's ghost and as fast-talking as any Shakespearian clown, he riddles, mocks and bamboozles his way out of being definitively signified. As such, he remains true to the enigmatic, impossible object of his desire, cultivating a lack of being which remains unfulfilled even in death. As Lacan observes, 'He sets everything up so that the object of his desire becomes the signifier of this impossibility.'[14]

It is Sophocles's Antigone who in Lacan's view most strikingly incarnates an ethics of the Real; yet she has an English equivalent in this respect. Clarissa Harlowe, heroine of Samuel Richardson's eighteenth-century masterpiece *Clarissa*, is another remarkable female figure of world literature who dies of refusing to relinquish her desire.[15] After the trauma of her rape by Lovelace, Clarissa proceeds in meticulously ritual fashion to withdraw her body from the symbolic order, speaking of herself as 'nothing' and declaring that 'I am nobody's.' By being resolute for death, she refuses to figure as an item of exchange in the symbolic currency of her culture. Instead, in a surreal act of resignation from a power-system which she has seen through, she becomes nothing, errant, schizoid, a non-place and non-person. By scripting and performing her death so punctiliously, Clarissa turns it into the meaning of her life. Unlike Barnardine, her death is an event in her life – *the* event, in fact – rather than simply the biological end point of it. It is no wonder that so many critics have castigated the novel as intolerably morbid. In yielding her body up to the obscene pleasures of the death drive, Richardson's heroine turns upon her own flesh and blood a mortal aggression which predators like Lovelace wreak injuriously upon others. As such, she presides over a publicly staged sacrificial ritual in which she herself is both ministering priest and mutilated victim, and in doing so passes like the sacrificial offering of antiquity from weakness to power, death to glorification. Clarissa is aware that in her own society, marked as it is by an original sin which is symbolised in her own status as a 'guilty innocent', such a renewal is accessible only by a sacrificial passage through death.[16] As a version of the *pharmakos*, the scapegoat who bears the collective sins of the community, her polluted body incarnates the crimes and contradictions of a more modern-day symbolic order. Her violated flesh symbolises the monstrous Real which must be confronted if this property-obsessed society is to refashion itself. It is this *metanoia* or spiritual transformation which will later be given the name of political revolution.[17]

[14]   Lacan, 'Desire and the Interpretation of Desire in *Hamlet*', p. 36.
[15]   See Terry Eagleton, *The Rape of Clarissa* (Oxford, 1982).
[16]   The phrase 'guilty innocent' is Paul Ricoeur's, in his *The Symbolism of Evil* (Boston, 1969), p. 225.
[17]   For the political implications of sacrifice, see Terry Eagleton, *Sweet Violence: The Idea of the Tragic* (Oxford, 2003), Ch. 10.

Conscious that this is no civilisation for a woman to live in, Clarissa transports her plundered body out of harm's way, converting her dying into a ceremonious public spectacle and steadfastly refusing all calls for compromise from her distraught friends and kinsfolk. Like every votary of the Real, she becomes one of the living dead. Her physical death will merely consummate her spiritual one. In this state of extremity, the only way to safeguard the self is to surrender it. Richardson's heroine coolly hands herself over to the erotic seduction of *Thanatos*, transforming her body into a silent negation of the regime which has hounded her to death, and leaving her humiliated tormentors with blood on their hands. Rarely before the fiction of Henry James has masochism proved so potent a political weapon, as Clarissa, in the spirit of the classical tragic protagonist, plucks a formidable power from her own feebleness. A just social order could be founded only on this solitary, unsociable fidelity to truth. Clarissa's masochism is extreme; but this extremity is a measure of just what it would take in these conditions for truth and justice to be born.

The martyr takes his or her stand directly in the Real, short-circuiting the symbolic and testifying to an alternative truth by repudiating the ways of the world even unto death. Martyrs take what Walter Benjamin would call a tiger's leap into the future, gazing upon the present as though they were already dead and the present were already the past. The martyr harnesses the death drive to a cause which might mean more abundant life for others – an abundance of life which springs from the cessation of his or her own. This is bound to seem ultra-leftist folly to many of those who work pragmatically for a more equitable social order, and who must therefore to some degree abide by the rules of its game. But there is a difference between working for justice and incarnating it, however negatively one might do the latter; and in societies where women are excluded from political life, it is they who, like Clarissa Harlowe, are more likely to prove exemplary of this second form of political dissent. Clarissa testifies to the good life not by agitating for it or preaching in its name, but by converting her flesh into a political signifier, disclosing the lamentable lack of justice around her by the act of putting her ravished body on public show. As David Wood remarks, 'To be a sacrifice is to transform one's individual life into something whose significance transcends that individuality.'[18]

There is a sense in which we all undergo this conversion from flesh to sign in the process of entering the symbolic order; but the martyr is one

[18] David Wood, *The Step Back: Ethics and Politics After Deconstruction* (Albany, NY, 2005), p. 89.

who raises it, so to speak, to the second power. Like the scapegoat, Clarissa 'becomes sin', in St Paul's description of Christ. The more she does so – the more she manifests the criminal violence of the social order in her own body – the more she attests to her own saintliness. The more besmirched the scapegoat, the more immaculate it becomes. In this condition, poison and cure are one. By distilling the essence of an unjust society, the scapegoat points beyond it. What Lacan writes of Oedipus applies to Richardson's heroine too: 'He doesn't die like everybody else, that is to say accidentally; he dies from a true death in which he erases his own being. The malediction is freely accepted on the basis of the true subsistence of a human being, the subsistence of a subtraction of himself from the order of the world. It's a beautiful attitude. . . .'[19] One is reminded of Rilke's distinction between *der kleine Tod*, meaning death as sheer biological event, and *der eigne Tod*, the actively seized-upon, personally authenticated death which grows with a certain moral logic out of one's life. Lacan writes of Antigone that she presses to the limit a pure desire for death as such; and this, too, is the case with the cursed and saintly Clarissa.

Clarissa dies because she values her biological existence less than that within her which is more than herself, and to which the novel itself gives the name of honour or chastity. The Real which she refuses to give up on, the undeniable essence of her being, is given by her devoutly Protestant author the name of God. The heroine's unworldliness springs not from rejecting desire but from remaining true to it. She has come to recognise that no object in this culture of exploitation is worthy of her craving, which is why she quietly disinvests herself of them all. It is this revolutionary, impeccably conformist figure, one who triumphs like a Jamesian heroine by a principled abstention from action, whom the critics have branded as dull, prudish, priggish, morbid, perverse, narcissistic, masochistic, sanctimonious and inflexible. What they fail to point out is just how commendable some of these qualities are for an unprotected woman in patriarchal England.

For most of the past two centuries, critical commentary on William Wordsworth has viewed his work through an imaginary optic. It is the sealed, symbiotic unity between a bountiful Nature and a beneficent humanity

---

[19] Lacan, *Ethics of Psychoanalysis*, p. 303.

which has seized the critics' attention, in what one might call an angelic reading of his poetry. Only with the appearance in 1964 of Geoffrey Hartman's uninspiringly entitled *Wordsworth's Poetry 1787–1814*, still perhaps the single finest monograph on the poet, did this sanguine version of his world yield to a more sceptical, demonic reading. The imagination in Wordsworth's writing (the human capacity most uncritically revered by orthodox literary criticism) stands scandalously exposed in Hartman's study as a death-dealing, obsessional, annihilating power. It is, in a word, an emanation of the Real, rather than a unifying principle of the imaginary.

There is a recurrent scenario in Wordsworth's poetry, portrayed by Hartman with splendid acuity, which bears all the hallmarks of a traumatic encounter with the Real. In a moment of apocalyptic dissolution, one which instantly brings thoughts of death and judgement, the self knows an uncanny moment of arrest or disruption, in which the everyday continuum of existence is abruptly shattered, the light of the senses is blotted out, and the abyss of the imagination opens beneath one's feet. The imagination is a self-begotten, 'unfathered' power, as excessive (Wordsworth comments) as the overflowing Nile; and its consequence is to wrench the self violently from Nature, its familiar habitat and a securely centred existence, plunging it instead into an acute sense of lostness and solitude. In this 'terminal experience', as Hartman describes it, the soul feels itself alien to the world, divorced from a daily existence which now seems so much unreal trifling. But the obverse of this sense of self-dissolution, as with the experience of the sublime, is a triumph of self-affirmation, as the human subject, estranged from all upon which it was previously dependent, exults in its inner strength, feels its consciousness raised to an apocalyptic pitch, and knows itself to be autonomous of all mere circumstance. In particular, it knows itself to be eternally separate from human companionship. The imagination in Wordsworth is not at root a sociable force but an isolating one. It is, as Hartman observes, essentially apocalyptic, and must desecrate the world of common objects and relationships. It is associated with murder, ruins, sacrifice, the inhuman and a kind of 'apocalyptic wounding', not (as the poet himself would prefer to believe) with a joyful binding of the self to others and its surroundings. Wordsworth's poetry is full of stark, fixed, solitary figures, all of whom have a strange power to shatter and transform everyday consciousness. When the poet sees a blind beggar in London in *The Prelude*, his 'mind turned round / As with the might of waters' at the sight of this haunting hieroglyph.

What is glimpsed in these terrifying, inspiring epiphanies is a power of imagination which could not be satisfied by anything in Nature, however sublime; and this, perhaps, is the Wordsworthian equivalent of psychoanalytic desire. As the poet writes in Book 6 of *The Prelude*:

> Our destiny, our being's heart and home,
> Is with infinitude, and only there;
> With hope it is, hope that can never die,
> Effort, and expectation, and desire,
> And something evermore about to be.

No doubt such sentiments had a pious enough ring to Wordsworth's Christian readers; but the implications of such passages are far more subversive than such respectable souls would have recognised. The mighty prophet of Nature, with his message of benevolence and tranquillity, admonishes us that Nature is so much dross in contrast with some unnameable power whose effect is to blot out our vision, rupture our self-repletion and render us eternally dissatisfied. It is true, as Hartman insists, that much of Wordsworth's effort consists in resisting this traumatic truth, reabsorbing disruption into continuity and seeking to naturalise or domesticate the imagination's terrors. He will come to suspect that the French Revolution is a work of the apocalyptic imagination, to be repelled by a very English organicism. Nature's task is to seduce the human subject into obliviousness of its secret infinity, anchoring it instead in the sublunary world. But this is no easy achievement. The faculty of imagination, Hartman observes, is profoundly conservative: it strives to nurture in men and women memories and recollections of a previous, immortal existence, as in the celebrated 'Intimations of Immortality' ode. To this extent, it is not entirely remote from the Freudian death drive, another preservative power which seeks to return us to our immortal origins. The poet wants to believe that Nature and subjectivity are co-partners, not eternal antagonists. But if Wordsworth strives in this sense to be a poet of the imaginary or symbolic, it is because he is fundamentally an apostle of the Real.

The moment of apocalyptic stasis or arrest is also one of spiritual conversion. The subject casts out anything which might intervene between itself and the infinite, at whatever mortal risk to itself. In what Hartman portrays as a 'catastrophic turn to terrible beauty', an old world passes away and a new form of consciousness is born. There is a 'blinding' initiation, in which the poet travels beyond a familiar landscape into (Hartman's words once more) a 'strait between states of being'. The self seized by the imagination becomes one of the living dead, wandering in some purgatory or border region between finitude and infinity. 'I seemed a Being who had passed alone / Into a region of futurity', Wordsworth's demonic character Oswald remarks of himself in *The Borderers*. Oswald commits one of the many acts of betrayal in Wordsworth's art, a term which Lacan employs of the condition of the Real. He has broken blasphemously with custom, tradition and natural law – an impiety which his creator formally castigates yet for which he harbours every secret sympathy. In fact, at the time of writing *The Borderers*, Wordsworth suspected that life, consciousness and civilisation themselves were based upon some primordial murder or crime against Nature.

Divorced by an unfathomable gulf from Nature and the everyday, the subject seeks to vanquish its sense of estrangement by clinging obsessively to some single object or idea, with a tenacity which Hartman sees as at once pathetic and alarming. *Lyrical Ballads* is full of such cherished bits and pieces, in which it is not hard to discern the shadow of Lacan's *objet petit a*. Even when Wordsworth's characters suffer a quite ordinary loss, the passion with which they experience it is extraordinary, so deeply have they invested these common-or-garden things with their desire. Tenacity and resolution, Hartman points out, are keynotes of the poetry, as they are indices of the desire of the Real. There is a kind of crazed, perverse, inhuman persistence about many of Wordsworth's figures, of the kind we have observed in the case of Kohlhaas and Shylock.

In the fearfully apocalyptic dream recounted in Book 5 of *The Prelude*, the poet finds himself in a trackless, boundless wilderness 'all black and void' – a common enough sign in Wordsworth of the solitude and loss of bearings associated with the advent of the Real. A guide appears holding symbols of what binds one human being to another: a stone which denotes geometry, and thus, in Hartman's phrase, dispassionate eternal relations; and a shell to signify poetry, or passionate human relations. The guide's emblematic objects, one might claim, exalt both the symbolic and imaginary dimensions of human existence: abstract relations on the one hand, affective ones on the other. Yet the dream is shot through with images of the impending destruction of both Nature and humanity – of a stark confrontation with the Real which the poet both fears and yearns for, while the guide who might rescue him from this catastrophe hurries on ahead. Unable to catch up with him, the dreamer wakes in terror. The greatest English poet of Nature, humanitarian feeling and organic continuity is driven to write by a power which negates all three.

If *Clarissa* is one of the rare tragic novels in England before the work of Thomas Hardy, it is not least since the aim of middle-class art in this era is to edify rather than dispirit. Another such literary rarity is Emily Brontë's *Wuthering Heights*.[20] That Richardson and Brontë's works are both fictions of the Real is no doubt one reason for this peculiar tragic status, in a society which preferred its narratives to end on an uplifting note of marriage, property settlement, the success of the virtuous and the worsting of the wicked. Or, as Henry James puts it, 'on a distribution at the last of prizes, pensions, husbands, wives, babies, millions, appended paragraphs, and cheerful remarks'.[21] *Wuthering Heights* does indeed tentatively sound such a sanguine note at its conclusion; but it is a notably fragile strain of hope, lurking as it does in the shadow cast by the tempestuous tragedy of Catherine and Heathcliff.

It is hard to describe the bond between the two as a relationship, since it seems to lack all sense of alterity. It is also a strangely sexless rapport. If it is harder still to apply to it a conventional moral discourse of love or affection, it is because there is something curiously inhuman about this violent symbiosis of selves which proves recalcitrant to a symbolic ethics. Driven by an elemental hunger which is foreign to tenderness, Catherine and Heathcliff are more likely to tear each other to pieces than end up side by side before a clergyman, and throughout the narrative set an inexorable course towards death. What compels them is less *Eros* than *Thanatos*, as when Catherine peevishly seeks to do away with herself, or when Heathcliff, an image of the living dead, stands petrified like a statue outside her window. Their frenzied need for one another is a passion for the Real, one which bears them beyond the civilities of the symbolic order into that trackless wilderness which the novel calls Nature.

The fictions of Emily's sister Charlotte are strategies for reconciling desire and social convention. Jane Eyre will be allowed to fulfil her yearning for the glamorously Byronic Rochester, but only in a way which does not transgress social propriety, and so leave her dangerously exposed. No such judicious compromise between desire and convention is possible in *Wuthering Heights*. Instead, Catherine is forced to choose sexually between Heathcliff and Edgar Linton, and in opting for Linton, the most prosperous landowner in the region, hopes to pay her dues to the symbolic order while

[20] See Terry Eagleton, *Myths of Power: A Marxist Study of the Brontës* (London, 1975), Ch. 6.
[21] Henry James, 'The Art of Fiction', in *Henry James: Selected Literary Criticism* (London, 1963), p. 82.

preserving an imaginary bond with her childhood soulmate. By this device she will sustain two selves, phenomenal and noumenal, so to speak, at the same time. Her celebrated cry 'I am Heathcliff!' signifies an imaginary symbiosis with her lover, one marked as much by murderous aggression as by mutual need. Catherine chooses Linton rather than Heathcliff in an act of social prudence – but also because when it comes to Heathcliff, a companion who is as much a necessity of her being as breathing, choice is not in any case a relevant concept. It is possible that the lovers are half-siblings, which might cast light on their sense of each other as alter egos as well as on their asexuality. Yet if this is the case, a hint of incest hangs over their relationship; and since incest is a sign of the traumatic horror at the heart of the symbolic order, its rigorously excluded ground of possibility, it has an intimate relation to the Real. In this death-driven liaison, the symbolic order is outflanked both by the imaginary and the Real.

This is why Catherine's striving for a Charlotte-like compromise is doomed to fail, for the Real permits of no such trade-offs or half-measures. Heathcliff is a visitor from this outlandish region as well as an imaginary complement to his lover, an uncivilised thug who figures as the joker in the pack of the symbolic order. He has no natural place in the restricted economy of the Heights, and his presence there pitches the marriage-and-property market into violent disarray. For Catherine, he represents the eternal rock beneath the woods, the hard core of the Real within the malleable stuff of culture. As an outcast adopted by the Heights but an internal exile within its walls, this well-spoken savage has the ambiguous insider/outsider status of Nature itself, which figures in the novel both as cultivated estate (and thus as a dimension of human culture) and as a barbarous yet fertile region beyond the bounds of civilised existence.

Heathcliff has the Janus-faced quality of the Real, as both death-dealing and life-bestowing. As a child he is a *pharmakos*-like figure, who in old Earnshaw's words is a gift of God but one as dark as the devil. As an adult, he brings both life and death to Catherine, as the agent of a drive which ruins and regenerates simultaneously. Like many a figure of the Real, he is a brutal monomaniac who will wade through blood rather than give up on his desire. The preternatural intensity of his desire is a foretaste of the absoluteness of the death he comes to crave. Yet the novel does not rush to endorse what Heathcliff represents. It does not entirely share his macho contempt for the overbred Edgar Linton, who may well be something of a wimp, but whose love for Catherine is tender and steadfast. Against the 'Heights' reading of Heathcliff as a source of transcendent energy, the text counterposes the 'Grange' view of him as a wolfish exploiter, a pitiless property baron to whom no tie or tradition is sacred. Heathcliff is inhuman because what he signifies transcends the domain of the personal; but he is also inhuman in a rather less exalted sense of the word, as a man who is driven by Catherine's rejection of him into outdoing his oppressors in their own marriage-and-property machinations.

Even so, for all his malevolence, Heathcliff behaves like a dead man walking. His soul is buried with the dead Catherine, and the cultural capital he amasses during his mysterious disappearance from the Heights is expended purely to bring to their knees those who snatched her from him. The more he invests as a heartless capitalist, the less spiritual investment he has in such schemes, driven as they are purely by vengeance against those who severed him from his lover. His worldly wheeler-dealing is wholly in the name of the unworldly. The Real to which Heathcliff clings with such pathological persistence reduces his actual surroundings to unreality, as he is gripped by a drive which brooks no earthly confine. The desire of this hard-headed virtuoso of law, finance and property is as extraterrestrial as the faith of an eremite, which is why death comes to him as a friend rather than a stranger.

Yet the novel sees what is sterile as well as splendid about this ethics of the Real. From the viewpoint of the Grange, with its civilised affections and urbane mores, Catherine and Heathcliff are a pair of brawling brats whose rejection of the symbolic order is a badge of their eternal immaturity. Unable to relinquish an idealised childhood, they turn respectively into a petulantly self-destructive adolescent and a monstrous predator. On this view, the couple's love for one another is both regressive and narcissistic, stuck fast in a lost mythological world from which it could never have evolved into history proper. It is hard to imagine Heathcliff stacking the dishwasher or bathing the baby.

The view from the Heights, however, or at least from the critical apologists for the place, is rather different. If the protagonists' relationship is driven to self-destruction, it is because there is no place for such a pure mutuality of selves in conventional society. The intense communion between the pair is out of joint not because it is regressive but because it is utopian. If their relationship is pre- or anti-social, natural rather than cultural, it is because this is the only authentic form of existence open to them in an exploitative social order. Because the new possibilities they point to cannot yet be made actual, they must be relegated instead to the domain of Nature, myth and the imagination. As a 'gift of God', Heathcliff's presence in the Heights is radically gratuitous: he is received into this domestic-cum-economic unit as an outsider, with no allotted role within its spare, family-centred structure. As surplus to its economy, a stranger in a world in which history is effectively genealogy, he is thus to be embraced or rebuffed simply for what he is, laying claim to no status but a human one. The fearfully polluted *pharmakos* represents the dregs and refuse of humanity; but if it can be gazed upon fearlessly and welcomed within one's walls, this stranger at the gates is capable of releasing an unfathomable power for good.[22]

Catherine, likewise, is superfluous to the yeoman economy of the Earnshaws; as a mere daughter, she is not expected to inherit. But the Heights can find no use for these wild cards other than to abuse and neglect them, abandoning the pair to their own devices. Love is all very well for those who have the leisure and resources to lavish on it. The tight-fisted, hardheaded Heights can make no sense of a relationship bereft of social, familial or economic foundation – one, moreover, which involves a profound equality of being within what the novel consistently portrays as a stratified, brutally domineering regime. One of *Wuthering Height*'s most audacious accomplishments is to unmask the Victorian family hearth as a cockpit of grotesque violence and squalid power-struggles. It is in this sense that the relationship between Catherine and Heathcliff can be read as utopian. The Real involves the possibility of inaugurating a new style of being which breaks with the oppressive past, as well as the reality of unleashing a fearful havoc in the present.

Just as there is a desire at the centre of Emily Brontë's novel which resists signification, so the very form of her text, with its flagrantly biased narrators, contending voices and Babushka-like embedding of accounts within accounts, is enough to baffle any straightforward reading of the story. The device of stacking one potentially unreliable narrative within another not entirely trustworthy one also involves a dismantling of chronology, as history in the text curves in upon itself in a forward-and-backward motion. This, too, is in marked contrast to the unilinear unfolding of a Charlotte tale, with its implicit trust in moral and historical evolution. There is something about the Real which disrupts the historical, as a diversity of characters, episodes and events swirl around its vortex in a kind of whirligig of time.

With a Charlotte Brontë novel, we are never left in much doubt about what to think, as the voice of the omniscient narrator cues our readerly responses with the brisk authority of a schoolmistress. *Wuthering Heights*, by contrast, lacks a meta-narrative, as though the opaqueness at its core

---

[22] See Eagleton, *Sweet Violence*, Ch. 9.

can be approached not directly but perspectivally, glimpsed in the hiatus between one tendentious report and another. The novel thus forestalls any simple choice between the symbolic and the Real, Heathcliff as surly obsessive and Heathcliff as revolutionary new horizon. We are meant to understand that the man is a sadistic scoundrel, not an engaging rogue or rough diamond; yet we are also invited to recognise that it was ill-treatment at the hands of the Earnshaws which transformed him from a plucky child into a heartless crook. Once his desire for Catherine is rejected, it twists into a pathological drive for death, negation and self-violence; yet the desire itself is entirely reasonable, thwarted only by the rigours of the class-structure. Heathcliff is denied respect and recognition, first by the Earnshaws and then by his lover; and we have seen already how such a rejection can transform a Shylock, Kohlhaas or Clarissa from peaceable citizens into avatars of death and destruction. There is something in the fact of injustice, more than there is in envy or resentment or even hatred, which can drive men and women to madness.

In a similarly even-handed way, the novel intends us to see that culture does not go all the way down – that there is a materiality about human existence which proves refractory to it. Yet we are also meant to acknowledge that culture is not in the least skin-deep, and that a Heathcliff-like contempt for it as brittle and effete is no more than a macho prejudice. As far as ambiguity goes, it is even difficult for the reader to get the status of the action in focus. Is this a tale of tragic heroism or of squabbling urchins? Does the truth, after all, lie with the dismissive, down-to-earth Nelly Dean? Desire has been unmasked as a profoundly subversive force, perilously indifferent to social distinctions; yet not all desire is to be affirmed, and not all social convention is bogus. The symbolic order is protective as well as repressive, just as the Real is both transformative and traumatising.

Four years after the appearance of Emily Brontë's novel, an even more magnificent fable of the Real broke upon the literary scene. The white whale which the demonic Ahab of *Moby-Dick* pursues all the way into death is 'inscrutable', as impenetrable to knowledge as the Kantian *noumenon*: 'Dissect him how I may, then', the narrator Ishmael laments, 'I but go skin deep; I know him not, and never will.' Moby-Dick's whiteness is a sign of holiness, of something 'sweet, and honourable, and sublime'; yet 'there lurks an elusive something in the innermost idea of this hue, which strikes more of panic to the soul than that redness which affrights in blood'. Whiteness is pure, but also pure negation; and Moby-Dick, like the sublimity of God or the power of the Real, is terrifying as well as enthralling, accursed as well as sacred, an uncanny, abysmal nothingness which one can gaze upon only at the risk of being struck blind. Like the Real, the whale is both pure negativity and positive force – a cipher which eludes cognition, but also a raging power of annihilation with which the death-haunted Ahab falls catastrophically in love. Moby-Dick's monstrous indeterminacy, an indefiniteness which deranges all zoological categories, reminds the narrator of annihilation, of the 'heartless voids and immensities of the universe'. Landlessness, Ishmael remarks, is as indefinite as God.

If the whale disorders zoological tidiness, it also deranges the novel's tragic protagonist, who sees it as the living incarnation of 'all that most maddens and torments; all that stirs up the lees of things; all truth with malice in it; all that cracks the sinews and cakes the brain; all the subtle demonisms of life and thought; all evil . . .'. For the unregenerate Ahab, Moby-Dick signifies the askew, cross-grained nature of the Real, the subtle flaw in the symmetry of Nature. Just as the Real defeats the signifier in its brute yet elusive thereness, so even the highest earthly felicities, Ahab reflects, have 'a certain unsignifying pettiness lurking in them'. What he discerns in the *tabula rasa* of the whale is the pure malice of the death drive, the cackle of demonic meaninglessness which resounds throughout the universe. But this is because the captain's vision of Moby-Dick resembles the Satanic view of God – which is to say, God seen as oppressor, as judge and patriarch rather than friend and lover. Moby-Dick is in Ahab's view an 'accursed thing', though viewed through less malevolent eyes he shines with a transcendent splendour. You can see the whale as devil or archangel, so we are informed, depending on your mood.

Like all sacred things, the beast is both blessed and cursed; and Ahab's monomaniacal desire for him is both love and lethal aggression, *Eros* and *Thanatos* intertwined. Like the classically demoniac figure, Ahab can reap an *ersatz* kind of vitality only from the pain which his self-lacerating hatred of the whale affords him. It is this self-tormenting condition which is traditionally seen as hell, and the captain is one of a venerable literary lineage of diabolical transgressors. He belongs to the Satanic elect, 'gifted', as he observes himself, 'with the highest perception . . . damned, most subtly and malignantly!' Only the devil – a fallen angel – is on terms with the Creator, valuing destruction for its own sake rather as God creates for the sheer delight of it. Ahab has strayed beyond the frontiers of humanity into some desolate no man's land in which, as he cries in the manner of Milton's Satan, 'all loveliness is anguish to me'. He is one of the living dead, and the whole of his self-annihilating existence is caught up in a fanatical being-towards-death. Even his ivory leg, every echo of which on deck sounds like a rap on a coffin, is a piece of dead matter literally incorporated into his flesh and blood. The captain has done what is demanded of Antonio in the *Merchant*: he has sacrificed a piece of his body to the Other, yet has still received no recognition from the monstrous spectre he fruitlessly pursues. As usual with such intractable desires, everyday reality shrinks to so much gaudy façade, emptied of its ontological substance: 'all visible objects', Ahab considers, 'are but as pasteboard masks'. Acolytes of the Real are natural-born Platonists.

'Thy thoughts have created a creature in thee', Ishmael reflects, contemplating his captain's forlorn condition. It is the alien wedge of the Real within him which shatters Ahab's being, driving him on to attain an impossible object; but it is also this crazed, undeviating desire which constitutes his greatness. Like all protagonists of the Real, he is possessed by a passionate longing for infinity: 'Truth hath no confines', he protests. He is prepared to risk his life in pursuit of his desire; and in this sense he presses to a tragic extreme the routine behaviour of his fellow mariners, who reap life from death by plucking a livelihood out of the ocean. They, too, are *pharmakoi* like himself, outcasts from humanity whose trade is marked by 'uncleanliness'; yet though the world spurns these traffickers in the inhuman, it also pays them homage as Promethean bringers of fire, providers of oil for the lamps of their homes and workplaces. Human civilisation itself is a matter of dredging life from death, pressing an intractable Nature into the service of culture; and to this extent the doubleness of Ahab reflects the civilised norm rather than the unsociable deviation. It is humanity, constituted as it is by the impossible, Janus-faced Real of its desire, which is the true *pharmakos*, capable of both redemption and damnation in a way beyond even the most superb of sea creatures. If Ahab is an aberration on the face of the earth, it is because he forces the logic of the human to an unthinkable limit – a limit at which humanity reveals itself at a stroke both as inhuman and as most authentically itself. This is the region of the Real, where, for both good and ill, neither the apologists of the imaginary nor the advocates of the symbolic are able to venture.

A much less resplendent novel than Melville's, Arnold Bennett's *The Old Wives' Tale*, contains an extraordinary moment in which Harold Povey, a nondescript North Midlands draper of impeccably petty-bourgeois mores, is transfigured by the unjust execution of his cousin into a frighteningly unrecognisable figure. Racked by pneumonia, Harold stumbles from his sick bed to visit his condemned kinsman in prison, and then to consult with the local rector about a political demonstration against the sentence. The result of his preternatural exertions in the cause of justice is two deaths rather than one, as Povey expires of toxaemia. 'He lacked individuality', comments his author, 'He was little . . . But I liked and respected him . . . I have always been glad to think that, at the end of his life, destiny took hold of him and displayed, to the observant, the vein of greatness which runs through every soul without exception. He embraced a cause, lost it, and died of it.' 'In each of us', Lacan writes, 'the path of the hero is traced, and it is precisely as an ordinary man that one follows it to the end.'[23]

At the end of Arthur Miller's play *A View from the Bridge*, the lawyer Alfieri enters to deliver a Choric tribute to the dead protagonist of the piece, Eddie Carbone:

> Most of the time now we settle for half and I like it better. But the truth is holy, and even as I know how wrong (Eddie) was, and his death useless, I tremble, for I confess that something perversely pure calls to me from his memory – not purely good, but himself purely, for he allowed himself to be wholly known and for that I think I will love him more than all my sensible clients. And yet, it is better to settle for half – it must be. And so I mourn him – I admit it – with a certain . . . alarm.

The tone is not far from *The Old Wives' Tale*'s elegiac comment on the defeated but defiant Harold Povey. Alfieri's bemused response to Carbone reflects a proper ambivalence about the Real. The hero of the drama has rushed bull-headedly to his death in the name of his soiled reputation; and the play admires the tenacity with which he cleaves to his desire even as it presents him as tragically deluded. Much the same is true of *Death of a Salesman*'s view of its protagonist Willy Loman, a character who dies enmired in false consciousness, yet whose tragic dignity consists in the fact that he is unable to walk away from the problem of his own identity. One might say of this prototypical modern hero that he preserves 'the authentic place of (his) *jouissance*, even if it is empty', as Lacan remarks in another context.[24] Loman is another literary figure who moves among the ranks of

---

[23] Lacan, *Ethics of Psychoanalysis*, p. 319.
[24] Ibid., p. 190.

the living dead, marching inexorably to his encounter with the death which the play's title, a piece of destiny in itself, has in store for him from the outset. What Miller himself admires about his hero is 'the intensity, the human passion to surpass his given bounds, the fanatical insistence on his self-conceived role'. Like many a protagonist of the Real, Willy is haunted by the banality of the everyday, dismayed by the contrast between his own sublimely unswerving demand and, in his author's own phrase, 'the hollowness of all he had placed his faith in'. 'I take it', Miller goes on, '. . . that the less capable a man is of walking away from the central conflict of the play, the closer he approaches a tragic existence. In turn, this implies that the closer a man approaches tragedy the more intense is his concentration of emotion upon the fixed point of his commitment, which is to say the closer he approaches what in life we call fanaticism.'[25]

It is easy, then, to understand Alfieri's rueful head-scratching over his murdered client in A View from the Bridge, not least because the lawyer is a product of the pen which also composed The Crucible. In an age shorn of heroic ideals, the only nobility within one's grasp lies not in the nature of one's desire, but in the intensity with which one remains loyal to it. Yet that intensity is always potentially pathological. We are dealing, then, with a purely formalistic ethic – one which has a touch of glamour about it but a smack of recklessness, too. Indeed, Lacan's 'Do not give way on your desire' is one in a lineage of such formalistic doctrines, of which the existentialist 'Act authentically!' is a remote precursor. 'What makes Philoctetes a hero?', Lacan asks, and replies: 'Nothing more than the fact that he remains fiercely committed to his hate right to the end.'[26] Whether a man who remains fiercely committed to his paedophilia right to the end also qualifies for morally heroic stature remains unclear. It is just such a formalist ethic which Lacan admires in Antigone, poised as she is at a frontier of the symbolic order so far-flung that she can affirm the unique value of her slain brother without reference to the moral quality or social effects of his actions. In a tradition from Heidegger to Sartre and Lacan, the distinction which counts is not one between good and bad but between authentic and inauthentic, however imprecise the latter adjective may be in the case of Lacan. One is invited to admire the sublime or beautiful form of an action, or to commend its dauntless extremity, regardless of its perilous or prosaic content.

[25]   Arthur Miller, Collected Works (London, 1961), pp. 33, 37.
[26]   Lacan, Ethics of Psychoanalysis, p. 320.

Fictions of the Real, however, tend to be more nuanced in this respect than some theory of it. Both Loman and Carbone do the wrong thing for the right reason; but the dramas in which they appear, rather than simply affirming the clenched persistence of their desire, play it off against its unworthy object. The fact that these characters cannot walk away from themselves is seen as both folly and victory; and this dual vision is part of Miller's Ibsenite inheritance. Those who edge too near to the Real are likely to perish of the truth – but perishing of the truth may be preferable all the same to never having clapped eyes on it. In a sense, Miller's protagonists are caught between both camps, fixated on various specious objects of desire yet investing a passionate truth in these painted idols. In this sense, Loman has not, in Lacan's phrase, 'gone to the end of his desire' – a point at which, as Lacan colloquially remarks, one sees that life isn't a bed of roses, but has one's eyes opened all the same 'to the wholly relative value of beneficial reasons, attachments or pathological interests'.[27] Willy is justified in his demand for recognition, but deluded to imagine that the forms of it socially available to him are worth having. Carbone is right to demand back his 'name' or public honour, but fails to acknowledge that it has been justly forfeited. In a society where traditional moral goods have become increasingly tarnished, and where the quarrel between this or that conception of the good life has grown acute, ethics is bound to become largely a question of form. An ethics of the Real is the latest version of this formalism.

In a passage in *The Ethics of Psychoanalysis*, Jacques Lacan writes of the betrayal involved in abandoning one's desire:

> What I call 'giving ground relative to one's desire' is always accompanied in the destiny of the subject by some betrayal – you will observe it in every case and should note its importance. Either the subject betrays his own way, betrays himself, and the result is significant for him, or, more simply, he tolerates the fact that someone with whom he has more or less vowed to do something betrays his hope and doesn't do for him what their pact entailed – whatever that pact may be, fated or ill-fated, risky, short-sighted, or indeed a matter of rebellion or flight, it doesn't matter.

Something is played out in betrayal if one tolerates it, if driven by the idea of the good – and by that I mean the good of the one who has just committed the act of betrayal – one gives ground to the point of giving up one's

---

[27] Ibid., p. 323.

own claim and says to oneself, 'Well, if that's how things are, we should abandon our position; neither of us is worth that much, especially me, so we should just return to the common path.'[28]

The subject who betrays himself is Eddie Carbone, while both Shylock and Kohlhaas confront enemies who renege on their solemn pacts. As for those who seek to abandon their claims and settle for half, the final sentence of Lacan's paragraph could almost be a paraphrase of Biff Loman's desperate appeal to his father to back down from his destiny: 'Pop, I'm a dime a dozen, and so are you!' Willy's own view of the matter, by contrast, is crystallised in a laconic exchange with his nephew Bernard:

BERNARD: But sometimes, Willy, it's better for a man just to walk away.
WILLY: Walk away?
BERNARD: That's right.
WILLY: But if you can't walk away?
BERNARD: I guess that's when it's tough.

[28]   Ibid., p. 321.

9

Levinas, Derrida and Badiou

No two ethical theories would seem less akin than British eighteenth-century benevolentism and the philosophy of Emmanuel Levinas.[1] Yet Levinas's thought represents among other things a return to an ethics based upon sentience and sensibility, emerging from the chilling shadow cast by Immanuel Kant to place moral values once more in the context of the needy, afflicted, compassionate body. One might add that there had been an important earlier project of this kind: the young Marx's attempt to argue his way up from the sensible body to a communist ethics in his *Economic and Philosophical Manuscripts*. Levinas himself, for whom (like Alain Badiou) the ethical is contrary to nature, sets his face sternly against any such naturalistic theory, indeed against ethical theory as such. In his view, such talk of the biological species has inescapable resonances of the Third Reich. Ethics for him is rooted in the body, but is also a transcendence of it. And this mode of transcendence is known as the personal.

To be a subject for Levinas is to be subjected – which is to say, exposed to the bruising demand of the Other, a demand which registers itself not in the mind but 'on the surface of the skin, at the edge of the nerves'.[2] 'Subjectivity', as Simon Critchley comments, 'is founded in sensibility.' Levinas has much in common with Kant; but he does not share his distrust of sensibility. Life for Levinas is in Critchley's words 'sentience, enjoyment and nourishment. It is *jouissance* and *joie de vivre*'[3] – though given the extreme austerity of these wilfully esoteric texts, one could be forgiven for overlooking the fact. Nourishment and enjoyment in Levinas's eyes form a sort of prehistoric structure off which the life of consciousness feeds, but which are

---

[1]   See in particular Emmanuel Levinas, *Totality and Infinity* (Pittsburgh, 1969), *Otherwise than Being* (Pittsburgh, 1981), *Ethics and Infinity* (Pittsburgh, 1985) and *Time and the Other* (Pittsburgh, 1987).

[2]   Levinas, *Otherwise than Being*, p. 81.

[3]   Simon Critchley, *Ethics–Politics–Subjectivity* (London, 1999), p. 189.

always radically anterior to it. As with the eighteenth-century imaginary, will, reflection and cognition are latecomers to the ethical scene, pallid derivatives of something considerably more primordial. Critchley is right to see that the ethical subject in Levinas is a creature of flesh and blood, as in his celebrated comments that 'only a being that eats can be for the other' and (a smack at Heidegger) '*Dasein* does not eat.' Ethics, he declares, is 'not a gift from the heart, but of the bread from one's mouth'.[4] The other, he remarks, is someone one has under one's skin, an image which is meant to suggest an irritant rather than an agreeable merging of egos. The ethical is to be approached through sensibility rather than cognition. We exist in so far as we are affected. As an infinite openness to an 'outside', sensibility is itself a form of transcendence. The sublime is inscribed in our sensations.

In a grandly hyperbolic reaction to Enlightenment thought, then, we have abandoned the world of free, voluntaristic, self-determining agents for an ethical sphere of victimage and dependency, obligations rather than options, in which what reigns sovereign is not freedom of will but a fearful susceptibility. Death, Levinas writes, is the impossibility of having a project. The traditional ethical question 'What am I to do?' becomes 'What does the Other want of me?' Ethics is no longer a matter of reasoning about how to act, or about what constitutes the good life. Levinas has a Lacanian distaste for such notions of the supreme good, which in his view lead only to failure and frustration. Ethics is too momentous an affair to be reduced to such sublunary considerations as happiness, fulfilment or well-being. He also has scant patience with the classical conception of ethics as a reflection on particular situations so as to discover how to act most fruitfully within them. The idea of adducing sound reasons in order to attain rational ends is not one which especially enthrals him. The ethical is more a matter of being chosen than choosing. We have seen how much the same vein of wise passiveness can be found in the empathetic world of the sentimentalists, for whom pity or disgust lie beyond one's conscious mastery. Levinas's is an ethics of breakdown and vulnerability rather than of robust achievement, and as such belongs not to the world of politics and technology but to those fellow Jews who have been done to death by such things. He is out to retrieve the finitude of human existence from the hubris of the unbounded will; but infinity, as we shall see, is smuggled back in even so, in the inexhaustible responsibility we bear towards each other. It is, Levinas writes, in language reminiscent of the Lacanian Real, the 'more in me than I can contain'.

---

[4]   Levinas, *Otherwise than Being*, p. 74.

At the centre of Levinas's moral thought lies a relation with the Other, which – since the Other is *wholly* other, enigmatic and inaccessible – is also a non-relation. Like the Lawrence of *The Rainbow* and *Women in Love*, Levinas is in pursuit of a relationship beyond relationship – one which in Lawrentian style has left behind the whole clapped-out conventional discourse of will, consciousness, psychology, emotion, social mores, moral laws, humanitarian sympathies and the like for a realm beyond being itself, a country of the spirit far beyond ontology. The dangers of human domination are now so insistent that it is almost as though relationship itself, which can never be innocent of power, must be forsworn. It is in being open to an unmasterable otherness, to a transcendence encountered at the very core of subjectivity with which (as with the transcendent God) no bartering, wheeler-dealing, exchange or reciprocity is conceivable, that my guilt-ridden existence is grounded. We are speaking, in other words, not of empirical encounters with this person or that, but with a primordial or transcendental encounter which is the condition of any empirical relationship whatsoever, and which constitutes the matrix within which all such liaisons move. The self is no more than an echo of something which outstrips it. It is not even the Other who evokes my sense of responsibility, but the Law or Infinite which in its imperious fashion addresses the Other to my responsibility. If there is no question of symmetry, equality or reciprocity here – which is to say, no question of a symbolic ethics – it is because the Other, in that pure, palpitating vulnerability which is signified by the 'face', robs me of my autonomy and casts me into a kind of traumatised abjection. I am taken hostage by this infinitely accusative Other, called forth by him in my utter nakedness to a meaning beyond being. As a sign of the absolutely unknowable which breaches my self-mastery, this epiphany of the infinite is also a harbinger of my death.

It is in trauma, then – in one's exposure to an absolute, well-nigh unbearable alterity, one which for Lacan would be the very mark of psychosis – that the ethical has its inhuman origin. Being is exteriority. What shatters the self into subjectivity is the shockingly unmediated nature of this exposure to the Other, the well-nigh intolerable intensity of affect it occasions, which eludes the impersonal exchanges of the symbolic order and does not pass through the defiles of the signifier. Since it is this confrontation which brings me to birth as a subject, my 'election' is also my subjection. The good is prior to being, since it is through a commitment to the Other that we are brought into subjective existence ourselves. Since I can never grasp, know, thematise or conceptualise the Other, all of which would be to reduce her to an imaginary identity with myself, she signifies for me an absolute alterity – strange, exorbitant, unconditional, non-representable, scandalous, incommensurable, utterly singular, impenetrable to my desire – and is thus as transcendent of my own selfhood as the God who lives in us both. In fact, Levinas effectively transposes the latter (non)relation into the former. A current of modern ethics, sceptical that the Almighty is any longer at home, simply shifts his transcendence to the person of the Other. In doing so himself, Levinas presses to an extreme limit the familiar paradox that all human relationship requires some undecidable blending of affinity and autonomy, and does so to the point where both conditions are undermined. Not only is there not a scrap of identity or common ground between myself and the Other, but his plangent appeal confiscates my independence, reducing me to a sort of spiritual slave in his numinous presence.

Yet though the Other is remote and incomprehensible, experienced in the manner of the superego as an impossible demand, crushing burden or unrebuttable accusation, he is at the same time overpoweringly intimate, a kind of alterity within my own body, and as such manifests something of the dual nature of the Real. The Other is at once proximate and unpossessable, too near to avoid but too remote to grasp. He is, so to speak, given to me spontaneously in his ungivenness, without detriment to his absolute transcendence of myself, and his skin makes visible his utter invisibility. In confronting me with a claim on my own being which is absolute, one which like the Kantian moral law I can neither make adequate nor avoid, the Other disrupts my settled location within the symbolic order, breaking violently in on the narcissistic totality of my world, casting me adrift, thrusting me from my home and summoning me to shoulder the burden of an infinite responsibility on his behalf. One is never quits as regards the Other, who is modelled in this sense on an unappeasable God. Levinas does not consider in this respect the paradox of the New Testament – that this terrible demand is a form of loving, a love which for all its ruthless absolutism understands our frailty through and through, and rejoices in us just as we are. Rather as Jesus pointedly does not ask sinners to repent before enjoying his company, so God loves his creatures unconditionally – which is to say, in all their unregeneracy. It is this which the morally self-righteous, pre-empted in their personal improvement programmes, find too scandalous to accept.

Entangled in this bruising encounter, the subject feels 'uneasy in his skin', 'exiled from himself', invested in an irremissible guilt as though wearing a Nessus tunic. As with the benevolentists, the Other inaugurates a decentring of the self, though one far more terrifying and vertiginous in Levinas's eyes than for the eminently civilised eighteenth century. One's obligations towards him stretch well beyond the civic reasonableness of a Hume or Burke, towards that measureless self-giving which is commanded by Judaeo-Christianity. It is the Other's absolute status, along with the infinity of his demand, which is so traumatic. Faced with this intractable presence, the subject is fractured into non-self-identity, abject rather than autonomous, perpetually unable to coincide with itself. All this, like the ethics of sentimentalism, occurs in some pre-reflective, pre-historical depths of the self, prior to knowledge, intention, commitment, consciousness or free decision. This Other is troublingly eternal, existing outside all social or historical context, denuded of all definitive cultural markers, transcending all moral or psychological factors. What his face opens up to me is humanity in its purest state. Levinas seems not to recognise that to strip the subject of its social context is to render it more abstract rather than more immediate, and thus more akin to the bloodless Enlightenment subject he detests.

It is the archaeology of the ethical which Levinas is out to investigate, that epiphany of originary otherness which runs so deep in our pre-conscious constitution that it cannot even be spoken of as an event or an experience, and certainly gives the slip to anything as lamentably prosaic as a mental representation. (At the same time, he will have no truck with the supposed science of this originary otherness, psychoanalysis.) This primordial ethical encounter is the source of all knowledge and reflection, and thus looms up as the origin of subjectivity itself. It lies at the genesis of truth, for truth is the event of one's reckless self-exposure to the Other prior to all speculative discourse. It is also the wellspring of epistemology, as it is through our dealings with others that we establish an objective world in common. The objectivity of the Other, his sheer phenomenological insistence on my horizon, is the paradigm of objectivity in general.

Moreover, it is the Other who lies at the source of the self, and being-for-the-Other is the precondition of being-for-oneself. The self is the Other in the same, and its uniqueness is constituted by its assuming the Other's burden of sin and guilt, in the inimitable way that only you or I can. My responsibility for this mesmerising Other is a primordial one, anterior to all particular social or moral obligations, prior to all universal codes or precepts, indeed before all discourse. Indeed, it is the Other who gives birth to language, since the origin of speech lies in an articulate response to his unsettling presence. The Other is also prior to freedom, since freedom is not a question of individual choice but of being 'obliged by the Other', commanded by his stricken plea, coerced in the depths of one's being by his unignorable cry. In an encounter with the Other, the freedom of the self is given meaning through its responsibility. Only a free being can be responsible – which is to say, not actually free at all, in any sense of the word familiar to the modern liberal legacy from which Levinas is concerned to distance himself. In the presence of the Other, one can make neither an unconstrained act of will nor an impartial decision. We are speaking of compulsion rather than choice.

The Other's demand, like that of the Kantian moral law or Freudian superego, is infinite, excessive, inarticulable, unfulfillable, beyond all comprehension; and so too is the response he evokes in me. I must consider myself infinitely responsible for all Others – responsible even for their own responsibility, responsible for their deaths (rather than, as with Heidegger, preoccupied in the first place with my own), as well as responsible for the crimes inflicted upon them by evildoers. I am even responsible for their persecution of me. One might wonder whether there is not a certain strain of inverted megalomania in this supreme self-abnegation. To be responsible for everyone sounds more like a neurosis than an ethics. I am arraigned, persecuted, even obsessed by the implacable demand of the Other, 'turned inside out', racked and tormented, driven back by him upon the speechless void of my own being. On hearing his mute appeal, I am forced to question the worth of my own paltry existence, stirred to self-loathing and stripped of my meagre resources at the very moment that the claim of the other summons me to decisive action on his behalf. The very act that constitutes me as a subject also places me at a distance from my own being. Before the Other I am always in the wrong, always a guilty innocent. It is as a scapegoat that the subject comes into being.

Yet one's responsibility for the Other is not founded in anything beyond itself. It is not validated by any code, norms or set of values, since it is anterior to them. It is simply a sublimely unknowable imperative – 'Be responsible!' – which resounds from one knows not where, and to which one is compelled to hearken without knowing why. Like many a modern French thinker, Levinas makes a virtue out of ignorance. Yet this mysterious imperative is also the ground of the indicative – of law, knowledge, justice, morality, ontology, politics and the like. The 'face', the sheer aching vulnerability of the other, comes before all moral and political discourse; and though it opens these issues up for us, they must never stray too far from their home in the face-to-face encounter. The symbolic order, in short, has its ground in the Real – for the ethical is Levinas's own version of this Lacanian conception, one in which the 'relation' to the other has all the traumatic force, absolutism, self-estrangement, steadfastness, disruptiveness, ahistoricity, infinity, singularity, non-relatedness, impossibility, obsessiveness and transformative power of the ethics-beyond-ethics of Jacques Lacan. As we shall see later with Alain Badiou's 'event', the Other for Levinas is an unforeseeable revelation which violently breaches the known and knowable, and in doing so gives birth to a new species of truth on a terrain far distant from commonplace cognition. If the Real also involves dicing with death, then such extremities of risk and self-exposure are present in Levinas in the form of our self-abandonment to the 'hateful' other, who like Freud's hostile neighbour threatens at every moment to annihilate us with his animosity.

In fact, all three Lacanian registers are interwoven in Levinas's work. At the centre of his thought lies the unique, irreducible face-to-face relationship of pity, compassion and responsibility, a clear allusion in our own scheme of things to the imaginary. It is true that the place of the other as object of benevolence is now occupied by the dreaded neighbour-as-stranger, by an horrific epiphany of the Real; but the privileged status of the face-to-face relation remains largely unaltered. The face of the Other is an epiphany or revelation which 'calls my name', 'hails' or interpellates me rather as in Althusser's imaginary version of ideology, even if the result of this interpellation in Levinas's case is to leave me destitute rather than comfortably ensconced in a familiar social landscape. Along with the benevolentists, Levinas is out to undermine an ethics of egoism – though if the bugbear in their case was Hobbes, in his case it is Husserl. It is the proximity of subjects that is at stake here, the semi-erotic 'caress', 'stroking' or 'contact' which occurs between them. The encounter they undergo is unmediated by content; instead, it is what Levinas portentously describes as 'pure communication as the communication of communication'.[5] Nothing as prosaic or 'symbolic' as conversation takes place in this sacred sphere.

'The immediacy of the sensible', Levinas claims, 'is an event of proximity and not of knowledge.'[6] We are not to mistake the sensible, or 'passibility' as Levinas sometimes dubs it, for some lowly matter of empirical experience *à la* Hume or Smith. 'Proximity' is a form of contact between human subjects more inward and intimate than any sort of cognition, but also than

---

[5] Quoted in Jeffrey Bloechl (ed.), *The Face of the Other and the Trace of God* (New York, 2000), p. 99.
[6] Ibid., p. 100.

any conceivable sensation or intuition. The presence of the other is given to me as swiftly and pre-reflectively as it is for Hutcheson or Hume; it does not depend on any act, intention or initiative of my own. We are not speaking here of the mediations of the symbolic order, where consciousness is constituted as a loss of immediacy, born of the gap between the subject's act of sensing and what is sensed. Subjects and objects in the familiar sense of the terms are not at issue at all. If the Other were an object of knowledge, then it would be of *my* knowledge, and in thus failing to escape the all-consuming ego would not be Other at all.

Yet it is an imaginary transformed almost out of recognition, in which the Other shatters rather than supports me. The privileged relation between self and Other is carried over from the imaginary realm, but with nothing of its complacency or mindless reciprocity. The potentially endless mirroring of selves of the eighteenth-century philosophers is now brought up short by the unbearable burden of my responsibility. 'The vortex', Levinas writes, '. . . suffering of the other, my pity for his suffering, his pain over my pity, my pain at his pain, etc. – stops at me.'[7] Reciprocity tilts into asymmetry. The sphere of the face-to-face retains its claustrophobic, pre-reflective intimacy, but the fluid, affective bonds between self and other are severed, so that the Other retreats with the majestic aura of the Real into some region beyond all natural humanity or recognisable relationship. If the imaginary is a domain of spontaneity, the Levinasian encounter displaces and upends the subject, throwing the spontaneity of the self violently into question. The Other, Levinas insists, is by no means myself, and we do not share an existence in common. What links us, so to speak, is our difference: it is the unbridgeable gulf between myself and the Other, the measureless imbalance of our (non)relation, which makes me what I am. Desire is the desire of the absolutely Other.

Yet whatever else this Other may be, he is not in the ordinary sense gratifying or desirable. It is pure, bruising strangeness and alterity, rather than the pleasurable alter ego of the imaginary, which is at issue here. We are in the realm of Judaic transcendence rather than Greek determinable presence. In his customarily counter-Enlightenment style, Levinas detests the notion of identification, so that empathy with the Other's feelings is not at all in question. In this sense, indeed, his ethics are the very antithesis of the imaginary. Whereas for Francis Hutcheson the other's face speaks of this or that emotion, what it speaks of for Levinas is infinity. In *Totality and Infinity*, the imaginary is where we are enjoyably at home, recuperating

---

[7]   Ibid, p. 101.

the non-self within the sovereignty of sameness and selfhood. In this condi-tion, the world is given over to my desire, and the other is taken into the self as a source of *jouissance*, so that otherness becomes not a threat but a pleasure. Here, then, is Levinas's equivalent of the mirror stage, which in his view is very far from an authentic ethics.

There is something oppressively inhuman about the Levinasian Other, whose fleshly presence is more an intimidatory law than a ground of friendship. It is as though the language of affectivity is being used of a domain which lies immeasurably beyond it. If this is a carnal world, it is of a rebarbatively high-toned kind, remote from the workaday sympathies of Hutcheson and Hume. There is nothing congenial or *gemütlich* here, no high-spirited delight in one another's being. One is reminded of Bruce Robbins's comment on a passage from Zygmunt Bauman: 'The other side of Bauman's sacralisation of dying for the Other is an ostentatious contempt for ordinary life, a blank incomprehension of what else might possibly make (life) worth living.'[8] We are speaking not of harmony, communion, sympathy and the like, but of a 'relationship' or mute epiphany which seems to transcend such common-or-garden moral discourse altogether. We are, in brief, somewhere on the far side of the pleasure principle. David Wood suggests in *The Step Back* that the asymmetrical relationship of obligation can be conjoined with relationships of friendship and cooperation. But not fundamentally, it would seem, for Levinas.

In its upbraiding, accusative aspect, the Other has a smack of the sym-bolic law as well as of the abrasive Real – a law which like Kant's is without tangible moral content. This resolves a certain difficulty for Levinas – one which, as we shall see, he shares in common with a number of his French *confrères*. For his imagination is hardly gripped by the thought of the sym-bolic order, which stands for so much that the encounter with the Other is meant to rebuff: freedom, identity, autonomy, equality, reciprocity, representation, legality, communality, normativity, conceptuality, calcula-bility, commensurability, substitutability and so on. For the most part, Levinas has the cavalier way of a Kierkegaard with all of these humdrum phenomena. If, however, the symbolic order is reduced to no more than an imperious but empty command – if the Kantian Ought is retained, but the accompanying vision of free, equal, exchangeable human subjects is discarded – then what is most distasteful about the symbolic domain can

---

[8] Bruce Robbins, *Feeling Global: Internationalism in Distress* (New York and London, 1999), p. 172.

be consigned to the dustbin of philosophical history. One might say that Levinas's Kant, like Jacques Derrida's, is a matter of obligation without economy. One consequence of this shift is that the symbolic imperative then begins to merge into the mysterious command of the Real. Once deprived of the rational foundation which Kant affords it, it looms up as cryptic and ungrounded, still absolute in its force yet – precisely because the absolute is inarticulable – beyond all reason or regulation. It is therefore just the kind of imperative required by post-structuralist thinkers who wish to speak of ethical obligation while clinging to their notions of ambiguity and indeterminacy, as well as preserving a certain aura of infinity.

Levinas, to be sure, has his own conception of substitutability. I must be prepared to stand in for all others even to the point of dying on their behalf. In fact, it is this place-taking for others which constitutes the birth of the subject. It is in putting myself in another's place that I come to be who I am. Freedom is the replacing of my will with yours. But this relation of responsibility to others is not reversible, as it is in a symbolic economy: these others can never substitute for me in their turn, since I am always more responsible than they are. There is a kind of curious out-abnegating at work here, like two people striving to outdo each other in the business of bowing low. To apprehend one's own death and to experience one's absolute irreplaceability amount to much the same thing. The other can therefore never die for me; but neither can I assume the other's death, even if I die in her place; and this, too, is an index of my irreducible singularity. It is not in fact clear that the logic of 'I cannot die for another' differs substantially from that of 'I cannot sleep for another', or 'I cannot play the tin whistle for him'; but death in Levinas's eyes marks the subject's ultimate solitude. Jacques Derrida notes similarly in *The Gift of Death* that one can die for someone in the sense of taking their place, but not in the sense that one can deliver the other from her mortality. To do this, as in the Christian doctrine of resurrection, would be the ultimate gift. Symbolic exchange thus yields to the singularity of the Real. My death, in Derrida's words, cannot be taken, borrowed, transferred, delivered, promised or transmitted. The absolute non-fungibility of death is for both thinkers the final refutation of the symbolic order. It does not seem to strike them that one might say as much about one's style of walking or pattern of speech. Perhaps this is because, since the early writings of Heidegger, the subject of death has become an index of one's philosophical depth.

For the eighteenth-century moralists, the principle of substitution works at the level of the ego. For Levinas, it is active at a far deeper level, in a place where one is a stranger to oneself, not at home in one's being, a tenant rather than a proprietor, 'hunted down in one's own home' as Levinas has it in *Otherwise than Being*. The truth is that I am not just one being among others, and neither are the others. I am not part of the totality to which others belong, and neither, from their standpoint, are they. Rather, the self is an inequality with itself. It is a part which is no part, the ruin of all genre, scheme or grand narrative. Ethics is in this sense the end of ontology. Human subjects cannot be totalised, and the ontologies which seek to do so can easily serve to underpin political totalitarianism. In this sense, Levinas is one of the earliest postmodern thinkers. His extreme wariness of identity and generality has its roots in a history of fascist and Stalinist barbarism. For him, as for some of his postmodern progeny, there is a discernible path from the generic to the Gulag. This is why, like Derrida, he regards the idea of community as being an inherently imaginary affair – a specular reflection of each in the other in some organicist, ominously transparent whole. No more sophisticated notion of human fellowship is permitted. When Levinas thinks of solidarity he thinks of fascism, not of the resistance movements which fought to overcome it. As with Derrida, his ethical thought is among other things symptomatic of an era in which the whole concept of human communality has been damaged almost beyond repair, both by its advocates and its antagonists. At its most negative, it is the sign of the gradual atrophy of the sense of society. Politics is now the problem, not the solution.

Yet it was not a jealous singularity which put a stop to Stalinism. Neither were the armies which put paid to Hitler suffused by an experience of transcendent otherness. What one might loosely call post-structuralist or postmodern ethics reflects among other things a massive failure of political nerve on the part of a European intelligentsia confronted not only with the formidable power of global corporate capitalism, but still languishing guiltily in the long shadow of the Gulag and the gas chambers. This failure of nerve is not to be dismissed simply as the bad faith of ex-Trotskyist turncoats, in some flourish of leftist triumphalism. Belief can indeed be perilous, as an era awash with various crazed fundamentalisms scarcely needs reminding. We need a degree of certainty in order to thrive, but too much of the stuff can prove fatal. A cautious liberal pragmatism, coupled with a salutary scepticism of grand narratives, may thus appear the order of the day. But though such pragmatism can valuably contest dogmatic irrationalism, it is powerless to transform the conditions which give birth to it. Besides, if the twenty-first-century conflict between capitalism and the *Qur'an* (or a tendentious reading of that text) does not constitute a grand narrative, it is hard to know what does.

If, then, one transposes the moral law into the call of the sublimely inaccessible Other, an Other who is singular and unique rather than remote and anonymous, one can cling to the mysterious Kantian imperative while retrieving it from the symbolic order it regulates. Levinas deploys the deontological language of the symbolic, with its idiom of obligation, command, duty, guilt, responsibility and the like; but he does so in a style which undermines the familiar furnishings of the symbolic order, such as law, moral discourse, social relations and collective political practice. At the same time, he adopts the idiom of the imaginary – creatureliness, corporeality, life, enjoyment, sensibility, suffering, pain, passivity and so on – in a way which also puts the symbolic at arm's length. Like Lacan, Levinas seems to assume (falsely, as we shall see) that ethics is primarily about obligation; but to stage this obligation as a matter of flesh and living presence, self and inimitable Other, is to rescue the idea from what can be seen as the less palatable, aridly rationalist aspects of the Kantian tradition.

In one sense, the law is non-identical with the Other, since it is bestowed from some place infinitely beyond both him and myself. In another sense, the law is no less than this Other in person. Deontology becomes phenomenology, as the intolerable millstone of the moral law becomes incarnate in the well-nigh unbearable burden of the other's ineluctable demand. The harshness of the Kantian moral law remains firmly in place; but its brutal lack of realism is tempered by a phenomenological vocabulary (openness, otherness, bodiliness and so on) more hospitable to a late modern or postmodern age. Sensibility becomes the medium of obligation. The law retains all its inhuman transcendence; it is as unconditional an imperative as Kant's; but it is now fleshed out in the corporeal form of a feeling, afflicted fellow creature. In this sense, one might claim, the moral law is both returned to the imaginary and converted to the Real. It is as though the familiar alter ego of the imaginary, once invested with the awesome imperative of the symbolic law, becomes the singular, enigmatic subject of the Real.

In this way, too, the fraught relation of law and love can be resolved – for the Other, as the object of one's love, is imbued with the absolute force of an edict, just as one's response to him has a law-like necessity about it. In his Judaic fashion, Levinas severs the sentimental bond between *agape* and affection – which for him is also to cut the link between affection and the affective. We feel the Other affectively, on our pulses or in the crawling of our skin; but this must be distinguished from some common-or-garden affectionateness. The love Levinas speaks of is one located in the Real, far removed from the genial empathy of an Adam Smith. Ethics is what hurts. If the relation with the Other has the nearness of the imaginary, the Other in question is not Smith's or Hume's cherished companion. He is, in Levinas's own word, anyone who happens to 'befall' us, and is thus always a potentially hostile stranger. As with the eighteenth-century moralists, however, one needs to put a face on this Other, stranger or not. In speaking of the Other, Levinas is not promoting an ethics of anonymity, a phrase he would no doubt find oxymoronic. It is *proximate* strangers, not far-flung or abstractly apprehended ones, who command our response. Our anonymous relations with others are for the most part taken care of not by ethics but by politics.

There are negative as well as positive consequences to this rupture with the imaginary. Negatively speaking, it is also a break with the everyday virtues of affection, benevolence, companionship, equality, mutuality, taken-for-granted intimacy and – anathema to Levinas and the postmodern sensibility he has helped to mould – a delight in sameness as well as difference. It belongs to the good life to enjoy the company of those like ourselves, as long as it is not injurious to those who are excluded. Only the Stoic or hard-line rationalist insists that our feeling for intimates must differ not a whit from our response to strangers. Yet Levinas is too nervous of converting the Other to an imaginary alter ego to endorse such commonplace affinities. Orthodox philosophy, he declares, is from start to finish the reduction of otherness to sameness – an extravagantly homogenising claim if ever there was one. The Levinasian subject would doubtless go to the gallows for you, but he would be unlikely to prove the liveliest of companions in the pub. Nor would he be the most trustworthy consultant on, say, immigration legislation or animal rights, empirical matters from which his thought is loftily removed. These are merely moral affairs, fit meat for the parson rather than the philosopher. It is not clear how one moves from an infinite openness to the other to the business of tackling tax evasion. And for a good many tangible others (Asians, for example, or Arabs), this robustly Eurocentric thinker betrays a mixture of aversion and distaste.

Ethics is generally regarded as the science of morality, and so is already at one remove from actual behaviour; but Levinas's moral philosophy is intended as a species of meta-ethics, a reflection on the conditions of possibility of the ethical itself, and thus stands at two removes from empirical conduct. One might even risk calling it a matter of the ethical unconscious, despite Levinas's suspicion of the anti-humanist Freud. Run-of-the-mill morality is not to be confounded with the sublimity of the ethical life, which is accordingly emptied of specific content. Yet the more portentously empty the ethical imperative ('Be infinitely responsible!'), the more beguiling mystery it radiates, and so the more vacuously authoritative it grows. When Levinas does deign to descend to the sphere of mundane morality, his judgements are not always entirely trustworthy. 'Don't kill me!' is in his view what the face of the Other entreats; yet killing, as Aquinas understood, may be not only permissible but obligatory. What if the 'face' you confront is that of a psychopath with a machine-gun trained on a classroom of schoolchildren? Levinas has an immanent view of ethics, hearing the call of the infinite in the destitute and dispossessed; yet the style of thought in which he frames this view only succeeds in disincarnating it. For this champion of Zionism, for example, the dispossessed are certainly not the Palestinians. If he calls upon the human subject to shed its imperial pretentions, he fails to address the same demand to the state of Israel. There is a sense that to put an empirical countenance on the face, or lend a degree of determinacy to its demand, would be to diminish its absolute authority. Like Heidegger, he invests the ordinary with a depth which at once enhances and diminishes it. He is, so to speak, far too deep a thinker.

In any case, it is far from clear that all ethical questions can be reduced to the elevation of otherness over identity. This anti-reductionism is itself reductionist. The protection of the planet, campaigns against political corruption, the banning of black marketeering or mendacious advertising are not easily reducible to a reverence for the Other. Levinas would no doubt object to lying as a violation of the Other's trust; Thomas Aquinas objects to it as a devaluation of the currency of the symbolic order. If men respected women's otherness, would there then be no need for equal wages? And how does the latter follow from the former? And what if the Other is destitute because we are not? What if it is this – the condition of exploitation – which constitutes the most vital ethical relationship between us? Will phenomenology alone inform us of this fact?

In any case, is not an openness to alterity a condition of ethics rather than the thing itself? And would not this be more evident if one began in Aristotelian style from the premise that ethics is a practice rather than a state of being, not to speak of a state beyond being? What would it mean to be open to the otherness of Joseph Stalin or Rupert Murdoch? Is not the notion of absolute openness, along with absolute otherness and absolute responsibility, a logical absurdity? Jacques Derrida asserts that wherever there is absolute otherness, there is God, which seems a convenient enough way of demonstrating his non-existence. Otherness is not a given: it is constituted by our dealings with each other, and is therefore bound up with identity and reciprocity. Human interaction involves identity as well as difference. The notion of communication is the ruin of both absolute identity and absolute alterity. Forms of otherness like the kettle, which can enter into dialogue with human beings only in fairy tales, are by no means of the same order as the otherness of other humans. Peaches are not unique in the way that persons are. To respect your otherness, I must be aware that I am in the presence of an autonomy of a specifically human kind, not, say, of a leaf-like or computer-like kind; and I cannot know this without implicit reference to a shared humanity.

Absolute responsibility, likewise, is really a case of Hegel's 'bad infinity'. It is ridiculous to claim that I am absolutely responsible for the secret police who are torturing me. As for openness, must it not already be secretly informed by moral criteria of a codifiable kind if we are to distinguish between being open to the starving who beg us for bread, and being open to those who traffic heroin to schoolchildren? No doubt we should respect the autonomous being of such traffickers, feeling ourselves suitably traumatised and abjected by their transcendent presence; but ethics is to do with stopping them in their tracks, not with a numinous sense of their difference. Iago is open to Othello; it is just that the mode of this supersensitivity is known as implacable hatred. Like sincerity, openness is a *sine qua non* which means nothing in itself. Taken in itself, it is as portentously hollow as the Kantian categorical imperative. The Judaeo-Christian commandment is to love one's neighbour *in* her otherness, which is to say, 'in the Real', not to love her otherness.

Levinas's ethical thought manages at times to obscure this truth, since it attends to the subject's selfless relation to the Other; and it does so because to think of the Other in terms of the self would seem to rehearse a customary Western vice. Self and Other, as we have seen, are supposedly incommensurate, in the sense that though I can substitute myself for you, you cannot do the same for me. But this, of course, is true only phenomenologically. From the viewpoint of what Levinas calls 'the third' or the symbolic order, it is clear enough that the Other bears the same responsibility for me as I do for him, a fact of which Levinas is naturally aware. He thus presents us with a kind of modified Spinozism. For Spinoza, as we have seen, we exist phenomenologically speaking as though the world were centred upon ourselves, while being theoretically aware that this egocentrism, since it is true of all men and women, is self-negating. For Levinas, to live ethically is to live non-egocentrically, conscious that of all human

beings I am the most abject and decentred, while being aware that from a
theoretical standpoint this is a necessary fiction. It is a fiction because if it
is universalised to all men and women, as it must be, it cancels through.
What is true for me phenomenologically really is true; but it is, as it were,
folly to Greeks, and not the truth as it presents itself to philosophy. What
ethics reveals is not what ontology could ever hope to acknowledge. The
latter deals with what we have in common, while the former trades in singularity. But what if ethics and ontology were not so opposed? What if an
immeasurable abjection were what we had in common? If the Other relates
to me (as abjected, traumatised, held hostage and the like) just as I relate
to him, then the non-relation between us, so to speak, becomes symmetrical. Equality and commensurability are thus not so quickly banished by the
all-demanding Other. It is on the ground of our shared trauma – which is
to say, on the common terrain of the Real – that a free, equal and fulfilling
encounter between us becomes possible.

The phenomenological paradox is that I can only register the density of
Otherness as I feel it on my own pulses, thus courting the risk of confiscat-
ing it in that very act. To this extent, there is a danger of Levinas's phenomenological method running contrary to his moral doctrine. He himself,
however, claims that this need not land us in the egological quagmire of a
Husserl – not only because the Other is present to me at some level incomparably deeper than the egoic (indeed, incomparably deeper than mere
'presence'), but because what a phenomenology of the Other reveals is that
my own precious selfhood is no more than a fraught relation to alterity.
The meaning of my life is in every sense beyond me. The self-brooding ego
is accordingly chastened, abruptly relieved by the Other of its narcissistic
delusions. Yet all this remains within the frame of a certain phenomenological relation to the Other, and Levinas's moral reflections are constrained by this fact. For by stepping outside this phenomenological
framework, within which the Other is always perceived as my superior, I
am able to perceive that he is in fact no more than a guilt-ridden mode of
subjection to myself, as I am to him; and if this is so, then this reciprocal
service or self-giving, suitably transfigured, might lay the ground for a different form of relationship altogether – one in which mutual dependency
becomes the condition of mutual freedom, self-bestowal the source of self-
fulfilment. This, among other things, would be one way of negotiating the
passage from the ethical to the political, as Levinas himself characterises
those spheres. Since the 'law' one confronts in this condition is no longer
some imperious superego, but the law of one's own fulfilment in and
through the fulfilment of the other, the result is a diminishing of the guilt

which in Levinas's view lies at the very core of the ethical. One might claim that true morality is more or less the opposite of guilt; so that an ethical theory like Levinas's or Derrida's in which guilt plays so prominent a role, not to speak of one to which the notion of human flourishing is largely alien, is seriously defective. Levinas feels guilty not only in the presence of the Other, but about ideas of happiness, freedom, gratification and self-fulfilment. It is hard to see how his guilt over such notions, not to say his occasional contempt for them, can truly be of service to the Other. The Other is not best served by self-laceration.

The eighteenth-century moralists we have examined advocate an exchange of sympathies with others, but one, perhaps, with a certain suspicious facility. This kind of sympathy seems too warmly spontaneous to be entirely ethical. Kant and Levinas, by contrast, are bent on the subjugation of men and women to the moral law or the Other. From a Judaeo-Christian viewpoint, both styles of ethical thought, sympathetic and sacrificial, are disfigured by their separation from one another. The advocates of self-fulfilment generally fail to grasp just what painful self-abandonment this would actually entail, not least if it were to be politically available to everyone. For their part, the purveyors of a sacrificial ethics seem not to see that if this self-abnegation is not made in the name of a more prodigal abundance of life all round, it remains no more than a morbid compulsion. Sacrifice is a revolutionary passage from victimage to power, a turbulent transition from destitution to riches. It is not an end in itself. Tragically, however, it may prove the essential precondition of what appears at first sight its opposite: an ethics of pleasure, well-being and self-fulfilment in the service of others. That this is so is much to be regretted.

The infinite is alive for Levinas in persons, since to be a person is to manifest an absolute otherness which can be no more weighed or measured than infinity itself. There is a peculiar kind of paradox here. To be mortal is to be finite; but it is also to be aware of the finitude signified by one's death, and thus (since nobody can do my dying for me) of one's inimitable singularity. Such singularity, however, exactly because it is irreplaceable, incommensurable and non-replicable, can be seen as a kind of infinity. Like Kierkegaard, Levinas is gripped by the mind-warping fact, at once momentous and banal, that one is oneself and not someone else from all eternity. So finitude, ironically, breeds an awareness of its opposite, as it does in Kant's aesthetics of the sublime. It is not, however, an infinity which in Levinas's view is incarnate in history, politics, Nature, biology or run-of-the-mill moral issues – in a word, in everyday life, for which, like a number of his Gallic philosophical colleagues, he maintains a certain fine disdain.

Transcendence must not be compromised by immanence: it is irreducible to presence, and is therefore, except in the unpresentable face of the Other, disincarnate. The Other, who is pure transcendence, may offer a means of redemption; but the *polis*, with its abstract, anonymous life-forms, is not up to such a task. There can be no institutional redemption, no radically transformative politics. Politics left to itself, Levinas announces, courts the risk of tyranny. There is a problem, in other words, about the faceless, just as there is for Hume and Smith. After our trek through the symbolic order, we seem to have come full circle – though the name of what resists the anonymity of the symbolic is now not the imaginary but the Real. It is as though Levinas turns his back on the imaginary, of which he retains only the barest outline; but in doing so he bypasses the symbolic and moves straight to the Real. He can deal, to be sure, with the *proximate* stranger – which is to say, with whatever member of the symbolic order happens for the moment to occupy the location of neighbour. One's relationship to this figure mixes elements of the imaginary and the Real: the imaginary, because what is at stake here is a corporeal compassion for one close to hand; the Real, because this neighbour, even if she happens to be your daughter or sister, is an inscrutable avatar of the infinite, and can be dealt with appropriately only if she is seen against this luminous backdrop. What is harder for so intimate an ethics to grasp is the domain of the symbolic as such, which risks in a pincer movement being squeezed out by the other two. We shall see in a moment, however, that Levinas is well aware of this difficulty, which is nothing less than the problem of politics, and seeks to address it without relaxing his grip on his highly idiosyncratic brand of moral thought.

For all its seductive carnality, there is something altogether too high-pitched and portentous about Levinas's style of moral discourse. A Christian or Jew would no doubt want to insist that he has a magnificent sense of the transcendence of God, but for just that reason fails to grasp how this ineffable enigma is incarnate not only in the otherness of the Other, but in his or her routine availability, in everyday fellowship and familiarity. The Levinasian Other, in Burkean terms, is more sublime than beautiful. Such an ethics is far from the Christian notion that men and women have been invited through the humanity of Christ to share in God's friendship, not simply to feel his numinous presence in the Other like an agonising wound or guilty start from slumber. Ethical responsibility for Levinas is not really part of the phenomenal world, though it is there that it must manifest itself. He consequently shares something of Kant's difficulty in explaining how the spirit of ethics is to be made flesh. There is the totality of determinable objects, and there is, as in the thought of Alain Badiou, a quite separate sphere of infinity which cuts across it in a violently dislocating gesture; but it is hard to see how the two can be reconciled.

How, then, is the problem of the faceless, those who fall outside the numinous circuit of self and Other, to be addressed? If this is a vital issue, as it is for the benevolentists, it is because it raises nothing less than the question of politics – of how ethics bears upon all those issues which are more than interpersonal. Levinas's problem here is that he has framed the ethical in such full-bloodedly non-social terms, in a language so aloofly indifferent to community, consensus, equality, civil rights, legality, universality, reciprocity, natural qualities, the generic and so on, that he makes it well-nigh impossible for himself to conjure a politics from it, beyond the most banal variety of liberal pluralism. This, indeed, is a truth almost universally acknowledged among his commentators. Like Derrida, Levinas acknowledges the inescapability of the political; but one feels at times that he would rather that it went away. By and large, the symbolic order proves to be a stumbling block to his remarkable amalgam of the imaginary and the Real. There is a bathetic contrast in the writings of both Levinas and Derrida between the arresting, avant-garde pitch of their theory and the tediously familiar brand of multiculturalism which it seems to involve in practice. Like David Hume, Levinas has trouble with strangers – not, to be sure, with those of them who are 'proximate', but with the anonymous masses who at any given moment happen not to be so. (The case is even worse when the masses in question are non-European: witness his deep distaste for what he calls the 'yellow peril' in *Les Imprévus de l'histoire*.) If the champions of the imaginary find it hard to cope with those beyond their own charmed circle, so in a different way do the sponsors of the Real.

Even so, Levinas has various shots at a solution.[9] In one's encounter with the privileged Other, the potential presence of countless others is implicitly revealed. In this sense, what Levinas names *le tiers* or third party already stages an appearance on this primal scene in what one might call the Levinasian Oedipal moment, rupturing the relationship between self and other. At times in Levinas's writings, the third party would seem to arrive on the scene subsequent to the face-to-face relation, a case which differs sharply from that of Lacan. If Lacan writes the other as Other, it is to insist that there can be no unmediated relation with it – no liaison with the 'unique'

---

[9]   For an excellent account, see Howard Caygill, *Levinas and the Political* (London and New York, 2002).

other which does not pass through the refractions of the symbolic order as a whole. What Levinas would call the 'third' is thus inscribed within any face-to-face encounter from the outset, as an estranging dimension of that rapport.

At other times, however, the presence of the third party for Levinas informs the relation with the Other from the outset. When this is the case, the epiphany of the face opens up to me the whole of destitute humanity, along with the discourse of universal reason and justice. The face of the Other itself places one in relation to the third, which in turn opens up the continent of law, the state and political institutions. In an alternative formulation, the face discloses the 'Other of the Other' – which is to say yet another asymmetrical relation between my Other and *his* Other, suggesting that society is no more than a multiplicity of singular selves. The Other is now an unforgettable face among a whole array of unforgettable faces. Yet the face-to-face relationship remains originary – not only in the sense that, being prior to freedom, autonomy, decision and so on, it pre-dates all questions of politics or justice, but also because it is the place where we are first turned outward to the symbolic order, as we become conscious of a network of responsibilities stretching beyond the irreplaceable Other. Through the presence of the third party there emerges justice, objective knowledge, equality, ontological stability, reciprocity and the rest of that symbolic baggage.

In this sense, the passage from ethics to politics is immanent in what one might call the primal scene, even if that scene also serves as a permanent critique of the political. The Other in *Totality and Infinity* is an epiphany of equality (in the form of the third party) as well as asymmetry. The unique Other implies the possibility of others, who might always become Others too. Others, then, may be of concern to the self without entering into conjunction with it – a condition which belongs to what Levinas names *illeity*, and which is among other things his own idiosyncratic term for the symbolic order. The privileged relationship with the unique Other must be 'moderated' so that law, justice, equality and social conscience may emerge. Love of one's neighbour already implies justice, since it must happen within the context of that neighbour's relations to third parties. I must consider not only my relation to the Other, but my relation to the relations between others. Justice is to that degree 'necessary' – a term which, so one might think, scarcely captures the traditional Judaic thirst for it.

So there are pathways from ethics to politics. All the same, questions of justice, liberation, equality and so on derive from the primordial encounter with the Other (a confrontation which is closed to outside knowledge), and must find their way back to it as a traveller in the desert must return for periodic replenishment to a spring. Ethics is the phenomenological ground of politics, and the prophet is the discomforting figure who recalls us from the shabby compromises of the latter to the purity of heart of the former. 'Justice', Levinas writes, 'is impossible without the one who renders it finding himself in proximity.'[10] This, one takes it, means not that we must be personally acquainted with those to whom we do justice, but that the infinite responsibility of the proximate must be the source from which our less proximate moral dealings flow. Yet the relation between these two spheres remains elusive. Ethics must govern routine behaviour, but cannot be reduced to it. As an infinite obligation to the Other, it is the source of everyday morality; but it also appears as a domain quite distinct from it. The ethical must not be confounded with the quantifying, workaday world of rules, codes, obligations, conventions and specific injunctions. Yet general codes and institutions (politics) must somehow be derived from an irreducibly singular relationship (ethics). The incommensurable must give birth to the commensurable.

We have seen, however, that Levinas is deeply sceptical of the generic, universal, normative, conventional, commensurable, reciprocal and so on, which would seem to risk subverting the very ethical foundation from which they are supposed to spring. The ethical is in perpetual danger of being negated by a system of universal laws which it nonetheless requires. It resists the identificatory logic of a *polis* on which it is nevertheless dependent. The demand of justice germinates in the ethical sphere, but is also controverted, even betrayed, by that realm's non-reciprocal nature. An abyss yawns between the disinterested province of the ethical and the considerably less glamorous world of mundane moral interests. In his characteristically backwoods, anti-Enlightenment way, Levinas fears what he calls in *Totality and Infinity* 'the tyranny of the universal and impersonal'; but he must acknowledge all the same that a 'comparison of incomparables' is essential if justice is to flourish. This in turn, he confesses, requires a form of reason that synthesises and synchronises – operations for which one suspects he has almost as little enthusiasm as he has for Arab nationalism. It would not be too much to claim that the symbolic order is the implacable enemy of his most cherished values, even though as a moralist he must of course address it.

---

[10] Levinas, *Otherwise than Being*, p. 159.

The ethical for Levinas is a relation between one absolute singularity and another – the love, in effect, of stranger for stranger, even if the two involved are intimate friends, which takes place outside all political community. If ethics is defined as the absolute irreducibility of the other to the same (a deeply questionable proposal, to be sure), then it lies askew to the comparisons and equivalences of the public sphere. The ethical subject is distinct from the citizen, even though (like Kant's noumenal and phenomenal realms) they both inhabit the same body. Though both spheres must be affirmed, there seems a chronic state of conflict between them. The ethical 'interrupts' the political – a case which implies that difference, otherness and a sense of the infinite must be brought to the political realm from the outside. Politics, it would seem, is not immanently capable of generating such values, despite the curious prevalence of multiculturalism, cultures of respect, cults of social difference and so on which surround us on all sides. Ethics, then, irrupts into the political arena, but it does not fundamentally transform it. The political tends naturally to the uniform and degenerate, and the most ethics would appear capable of is to shake it up from time to time. One might contrast this with a socialist or feminist morality, for which political change is the ground of transformed ethical relations between individuals. Such politics involve a transformation of the very meaning of the political. Ethics on this view is not simply a superaddition to existing modes of political existence. Far from being an outside intervention into the *polis*, it is a specific way of describing it.

At his least inspirational, Levinas portrays political society as riven by a state of permanent warfare, a Hobbesian struggle for power amongst wolfish competitors. At best, the *polis* is portrayed as a largely neutral sphere, an indispensable but unedifying province of norms and exchanges. Whereas the ethical has all the turbulent passion of high drama, the political is a second-rate documentary. A view of the *polis* as a place of alienation reflects an alienated view of politics. Levinas speaks in an interview of 'the socio-political order of organising and improving our human survival', a piece of bureaucratese which would scarcely serve as an adequate description of politics for Rousseau, Burke or Marx. If politics appears to have been drained of much of its value, reduced to a sphere of arbitrary decisions and administrative devices, then one can see why ethics will need to parachute in a set of self-grounding values from some spiritual outer space. The business of how the two realms are conjoined is then bound to prove tortuous. But this need not be the case if one were to begin with a less jaundiced view of the political. One is reminded of those late nineteenth-century neo-Kantian Marxists who were driven to Kant's ethics in order to lend value to a history which they, through their own determinism had bleached of moral purpose. Without the ethical to challenge, disrupt and renew it, political society can engender no profound value in itself. Ethics is essential partly because politics is spiritually bankrupt. The idea that the political might in turn pose a challenge to the ethical – that, say, a mode of treating others might be transformed by institutional change – passes largely unregarded.

Much the same, as we shall see in a moment, is true of the later Jacques Derrida. In the wake of the heady events of 1968, as Western capitalism consolidated its power and whole sectors of the political left sank accordingly into disillusion, the very concept of politics came increasingly under philosophical fire, not least in a France whose intelligentsia were sliding rapidly into strident reaction. A handful of these disaffected spirits reached back to a previous epoch of political disenchantment – the bitter experience of fascism and Stalinism, in the light of which all collective or utopian projects seemed doomed to spawn monstrous despotisms. Jacques Derrida's debt to Emmanuel Levinas, a man who spent time in a Nazi labour camp, is one such conjuncture between two different historical moments.

One difference for Levinas between the sphere of the Other and the province of politics is that relations in the former are asymmetrical, and in the latter a question of equality or reciprocity. But the distinction needs to be queried. It is true, as we have seen, that the condition which Levinas takes as his moral prototype involves asymmetry and abjection, since the Other is lowlier and needier than myself and therefore, in the annals of Judaic wisdom, higher as well. But this is not in fact the prototype of human love. In the fullest sense of the term, there can be no love without equality and mutuality. It is true that the New Testament commands the unilateral love of enemies, just as it is true that we can have genuine love for creatures such as infants, not to speak of rabbits, who are unable fully to return our affection. But though unilateral love – love which involves reckless, fruitless self-expenditure, gritting its teeth in the face of malice and mockery – is more morally deserving than love which is mutual, not least because it is incomparably more taxing, it is also in a sense less perfect. It is less perfect because in this situation one of the partners does not flourish in and through the flourishing of the other(s), which is what love in the fullest sense involves. That love in the most complete sense is possible only among equals is why, in Christian doctrine, the Father loves his creatures in and through the humanity of their elder brother his Son, in whom they are raised from mere creaturehood to friendship and equality with him. Otherwise God could love us only as we might love our hamsters or Volvos. Not to acknowledge that love and equality are interwoven in this way is to reinforce the frontiers between ethics and politics, or love and justice. It is also, as we shall see later, to overlook the concept of political love, which similarly breaches the barriers between the two domains.

There is another sense in which equality and singularity are not as discrepant as Levinas would assume. To treat others equally is not to treat them the same, the upshot of which would be flagrant injustice, but to address oneself with equal, disinterested attentiveness to their uniquely different needs. Identity and difference are not in this sense naturally at loggerheads. Sylviane Agacinski, who like Levinas contrasts a relationship between absolute singularities with the impersonal equivalences of the symbolic order, is thus mistaken to claim that 'in a case of ethical respect or dutiful loving, my relationship flows from a requirement which is indifferent to the individuality of the other . . .'.[11] It is only because Levinas assumes a bourgeois notion of equality as abstract equivalence that he is forced to consign the concept to the ancillary sphere of the political, while singularity becomes the preserve of the ethical.

For Marx, by contrast, all men and women must be granted equal respect, but it belongs to that respect to acknowledge that their needs are uniquely different. This is one reason why he opposes the idea of equality of income in his *Critique of the Gotha Programme*. Abstract equality is not a socialist virtue, however progressive a value it may have been in its day. Equality for Marx, a thinker who is indebted both to Romantic particularism and Enlightenment universalism, must be incarnate in human difference, rather than riding roughshod over it. The Marxian species of socialism means simply this: that the material means have now been established for human community, which has so far tended to flourish at the cost of individual freedom, to be reinvented at the level of the unique, richly evolved individual. This is why Marxism celebrates as well as castigates the great middle-class liberal heritage. In a socialist democracy, all men and women will have an equal right to participate in the determination of the common life; but how they do so will depend on their individual capabilities.

---

[11]   Sylviane Agacinski, 'We Are Not Sublime: Love and Sacrifice, Abraham and Ourselves', in Jonathan Rée and Jane Chamberlain (eds), *Kierkegaard: A Critical Reader* (Oxford, 1998), p. 146.

The ethical thought of Jacques Derrida need not detain us long. It is for the most part an extended footnote to Levinas's own meditations, with which Derrida, rather oddly in the light of his various critiques of the senior philosopher, once declared himself in entire agreement. Derrida writes excitedly of Levinas having revolutionised the whole meaning of ethics; but this overlooks the way in which the latter's work is still indebted to a traditional (deeply suspect) notion of ethics primarily as obligation, as indeed is Derrida himself. The prominence of Kant in French academia is enough to ensure that even the most outlandishly bohemian of Parisian thinkers pay homage to notions of moral duty which are elsewhere being steadily consigned to the ashcan of history. Taking his cue from his older colleague, Derrida assumes without question that an authentic ethics must pivot on the idea of responsibility – an assumption which would have come as something of a surprise to Aristotle, Hume, Bentham or Nietzsche. The ethical thought of Levinas and Derrida remains caught within the confines of the deontological. It is just that it manages to translate a rather pedestrian discourse of laws, rights and universal subjects into an altogether more poetic or phenomenological idiom, a rhetoric of risk, call, command, adventure, alterity, enigma, infinity and impossibility. With Levinas and Derrida, we are offered a kind of mystified version of Kantian ethics, one which invests it with the poetic resonance in which the sage of Königsberg is so painfully lacking. Derrida's early work is not notable for its engagement with the ethical; but in his late essay 'Force of Law' he is to be found arguing that deconstruction *is* justice, rather as he claims in *Spectres of Marx* that he has regarded deconstruction all along as a radicalised form of Marxism. It is hard to say which of the two theoretical camps in question found the latter claim more astonishing.

Like Levinas, Derrida deploys the ethical to denigrate the socio-political. 'There is no responsibility', he writes, 'without a dissident and inventive rupture with respect to tradition, authority, orthodoxy, rule, or doctrine.'[12] The ethical is a form of spiritual vanguardism which breaks disruptively into the self-satisfied inertia of everyday life. It does not seem to occur to Derrida, caught as he is in a rigid opposition between the dissident and the normative, that there are inventive traditions as well as oppressive ones, enlightened as well as barbarous orthodoxies, revolutionary as well as repressive norms, protective as well as bureaucratic rules, or benign as well as noxious forms of authority. There are also plenty of deeply unpleasant kinds of marginality, criminal modes of transgression, benighted styles of

---

[12] Jacques Derrida, *The Gift of Death* (Chicago, 1995), p. 51.

dissent and injurious forms of rule-breaking. Consensus can be radical, and nonconformity odiously privileged. Community – a concept of which, so Derrida informs us in *On the Name*, he has always been suspicious – can be nourishing as well as stifling. So hostile to the notion is Derrida, however, that J. Hillis Miller can write with some justice that his work is marked by 'the fundamental assumption that every self or *Dasein* is absolutely isolated from all the others'. 'Between my world and every other world', he quotes Derrida as writing in a personal file, '. . . there is . . . an interruption incommensurable with all attempts at passage, of bridge, of isthmus, of communication, of translation, of trope, and of transfer. There is no world, there are only islands.'[13] We are dealing not with alterity but with monadology.

Whatever Derrida may think, the ethical is not spontaneously at odds with the commonplace, determinate, orthodox or consensual. The word 'doctrine' simply means 'what is taught', with no necessary suggestion of dogmatism. The work in which Derrida makes this tiresomely fashionable observation is a work of doctrine, and is none the worse for that. Nor do you escape determinate propositions by deploying Derrida's favourite, much overlaboured stylistic device, the rhetorical question ('What is it, to giggle? Can there be a kind of pure giggling free of law, duty, debt, obligation? Is this question even intelligible? And how about that one?'),[14] a device which insinuates a distinctive viewpoint while breeding a sense of excited openness.

Doctrine, however, belongs to the symbolic order, which is why Derrida is so shy of it. The ethical is the foe of the conceptually determinate. Responsibility involves 'absolute decisions made outside of knowledge and given norms, made therefore through the very ordeal of the undecidable'.[15] It is not clear whether the decision to have an abortion should be made outside the knowledge of how far advanced your pregnancy is; but Derrida is clearly not speaking of such vulgarly mundane matters. Instead, he holds the eccentric view that since decisions are not reducible to norms or criteria, they are a form of 'madness'.

In theological terms, Derrida is a fideist with a Protestant suspicion of rationality. In Kierkegaardian style, he holds that the leap of faith involved in ethical decisions is independent of reason. But decisions may be dependent upon reasons without being reducible to them. He points out that

---

[13]   J. Hillis Miller, 'Don't Count Me In', *Textual Practice*, 2:2 (June 2007), p. 285.

[14]   I trust that it is unnecessary to point out that this is my own invention.

[15]   Derrida, *Gift of Death*, p. 76.

moral choices cannot be 'insured' by a rule; but this is not to say that they cannot be guided by one. If he feels the need to insulate such decisions from reason, it is because he wants to rescue them from the ignominy of being no more than deductions from *a priori* principles. But this is like rescuing a swimmer who is palpably not drowning. Decisions can be reasonable without being rigorously deduced from principles, just as utterances can be grammatical without being mechanically predictable. Derrida seems not to recognise that to adduce reasons for one's commitments – reasons why one is hopelessly in love with one's chauffeur, for example – is not to reduce those commitments to such reasons. Someone else may feel the full force of my reasons yet not be in love with my chauffeur himself. Commitments must indeed be reasonable; but to insist on this requirement is not to resolve the question of why we take them up, since incompatible cases may be equally rational. It is how their reasonability engages us that matters; but this is not the same as a decision made in empty space.

If one were really to choose a course of action independently of all norms or criteria, it is hard to know in what sense it could be called a decision. It would be rather like calling a rumbling of the gut a royal proclamation. What so-called decisionism fails to recognise is that I cannot call what I do a choice if there are no criteria by which to choose. Ethics, so Derrida claims, is a matter of absolute decisions which are at once necessary and 'impossible' – a kind of implacable destiny for which, like Oedipus, we are none the less entirely to blame. One can only feel relief that he is no longer eligible for the jury when one's case comes up in court.

Like Levinas, Derridean ethics are founded largely on guilt, which one might see as the obverse of responsibility. My responsibility for the other must be absolute; yet if I am to be responsible for everyone, how can this be so? To dissolve my singularity in the collective or the general concept is to act irresponsibly; yet without such generic concepts, how can I conduct myself responsibly all round? All responsibility is absolute, singular, exceptional and extraordinary; yet any particular manifestation of it must therefore constitute a betrayal of my responsibility to everyone else. It is, as we shall see in a moment, a flagrantly false dilemma. Moreover, actual responsibility must involve calculation, one of the many motifs of the symbolic order which Derrida finds both distasteful and unavoidable. The term 'economy' is another such bugbear of his, suggesting as it does a drearily regulated exchange of goods, duties or services, one far removed from the madness of unlimited expenditure, the perilous venture of a commitment beyond norms, the fear and trembling of an absolute exposure to the Other. To be authentic, that exposure must be of a kind which 'doesn't keep account or give an account, neither to man, to humans, to society, to one's fellows, or to one's own'.[16] Accountability, Derrida insists, has its place; but one gathers from his tone that it is largely for dentists and grocers. One must render unto Caesar the things that are Caesar's, and to the absolute the things that are its own. To demand accounts and justifications is a form of 'violence' – a typically overblown post-structuralist flourish. Is this the case with holding railway companies to account for their negligence in causing accidents, or are we speaking at some altogether more sublime level?

Responsibility, Derrida writes, 'demands on the one hand an accounting, a general answering-for-oneself with respect to the general and before the generality, hence the idea of substitution, and on the other hand uniqueness, absolute singularity, hence non-substitution, non-repetition, silence and secrecy'.[17] We have seen already that this polarity can be deconstructed. True generality involves attending to the specific, not closing one's eyes to its peculiar claims in hot pursuit of the universal. The force of the term 'general' or 'universal' here is simply to remind us that we are speaking of any specificity whatsoever. There is no attempt here on Derrida's part to negotiate a passage from the singular to the universal, as there is, however laboriously and ambiguously, in the writings of Levinas. Like Kant's noumenal and phenomenal spheres, the two worlds exist cheek-by-jowl, divided by an unspannable abyss. Derrida is not a man for resolutions, which he unjustly suspects of being almost always anodyne and organicist. Ethics and politics exist in permanent conflict. Both, to be sure, are essential; but a distressing amount appears to be lost in the translation from the one to the other.

The Real of ethics resists the false consolations of the imaginary, while at the same time rebuffing the necessities of the symbolic. It sets its face against what Derrida dismissively terms the 'smooth functioning' of civil society, 'the monotonous complacency of its discourses on morality, politics, and the law, and the exercise of rights . . .'.[18] Do all forms of politics and morality, then, serve simply to buttress the smooth functioning of the status quo? Are all of civil society's discourses on politics, law and morality monotonously complacent? What of campaigns against war and poverty, laws against child abuse or struggles for the rights of immigrants? Where

[16]   Ibid., p. 101.
[17]   Ibid., p. 82.
[18]   Ibid., p. 71.

are the contradictions in this apparently monolithic social order? Why such violent homogenising of social existence from the pen of an apostle of difference? Derrida has much to say of the violence of law; but like most libertarian leftists he is silent on its capacity to safeguard, nurture and educate. Political emancipation is allotted an urgency which is foreign to the conservative Levinas; yet it is the notion of infinity, not politics, which fires the Derridean imagination. Simon Critchley adopts a similar view when he writes of ethics as 'anarchic meta-politics', or 'the continual questioning from below of any attempt to impose order from above . . . politics is the manifestation of dissensus, the cultivation of an anarchic multiplicity that calls into question the authority and legitimacy of the state'.[19] But what if the state in question is struggling to free itself from colonialism by revolutionary force? What if a particular current of dissent is reactionary? Can there be no radical consensus?

Derrida's essay 'Force of Law' is a classic instance of these prejudices. Law for Derrida is finite, determinate and largely negative, whereas justice is infinite, undecidable and supremely positive. It is as though justice, a precious keystone of the symbolic order, must be salvaged from that largely disreputable domain and invested instead with a quasi-religious aura. Levinas is more equivocal about the matter, uncertain at times whether to include justice in the ethical or political sphere. What seizes Derrida's attention is not run-of-the-mill legality, but a kind of justice which 'not only exceeds or contradicts law but also, perhaps, has no relation to law, or maintains such a strange relation to it that it may just as well demand law as exclude it'.[20] What he cherishes above all is the elusive, transgressive and undecidable, all of which are rather more glamorous than the drab determinacies of everyday existence. Like dentistry, the determinate in Derridean eyes is inevitable but unappealing. By and large, what is unequivocal is in his view uninspiring. It is a curiously rigid kind of doctrine. Derrida does not seem to appreciate that there are enthrallingly unambiguous utterances as well as tritely polyvalent ones. True pluralists understand that we sometimes need accounts as exact as we can make them, and sometimes not. Definitions may be emancipatory, or just (as Wittgenstein remarks) a kind of ornamental coping. For all the formidable power and originality of his work (he is surely one of the most eminent philosophers of his century), Derrida is the kind of thinker who in Bernard Williams's

---

[19]   Simon Critchley, *Infinitely Demanding* (London, 2007), p. 13.
[20]   'The Force of Law: The "Mystical Foundation of Authority"', in Jacques Derrida, *Acts of Religion* (New York and London, 2002), p. 223.

words 'makes a virtue out of uncertainty itself and, in place of conviction, enjoys the satisfactions . . . of a refined indecision'.[21] This is not to suggest that he has no convictions whatsoever.

Law for Derrida involves calculability, whereas justice is incalculable. The terms of the contrast are by now wearily predictable: law is a 'stabilisable, statutory and calculable apparatus, a system of regulated and coded prescriptions', an account which feigns neutrality but betrays a covert animus in its every word. Justice, by contrast, is 'infinite, incalculable, rebellious to rule and foreign to symmetry, heterogeneous and heterotropic'.[22] It exceeds rules, programmes and calculations. It is clear enough which pole of this opposition Derrida finds more seductive, even if it is the one which involves an aversion to taking sides. A somewhat perfunctory attempt at equity then follows. Equality and universal rights, so he claims, are as imperative as the heterogeneous and uniquely singular. One must deliver oneself over to ' the impossible decision' while 'taking account' of laws and rules. The excess of justice over law should not become an alibi for avoiding juridico-political battles. But this effort at equipoise is undermined by Derrida's ethical decisionism, which seems to regard authentic moral choices as transcendent of rules and reasons. If he were to allow the determinate due weight, he might bring himself to acknowledge that moral choices are still choices even when they are code-bound and rule-governed. For to follow a rule, as Wittgenstein points out in *Philosophical Investigations*, is not the same as being bound by a law. Applying rules is itself a creative practice. In fact, there would be no liberty without it. There is thus no need to rescue decisions from rules in order to preserve their freedom. Decisions are not a form of madness, as Derrida seems to consider. It is a form of madness to think so.

What does it mean to claim that justice is infinite? It is infinite, perhaps, in the sense that the passion for it is, as we have seen in the case of Shakespeare's Shylock and Kleist's Michael Kohlhaas; or in the sense that since there is no apparent end to injustice, there is no end to justice either. But justice is more properly to be seen as finite. Shylock's thirst for it may be unslakeable, but the object of his desire is one which he regards simply as his due. It is impartiality which he is after. Like revenge, justice is a question of tit for tat. It is a matter of weighing merits and calculating returns, practices which are by no means inherently mean-spirited or small-minded, as the ethical Realists seem to suspect. There is nothing small-minded

[21] Bernard Williams, *Ethics and the Limits of Philosophy* (Cambridge, MA, 1985), p. 169.
[22] Derrida, 'Force of Law', p. 250.

about asking for a loan which has left you semi-destitute to be returned now that your debtor has inherited a capacious estate. If the idea of justice poses something of a problem for both Levinas and Derrida, it is because both of them (not least because of their Judaic provenance) are passionately committed to it in practice, yet are at the same time wary of law, measure, rule and reciprocity, all of which they unjustly denigrate as an ethics of suburbia rather than of the sublime.

There is a sense in which Derrida manages to have his symbolic cake and eat it. If he abandons ethics, in the sense of the monotonous complacency of discourses on child abuse, he does so for the sake of ethics, in the sense of being answerable to the demand of the Real. In this sense, he rehearses the paradox of the potential child abuser Abraham in Kierkegaard's *Fear and Trembling*, torn as he is between his absolute duty to an apparently sadistic God and his love for his son Isaac. Or, in another idiom, caught between ethics, which for Derrida (though not for Levinas) is a question of generality, and the singularity of faith. Abraham, commanded by divine edict to slay his son, chooses God over the universal, the absolute singularity of his faith in the Almighty over general laws, and is thus both responsible and irresponsible. He opts for the Real, which is always an excess over and above the ethical, rather than for the obligations of the symbolic order. 'The absolutes of duty and of responsibility', insists Derrida, 'presume that one denounce, refute, and transcend, at the same time, all duty, all responsibility, and every human law.'[23] Yet those symbolic bonds are also to be cherished – for if Abraham did not love his son so dearly, slaughtering him would not of course count as a sacrifice. He must, as it were, hate Isaac in so far as he loves him, and in the act of destroying him immolate ethics as well. But this, too, would be no genuine sacrifice unless the value of the ethical were also acknowledged.

Abraham's outlook is not exactly dewy-eyed, yet he has the virtue of radical hope. It is a distinction between hope and optimism usefully illuminated by the American philosopher Jonathan Lear.[24] Abraham refuses to give up on his desire for the impossible – for a God whose commands are at one with the decrees of the symbolic order – in the unthinkable paradox known as 'faith', and it is because he clings so tenaciously to the impossible that it comes to pass, as God stays his hand and saves his son. His acceptance of the apparent fruitlessness of his deed is what finally

---

[23] Ibid., p. 78.
[24] See Jonathan Lear, *Radical Hope: Ethics in the Face of Cultural Devastation* (Cambridge, MA, 2006).

brings him through. He is, as Kierkegaard observes, 'great with that power which is powerless'. As in many a tragic plot, something will only come of nothing.

In Kierkegaard's view, the classical tragic hero moves within the sphere of the ethical, which means that his fate, however unenviable, is at least intelligible. Abraham, by contrast, bypasses the mediations of the ethical, in which all particulars are indifferently interchangeable, to establish an immediate relation with the absolute, one which pitches him beyond the frontiers of moral discourse and rational comprehension. Aesthetically speaking, one might claim that he resembles the Romantic symbol more than he does the practice of allegory. In being prepared to flout the claims of the ethical in the name of the Real, Abraham proves himself a living affront not only to conventional mores but to the Hegelian dialectic. He elevates the particular over the universal, opting for the illegible mystery of Yahweh's will as against the translucent representations of the symbolic order. To the eye of faith, there is an Other even beyond the symbolic Other. In this sense, Abraham dares to venture upon what for Kierkegaard is the most fearful project of all: existing as an individual. As we have seen already, individuals in this radical Protestant view are pure singularities, wholly incommensurable with one another. As such, they represent the ultimate ruin of the symbolic order, as well as of any rational politics. That which is purely and eternally itself is bound to elude the concept.

In behaving as he does, Abraham anticipates the tragic drama of Jesus's crucifixion. Only if Jesus is in the dark about his own destiny, his tormented pleadings on Calvary greeted by the resonant silence which is his Father, can he be raised in glory from the dead. Otherwise, he remains trapped in the logic of tit for tat or symbolic exchange: this ephemeral agony in return for heavenly bliss. Yet having manifested his faith in a God who transcends all such transparencies and equivalences, Abraham is returned to the symbolic order, united once more with his son Isaac. And this is a sign that the law of human love is indeed the medium of God's presence in the world. The ethical is suspended but not annulled. The structure of the fable is an ironic one. Indeed, the fable in its Kierkegaardian form comes from the pen of one of the great masters of irony of the modern age. Faith cannot be translated into ethical discourse without an illegible remainder; but neither do the two inhabit incommunicable worlds. If faith is folly to the wise, a species of enigma and sublimity which refuses to calculate returns, it is also incarnate in everyday human love; and human love is what the Abraham myth finally vindicates, as the son is joyfully restored to the father.

It is God's mercy, then, which rescues Isaac from his doom; but we should not thereby complacently assume that his logic is ours; and he has just granted Abraham a timely reminder of this inconvenient truth by the brutal *acte gratuit* of demanding his son's life. Derrida, by contrast, seeks to press the fable into the service of a certain radical Protestantism. God on this reading is a capricious, overbearing personage, as full of fads and whims as a pampered rock star. This, indeed, is what the average liberal humanist finds so distasteful about the tale; but it is what Derrida himself finds so alluring. Since he admires the gratuitous more than he does the reasonable – which is to say, since he associates reason with the political status quo, rather than (as with Hegel) with its political transformation – he finds this wayward, Pascalian sort of God by no means unpalatable. Fear and trembling are not entirely disagreeable emotions.

A fidelity to the Real (Derrida does not use the term, but he speaks of the experience of God as one of 'stupefied horror') will 'compel the (Kierkegaardian) knight of faith to say and do things that will appear (and must even be) atrocious'.[25] It is hard to know whether Derrida really means this – one *must* do things which are (literally?) atrocious? – or whether it is to be taken as yet another flamboyant rhetorical flourish. In any case, it does scant justice to the story of Abraham, whom Derrida portrays luridly at one point as a 'murderer'. But of course he isn't. Abraham does not slay his son, and it seems a touch short-sighted of Derrida to overlook this rather vital twist in the storyline. It is akin to supposing that Desdemona survives with a few minor scratches. Sylviane Agacinski makes a similar mistake, writing repeatedly of Abraham's 'crime'. But Abraham commits no crime, unless one happens to be a devotee of the thought police. There is, in the end, no conflict between the demand of the Real and the decencies of the symbolic. God is simply testing his disciple's faith. The fable is a dark parody of the creative recklessness of faith. The symbolic law – the command not to murder – *is* the demand of the Real. There is no contest at this level between immanence and transcendence. As the Judaeo-Christian tradition proclaims, God is present to us in so far as we are present to one another. He is incarnate in flesh and blood, not simply (as Derrida considers in his Jansenist fashion) an eternally inaccessible non-presence who puts a paltry human reason in its place. The fact that God and humanity are not ultimately at cross-purposes is known to Christian faith as the doctrine of the Incarnation. If God is indeed in one sense utterly other, he is also made manifest in the tortured body of a reviled political criminal. And this body,

---

[25] Derrida, *Gift of Death*, p. 77.

like all *pharmakoi* or monstrously polluted scapegoats, is 'other' or inhuman enough to be a suitable sign of him. The ghastly good news of the gospel is that being done to death by the state for speaking up for love and justice is the status to which we must all aspire. The message of the New Testament is that if you don't love you are dead, and if you do, they will kill you. Here, then, is your pie in the sky and your opium of the people. It is a message scandalous alike to the civilised liberal, the militant humanist and the wide-eyed progressivist.

That God is not wholly obscure is a point well understood by Levinas, for whom our access to transcendence is the face of the Other. Derrida, on the other hand, presses the conflict between Real and symbolic, God and neighbour, religious faith and social ethics, to a point of implausible dead-lock. The message of the Abraham saga is that Yahweh is indeed immanent in human love, but that we should not exploit this truth by treating him idolatrously as a supersized version of ourselves. To do so would be to view him in the imaginary – to reduce this non-god to a consoling alter ego, whose forbidden name we might then manipulate for our own ends. This manipulation, which turns faith into ideology, is known as the history of religion. So the absolute difference of Yahweh must be stressed along with his immanence – his non-being, his transcendence of human wheeler-dealing, the way he gives the slip to our reifying schemas and acts as a relentless critique of them all in his terrifyingly unconditional love. God is not himself an ethical being, though he is the cause of ethics in others. He is not an impeccably well-behaved mega-person of whom moral qualities can be predicated. He cannot be the subject of a purely rational theology *à la* Kant, with its tedious civic reasonableness. All this Derrida rightly perceives. But neither is Yahweh to be divorced from human ethics in some fit of fideism or post-structuralist flirtation with the mad, violent, absurd, irrational, gratuitous and impossible. The political in Derrida's view is at once the domain of the 'decision' and the zone of administration – which is to say that he overglamorises and devalues it at the same time. If the decisionism of the Nazi philosopher Carl Schmitt arises from a convulsion of Enlightenment rationality, that of Derrida and his acolytes is the symptom of a later historical crisis. It belongs to an era for which there can apparently be no rational basis for a radical politics.

What religious faith is for Kierkegaard, a numinous form of ethics is for Levinas and Derrida. If the Danish philosopher promotes religion over ethics, his French counterparts elevate an ethics of the Real over one of the symbolic. The Other is now the last trace of transcendence in a profane world. But it is a mistake to take the Abraham story as a paradigm of ethical existence. This, by and large, is the view of those who require their ethics to be more spiritually exalted than campaigns against supermarkets, more resonant with absurdities and impossibilities, aporias and infinities than the struggle to preserve a playschool. The Old Testament myth indeed concerns the absurdity of faith in the eyes of the theorists and philosophers; but the faith in question is in a Yahweh who fills the hungry with good things and sends the rich away empty. It is not, then, a question of faith versus ethics, or religion *contra* morality. It is rather that Abraham, in the teeth of all tangible evidence, clings steadfastly to the God of ethics and politics – the defender of the destitute, champion of the immigrant and liberator of the enslaved, the anti-religious god who despises the burnt offerings of the Hebrews and fulminates against the oppressors of the poor. A Derridean ethics might seem at first glance in line with the New Testament injunction to render unto Caesar what is his due, while granting God the things that are properly his. The claims of both spheres, symbolic and Real, must be satisfied; but there would seem more antagonism than affinity between the two. Politics and religion don't mix. Yet it is highly unlikely that this is how a devout first-century Jew would have understood Jesus's command. For the things that are God's include justice, mercy and righteousness, which for the Old Testament are made manifest in protecting the weak and welcoming the outcast. Modern distinctions between politics and religion are anachronistic here.

Abraham is traditionally treated as a prototype of the crucified Jesus, another figure who remains loyal in torment and bewilderment to a Father who seems to have failed him. But the two scriptural figures are alike in another sense, too. Both are abrasively critical of the symbolic order in the sense of kinship: Abraham because he is prepared to kill his own flesh and blood, Jesus because his attitude to the family is for the most part brutally dismissive. A new form of symbolic order or mass movement is to be carved out, one which will cut violently across sovereignties, blood relations and entrenched loyalties, dividing parents from children, setting neighbours violently at odds and ripping one generation from the arms of another.

The Derridean conflict between absolute singularity and universal responsibility – a conflict which in Derrida's view should be open to nothing as simple-minded as a solution – is a version of the Levinasian tension between ethics and politics. But it is also for the most part a false dilemma. The fact that in feeding my own cat (Derrida's own solemnly ludicrous example in *The Gift of Death*) I am inevitably neglecting all the other needy cats in the world is not, as Derrida considers, a matter of culpability; and I can only reasonably feel guilt over actions or omissions for which I am culpable. I cannot feed all the cats on the planet, not with the best will in the world and a fleet of trucks laden with minced liver. Responsibility is not in this sense infinite, and it is pointlessly hyperbolic to claim that it is. There are enough genuine occasions for guilt in the world without Parisian intellectuals concocting a few bogus additions. With equally grandiloquent absurdity, Levinas observes in the manner of some befuddled campaigning rock star that when we drink coffee each morning, we 'kill' an Ethiopian who has no coffee to drink himself. This, one might venture, is a vein of melodramatic hyperbole typical of some modern French philosophy, with its exorbitant vocabulary of 'madness', 'monstrosity', 'violence', 'impossibility', 'pure difference', 'absolute singularity' and the like. The tediously sober truth is that I am not at the moment of writing guilty of injustice to a suffering child in the Sudan whom I do not know, rather as by choosing to be in Galway I am in no sense casting aspersions on Nashville or Newcastle. The true resolution to the conflict of singularity and universality is one we have encountered already. One must grant full attention to the stranger who happens at the moment to occupy the location of neighbour, while doing just the same for the next any-old-body who chances along. Universality means being responsible for anyone, not, *per impossible*, for everyone at the same time. To assume that it does, even while insisting on its impossibility, betrays a certain hubris of the infinite, however apologetic and self-castigating in tone.

Levinas is surely right to hold that responsibility is infinite in at least this sense, that I must be ready to die for the Other. This is so even if she is a stranger or an enemy, which in a sense she always is. In fact, if others are enemies, it is partly because we might always be required to lay down our lives for them. One can only devoutly hope that so grossly inconvenient a demand never comes one's way, even though guerrilla fighters confront it all the time. In so far as one must be prepared to die for anyone without distinction, given the appropriate circumstances, equality and universality are bound up with love or ethics; they are not confined to the political sphere, as Levinas appears to imagine, just as love is not confined to the personal. (Alain Badiou is another who makes this stereotypically Gallic mistake about love, defining it largely in erotic terms and claiming that love begins where politics ends.) But one cannot, after all, die for everybody. Nor should one be excessively eager to relieve others of responsibility for themselves. Like any other human good, responsibility for others must operate within the constraints of prudence and realism. There is a proper kind of recklessness, which consists, for example, in dying for the sake of a stranger, and an improper kind, which consists (say) in throwing oneself in front of a truck so that a stranger may cross the street without the inconvenience of dropping his ice cream.

There is, then, something hopelessly cerebral about talk of infinity here. It is not, as Levinas seems occasionally to imagine, that my responsibility for the Other is infinite, whereas my debts to the faceless citizens of the symbolic order are strictly regulated. For one thing, I must be prepared in extreme circumstances to lay down my life for the faceless, not simply for those of them who have wandered into numinous proximity to me. For another thing, even when an erstwhile anonymous citizen assumes this location as Other, my relationship to him must continue to be governed by the requirements of prudence and justice. Justice is not simply a relation between anonymous citizens. It bears on our treatment of the Other as well. This is one of several reasons why no sharp distinction between ethics and politics can be sustained, a topic we shall be returning to in our Conclusion.

For Derrida as for Levinas, Otherness is a matter of absolute singularity, 'inaccessible, solitary, transcendent, non-manifest . . .'.[26] Solitary, because while ethics is a matter of right relations between oneself and others, it is not in the Realists' view a question of sharing one's life with them. As far as that goes, ethical Realism is as anti-social as the Kant whose gigantic bulk continues to overshadow it. In good, old-fashioned, deontological style, such an ethics bears on our obligations to others, not our enjoyment of them. Otherness here is not primarily the ground of friendship and affinity; instead, it is reified to an absolute condition, in which one's friends and neighbours become as awesomely inaccessible as the Satanic view of Yahweh. The terror that others will seek to assimilate us to themselves – the mighty neurosis of the postmodern – is now so acute that it licenses a mutual impenetrability. For the Lacanians, this is where ethics must begin. We must shape an existence with others founded on this shared strangeness. For Levinas and Derrida, an acknowledgement of this fearful opacity is often enough where ethics ends.

In the writings of Alain Badiou, perhaps the most influential of all contemporary French philosophers, the Real becomes the Event – that miraculous occurrence which surges up from an historical situation to which it

---

[26] Ibid., p. 41.

simultaneously does not belong. Events for Badiou are not bald historical facts but objects of faith. They are utterly original happenings founded purely in themselves, pure breaks and beginnings which are out of joint with their historical 'site', in excess of their contexts, sprung randomly and (as it were) *ex nihilo* from an established orthodoxy which could not have foreseen them. They are purely haphazard acts, as incalculable as grace or the strategies of a Mallarmé poem.

Truth events, as Badiou calls them, come in various shapes and sizes, all the way from the resurrection of Jesus to Jacobinism, falling in love to making a scientific discovery, the Bolshevik insurrection to the moment of Cubism, Schoenberg's atonal composition to the Chinese cultural revolution, and (Badiou's own personal, subject-constituting instance) the political turbulence of May 1968. All these avant-garde ruptures represent for him a 'void' in the situation of which they are formally part, a making present of an infinity which lurks within that situation but which cannot be fully articulated. In Badiou's view, there is an infinity of elements in any situation, a fact which provides a potential for anarchy or unpredictability which conventional power must police. It is this anarchic multiplicity, figuring as it does as a sort of transcendental *a priori* or unthinkable anteriority, which he sees as the 'void' within a situation – that which inheres in it but cannot be represented; and it is from this singular point of 'nothingness' that what he calls an event springs forth.

This, one might claim, is Badiou's rewriting of the Lacanian Real. An event is what evades the count; it is supernumerary, that which counts for nothing, that whose existence is purely undecidable from the viewpoint of the situation in which it occurs. Rather as not even the most obdurate of theological literalists could have taken a photograph of the Resurrection, so an event is unnameable within the situation in which it occurs. Like some stupendously avant-garde artefact, it signifies a pure origin or absolute novelty – one which bears no relation to the context to which it formally belongs, and which certainly cannot be captured in the woefully restricted lexicon of its speech. A situation can pronounce nothing of its own void. What the event itself grasps as truth, the situation in which it takes place regards as void of value.

Being in Badiou's view is an inexhaustible multiple, which comes to us in recognisable chunks or distinct situations only through the operation of being 'one-ed' or provisionally unified by a human subject. Otherwise, it is as infinitely inaccessible to us as Kant's noumenal sphere. In the presence of an event, however, it is as though the 'inconsistent multiplicity' which this counting-as-one conceals bursts momentarily out again, granting us a privileged glimpse of the disorderly infinity of pure Being. Events are explosive, ineffable exceptions to the rule, epiphanies of truth entirely without foundation. Like the Iranian revolution for Michel Foucault, they signify an ultimately inexplicable break with routine historical causality.[27] As such, they fly in the face of knowledge, reflection, ontology, calculability, law and morality – in brief, all of those orthodox categories for which the very existence of such events, like mathematical sets which belong purely to themselves, is strictly speaking impossible.

One might take leave to inquire how we are to determine what counts as such an event, or how we can know, say, that situations are infinitely multiple, unless the notion of truth is already in play from the outset. But truth for Badiou is more performative than propositional. Rather more gravely, one might also question the soundness of an ethics for which morality, in the sense of everyday estimations of right and wrong, is scathingly dismissed. Defending revolutionary violence in a hymn of praise to Mao's cultural revolution, Badiou remarks that the 'theme of total emancipation . . . is always situated beyond good and evil . . . The Leninist passion for the real . . . knows no morality. Morality, as Nietzsche was aware, has only the status of a genealogy. It is a leftover from the old world.'[28] Ethics is avant-garde, whereas morality is petty bourgeois and *passé*. Nietzschean elitism sits well with revolutionary purism.

The absolute novelty of Badiou's 'event', ironically enough, is something of an *idée reçu*. Nothing is more traditionally modernist than the dream of such an ineffable rupture with the actual. One thinks, for example, of the fiction of Joseph Conrad, in which many of the key narrative events – Lord Jim's crucial jump, the unspeakable rites surrounding Kurtz in *Heart of Darkness*, Winnie Verloc's murder of her husband in *The Secret Agent*, the blowing up of Stevie in the same novel, Decoud's gradual disintegration in *Nostromo* – take place, so to speak, behind the back of the reader, squinted at sideways rather than viewed head-on. In a drably deterministic world, truth, freedom and subjectivity are bound to remain enigmas as impenetrable as Africa. So it is that Conrad's characters are granted a sublime moment of transcendence, only to witness this quasi-miraculous event being inexorably reabsorbed by the phenomenal world, sucked back into the flow of meaningless matter and degenerate time until the erstwhile free subject now confronts his or her own existence as pure facticity. The act

---

[27] See Janet Afary and Kevin B. Anderson, *Foucault and the Iranian Revolution* (Chicago, 2005).

[28] Alain Badiou, 'One Divides Itself into Two', in S. Budgeon, S. Kouvelakis and S. Žižek (eds), *Lenin Reloaded* (Durham and London, 2007), pp. 13–14.

of jumping may be a free decision, but it hands you over to natural forces over which you have no control.

Truth events, as Badiou calls them, cannot be known at the time of their occurrence. Their existence can be decided only retrospectively, as St Paul declares the Jesus he never encountered in the flesh to be Lord or *Kyrios*. There is no truth event without the decisive act of a subject; and in a chicken-and-egg paradox there is no subject other than the one who is brought into existence by his or her persistent, laborious, sometimes heroic fidelity to this primal revelation. Badiou inherits the dubious avant-garde doctrine that the human subject is authentic only when audaciously staking its existence *in extremis*. Truth is a matter of all or nothing. Otherwise, in a kind of secularised version of the doctrine of election, we are merely finite biological individuals, who have yet to be transformed into genuine or infinite subjects by force of such a commitment. The individual is a kind of nothing, a cipher who must be cancelled and reborn by her faith in some road-to-Damascus event which remains rationally undemonstrable, extrinsic to the order of being. The human subject is always the subject of a truth event. What provokes it into existence is an eternal, incorruptible, exceptional, utterly particular truth. Subjectivation is conversion. Only such a subject can affirm that a truth event actually took place, rather as our knowledge of God for Judaeo-Christian belief moves within the domain of faith. The Resurrection for Paul is no more a question of eyewitnesses than the gas chambers are for us today.

This fidelity to an event which opens up a new order of truth is what Badiou means by the ethical. Like divine grace, it is an invitation which is available to anyone, so that in this sense Badiou champions the equality and universality of the symbolic order. But since the truth upon which one wager's one's existence is always singular, traumatic, infinite, transformative and ultimately ineffable, it belongs to the register of the Real. It partakes of the Real, too, in its stark Protestant solitude. Rather as the Lacanian subject of the Real exists at some extreme, unsociable limit, refusing the seductive amenities of the *polis*, so Badiou's knight of faith is a pure singularity. This condition is not just ethical but ontological. One of the more controversial aspects of Badiou's thought is his insistence on the non-relatedness of beings – on their random proliferations, chance intersections, contingent encounters and resistance to orderly connection. Human subjects may cooperate in a kind of 'we-being' or 'communism of singularities', but human subjects are not constitutively relational. Badiou has a belief in collectives; but lending them a name and determinate shape is always in his view a political catastrophe. In an anti-structuralist gesture, it is discrete elements which take priority, not the relations between them. It is no wonder that the philosopher of the event is an admirer of Gilles Deleuze.

It follows from this fondness for the discrete that Badiou the left activist is as hostile to the idea of a global capitalist *system* as the most benighted of political commentators. His vision of the unrelatable solitude of Being is classically modernist. Much the same might be said of Lacan's ethical heroes of the Real – of the Oedipuses and Antigones on whom he expends such praise. Truth, like mathematics or symbolist poetry, is self-founded, self-constitutive, self-validating and self-referential. It is detached from the workaday province of Nature, history and biology, just as politics for Badiou the ex-Maoist is an affair of the will and spirit – of decision, exception and axiomatic conviction, remote from the sublunary zone of the social and economic. Politics is about the subject, not the organising of food supplies. As Peter Hallward remarks, Badiou has an 'exalted' conception of politics[29] – one coupled with an ultra-leftist contempt for trade unionism, socio-political agendas, social democracy and other such theoretically unglamorous phenomena. In true Pauline spirit, one must not conform oneself to the world – a doctrine which in Badiou's hands becomes a kind of ultra-leftist purism. Paul, at least, had an excuse for his abstentionism: like the early church in general, he doubtless believed that the second coming of Christ was imminent, an event which would put paid to historical practice because it would put paid to history. This is one reason why the New Testament has no real concept of political action. There simply isn't time. Jesus himself seems to have believed that history would come to an end while some of his disciples were still alive.

It is true that Badiou himself has remained a political activist; but one is reminded of the Derrida of *Spectres of Marx*, with his desire for a Marxism without doctrine, programme, party, orthodoxy or institution. It is rather like the ultra-liberal Anglican who seeks a Christianity unencumbered by such embarrassments as God, Jesus, heaven, hell, sin and repentance. The most Derrida can muster is a Marxism without a name, a shamefaced socialism absolved from the crimes of its forebears only at the price of being politically vacuous. One thinks of the symbolist dream of the ideal poem, one so untainted by a fallen world that it is nothing but a blank sheet of paper. In their pathological nervousness of the positive, the French leftist

---

[29]   Peter Hallward, *Badiou: A Subject to Truth* (Minneapolis, 2003), p. 226.

intelligentsia remained stymied by the guilt of Stalinism and the shadow of fascism. For Badiou, one cannot and must not speak the whole truth, as though any complete declaration must inevitably be despotic. For Derrida, one may propose – but only in fear and trembling, irony and self-subversion. This style of reticence (one may claim something of the same of Adorno) may well pay oblique homage to the victims of oppression; but it is hard to see how it might prove effective in preventing its recurrence. In this sense, its homage is more compromised than it confesses.

Against the squalid calculation of social interests, Badiou takes his stand on infinity. This enmity towards human interests is one way in which he remains true to the legacy of Kant – ironically, the great prophet of human finitude. Justice is a matter of immortality rather than finitude. The event inaugurates its own peculiar time, one quite autonomous of common-or-garden history. Truth in this profoundly otherworldly perspective is at daggers drawn with the given and largely indifferent to the sensible or empirical. In this, too, Badiou is at one with Kant. Ethics must be severed from animality. Badiou may be fascinated by singularity, but he has a Platonic disdain for particularity. A naturalistic ethics, one founded in finitude and the body, is accordingly spurned for an ethics of the infinite – which is to say, for that tenacious commitment to a truth event which raises us above our creatureliness, and in doing so constitutes a kind of eternality. It is the ethics of a mathematician, as well as of a former Althusserian. But there is also a Kantian strain in the conviction that the ethical is transcendent – that its truth leads us beyond Nature to our home in eternity.

Like Levinas and Derrida, Badiou finds in ethics the scourge of everyday morality. For all his ferocious antagonism to their thought (the cult of the Other is tersely, scurrilously dismissed in his *Ethics* as 'a dog's dinner'), aspects of his own theory run in much the same grooves as the custodians of Otherness about whom he is so refreshingly rude. For all his invective, he shares their high-minded distaste for theory, consensus, knowledge, community, legality, interests, reformism, calculation, civil rights, humanitarianism, civic responsibilities, social orthodoxies and the rest of that by now familiar baggage. Politics concerns the human subject, not human rights, mass democracy or the economy.[30] All consensus, Badiou remarks, seeks to avoid division, conveniently forgetful of the solidarity which

---

[30]   See, for example, Badiou's *Metapolitics* (London, 2005), in which he argues that mass democracy is indistinguishable from dictatorship.

toppled apartheid and overturned neo-Stalinism. He also shares his Parisian colleagues' dim view of pleasure, happiness, well-being, utility and sensibility. Like Lacan, as Peter Hallward observes, Badiou repudiates 'all consensual social norms (happiness, pleasure, faith, etc) in favour of an essentially asocial, essentially traumatic exception'.[31] What he rejects is what Slavoj Žižek calls with equal off-handedness 'the smooth running of affairs in the domain of Being',[32] as though anything short of an ethics of the Real is simply a tedious matter of clerical administration. 'For Badiou no less than for Lacan and Žižek', Hallward comments, 'subjectivation is essentially indifferent to the business and requirements of life as such.'[33] It seems a strange kind of ethics which regards the business of life as of minor importance. In place of these degraded goals, Badiou himself proposes an ethics of 'superhuman tenacity', one which boils down to the slogan 'Don't give up!' or 'Keep the faith!', and which has more than an echo of Lacan's 'Don't give way on your desire.' (Badiou regards Lacan as 'the greatest of our dead'.) In both cases, it is ethics as a rearguard action, a flamboyant, last-ditch gesture of defiance to a world now portrayed as chronically unregenerate. As such, these apparently universal battle-cries have their own peculiar historical conditions.

Adherence to a truth event for Badiou, as for the Pascal he admires, is a purely fideistic affair. In a strain of Maoist spontaneism, knowledge and reflection are the enemies of faith, not its essential undergirding. Analysis and political practice must remain distinct. Ethics is a lived relationship to truth, not a question of speculating on what one should do. Truth itself is axiomatic rather than deliberative, a dogmatism with which Mao might well have found himself in hearty agreement. It has little to do with reflection, existing as it does on the extreme edge of knowledge. We are offered, then, a series of stark, eminently deconstructible oppositions: truth (or faith) versus knowledge, politics *contra* everyday life, infinity rather than finitude, event versus ontology, chance against system, subject rather than object, rebellion over consensus, autonomy versus causality, transcendence over historical immanence, eternity as against time. Since all truth events are at imminent peril of being neutralised and absorbed by social orthodoxy, we might add a familiar Weberian couplet to these polarities: charisma and bureaucracy.

---

[31] Hallward, *Badiou*, p. 265.
[32] Slavoj Žižek, *The Ticklish Subject* (London, 1999), p. 143.
[33] Hallward, *Badiou*, p. 134.

Like Derrida – indeed, like postmodern thought in general – Badiou shares the banal assumption that all orthodoxies are oppressive, all consensus stifling and all heterodoxies to be applauded. Yet it is hard to see why the orthodox doctrine that workers may sometimes withdraw their labour should be pilloried, just as it is difficult to grasp quite what is enlightened about devil-worshipping dissenters. Those who are supposed to look with a cold eye on binary oppositions end up with a demonised political system on the one hand and an inherently creative dissidence on the other. Truth is always oppositional. If it can inaugurate a new regime, it cannot trigger a general political trans-formation. In Badiou's eyes, the age of revolutions is over. The political status quo can be disrupted but not overthrown, a proposition which the leaders of the Soviet Union in the late 1980s might have greeted with a degree of surprise. In trusting to subversion rather than transformation, Badiou is at one with the postmodernist theory he detests. He also shares with Lacan and Derrida what one might call the avant-gardist fallacy: the belief that radical innovation is always to be prized, breaking as it does with a past caricatured as uniformly sterile. In its naive counterpointing of tradi-tion and innovation, this callow iconoclasm forgets the regenerative power of the past and is oblivious to the noxious nature of much making-new. No form of life is more innovative, subversive and disruptive than capital-ism. For all its cult of the diverse and differential, this style of thought portrays both past and present as drearily uniform, miraculously void of internal contradiction. A philosophy which exalts the political is thus symptomatic of a crisis of politics. All value is transcendent rather than immanent. In a dogmatism of deviation, every authentic truth springs from an exception to the rules. We are not far from the banal Romantic cult of the wayward genius (Lenin, Robespierre, Cézanne) who breaks the mould.

In rejecting an ethics of the Other, Badiou takes a militant, refreshingly unfashionable stand on the politics of the Same. Ethics, he believes, has come in our age to displace politics, as a bogus humanitarian ideology of victimage, otherness, identity and human rights thrusts aside political proj-ects. (The other great political displacement of our time, he might have added, bears the name of culture.) The voguish idiom of difference and otherness reflects what he calls a 'tourist's fascination' with moral and cultural diversity, while the cult of human rights divides the world between powerless victims and self-satisfied benefactors. Since multiculturalism tol-erates only the 'good' other (that is to say, one much like myself), it toler-ates no other at all. In this sense, it remains immured in the imaginary.

It fails to respect the difference of those who fail to respect its own most cherished differences. There is a good deal of truth in this case, as well as a good deal of typically Gallic hyperbole. In an audacious reversion to universality, hardly *à la mode* among the Parisian intelligentsia, Badiou claims instead that difference or alterity is the mark of the status quo, and that the struggle which counts is one for the achievement of sameness. The political task, in short, is what it has been since the radical Enlightenment: to resist unequal, particularist interests in the name of the revolutionary universal. Badiou's notion of universality, to be sure, is idiosyncratic enough: the domain of the universal is not given but constructed, not a received fact but a subjective operation. In this sense, every universal is exceptional, as the product of a subjective decision. Yet his hostility to the anti-universalism of Levinas, Derrida, Lyotard and Foucault remains stead-fast. Philosophy, he considers, has always constituted itself in the teeth of Sophism, from Plato's wranglings with Protagoras to Kant's contention with Hume; and the postmodernists are simply the latest sophistical crew to be contested.

It is these universalist, egalitarian aspects of Badiou's thinking which ally him to a symbolic ethics. Truths are the same for everyone, and anyone at all can proclaim them. They fly in the face of all local, ethnic, communitarian *doxa*. Yet truths in themselves are stubbornly singular. In fact, there are as many truths as there are human subjects. Unlike the truths of the symbolic order, they are not theoretical, rule-governed or propositional, but event-like, non-conceptual, revelatory and subject-constituting. Truth is less Kantian than Kierkegaardian. In this sense, then, the symbolic and the Real are allied: truths belong to the order of the Real, but must be universalised by certain attested procedures throughout the symbolic order. For the Badiou of the superb little study *Saint Paul: The Foundation of Universalism*, the relation between Christ and St Paul is an allegory of this alliance, as the Real of Christ's crucifixion and resurrection – events inscrutable to theory, knowledge, moral discourse, symbolisation and the like – are promulgated by Paul as a universal gospel. A new form of symbolic order or church, in which all members are equal and identical in Christ, cuts violently across the conventional symbolic order's distinctions of gender, kinship, class and ethnicity. As such, it launches the first truly universal movement in human history, as well as the most enduring over nations and centuries. The symbolic encounters the Real by reconfiguring it in its own image and likeness. The Christian church carves out of existing social orders a new form of community, one united around the Real of Christ's death and destitution.

Against the postmodernists and multiculturalists, Badiou adopts a Kantian indifference to particularity; yet at the same time he rids that Kantianism of its norms and obligations. We have seen a similarly selective version of Kant in the case of Levinas. Badiou's thought is a curious *mélange* of Enlightenment rationalism and a Romantic faith in truth as sublime revelation. There is one sense, however, in which this notion of truth differs from that of those ethical Realists who prefer disruption to continuity, epiphanic enigma to the dreary persistence of history. For the whole thrust of his ethics is an attempt to live in perpetual fidelity to a revealed truth – to 'persevere in the disruption', as he puts it – and thus to clip together both innovation and continuity. The big bang of truth must be combined with the steady state of ethics. In this sense, Badiou's thought differs from those radicals for whom the problem is what to do when the General Strike is finished, the public clocks have been shot at, the Dadaist happening is over almost as soon as begun, the epiphany has faded and *jouissance* is no more than a fond middle-aged memory. In contrast to this disenchanted crew, Badiou wishes to insert eternity into time, negotiate the passage between truth event and everyday life, which is what we generally know as politics. Those who insist on the pure unrelatability of the event, isolating it from its temporal consequences in the symbolic order, are written off as 'Mystics'.

Yet it is not as though the event and everyday life completely intersect. For the 'time' of one's perseverance in the truth is not the time of the symbolic order as such. It belongs entirely to the subjective sphere. There is no single history to which events can be related, only the multiple histories which they themselves inaugurate. The contrast between the ordinary and the epiphanic, the immanent and the transcendent, is thus sustained. Badiou does not grant the commonplace world enough credence to trust that there may be forces immanent within it which are capable of transforming it. Everyday life is characterised in quasi-biological terms as the province of appetite, self-interest and dull compulsion. There is a Hobbesian quality about his vision of the quotidian. If he had a less jaundiced view of it, he might have need of a less exalted alternative. Is there really no courage, compassion or selflessness in this sphere? Is there no grace in the normative, no miracle of the ordinary? Or does the life of virtue spring only from a fidelity to exceptionalist truth events? In one sense, the symbolic order is given its proper due, as liberty, equality and universality are acknowledged as precious political goals; yet all this must be 'organised around the Real of a radical fraternity', as Peter Hallward puts it – a fraternity which cannot be represented, and which in its militancy shatters the gentri-fied symmetries of the symbolic.

Badiou gives short shrift to Aristotelian virtue ethics, a lineage which we shall be glancing at later. (One might say the same of J. M. Bernstein's magisterial study *Adorno: Disenchantment and Ethics*, which in a span of some 450 pages has scarcely anything to say of Aristotle.) In Badiou's case, this is largely because virtue ethics is concerned not with truth, but with such tainted moral goods as happiness and well-being. But it is also because they involve our animal constitution or (in Marxian phrase) species-being, and thus, from Badiou's Platonic-rationalist viewpoint, belong to the sub-sidiary domain of Nature, history and the everyday. Ethics for Badiou involves a death-defying leap from this cheerless zone of inauthenticity to the infinity of a commitment to truth. Only by such a reckless venture does one become an 'immortal' subject rather than a biology-bound, death-oriented animal. He does not accept that the infinite, if the term has valid-ity, may be encountered only by a tragic confrontation with one's finitude. 'Man', remarks Milan Kundera in his novel *Immortality*, 'doesn't know how to be mortal.' It is not easy to grasp that immortality is the illusion into which we are born, and that undoing this lethal fantasy, one which dismembers bodies and destroys communities, involves a strenuous moral labour. If we were more conscious of our finitude, we might be less tempted to forget that all our appetites and animosities will end in dust. Finitude in Badiou's view, however, belongs to the menial sphere of our species being. It is the very antipode of an authentic ethics. His own ambition, he declares, is 'to have done with the finite'.[34]

Badiou's work thus takes sides in the battle between the avatars of the infinite and the apologists for finitude. From Heidegger's *Being and Time* to Georgio Agamben's *Homo Sacer* and Alasdair MacIntyre's *Dependent Rational Animals*, it is the vulnerable, death-ridden human creature which lays claim to our attention. Michel Foucault is also in his own way a poet of finitude, though with a mad undertow of longing for the illimitable. In Nietzschean fashion, Gilles Deleuze regards material process itself as a boundless flow of creativity, of which individual lives are no more than the perishable product. Actuality is consequently downgraded in the name of the virtual or potential, which is nothing less than the whole infinite con-tinuum of time.

---

[34] Alain Badiou, 'Philosophy and Mathematics: Infinity and the End of Romanticism', in R. Brassier and A. Tascano (eds), *Alain Badiou: Theoretical Writings* (London and New York, 2004), p. 25.

Emmanuel Levinas is a harder case to categorise, as a paladin of frailty and mortality who nevertheless urges the need for infinite responsibility. So, indeed, is the thinker from whom much of this talk of infinity stems, Søren Kierkegaard, who insists on the finitude of our condition yet sees men and women as shot through with the infinity of the spirit. Kant is at once the greatest modern philosopher of human finitude and the apologist for a sublimely unattainable Reason. Freud is a similarly ambiguous figure: as Eric Santner points out, human beings are more than creatures, but only because their existence is amplified by a death-driven singularity that makes them *more* creaturely than their fellow animals.[35] Because we are the only animals capable of reflecting upon our death, we enjoy an excess over and above other living creatures; yet because this reflection intensifies our sense of mortality, we become more purely animal than they are.

There are also those who turn from the finite to the infinite. The avant-garde French journal *Tel Quel*, home in the 1970s to a Maoist-tinged, materialist politics and poetics, changed its name, once those leftist currents had ebbed, to the rather less materialist *L'Infini*. Jacques Derrida, with his dream of absolute responsibility and the endless dance of the signifier, is undoubtedly an avatar of the infinite; and so in a different way is Alain Badiou, who callously observes that man as suffering victim is generally worth as little as man as torturer. Such figures are advocates of Burkean sublimity, rather than of the social symmetry Burke names beauty. An ethics of the mortal body is too unheroic for Badiou, as well as too naturalistic. Like most Realists, there is a strain of the superhuman about his vision, a refusal to cave in to anything as lowly and undignified as the flesh. The Lacanian philosopher Alenka Zupančič writes that 'the basis of ethics cannot be an imperative which commands us to endorse our finitude and renounce our "higher", "impossible" aspirations but, rather, an imperative which invites us to recognise as our own the "infinite" which can occur as something that is essentially a by-product of our own actions'.[36]

Yet the theory of tragedy which runs beneath Lacanian ethics really gives comfort to neither camp. Tragedy chastens the hubris of those whose reach exceeds their grasp, undoing their insane presumption, stripping them of

---

[35]   Eric Santner, 'Miracles Happen: Benjamin, Rosenzweig, Freud and the Matter of the Neighbor', in S. Žižek, E. Santner and K. Reinhard (eds), *The Neighbor* (London and Chicago, 2005), p. 47.
[36]   Alenka Zupančič, *Ethics of the Real*, p. 97.

their selfhood, and ushering them into the ghastly presence of the Real. Yet if these figures can gaze on the monstrosity of their condition without being struck blind or turned to stone, seeing in the mirror of themselves not an imaginary alter ego but a loathsome outcast, it is possible that the immeasurable power which allows them to acknowledge this thing of darkness as their own is also one which can bear them beyond the bleached bones and crushed skulls of those who have gone before them, to the remote domain of what Lacan calls in *The Four Fundamental Concepts of Psychoanalysis* 'a limitless love'. If the finite is to be transcended, it is not by spurning it but by staring it in the face. For this to come about, however, demands a state of destitution or descent into hell beyond anything that Badiou's more affirmative ethics can accommodate. As Slavoj Žižek writes of the ruined Oedipus: 'he is "excessively human", he has lived the "human condition" to the bitter end, realising its most fundamental possibility; and for that very reason, he is in a way "no longer human", and turns into an "inhuman monster", bound by no human laws or considerations . . . .' As one who encounters the death drive as the utmost limit of human experience, he 'pays the price by undergoing a radical "subjective destitution", by being reduced to an excremental remainder'.[37]

What Žižek does not add here (though he is doubtless well aware of it) is that this, for the cursed, polluted protagonist of *Oedipus at Colonus*, is the prelude to a kind of apotheosis. In becoming nothing but the scum and refuse of the *polis* – the 'shit of the earth', as St Paul racily describes the followers of Jesus, or the 'total loss of humanity' which Marx portrays as the proletariat – Oedipus is divested of his identity and authority and so can offer his lacerated body as the cornerstone of a new social order. Only those who count as nothing in the eyes of the current power-system are sufficiently askew to it to inaugurate a radically new dispensation. 'Am I made a man in this hour when I cease to be?' (or perhaps 'Am I to be counted as something only when I am nothing / am no longer human?'), the beggar king wonders aloud. To be divested of one's cultural difference, stripped to one's species being, is to exist as no more than a useless, excessive, dispensable piece of shit (since it is culture which constitutes our humanity); but it is also to become a living incarnation of what is most authentically human, an intolerable signifier of our shared mortality and fragility. It is this dialectic which tragedy understands most profoundly.

[37] Žižek, *The Ticklish Subject*, p. 156.

Only on this 'inhuman' foundation can a durable human community be constructed. If the imaginary is a question of sameness, and the symbolic one of difference, this unrepresentable vanishing point of humanity, to which Lacan gives the name of the Real, is a matter of both sameness and strangeness, allowing us to find ourselves mirrored in the very alienness, unrelatedness or deathly singularity of the other. To love another in her singularity is to love her in herself; but since what is most constitutive of the other is his or her sheer humanity, that void or vanishing-point where all differences dissolve, this love has a properly impersonal dimension, which is why we can speak of charity as a law. It is no wonder, then, that love is such an impossibility, given that those bereft of differential cultural markers are monsters, obscene creatures like the blinded Oedipus, destitute Lear or crucified Christ who are frightful to look upon. It is because Christianity believes at once in the necessity and impossibility of such love that it preaches the doctrine of redemptive grace.

Not many of us, gratifyingly enough, are called upon to be tragic protagonists. Most of us are not guerrilla fighters risking our lives for the well-being of others. There are, however, vicarious ways of negotiating this passage from self-dispossession to new life. One of them is the performative art known as psychoanalysis; another is the Christian practice of the Eucharist, in which the participants in this love feast or sacrificial meal establish solidarity with one another through the medium of a multilated body. In this way, they share at the level of sign or sacrament in Christ's own bloody passage from weakness to power, death to transfigured life. Badiou's St Paul, by contrast, is one who preaches resurrection alone, rather than the entire tragic action to which it belongs. In *Modern Tragedy*, Raymond Williams chides those commentators who isolate the moment of death and destruction in tragic art from the invigorated life which may survive it. But one can do the opposite as well, celebrating that surviving spirit without reckoning the terrible price it must pay in its passage through hell. Badiou is not in this sense a tragic thinker. Williams himself, whose work is occasionally marred by too doggedly affirmative a humanism, is not entirely innocent of this oversight himself. W. B. Yeats knew that nothing can be sole or whole that has not been rent; but this insight too often gives way in his writing to a Nietzschean strain of tragic triumphalism. Those who hold suffering and hope most finely in balance – the true tragic protagonists, so to speak – are those who rise up because they have little enough to lose, yet just for that reason have the power to transform their condition.

10

The Banality of Goodness

From Robespierre to Rimbaud, Breton to Lyotard, France has been one of the great homes of the avant-garde. The term itself is said to be the coinage of Claude Saint-Simon. Yet it is a vanguardism which has often shown itself contemptuous of the common life. Such contempt, contrary to popular wisdom, is not built into the idea of an avant-garde. In a sense, the opposite is true. For there is no advance guard without an army to which it is answerable, and on whose behalf it scouts the terrain up ahead. The very term implies a relationship to a less glamorous body of foot soldiers, as words like 'elite' or 'coterie' do not. The avant-garde is the first to feel those dim vibrations which will finally take shape as the future; but in doing so, it hopes to transmit these stirrings to those marching in the rear who are not yet attuned to them. If vanguards involve hierarchies, they are provisional rather than eternal. Like radical movements in general, they succeed only by doing themselves out of business. One day, if all goes well, the main body will heave over the horizon and catch up with them.

In practice, however, the line between vanguardists and elitists is fairly blurred. In the modern period, there has been plenty of two-way traffic across this frontier. The most successful elites, for example, are those with popular roots, linking a minority to the common people in mutual opposition to the strait-laced suburban masses. Fascism idealises the *Volk* just as much as Romantic leftism does. T. S. Eliot delighted in jazz and music hall and dreamed of a readership which would be semi-illiterate. W. B. Yeats sought an alliance between swash-buckling Anglo-Irish landowners and an Irish-speaking peasantry, all of whom would be vessels of timeless wisdom and a minority of whom would be colourfully crazed. For the Bolsheviks, the party was officially at the service of the workers' soviets, however scantily that vision was actually realised. Elites differ in this way from cliques, clubs, cabals and coteries, all of which are indeed jealously exclusive and non-populist.[1]

From Mallarmé and Sorel to Sartre and Badiou, a succession of French thinkers have dreamt of the moment of crisis which will blast open the inauthenticity of the everyday. Or they have imagined a realm of being which transcends the sterility of that existence altogether. The result has been a series of stark oppositions: *la poésie pure* versus common speech, myth against social illusion, the gift versus equal exchange, the Real *contra* the symbolic, the semiotic versus the symbolic, freedom over bad faith, theory against ideology, difference versus determinacy, the schizoid versus the paranoid, the event against ontology. Varied though these contrasts are, the project which underlies them remains remarkably consistent. It is to rescue true value from the clutches of the everyday – from the faceless conformism which Heidegger disdainfully terms *das Man*. Beneath these polarities runs a robust tradition of libertarian thought. Revolt is as Gallic as eroticism. Like sex, too, it is enjoyable for its own sake.

For the early Sartre, the contrast is one between the freedom of the *être-pour-soi* and the soulless inertia of the *être-en-soi*. Later, this ontological opposition will become a political one, between praxis and the practico-inert. For Jacques Derrida, the play of pure difference is confined by the straitjacket of metaphysics, only to burst out of it now and again like a madman exultantly eluding his keepers. For post-Nietzschean thinkers from Bataille to Deleuze, madness and transgression lay siege to the grey Apollonian pieties of the civic sphere. There are times when Michel Foucault treats the so-called life sciences or discourses of everyday life (biology, medicine, psychology, economics, demography and so on) as little more than the sinister handmaidens of social surveillance. There are dreams of some *acte gratuit*, moment of conversion or existential commitment that will catapult you out of the kingdom of necessity into the domain of freedom, abandoning the drearily prosaic stuff of tradition, biology, moral discourse and political orthodoxy for the heady *milieu* of liberty, desire, *engagement* and authentic selfhood. One can lend a deconstructive twist to this born-again narrative by insisting that nothing is ever *simply* abandoned – that each pole of the opposition inexorably implicates the other, that the metaphysical is not to be shucked off so simply, that power, law, lack, the ego, bad faith, closure and convention are finally inescapable. Even so, it is clear enough which option on offer is to be judged most precious.

---

[1] For a further discussion, see Terry Eagleton, *The Idea of Culture* (Oxford, 2000), Ch. 5.

In some recent French thinkers, this polarity involves a kind of split sensibility. On the one hand, there is the prudent face of Jacques Derrida, with his exemplarily scrupulous readings, his respect for Enlightenment and rational inquiry, his sober insistence that he is not *against* system, truth, the subject, dialectics, stability, universality and the like. On the other hand, running like a turbulent sub-current beneath this caution, there is a madder, more anarchic text altogether, revealed in a poetic out-burst here or a flash of utopian speculation there. Something of the same can be said of Michel Foucault, whose sombre archival investigations, rebuking all talk of negation, transcendence or repression, contrast with the wilder, more Dionysian figure who can be felt prowling around the edges of these clinical inquiries. This recusant Foucault will burst out sud-denly in some extravagant praise of Bataille or Deleuze, giving rein to an impulse which refuses all regime, resists all regulation, and trembles on the brink of articulation without ever quite speaking its name. An exception to this post-structuralist norm is Gilles Deleuze, for whom in Spinozist fashion a kind of 'transcendent' excess or infinity is immanent in material reality itself. Deleuze, for whom everything is both ordinary and miracu-lous, has a sense of the poetry of the commonplace closer to Surrealism than to Lacan or Badiou.

One might portray this divided sensibility as a form of libertarian pes-simism, in which the emancipatory impulse has by no means been laid to rest – in which the vision of 1968 can still be felt living and breathing – but which now, in the disenchanted aftermath of that epoch, must confess the naivety of dreaming that desire could ever be free from law or the subject innocent of power. On the whole, the French prefer to be thought wicked rather than wet behind the ears. One must, then, affirm desire and its impossibility, liberation and scepticism, in the same breath. There is much of this divided sensibility, at once rebellious and resigned, in Lacanian ethics. You must not give up on your delirious dreams of pure difference, free libidinal flows, the kingdom of justice, or a realm of love beyond the law; but you must not try to bring them about either, for that way lie psy-chosis, totalitarianism or some other ghastly graveyard of the spirit.

The avant-garde ambition to have done with history has a remarkably long history. The term 'modern' runs back to the Latin *modernus*, a word which according to Jürgen Habermas was used by fifth-century Christians to distinguish themselves from older, pagan believers.[2] Christianity on this

---

[2] See Jürgen Habermas, 'Modernity: An Incomplete Project', in Hal Foster (ed.), *Post-modern Culture* (London, 1985).

view was the earliest form of modernity, breaking with the old dispensation in its self-conscious newness. Yet attempts at absolute novelty simply pile more history on to what we have already. To announce the death of history is itself an historical act with material consequences, and in thus as self-refuting as announcing one's own demise. The avant-garde is mistaken to believe that the past always weighs like a nightmare on the brains of the living. Because the past is what we are made of, we can create the future only with the ambiguous resources it affords us. History is emancipation as well as oppression, and the avant-garde is as much new capitalist technology as political insurrection. To break with the past is among other things to break with the chance to transcend it. There are German avant-gardes as well as French ones; but because of the more dialectical cast of German thought, there is also a vision of what one might call revolutionary continuity, as, looking back on the past from the standpoint of a transfigured present, we can grasp how that present is both in line with and askew to it.

It might be claimed that if France is one of the great homes of avant-gardism, it is also the culture to which we owe the very conception of the everyday.[3] It is here above all that what Louis Aragon called 'le sentiment du merveilleux quotidien' is most in evidence. What of Charles Baudelaire, the first great poet of seedy urban existence, or the stray, workaday objects of Mallarmé and Apollinaire? Who else but Henri Lefebvre, in his monumental three-volume Critique of Everyday Life, placed the idea of the everyday on the intellectual map, to be followed by such later luminaries of daily life as Michel de Certeau and Georges Perec? 'In so far as the science of man exists', writes Lefebvre in the first volume of his magnum opus, 'it finds its material in the "trivial", the everyday.'[4]

It is a claim confirmed by the mighty heritage of fictional realism from Stendhal to Malraux. Franco Moretti has described the realist novel as 'a culture of everyday life', rather than a critique of it.[5] The Annales school's microscopically detailed landscapes of historical life, as well as Pierre Bourdieu's sociological investigations, are other cases in point. Even structuralism has a demotic touch, since the hidden codes it lays bare underlie wrestling as much as Rimbaud, fashion as well as Fourier. It is thus that the early Roland Barthes is the inheritor of earlier diagnosticians of

---

[3]   For a useful survey, see Michael Sheringham, Everyday Life: Theories and Practices from Surrealism to the Present (Oxford, 2006).

[4]   Henri Lefebvre, Critique of Everyday Life (London, 1991), vol. 1, p. 133.

[5]   Franco Moretti, The Way of the World (London, 1987), p. 35.

the everyday like Michael Leiris and Raymond Queneau. The greatest twentieth-century conspectus of the commonplace, Walter Benjamin's *Passagenarbeit*, is the work of a German yet is set in Paris. The writings of Maurice Merleau-Ponty desert the Platonic peaks of transcendental phenomenology for a hermeneutics of the everyday. Existentialism may convict the commonplace of inauthenticity; but it also thinks from within the day-to-day, which is why there can be an existentialist novel as opposed, say, to a logical-positivist one. It was Merleau-Ponty who suggested to a wide-eyed Jean-Paul Sartre that philosophy could be spun out of the ashtray. And what else are Surrealism and Situationism but the poetry of the inconsiderable?

The formidable richness of this work is not in question. Yet one should recall that several of these plunges into the quotidian were made from a standpoint which was sharply critical of it, or which sought to redeem it from its unregeneracy. If Baudelaire turns his gaze on whores and vagrants, it is to invest them with an aura of eternity. Lefebvre and the Situationists regard everyday experience as ineradicably ambiguous, as impoverished as it is precious. Guy Debord's vision of stupefied consumers enmired in administered well-being is hardly a hymn of praise to the creative energies of the everyday.[6] Lefebvre and the Situationists are full-blooded avant-gardists, looking eagerly in Lefebvre's words to the birth of the 'new man'. It is true that the Surrealists seek to distil the magic of the commonplace, fashioning new forms of urban mythology. Yet in Lefebvre's eyes they were guilty of a cult of the privileged moment which denigrated the day-to-day. He thought much the same about existentialism, which he rebukes for having 'drawn closer to life . . . only to discredit it', devaluing it in favour of 'pure or tragic moments – criticism of life through anguish or death – artificial criteria of authenticity, etc.'.[7] For André Breton and his acolytes, common morality is to be denounced as spinelessly petty bourgeois, in contrast to their own heroics of transgression. This doctrine will later find its way into an ethics of the Real. In the transition from realism to modernism, a fascination with the texture of everyday living gives way to a mandarin scepticism of it. Common experience is now the homeland of illusion, not the locus of truth. If the ethics of a Hume or Hutcheson are of a piece with the world of Smollett and Richardson, those of Derrida and Badiou belong to the era of symbolism, Formalism and abstraction.

---

[6] See Guy Debord, *Society of the Spectacle* (Detroit, 1970).
[7] Lefebvre, *Critique of Everyday Life*, vol. 1, pp. 130, 264.

One might contrast this strain of French culture with a certain English vein of preoccupation with the common life, all the way from William Cobbett, George Eliot and John Ruskin to William Morris, Thomas Hardy, F. R. Leavis, George Orwell, Richard Hoggart, Raymond Williams and E. P. Thompson. There are, to be sure, plenty of defects in this lineage, too. Too indulgent a view of the commonplace is an English vice, just as too condescending a way with it is a French one. Analytical philosophy in its heyday was all too eager to identify the sum-total of human wisdom with the daily idiom of North Oxford. Yet there is also a genuine esteem for the ordinary in this English tradition – one which can inspire political radicalism rather than finding itself at odds with it. There is a necessary tension in left-wing thought between a respect for the common life and a hostility to the powers and illusions which inform it. If the early Raymond Williams sometimes trades the hostility for the respect, the avant-garde generally makes the opposite mistake. Vanguardists who despise the common life sometimes do so because they confuse the everyday with the political system which regulates it, forgetful that there is daily resistance to that power as well as routine complicity. The later Wittgenstein was one of the few twentieth-century maestros to combine a deep trust in the workaday with a scathing dismissal of bourgeois politics.[8]

This divergence between French and English traditions is also a question of style. If one of the characteristic tropes of avant-garde French theory is hyperbole, the definitive figures for the English are bathos or litotes. There is a down-to-earth quality to some English writing in this area, a dry scepticism of the bombastic or overweening. One of its less reputable roots lies in a stout empiricist suspicion of fancy ideas. Even so, when David Wood writes in *The Step Back* of certain 'unknown moggies in Madras', *à propos* of Derrida's ridiculous breast-beating over not being able to feed every cat on the planet, he deploys a stylistic device which would be well-nigh unthinkable in the writing of Parisian philosophers. The slightest touch of earthiness would prove fatal to their high-toned compositions. It would be equally out of place in the impeccably academicised tones of much radical American writing. One can find the same wryly deflationary wit in, say, Simon Critchley, Jonathan Rée or Simon Blackburn. Rée writes of 'the English tradition from Hobbes to Shaftesbury to Bentham, which makes ridicule into the acid test of truth'.[9] In the lofty idiom of French theory, by

---

[8]   See Terry Eagleton, 'Wittgenstein's Friends', in *Against the Grain: Selected Essays 1975– 1985* (London, 1986).

[9]   Jonathan Rée, *Times Literary Supplement* (20 October 2006), p. 14.

contrast, even play or pleasure come to seem intimidating, distinctly uncongenial affairs. The carnivalesque remains distinctly cerebral. There are, to be sure, exceptions to this rule. Lacan is often upbraided for obscurantism, and not without excellent reason; yet those who chide him on this score generally put aside his abrupt obscenities, crashing colloquialisms, flashes of sportive good humour, ironic self-allusions and mischievous raillery at his audience.

If Slavoj Žižek manages to be both cerebral and scabrous, a mixture of highbrow philosopher and postmodern jester, it may be because he is a Slovenian as well as an honorary Frenchman. Small nations, as observers of the Irish have long been aware, generally tend to look with amusement as well as admiration on the solemn antics of their metropolitan neighbours. It is no accident that the most mundane and materialist of all the great avant-garde novelists is James Joyce. The work of his fellow-Dubliner Samuel Beckett reveals a similar unswerving fidelity to the ordinary. An earlier Dubliner, Edmund Burke, displayed an aesthetic sensitivity to the warp and woof of everyday customs and taken-for-granted pieties. Žižek's paradoxes, inversions and perversities are as much the mark of a small-nation intelligentsia as the wit of Oscar Wilde. Psychoanalysis is itself a form of bathos, a cranking down of gears from the sublime to the ridiculous which detects the lowliest of drives lurking within our most exalted sublimations. 'As far as Freud is concerned', Lacan observes, 'everything that moves towards reality requires a certain tempering, a lowering of tone.'[10] William Empson remarks wisely that 'the most refined desires are inherent in the plainest, and would be false if they weren't'.[11] For Lacan, the most humdrum of objects can become a torn-off fragment of the Real.

Many of the great intellectual currents of the twentieth century have harboured their suspicions of the everyday. For the Freudians, daily life is largely a matter of psychopathology. The Formalists can find value in ordinary language only when it is shattered and estranged, so that the everyday proposition reappears as that rarer, more burnished thing, the poetic utterance. Ordinary language can be unburdened of its rich freight of meaning only by being subjected to organised violence. Behind the aesthetics of Formalism, with its phenomenological brooding upon the word, lies a deep-seated scepticism of common speech. It is a distinctively modernist scepticism – the reverse, so to speak, of a too-credulous Habermasian

---

[10] Jacques Lacan, *The Ethics of Psychoanalysis* (London, 1999), p. 13.
[11] William Empson, *Some Versions of Pastoral* (London, 1966), p. 114.

faith in the resources of everyday utterance. In a similar way, hermeneutics refuses to assume that meaning is ready to hand.

Neo-Kantianism drives a coach and horses between what is the case and what is of value. The early Wittgenstein does much the same. For the *Tractatus Logico-Philosophicus*, value is not to be located in the common world at all. The writings of Heidegger are shot through from end to end with a distinction between heroism and mediocrity, the exceptional and the average, which was to culminate in the 1930s in his loyalty to the Führer. It is true that Heidegger is much taken with earth, dwelling and the common folk; but all this is invested in his writing with a quasi-mystical aura which raises it above the commonplace to some altogether more eminent domain. Modernism is full of this exoticism of the ordinary, all the way from its cult of peasants and primitives to a naturalism which wallows sensationally in the gutter. Phenomenology places the everyday social world in brackets in order to attend more vigilantly to the way it appears in consciousness. *Lebensphilosophie* privileges the *élan vital* over the empty husks of everyday institutions. There is a similar tension in the work of Max Weber between charisma and bureaucracy. Structuralism, like Marxism, Freudianism and scientific realism, refuses to be duped by the habitual appearances of things, searching instead for the invisible mechanisms which give birth to them.

Existentialism sets the fragile moment of authenticity against the *mauvaise foi* of daily life. A good deal of modernism contrasts the half-glimpsed absolute, sudden epiphany or stray intensity with the *longueurs* of the everyday. The Formalists find their enemy in what the Russians know as *byt*, the soul-destroying barrenness of day-to-day existence. Like Kierkegaard before him, Heidegger is oppressed by boredom, a concept which he manages to invest with pseudo-philosophical status. Sartre finds himself sunk in the viscous mess of the *être-en-soi*, while Levinas is haunted by a mixture of fatigue, listlessness and insomnia, a dull, anonymous rumbling in the background of one's existence to which he gives the name of the *il y a*. All of these thinkers are afflicted by the quotidian. They experience the commonplace as an affront, a soporific, a soul-killing state of ataraxia and *ennui*. Much modern ethical theory has its secret source in alienation. It reflects the catastrophic loss of a sense of common value and everyday solidarity.

There is a kind of solitary modernist hero who exists on some far-flung frontier of the spirit; and this figure stages a belated reappearance in an ethics of the Real. He or she usually belongs to that modernist current which makes the mistake of assuming that the truth reveals itself only *in extremis*. It is what one might call the Room 101 syndrome: what one stammers out under excruciating torture is bound to be the truth. In fact, as even the CIA may by now have discovered, this is unlikely to be the case. The modern doctrine that the true or the good will shine out only in such remote borderlands assumes that common experience is void of validity. The close-at-hand is always impoverished. Who says consciousness says false consciousness. The truth of humanity lies in the inhuman. It is on the outer threshold of experience that you prove yourself a man.

There is more than a smack of this purism in the writings of the ethical Realists. To this extent, they are late modernists rather than postmodernists. The sovereignty of desire is the theme of Surrealism from beginning to end. Lacan's Antigone is as much a high-modernist heroine as Jean Anouilh's. There are questions to be posed about the value of an ethics which seems confined to a coterie of spiritual extremists. Are the masses to be palmed off with mere morality, while the elect enjoy a hotline to the Real? It is a familiar form of ethical elitism, as disproportionately demonic as the symbolic is excessively angelic. T. S. Eliot's respectably suburban Hollow Men are too spiritually gutless even to be damned – and the damned, whatever else one might say of them, are at least metaphysically minded creatures in their own peculiar way, closer to the saved than they are to what one might call the moral middle classes.

To reject the supreme good involves being on nodding terms with it, which is more than one can say for the merely well-behaved. Besides, the evil are purely disinterested, wreaking havoc for its own sake, and thus bear a grisly resemblance to those who cling to their desire in the teeth of all reason and utility. In Kant's view, diabolical evil, could it but exist, would have much the same qualities as the supreme ethical act. Neither form of conduct arises from sensible impulse; both are performed entirely for their own sake, and neither is rationally intelligible. The purely evil make a point of transgressing the moral law, rather as the more naive sort of anarchist breaks rules as a rule. They do so even if it means acting contrary to their own interests, and even if it issues in their death. In this sense, they are mirror-images of Kant's ethical heroes.[12] Satan, as we have noted already, is a fallen angel, who has known both the horror and the glory. The evil know God by negation, as the merely ill-behaved do not. Evil yearns to annihilate the divine Creation because it is the only form of absolute

---

[12] See Alenka Zupančič, *Ethics of the Real* (London, 2000), p. 85.

creativity still open to it, the Almighty having inconsiderately cornered all the most gratifying forms of production for himself.

If the crazed anarchist professor of Joseph Conrad's novel *The Secret Agent* wishes to exterminate the whole of reality and start over again *ex nihilo*, the ethical act for Lacan and Badiou is precisely such an arresting new creation. Alenka Zupančič, seized by a typically avant-gardist belief that the new is invariably positive, writes of the authentic ethical act as one which oversteps given boundaries and is thus indistinguishable from evil.[13] The case is purely formalistic. From this viewpoint, actually existing morality is always false consciousness. Pinky, the malignant protagonist of Graham Greene's *Brighton Rock*, is spiritually superior to the suburban moralising of Ida Arnold precisely because he believes in God yet spits wilfully in his face. In this sense, he is a minor version of Dostoevsky's Ivan Karamazov. Greene, George Orwell commented in the *New Yorker* in 1948, 'appears to share the idea, which has been floating around ever since Baudelaire, that there is something rather *distingué* about being damned'. On this view, one shared by Hegel, all the great artists, innovators and lawgivers have had the courage to transgress. That some of the great exploiters, autocrats and imperialists have done much the same is greeted by this 'radical' case with a glacial silence.

The wicked, then, are as much on terms with salvation and perdition as the saints. There is a certain kind of evil, remarks Pascal in his *Pensées*, which is as rare as goodness, and easily confounded with it. Better to rule in hell than be a porter in paradise. Experience at an extreme, even the knowledge of evil, is preferable to moral mediocrity. The truly depraved are in touch with divinity. The devil has all the best tunes. The atheist is an inverted metaphysician. The devil in Thomas Mann's *Doctor Faustus* feels superior to petty-bourgeois banality, proudly declaring himself the sole custodian of theological truth. He means that evil is all that survives of the metaphysical in the modern age. Modernity has knowledge of the metaphysical only through its negation – above all, one might claim, in the shape of Auschwitz. All that lingers of the Creator is the forlorn shadow of his absence. In *Doctor Faustus*, the music of Mann's Satanic protagonist, Adrian Leverkuhn, reveals 'the substantial identity of the most blest with the most accursed'. Naphta, the austere Jesuitical absolutist of Mann's *The Magic Mountain*, regards God and Satan as united in their opposition to a tediously suburban reason and virtue.

It is a seductive, deeply dangerous mythology, far removed from the traditional view that evil is really a kind of lack or negation, an incapacity

---

[13]   Ibid., p. 94.

for life rather than an abundance of it. It is evil which is boring and brittle, not good, which is humorous and high-spirited. If we fail to appreciate the fact, it is partly because the middle classes have opted for all the most tame and tedious virtues. In some ways, an ethics of the Real is a latter-day version of the Baudelairian ideology. And this must be weighed against its properly tragic insight that authentic life must emerge from self-destitution. An ethics of the Real runs far deeper than one of the imaginary or symbolic; yet for just this reason it is also too hyperbolic, too privileged and quasi-sacred. The whole discussion, as with the symbolic ethics of a Kant, is pitched too high. When Kant speaks in the *Groundwork of the Metaphysics of Morals* of the 'contempt and disregard' in which the moral law holds fallible human inclinations, the great liberal reveals himself as one source of this spiritual elitism.

Sylviane Agacinski writes of her suspicion of what she sees as the 'exaltation of greatness, immensity and the absolute' in the writings of Kierkegaard, adding that 'The sublime call or demand that issues from the infinite or the absolute involves a condemnation of finitude, a condemnation which is present in all forms of nostalgia for the incommensurable.'[14] Agacinski might find her suspicions of Kierkegaardian sublimity confirmed by the fact that George Steiner, with his patrician distaste for the calculable and utilitarian, is so avid an enthusiast of it. It is, no doubt, a touch disquieting for those Realists who regard themselves as radicals to be greeted with such an ardent kiss of death from so flamboyant a reactionary, one of the few surviving exponents of *Kulturkritik* in the late modern age. 'Where morality is at its most elevated, in a Socrates, in a Kant', Steiner writes in a laudatory piece on Kierkegaard, 'inhumanity and irrational absurdity have no place.'[15] This, one should point out, is intended as a rebuke to Socrates and Kant, not as a commendation of them. Tragic inhumanity and irrational absurdity, which scarcely top the list of everyone's favourite states of being, are in Steiner's view a welcome respite from the petty-bourgeois *longueurs* of reason, morality, egalitarianism and mass democracy – in short, from a contemptible modernity more or less bereft of redeeming features. Abraham's act in preparing to sacrifice Isaac, the rightist Steiner declares in the spirit of the leftist Derrida, 'transcends all conceivable claims of intellectual accountability and ethical criteria', which

---

[14] Sylviane Agacinski, 'We Are Not Sublime: Love and Sacrifice, Abraham and Ourselves', in Jonathan Rée and Jane Chamberlain (eds), *Kierkegaard: A Critical Reader* (Oxford, 1998), pp. 129, 130.

[15] George Steiner, 'The Wound of Negativity: Two Kierkegaard Texts', in Rée and Chamberlain, *Kierkegaard*, p. 105.

are nothing compared to 'a private individual in the grip of infinity'.[16] Quite how Abraham is a private individual remains unclear. One does not normally associate him with middle-class suburbia.

The closeness of Steiner and Derrida is scarcely accidental. For there is a sense in which the Realists are among the latest inheritors of the *Kulturkritik* tradition.[17] What distinguishes that train of thought, as it descends from Coleridge, Arnold and Ruskin to F. R. Leavis, T. S. Eliot, the early Thomas Mann, Karl Mannheim and José Ortega y Gasset, is its aversion to Enlightenment and egalitarianism, its suspicion of liberalism, materialism and mass civilisation, its elevation of a few rare human spirits over popular democracy and the triumph of mediocrity. One of its finest expressions can be found in the fiction of Saul Bellow. It is a richly resourceful, politically catastrophic lineage, one which would far rather embrace an anguished absurdity than an administered well-being. Rationality is for shopkeepers rather than sages. There are, to be sure, clear points of divergence between this outlook and an ethics of the Real. With the notable exception of Levinas, the ethical Realists incline by and large to the left, and are not generally to be found lambasting socialism and democracy. Derrida mixes aspects of *Kulturkritik* with a distinguished career as a political dissident. Yet the Lacanian disdain for happiness, politics, utility, welfare, social consensus, worldly goods and middle-class morality is strikingly close to the idiom of a Leavis or an Eliot. There is an anti-bourgeois animus of the right as well as the left, one which gave birth to some of the most illustrious modernist writing. As Derrida's career unfurled, a left-wing dissent from capitalist civilisation slid gradually into a spiritual disdain for the political sphere as such, much as he bravely continued to do battle there.

Take, for example, the incongruous affinity between Lacan and D. H. Lawrence, an author who stands squarely in the tradition of *Kulturkritik*. Traditionally, moralists have quarrelled over whether ethics primarily concerns the good or the right. It has been a clash between utilitarians versus deontologists, the torchbearers for virtue and happiness as against the apologists for rights and obligations.[18] Lawrence and Lacan are at one in rejecting both styles of moral thought for an ethics of desire, one which confines both rights and virtues to inferior status. Rather as the only true guilt for Lacan lies in giving way on one's desire, so the only true crime for

---

[16]   Ibid., p. 108.
[17]   For an excellent account, see Francis Mulhern, *Culture/Metaculture* (London, 2000).
[18]   See Terry Eagleton, *The Illusions of Postmodernism* (Oxford, 1996), Ch. 4.

Lawrence is to disown the desire which is the essence of one's selfhood. It is to deny the 'god' in oneself, and as such constitutes a kind of blasphemy. In Lawrence's metaphysic, this desire, as with Lacan's desire of the Real, is implacably 'other' to those who are the bearers of it. It is an unfathomable, irresistible dimension of being, which will have its own sweet way with us whatever our conscious predilections. When Lawrence writes that 'A man's self is a law unto itself, not unto *himself*',[19] the difference in question is one between the realm of the ego and its petty appetites, and the majestic terrain of the Real. It is a choice between desire and desires – between a grand metaphysical abstraction on the one hand, and on the other hand the tangible wants and needs with which classical morality quite properly concerns itself.

Those who are loyal to their desire in Lawrence are aristocrats of the spirit, men and women caught up in a proud singleness of selfhood for whom the masses represent so much paltry non-being. Those who cannot fulfil or be fulfilled are almost literally non-existent, and will be swept peremptorily aside by the life-force. What matters is purity of soul, not human sympathy. In his more debased moments, as in *Fantasia of the Unconscious*, Lawrence rails virulently against 'beastly benevolence, and foul good-will, and stinking charity, and poisonous ideals'.[20] Liberalism and humanitarianism, like Lacan's 'service of goods', are the evasions of those well-bred suburbanites too craven to confront the Real. Lacan speaks in 'Kant with Sade' of the 'egoism of happiness', a view which Lawrence would surely have endorsed. For him, feeling, morality, consciousness and even humanity itself are simply so much spume on the dark surge of the life-force. As with much *Kulturkritik*, ethics, politics, society and rationality are all to be written off as so much soulless 'mechanism', or at best tolerated as necessary evils. Democracy and equality are odious threats to individual autonomy. What the soul or desire within you prompts you to do is what it is right to do. A murder committed in the name of spontaneous-creative life has more moral value than a dutiful feeding of the hungry.

One familiar home for *Kulturkritik* has been the idea of tragedy. If the tragic has bulked so large in modern Western culture, figuring among the preoccupations of one eminent philosopher after another, it is not, as one might have expected, because this philosophy springs from an era more burdened with surplus deaths than any other in human history. There have

[19] D. H. Lawrence, 'Democracy', in *Selected Essays* (Harmondsworth, 1962), p. 91.
[20] D. H. Lawrence, *Fantasia of the Unconscious* (New York, 1967), p. 34.

been, rather, four main reasons for the curious persistence of the tragic in an anti-heroic, post-metaphysical age. First, it has sought to serve as a substitute for religion in a secular world. In addressing the absolute and transcendent, it hijacks the halo of religion while leaving aside its discredited doctrinal content. Secondly, the idea of tragedy has sought to provide an aesthetic resolution of the paradox that modern men and women are everywhere free but everywhere in chains. It is a practical response, in short, to the theoretical question of freedom and determinism. The tragic hero who bows to the inevitable in a spirit of *amor fati*, making his destiny his choice, reveals in that very act an infinite freedom which transcends his dire condition. Nothing demonstrates such freedom more convincingly than the noble-hearted gesture of giving it away. Thirdly, tragedy has served as a modern-day form of theodicy, addressing itself to the problem of evil with as spectacularly little success as any other attempt to justify its existence. The existence of evil is an extremely strong argument against the existence of God.

  Finally, tragedy has done service as a displaced critique of modernity – of a rational, scientific, levelling, utilitarian, callowly progressivist, instantly intelligible culture which has turned its face from tragic art's mysteries, mythologies, cult of blood guilt, sacred rituals, hierarchies of being, absolute value, disdain for the contingent, spirit of transcendence and glamorous pantheon of gods, heroes and aristocrats.[21] It has been a lament for the decline of high culture, a numinous nostalgia for a more exalted world. Tragedy is a critique of hubristic reason, as the liberal subject's attempt to forge his own history is brought to nothing by an implacable destiny. Political hope is unmasked as self-delusion: no wide-eyed trust in material progress could patch up Philoctetes's foot, no social engineering retrieve Phaedra from her doom. Wisdom is to be preferred to knowledge. Oedipus is knowledge at the end of its tether. Reverence is the enemy of rational explanation. There is an imperishable human dignity beyond either the political mob or the scientist's laboratory. In the face of tragic catastrophe, the sentimental humanism of the middle classes is exposed as a contemptible sham. No taint of the mundane may enter this majestic world. As George Steiner remarks, with a resonant mixture of panache and *hauteur*: 'If there are bathrooms in the houses of tragedy, it is for Agamemnon to be murdered in.'[22] The opposite of tragedy is plumbing. For many a tragic theorist, Agamemnon is tragic but Auschwitz is not.

---

[21] See Terry Eagleton, *Sweet Violence: The Idea of the Tragic* (Oxford, 2003), especially Chs 1 & 2.
[22] George Steiner, *The Death of Tragedy* (London, 1961), p. 243.

It is not difficult to see an ethics of the Real as inheriting some of *Kulturkritik*'s patrician prejudices. Tragic theory at its least persuasive is a combination of nihilism and triumphalism. Existence is brutal and absurd, but the unconquerable will of the protagonist raises him serenely above it. Tragedy at its most powerful rebuffs both nihilism and triumphalism. It instructs us in how to hope without optimism. Like Lacanian ethics, it is therefore a suitable creed for those disenchanted radicals who wish to keep the faith without abandoning political realism. If you diminish the human spirit in the manner of the nihilist, you deprive men and women of the criteria by which they might take the measure of their unhappiness; and the consequence of this is that they risk viewing their wretchedness as inevitable rather than intolerable. If you inflate the human spirit in the mode of the triumphalist, human suffering begins to look like a fairly trifling affair.

Hope differs from optimism in that it does not confidently anticipate a positive outcome. This is where the *Kulturkritikers* have the edge over the bright-eyed progressivists. The only hope resilient enough to bring you through is one which is able to stare the possibility of failure steadily in the face. It is what we discover when our powers are broken and baffled, yet when something nevertheless survives to register the fact. As Edgar puts it in *King Lear*: 'The worst is not / So long as we can say "This is the worst"' (4.1.29–30). And this is neither nihilism nor triumphalism. If Jesus had submitted to his death with one canny eye on his imminent resurrection, he would not have been raised from the dead. But neither would he have been raised if he had given way on his desire – a desire which in his case consisted of that peculiar species of love known as faith. ('A believer, after all, is someone in love', writes Kierkegaard in *The Sickness Unto Death*.) Only if crucifixion is not some Houdini-like con-trick but a hellish encounter with the Real of destitution can it constitute the *transitus* to a transfigured life. Only if Jesus acknowledged that his mission had come to nothing, that he was a miserable failure deserted by his panic-stricken comrades, and yet maintained in the teeth of that confession his loving fidelity to what he regarded as the source of his being, could his death bear fruit in the lives of others.

This dialectic of acceptance and transfiguration is also one between the everyday and the extraordinary. It is here that it differs from the contrast between moral nobility and social banality on which *Kulturkritik*, 'high' tragic theory and ethical Realism all insist. It is notable that the New Testament nowhere presents Jesus's suffering as heroic. His death has nothing intrinsically glorious about it. Søren Kierkegaard remarks in *Fear and Trembling* that the tragic hero gives up what is certain for what is still more certain; but he also recognises that there are no guaranteed triumphs in return for acts of faith. Jesus's death is no more to be celebrated than any other human death. Suffering for the Judaeo-Christian culture which gave rise to the gospels is unequivocally evil. It is to be resisted rather than glorified. Jesus never once counsels the sick to be reconciled to their afflictions. On the contrary, he appears to subscribe to the myth that illness is the work of evil spirits. If you can pluck something positive out of your distress, then so much the better; but it would be better still if you did not need to.

Martyrdom – harnessing *Thanatos* to the cause of *Eros*, death to the service of the living – must involve accepting death as a tragic reality, rather than peering expectantly beyond it. Only for those who find that even in these conditions they cannot give up on their faith or love, however meagrely it may be realised or rewarded, can the barrier of death or self-destitution be transfigured into a horizon. Only for those who see death, failure and mortality as the last word, rather than as bargaining chips in some symbolic exchange, might these things prove not quite the last word after all, as the demoniac symphony which concludes Thomas Mann's *Doctor Faustus* ends with an impossible, infinitely hushed, scarcely audible note – a mere frail ghost or gesture on the air, a 'hope beyond hopelessness' which might just hint at some other way of looking and living altogether. Socialism, too, is a tragic project in this sense. It is a practice of solidarity with failure, and is aware that the only durable power is one which springs from a compact with such powerlessness. Only those with little to lose are likely to stake their scanty resources on the perilous chance of a more just future.

The crucifixion is traditionally regarded as the moment in which Christ assumes and redeems human guilt. The guilt in question springs from the lethal collusion of law and desire, as the law or superego drives us not only to punish ourselves for our illicit yearnings but to reap an obscene pleasure from the process, a pleasure which in turn provokes a deeper guilt and thus a more savage self-laceration. If the death of Christ is meant to break open this spiral, it is because, as we have seen, it reveals the law of the Father to be the law of love and justice rather than a death-dealing power. It proclaims the law as grace – as love, ecstasy, liberation, joyful abundance of life – rather than as a yoke of oppression.

Lacanian thought sees a tragic rift between the subject and the Other – between what we are as subjects, and what the inscrutable Other may demand of us. To say that Jesus is the 'Son', by contrast, is to claim that what he is for the Other known as God is also what he is for himself. The source of love, and the source of his personal existence, are identical. He is at one with the law of the Father, a transparent signifier (or 'Word') of it, born wholly of love rather than of the flesh; and it is because of this faithful identification with the roots of his identity, this refusal to give up on his loving trust in the ground of his being, that he is tortured and murdered. His fidelity to the law of the Father is itself an example of limitless love, and thus a revelation of the Father himself. God is not simply the object of his desire, but the source of it; so that the 'bad' infinity of Lacanian desire, whose object perpetually gives it the slip, yields to a desire for the good which is only possible if the good is somehow already enjoyed. One could not search for God, as the old Christian tag has it, unless one had already found him. In this sense, the infinity of desire gives way to an eternity of abundant life. It is charity which is most importantly limitless, not desire. Desire is no longer perpetual loss, once it has assumed the form of faith. Since, however, our morbid clamour is for the Other to chastise rather than forgive us, we are reluctant to relinquish the *jouissance* we reap from such self-punitive fantasies. It is hard to accept the scandal that there could be an Otherness which was actually on our side. To acknowledge this would mean forgoing the masochistic delight which binds us to the law, and would thus require a root-and-branch transformation of the self.

To claim that Jesus is the 'Son' of the Father, then, is to say that he is the authentic image of the Father, revealing him as friend, lover and fellow-victim rather than as patriarchal Nobodaddy, Satanic judge or bloodthirsty despot. Jesus was not murdered by his Father but by the Roman state and its supine colonial lackeys, who took fright at his message of mercy and justice, as well as at his enormous popularity with the poor, and did away with him in a highly volatile political situation. It did not help that a number of his closest comrades were probably Zealots or anti-imperialist revolutionaries. The holy terror of divine love thus becomes the holy terror of the guilty innocent, the scapegoat who is savaged for the sake of others. It is not that God has a benign presence but also an obscenely sadistic underside, but rather that he is a terrorist of love. The message of the crucifixion is that those who call in the tradition of the Old Testament prophets for the poor to come to power will be done to death by the state. The resurrection suggests that this victory is not quite the last word.

The idolatrous, superegoic image of the law is consequently toppled from its pride of place. Because of this, it is now possible in principle to love and desire without guilt. The lack of being which is desire can be seen as a trace of that deeper negativity which is God. We are thus set free from the tragic condition in which desire provokes the malicious sadism of the law, and thus nurtures in us that festering culture of guilt for which the classical Christian term is original sin. Astonishingly, a non-obscene form of *jouissance* or ecstasy now becomes possible. Like *Thanatos* or the death drive, this *jouissance* is in Lacanian phrase 'good for nothing', madly in excess of utility; but this is now the good-for-nothingness of Creation itself, which as pure, unmotivated gift and grace has absolutely no point beyond God's supreme self-delight. The law's terror stands unmasked as the implacable extremism of divine love – love itself exposed as a violent, disruptive, traumatic demand, and thus as nothing less than the Janus-faced Real. If desire is no longer illicit – if we can now love one another without guilt – it is because we have accepted the intolerable fact that the source of this love has always-already forgiven us, accepts us just as we are in all our moral squalor, and demands nothing from us other than that he should be allowed to love us. There is, astonishingly, a form of the Real which desires our welfare rather than disrupts it, and which will not let us founder. We are thereby rudely robbed of the obscene pleasure of our remorse, which at least assures us that we exist.

All this can be read as an allegory of an ethics of the Real. The Real, like the love of God, is a holy terror, at once sacred and cursed. It is the place where we fall prey to the vindictive fury of the death drive, yet also the place where we can be released from its shackles. The destitution of despair may be closer than it appears to the self-dispossession of love. By embracing the powers of death, we can shift in Lacan's view from the register of desire to that of the drive. In doing so, we are borne through the well-tilled terrain of the law and out the other side, into an outlaw region or Wild West of the spirit in which the only law that counts is the law of our desire. We have exchanged the symbolic law for the law of the Real. The burdensome necessity of the symbolic law gives way to the life-giving necessity of holding fast to one's desire, which like all genuine moral impulses is felt to be ineluctable. The only guilt to be feared now is the bad faith of giving way on this desire, which is affirmed as the very essence of one's being. In this respect, Lacan is in his own way as much an essentialist as Lawrence.

The living dead are those self-tormentors who are caught in the toils of the law, trapped in the eternal hell of a frozen dialectic between desire and self-loathing; but once death is seen as a threshold rather than a cul-de-sac, these zombie-like or vampiric creatures can now die for real, embracing their own finitude, seizing upon the death drive and converting it into the very dynamic of their desire. In doing so, they affirm a curious kind of immortality. No longer to be afraid of death is to enjoy a kind of eternal life. It is this condition which Lacan has in mind when he remarks that only in this province beyond the symbolic order 'may the signification of a limitless love emerge, because it is outside the limits of the law, where alone it may live'.[23] Only by renouncing the immediate objects of our affection, which Lacan sees as in Kant's sense 'pathological', can we affirm that purity of desire which is the Real. In doing so, we liberate ourselves from guilt and are therefore able to love unreservedly.

As with Christianity, then, Lacan's ethic is a sacrificial one. In fact, he once remarked that if any religion was true, which he did not credit for a moment, it was Christianity. But there are key differences between the two doctrines. Lacan contrasts a love of worldly things with the desire of the Real for which such things must be given up. Christianity, on the other hand, sees no such sharp opposition between worldliness and the Real. Christ relinquished the world out of love for it. He was prepared to lose everything for love for humanity. For an incarnational faith, the Real is not an alternative to the love of others, as it would appear to be for some Lacanians. Rather, it is realised through it. As Eric Santner writes: 'We don't . . . need God for the sake of divine things but for the sake of proper attentiveness to secular things.'[24] In this sense, there is no final antagonism for Christian faith between the Real and the symbolic, God and others, desire and love, the momentous and the mundane. Love-objects are not decoys on the path of desire, but the way in which the Real of divine love may be routinely encountered. Indeed, for Judaeo-Christian belief others are only truly objects of love when they are encountered 'in the Real' – which is to say, as the bearers of a sublime strangeness which resists the *égoisme à deux* of the imaginary and has its source in the transcendence of the Father.

The claim that one's repellently alien neighbour is to be loved 'as oneself' is a recipe for sweated labour, not for narcissism. This is because loving oneself is scarcely an easy task, involving as it does an acceptance of the disfiguring Real at the core of one's own identity. Yet this, in contrast to the mutual admiration of the imaginary, or those contractual arrangements between autonomous subjects which characterise the symbolic, can then become the solid ground on which human beings may meet. The twin scriptural commands – to love God, and to love one's neighbour as oneself – are in one sense to be taken as inseparable: love of one's neighbour is

---

[23] Jacques Lacan, *The Four Fundamental Concepts of Psychoanalysis* (London, 1977), p. 276.
[24] Eric Santner, 'Miracles Happen: Benjamin, Rosenzweig, Freud, and the Matter of the Neighbor', in S. Žižek, E. Santner and K. Reinhard (eds), *The Neighbor* (Chicago and London, 2005), p. 133.

only possible if it is grounded in the Real. Yet they are also to be distinguished, to make the point that not all love of neighbour is so well-founded. There are imaginary ways of loving one's neighbour which fall far short of the Real – that is to say, which lack the kind of impersonal, sacrificial, self-dispossessing love which would be necessary to bring a new social order into being.

In this sense, not all love of neighbour signifies the kind of secret narcissism to which some Lacanians seem eager to reduce it. The love that does not is of this sacrificial kind. It is the one which Marx portrays in his *Contribution to the Critique of Hegel's Philosophy of Right* as being required if a 'total loss of humanity' is to be converted into 'a total gain of humanity'. The scapegoat or sacrificial object – in Marx's case, the proletariat – is one who passes from weakness to power; and the psychoanalytical name for this movement from the lowly to the exalted is sublimation. As Hans Castorp comes to recognise in the great snow scene in Thomas Mann's *The Magic Mountain*, it is love, not reason, which is stronger than death, and from that insight alone can spring the sweetness of civilisation – but 'always in silent recognition of the blood sacrifice'. One must honour beauty and nobility of spirit, while acknowledging the horror and wretchedness which lie at their root.

In the end, the ethical thought of a Lacan, Levinas or Badiou is simply not boring or bathetic enough.[25] In an era which seems to many bereft of much inherent value, these thinkers are too ready to trade the immanent for the transcendent. In this respect, their thought contrasts unfavourably with a Christian ethics, for which there is no need to choose on this score. To give bread to the hungry is to live the life of divine grace. The ethical Realists are a good deal more ascetic, 'religious' and otherworldly than Judaeo-Christian morality, which is nothing if not materialist. Bathos is the constitutive figure of this latter legacy – as it is, for that matter, of psychoanalysis, for which the object will always fall lamentably short of the desire for it. There is no conflict here between immanence and transcendence, as there is for the Realists. The Yahweh of the Old Testament proclaims that his people shall know him for who he is when they welcome the immigrants, care for the destitute and protect the poor from the violence of the rich.

There is a carnivalesque quality about a faith for which the whole cosmos is at stake in the gift of a cup of water. The Son of Man sweeps majestically

[25]   For an excellent critique of Lacanian ethics from the viewpoint of comedy, see Simon Critchley, *Ethics–Politics–Subjectivity* (London, 1999), Ch. 10.

down on clouds of glory only to inquire prosaically whether you have visited the sick and fed the hungry. Conventional Messiahs tend to make their entrance into the national capital in bullet-proof limousines with police outriders, not on a donkey. Jesus is presented as a sick joke of a Saviour. Yet the Christian gospel sees in such humdrum activity as clothing the naked the foretaste of a transfiguration of the earth, one which is folly to the French. The exceptional and the everyday are not divided domains, as they are for the disciples of Lacan. The material world is the sole locus of redemption. As Graham Pechey writes, behind modern writing's 'junking of the classical "separation of styles" (*Stiltrennung*) and its discovery of the serious and the tragic in the everyday was a run-of-the-mill police action in Roman Judaea which has shaken the world'.[26]

The same is true of a socialist ethics, for which routine forms of comradeship in the present prefigure the revolutionary regime of the future. Classical Marxism adheres to the 'Real' of revolution, with its full panoply of drama, crisis and disruption; but this momentous rupture exists for the sake of the common life, and is wrought by the common people. If there is heroism, it is that of the anti-heroic masses. The Real and the symbolic are not to be riven apart. Neither are they for psychoanalysis, for which the death drive is the invisible colour of everyday life.

This tension between immanence and transcendence crops up in St John's gospel as one between loving and spurning the world. The world, in the sense of the dominant system of power, will vilify the apostles of justice, and is therefore to be rebuffed. Yet this is not some Derridean distaste for everyday existence, any more than it reflects the ultra-leftist otherworldliness of an Alain Badiou. For the world is also, so we are told, what God is in love with. Since it is his own creation, political dissent is not to be confused with an ascetic distaste for the fleshly and finite. The flesh, as Badiou recognises in his study of St Paul, signifies not the body, which is God's holy creation, but a corrupt and violent form of political life. Christianity and socialism are indeed otherworldly creeds: both look to a transformed humanity. But they do so because of their concern for actually existing men and women, not because they yearn for pie in the sky. There is little opiate delusion in Jesus's warning to his comrades that if they are true to his gospel they will be murdered. Those who scorn such otherworldliness are known as liberals or conservatives. They have fallen for the outlandish proposition that this, give or take the odd judicious reform, is

---

[26] Graham Pechey, *Mikhail Bakhtin: The Word in the World* (London, 2007), p. 155.

as good as it gets. It is this assumption which is naively unrealistic, not the belief that human existence could be feasibly much improved.

The voice of the (ethical) hero, Lacan writes in *The Ethics of Psychoanalysis*, 'trembles before nothing... and especially not before the good of the other'.[27] Altruism, equality and a respect for rights are the preserve of a symbolic ethics, to which Lacan respectfully pays his dues; but to his mind this ethics fails to cut deep enough. An ethics of the Real harbours a prejudice against philanthropy, which one imagines those in need of urgent assistance do not share quite so fervently. Ethics is not a matter of happiness, self-fulfilment or serving the good of others.

Yet Lacan's own arguments against this case in *The Ethics of Psychoanalysis* are remarkably feeble. The domain of goodness or virtue inevitably involves power, he points out, since who is to control and distribute the various social goods – goods which in his view are anyway no more than distractions on the path to realising one's desire? Yet a desire for the Real may surely involve power every bit as much. Certainly Clarissa Harlowe exerts an enormous authority by being so perversely resolute for death. Besides, Lacan claims, the question of the good raises the issue of whose good is at stake, as though this were enough to discredit it. Žižek and Zupančič advance just the same argument. They do not seem to appreciate that an endless wrangling about what and whose good is involved in any particular situation is precisely what is traditionally meant by ethics. Doing good does not allay one's guilt, Lacan sternly reminds us, as though anyone ever imagined that it did. Wanting what is good for others, he believes, is generally a matter of wanting what is good for oneself. Philanthropy, in short, is a kind of con trick. We must set our ethical sights on higher things than caring for others, which the welfare services can doubtless do on our behalf.

In an otherwise outstanding study, Alenka Zupančič speaks scornfully of the *jouissance* of an ethics of the Real being 'domesticated' by the love of one's neighbour.[28] This is not, one suspects, the view of those who have just been crushed under a truck on a street crowded with onlookers. The philosopher Catherine Chalier believes both Kant and Levinas are right to

---

[27]   Lacan, *Ethics of Psychoanalysis*, p. 323.
[28]   Zupančič, *Ethics of the Real*, p. 23.

reject an ethics of happiness, since it is bound to stem from self-love.[29] It is not clear why happiness is egoistic but not, say, desire. Levinas himself is deeply nervous of the notion of happiness, which risks anaesthetising us against the agony we ought to feel in the presence of the Other. We can, he fears, come to forget God in our enjoyment of sublunary things, rather as for Lacan such relish can lead us to forget the Real. Happiness is almost always regarded by Levinas as a kind of bovine complacency.[30] Another ethical Realist, Kenneth Reinhard, declares himself opposed to treating one's neighbour 'as my "fellow man", *mon semblable*, whose good (self-preservation, satisfaction of needs) I imagine in the mirror of my own ego'.[31] But there is no reason to suspect that all human charity is of this callowly narcissistic kind. Love of one's neighbour may result in one's death, as it does in the case of Antigone. Some Realists contrast the so-called animal pleasures of altruism (essentially an imaginary affair) with the sublime *jouissance* of the Real. But as Lacan himself teaches, *jouissance* involves an acceptance of death, and so does the love of others. Even if one does not die literally, as in the case of the martyr, death remains a metaphor of the self-abandonment which such love entails. There is no necessary conflict between compassion and the Real, the neighbourly and the alien. Clarissa turns her back on humankind and gives herself up to God, yet it is a tenet of the Christian faith to which she adheres that this God is most fundamentally present in the dispossessed. By being framed in a fiction, she dies on behalf of all the abused women of her time, not simply in glorious solitude.

Besides, one should not be too eager to dismiss the value of self-love, as Reinhard appears to do. It is a familiar moral insight that the good and just person will wish good and just things for herself, without which resources she will be less well-equipped to care for others. Not all self-love is smug and sterile. Why should I be licensed to treat myself more shabbily than I do anyone else? Why should I be dispensed from the universal law of charity just because I happen to be me? The injunction to behave towards others as I behave towards myself only works if I treat myself with a degree of respect. And there is no reason to suppose that this is a natural or spontaneous matter. For Christian belief, loving oneself requires the grace of God quite as much as loving others.

[29] Catherine Chalier, *What Ought I To Do? Morality in Kant and Levinas* (Ithaca, NY, 2002), p. 133.
[30] See, for example, Emmanuel Levinas, *Noms propres* (Montpellier, 1976), p. 169.
[31] Kenneth Reinhard, 'Towards a Political Theology of the Neighbor', in Žižek, Santner and Reinhard, *The Neighbor*, p. 48.

Sophocles's Creon, as representative of the *polis*, is engaged in the control and distribution of the good, a bureaucracy of the spirit which does not interest Lacan unduly. This is ethics as no more than the *'service des biens'*. What seizes the Lacanian imagination is not Creon, champion of Kantian practical reason, but Antigone – not a regulated economy of public goods but the excess of a solitary, death-driven desire, one which has travelled beyond all sublunary interests and gratifications. 'Only the martyrs know neither pity or fear', Lacan comments proudly, forgetful perhaps of the garden of Gethsemane, a scriptural scene which presents Jesus as badly panicking on the eve of his death.[32] The traditional martyr places his or her death at the service of the living, harnessing *Thanatos* to the ends of *Eros*; the Lacanian martyr-hero surrenders it to the cause or Thing within her which is her desire, experienced as some solitary *jouissance* beyond the far-flung outposts of social existence.

So it is that Zupančič can speak of the ethical refusal to be 'seduced' by pleasure, compassion, love of one's neighbour, happiness, public good and the like. To think of ethics along these sublunary lines – as bioethics, cultural ethics, medical ethics, environmental ethics and so on – reflects on this view a craven incapacity to contemplate an ethics of the Real.[33] Common-or-garden charity is an unconscious defence against the grisly splendours of *jouissance*, an expenditure which unlike social reform or soup kitchens is good for nothing. Mere moral 'actions' must be contrasted with revolutionary ethical 'acts', a term which elsewhere in Zupančič's account, as if to drive the point home, is transmogrified into the rather more dignified 'Acts'. If only such pure acts are truly ethical, then morality would seem in as short supply as political revolution. Slavoj Žižek speaks disparagingly of conventional or symbolic morality as 'the smooth running of affairs in the domain of Being',[34] as though the ethical were merely a perfunctory oiling of the administrative wheels. Ethics is aristocratic, whereas morality is petty bourgeois. From the Olympian vantage-point of the Real, everyday life looks tediously uniform and automated. It is not to be grasped first and foremost (as Žižek generally does) as an arena of ethical and political conflict. Compared to the sublime splendour of the Real, its internal struggles and contradictions appear relatively trifling. They are a question of suburban morality rather than of elitist ethics.

The aim of psychoanalysis, remarks John Rajchman, 'is not to make us more virtuous citizens or more productive workers'. The implication is

---

[32] Lacan, *Ethics of Psychoanalysis*, p. 267.
[33] Zupančič, *Ethics of the Real*, p. 95.
[34] Slavoj Žižek, *The Ticklish Subject* (London, 1999), p. 143.

that virtuous citizens are simply those rather sad, buttoned-down creatures who mindlessly support the state, rather than those, say, who exercise their virtue in order to call its power into question. If Edgar J. Hoover was a virtuous citizen, so was Robespierre. Similarly, breeding productive workers may have been a conservative project in Hitler's Germany, but it remains a constructive one in many a region of the post-colonial world. The stuff of psychoanalysis, as Rajchman claims, is indeed human discontent; but there is a rather vital distinction between being discontented with life in Nazi Germany and being distraught about the expulsion of the *ancien régime* from Castro's Cuba. If such differences are not noted, one is at risk of reproducing in rather more sophisticated guise the jaded Romantic contrast between lonely dissident and uniformly oppressive state. Much ethics of the Real falls into just this hackneyed posture.

There is a predictable dash of the Dionysian about Lacan's attitude to the ethical life. The desire of humanity in our age, so he considers, has been gentrified, castrated, lulled and domesticated by *bien-pensant* moralisers, reformists and educators. It is as though the moral is feminine while the ethical is masculine. Modern political culture, obsessed with the mere 'service of goods' – with happiness, welfare, well-being, civil rights and other such anodyne instances of the reality principle – has abandoned the key ethical question of Man's relation to his desire. The field of welfare, rights and so on, Lacan magnanimously concedes, 'exists, of course, and there is no point in denying that'.[35] It is just that one gleans the impression that, as with typhoid, he rather wishes that it didn't. Conscious perhaps of the perils of ethical elitism, he goes on to insist that there is no fundamental distinction between the tragic hero and the common individual. 'In each of us the path of the hero is traced', he writes, 'and it is precisely as an ordinary man that one follows it to the end.'[36] The hero experiences all the passions of the average person, 'except that in his case they are pure and he succeeds in supporting himself there fully'.[37] So the hero is really just the man next door; yet we are told in the same breath that he is nothing of the kind. Having generously annulled the difference between the exceptional and the average, Lacan instantly reinstates it. The average individual, he informs us, tends to back down on his desire when he is betrayed, returning to the inferior realm of the service of goods, whereas the hero remains true to his passion. Such egregious figures take their desire to the

---

[35] Ibid., p. 321.
[36] Ibid., p. 319.
[37] Ibid. p. 320.

point where it can no longer be represented, a point at which they perish of the truth.

Kant writes in *Religion within the Limits of Reason* of that revolution in an individual's disposition whereby he or she becomes a kind of new creation. It is this which we need if we are to move from the 'pathological' to the ethical. An ethics of the Real valuably inherits this doctrine, pivoting as it does on some 'impossible' revelation or extremity which turns our symbolic universe upside down, some tumultuous event which throws us out of joint, re-totalises our world and violently recasts the foundations of our existence. Only such a revolutionary ethics, the Realists are right to see, can answer to our unregenerate condition, whether personally or politically. When it comes to politics, only those who have thrown realism to the winds – liberals, conservatives, reformists and the like – could imagine that any change less deep-seated than this, given our calamitous political condition, would yield us anything like as much as we need.

One problem with this road-to-Damascus revelation, however, is what is to happen in its wake. There is little clue in Lacanian theory as to how the ethical hero's solitary encounter with the Real might forge a path to political transformation. As far as politics goes, this ethic is both too elitist and too unsociable to lend itself easily to such translation. Politics and ethics are for the most part on different sides of the fence. In any case, we need to ask whether all men and women must become Lears or Antigones in order to live well. The mistake of the Realists is to take as a paradigm of the moral life what is really a highly exceptional experience. In modernist fashion, the extreme defines the norm. But one needs an ethics appropriate to the orthopaedic hospital and pre-school playgroup, not just to the death camps and the barricades. An ethics which illuminates the moment of conversion, revelation, disruption or revolution, as this one valuably does, cannot be projected on to social life as a whole, which will inevitably prove unequal to it. The Real is thus in danger of behaving like the Freudian superego or Kantian moral law, rubbing our noses in our own frailty by making demands which we find impossible to fulfil.

For Alain Badiou, there can be translation of a kind from the one realm to the other. The answer to how the Real converges with the symbolic is to preserve a day-to-day fidelity to the truth which it makes manifest. This, so to speak, is Badiou's version of the Incarnation, the intersection of the infinite with the finite. It is not easy to see what it would mean to translate the exceptional into the ordinary in this way; but at least Badiou assumes some continuity between the two. In general, however, translating into political terms an ethics which is framed in large part against the *polis* proves a problem for ethical Realism. As Bernard Williams remarks in another context, one 'would have to admit that virtue as purity of heart, while it was the only good, could only be a minority accomplishment, and this would need another politics in its turn, in order to construct the relation of that virtue to unregenerate society'.[38] It is just this which, as we have seen, Levinas fumbles somewhat ineffectually to achieve.

Christianity has its own response to the question of whether all men and women must become Lears or Antigones, which is the doctrine that Christ's sacrifice was once and for all. Because he is scapegoat or *pharmakos* who assumed our guilt as the polluted signifier of pure humanity, his followers do not have literally to endure such bloody self-dispossession themselves. Instead, they share in it semiotically, at the level of sign or sacrament. The Eucharistic meal commemorates the turbulent passage from the old dispensation to the new, rather as Badiou's subject of truth stays faithful to the founding event. But though all Christians must be potential martyrs, prepared literally to lay down their lives for others, it is through the signifier that continuity with the original transformation is maintained. It is through the signifier, too, in the sense of the talking cure, that the patient in the scene of analysis negotiates the passage from an oppressed to an emancipated state. What is at stake, in Žižek's phrase, is 'subjective destitution' rather than a literal loss of self. As for politics, those who wish to see the poor come to power are not required to be poverty-stricken themselves, though it may enhance their political credibility not to own too many Picassos either. It is political solidarity that matters, not a literal sharing of others' deprivations.

It is not, however, primarily in sacramental terms that Christians re-enact the self-abandonment of Christ. It happens instead through run-of-the-mill love. It is in compassion and forgiveness, not first of all in ritual, burnt offerings, moral codes or elaborate diets, that Yahweh's love is made manifest. And in this human arena, it is made manifest first of all in the poor and dispossessed. The age of religion is superseded on Calvary: as the author of the *Letter to the Hebrews* observes, Christ is the last high priest, who has 'entered once and for all into the Holy Place, taking not the blood of goats and calves but his own blood, thus securing eternal redemption' (9.11). The only burnt offering that counts in the new dispensation is a broken human body. It is around this monstrous truth that a new kind of solidarity must be constructed, one which cuts uncompromisingly across the given roles of the symbolic order. This is one

---

[38] Bernard Williams, *Ethics and the Limits of Philosophy* (Cambridge, MA, 1985), p. 46.

reason why the New Testament is so indifferent to sexuality and so dismissive of the family.

In contrast to a Realist ethics, then, Christianity brings together the impossible and the everyday, transcendence and immanence, the Event and its historical aftermath, in what one might call the sublunary sublime. Kierkegaard speaks of the knight of faith as 'express(ing) the sublime in the pedestrian'.[39] Commonplace love re-enacts the crucifixion since it involves a metaphorical death or self-giving. This liaison between love and death is largely overlooked by Martin Heidegger's great philosophical classic *Being and Time*. Both being-with-others and being-towards-death are constitutive for Heidegger of *Dasein* or the human; yet he fails for the most part to grasp how the everyday form of dying-to-self which is love is a rehearsal for the final self-divestment which is death. Ethics is about love, not desire. There is no path from ethics as desire to the daily life of the *polis*; but there is, as we shall see, one from ethics as love.

With Christianity, then, there emerges a new esteem for the ordinary. Charles Taylor sees the Baconian revolution of early modern society as one which 'displaces the locus of the good life from some special range of higher activities and places it within "life" itself'.[40] Codes of honour and glory give way to a concern with labour, commerce, sexuality and family life. Spiritual value is no longer an elitist affair, but part of daily existence. It is above all the Reformation, with its sanctification of ordinary life, that erodes the barriers between sacred and profane; but Taylor finds the origins of this erosion in Judaeo-Christian spirituality as such, with its affirmation of the everyday. It is the preciousness of ordinary life which makes Jesus's execution tragic, whereas Socrates goes to his death in the belief that he is losing nothing of great value. Sacrifice implies the value of what is being surrendered. 'For the Christian', Taylor writes, 'what is renounced is thereby affirmed as good.'[41] Since all life stems from God, simply to be alive is now a value in itself, a view hardly shared by the kind of pagan warrior caste for whom honour outranks mere existence.

In his great study *Mimesis*, Erich Auerbach contrasts the essentially simple psychology of the Homeric poems with the intricate, multilayered, evolving human figures of the Hebrew scriptures. 'From the very first, in the Old Testament stories', he comments, 'the sublime, tragic and

[39]   Søren Kierkegaard, *Fear and Trembling and The Sickness Unto Death*, ed. Walter Lowrie (New York, 1954), p. 70.
[40]   Charles Taylor, *Sources of the Self* (Cambridge, 1989), p. 213.
[41]   Ibid., p. 219.

problematic take shape precisely in the domestic and commonplace.'[42] If the Homeric texts portray the affairs of an aristocracy, the Old Testament has a feel for the common people: 'Its activity is always discernible, it is often in ferment, it frequently intervenes in events not only as a whole but also in separate groups and through the medium of separate individuals who come forward; the origins of prophecy seem to lie in the irrepressible spontaneity of the people.'[43] It was this culture which was to produce in its Christian sequel the first universal movement of the common people known to history.

Alain Badiou, as we have seen, urges us to keep faith with the revolutionary event. Yet it is a mistake to imagine that a just society must remain in perpetual thrall to its moment of foundation. On the contrary, one index of its emancipation is that it no longer has need of such moral heroism. Once the 'Real' of political revolution has occurred, it is free to turn its back on this tragic drama and enjoy a fulfilling everyday existence. Here, as in Christian doctrine, crisis and conversion are to be seen as in the service of common existence, the Real regarded as the handmaiden of the symbolic. But the two are also at one in this sense – that to establish such unheroic, workaday virtues of justice and equality on a universal scale, given the kind of world we have, would require nothing short of a full-blooded transformation. For ethics to assume the fluency of the imaginary – for it to take on the ease of habit we know as virtue – requires, politically speaking, the agency and self-discipline of the symbolic, but also the traumatic discontinuities of the Real.

Lacan admires Aristotle, but finds his ethics irreparably lacking. Virtue ethics is too mundane a moral discourse for the champions of Oedipus and Antigone, too little a question of sublimity or transcendence. It belongs too stolidly to the symbolic rather than the Real. It is a line of inquiry which finds more to cherish in everyday social existence than the disciples of Lacan, Derrida and Badiou are prepared to stomach. Yet the moral tradition which flows from Aristotle offers an important challenge to the asceticism of the Realists. Set beside the sullen unsociability of a Realist ethics, a vein of moral thought for which human goods are deeply embedded in social and political existence is bound to appear inviting. Faced with the

---

[42] Erich Auerbach, *Mimesis: The Representation of Reality in Western Literature* (Princeton, NJ and Oxford, 2003), p. 2.
[43] Ibid., p. 21.

death-ridden ecstasy of *jouissance*, it is a relief to turn to an ethics for which the good consists in a high-spirited abundance of life – in the pleasurable fulfilment of one's distinctive animal nature. Whereas the Lacanians regard clinging to one's desire as an end in itself, virtue ethicists feel the same way about human flourishing. It is just that their idea of flourishing presumes rather more sense of a coherent self than postmodern thought is prepared to concede.

Faced with high-toned Kantian talk of law, right, duty, principle and obligation, one is bound to be struck by a virtue ethics which shows little concern for such matters (which is not to suggest that rights, imperatives and prohibitions, even absolute ones, need play no part in such a moral theory). Kantian ethics is modelled on the superego, whereas virtue ethics is not; and though this does not of course free us of this disagreeable power, it remains true that virtue ethics recommends a mode of human conduct which at least does not reinforce it. With virtue ethics, we are in a world of contexts rather than sibylline commands, social institutions rather than transcendent states of being.[44] The ethical is not a seductively unattainable ideal but a common material practice. There is nothing ineffable or exorbitant about it. We are speaking of the shape and texture of average lives, not of the aesthetic splendour of isolated acts.

Actions are not to be assessed simply in terms of what they get accomplished; we want to act in a certain way, not just to bring about certain states of affairs. Virtue ethics returns the study of action, will, feeling, intention, motive, consequence and so on to the 'moral personality', grasping them not as isolated phenomena but as products of an historical process of subject-formation, or (in an older idiom) 'character'. In thus resisting the ethical equivalent of the death of the author, it re-embeds moral discourse in the whole business of culture, childhood, upbringing, kinship, politics and education. As such, it is closer to the novel than to the Highway Code. To act well is not just to do the right thing, which is where this style of morality differs from some symbolic ethics; but neither is right action guaranteed by compassion and fellow-feeling, which is where it diverges from some imaginary moral discourse. Ethics for Aristotle is the science of human desire; but one reason why some Realists are so patronising about him is that the desires in question are this or that palpable want or need, not that modern form of metaphysics which is desire *tout court*. It is true that, given this empirical bent, virtue ethics can always lapse into a complacent acquiescence in the given, as the later Wittgenstein has been charged

---

[44] For a valuable account, see Rosalind Hursthouse, *On Virtue Ethics* (Oxford, 1999).

with doing. An embrace of the everyday can doubtless be conservative in effect. Even so, it may prove less politically injurious in the long run than an apocalypticism of the Real.

Virtue ethics discriminates among different qualities of action and character, rather than concerning itself with ontological hierarchies. Unlike the ethical Realists, it takes happiness, pleasure and well-being entirely seriously. For Aristotle, human happiness is an activity, not in the first place a state of mind. It is something we have to get good at. The fulfilled individual is the one who has made a success of the precarious project of being human. In the end, ethics is about knowing how to live enjoyably and abundantly, not about a fidelity to law or desire. It is about doing what you want to do (a difficult enough matter to determine, sure enough), as well as what it is right to do. Virtue ethics does not rate being true to one's deepest desire, or bowing to the moral law for its own sake, as goods superior to mercy or compassion. Laws and obligations are essential, but they are to be seen as the scaffolding of a form of life, not treated as fetishes to be revered in themselves. We could no more reduce morality to a set of rules than we could exhaustively codify our culture. Sabina Lovibond writes of 'the dependence of our powers of rational communication on a "likemindedness" not of our own making – one that goes beyond any mere collective adherence to a common code of rules'.[45] Imaginary resemblances rather than symbolic obligations are at work here. Practical reason involves a kind of tact, flair or (as Aristotle calls it) *phronesis*, which is where it is closer to the imaginary than to the symbolic. It is close to the imaginary, too, in that it sees virtue as rooted in the mimetic, beginning as it does in childhood imitation. Nor does this moral lineage imagine that there is a certain class of reasons for acting called 'moral' reasons, which differ in some vital way from other sorts of reasons. In this sense, so Bernard Williams maintains, ancient Greek thought 'basically lacks the concept of *morality* altogether'.[46] It was Kant, he claims, who introduced this curious notion to the world.

There are problems with virtue ethics, as there are with any other moral theory. It is an anthropological ethics, based in some cases on a theory of human nature which many nowadays would find implausible. Besides, Aristotle's own favoured virtues are not unreservedly appealing to the modern sensibility. His chief example of the virtuous individual, the

---

[45]   Sabina Lovibond, *Ethical Formation* (Cambridge, MA and London, 2002), p. 30.

[46]   Bernard Williams, 'Philosophy', in M. Finley (ed.), *The Legacy of Greece, 202–55* (Oxford, 1981), p. 251.

so-called 'great-souled man', is odiously condescending, priggishly unself-critical, arrogantly self-sufficient, too proud to be in the debt of others and possessed of a distinctly low opinion of them. If this is virtue, a spot of vice may well not come amiss. Such an ethics must also confront the psycho-analytic claim that there is that within our everyday desires which tends to play havoc with them. As for self-realisation, what is to count as an authentic model of this? Above all, virtue ethics would seem to lack much conception of the Real. It belongs wholly to the symbolic order, and fails to feel the full weight of such matters as death, sacrifice, tragedy, self-dispossession, loss, desire, negativity, impasse and the extreme strangeness of the self. In some respects, it is too gentrified an ethics for that. Aristotle is our first great theorist of tragedy, yet his *Ethics* is damagingly remote from his *Poetics*. He would not have understood that flourishing and loss are intimately allied.

Even so, there is more in the idea of virtue, excessively 'civic' though it may occasionally be, than the neurotic compulsion of habit, which is how Jacques Lacan seems to regard it. The unfashionability of virtue ethics in avant-garde Europe has doubtless much to do with its prizing of regularity, continuity, predictability and the coherent self. It would also seem to some conservative in its emphasis on the conventions of a given way of life – which is not to say that a radical virtue ethics is in the least out of the question.[47] But its unmodishness is also to do with the demoting of Hegel, the mighty inheritor of this current in modern times, in exchange for the virtual apotheosis of Kant. The latter has been treated by many a moral philosopher with the kind of reverence which he himself reserves for the moral law. Kant is undoubtedly more appealing than Hegel to an anti-totalising age which believes that it has seen off grand narratives. With his scrupulous distinctions between areas of inquiry, he is also congenial to an epoch which looks to ethics for an alternative to a failed politics. If politics have been fatally compromised, then ethics may furnish an alternative source of value. Yet Hegel, as a true disciple of Aristotle, makes no such sharp division between the two domains. In this he is true to his ancient Greek mentor. There is a science that studies the supreme good of man, Aristotle informs the reader at the start of his *Nicomachean Ethics*, adding somewhat surprisingly that its name is politics.

Indeed, whether or in what sense the ethical is a distinctive 'domain' is a question worth raising. Jacques Derrida denies that this is so in *Of Spirit*, while arguing often enough as though it was. He writes in 'Force of Law'

---

[47]   See, for example, Lovibond's excellent study, *Ethical Formation*.

of the ethical, political, economic and so on as 'fields', but also sees them as caught up with each other to the point where the term will no longer quite suffice.[48] The ethical is certainly a distinctive dimension of human existence for Søren Kierkegaard. Martin Heidegger argues in his *Letter on Humanism* that the question of the 'ought' as a special area of inquiry is a latecomer to human thought, arising only with the birth of Platonic philosophy. The whole tortuous business of relating the ethical to the political in the writings of Levinas springs from the assumption that they are two distinct provinces. The American critic J. Hillis Miller speaks of an ethical moment in reading which is 'neither cognitive, nor political, nor social, nor interpersonal, but properly and independently ethical'.[49] On any reasonably thick conception of the moral life, it would be hard to say what such a moment would look like; but if one adopts the thin Kantian version of morality, as Miller does, the answer, predictably, is an absolute imperative. Such an imperative, Miller considers, 'cannot be accounted for by the social and historical forces which impinge on it'.[50] The critic Paul de Man regards the ethical dimension of reading as a 'law of the text' which imposes itself upon us ineluctably.

Simon Critchley argues in *The Ethics of Deconstruction* that 'politics begins as ethics', a proposition which we shall later take leave to doubt; that the ethical and political communities are nonetheless simultaneous, since 'begins' here signals an ontological rather than temporal priority; and that society has a double structure, as at once a communality among equals (politics) and a more lopsided order based upon the inegalitarian moment of (Levinasian) ethics. Political space, Critchley suggests, 'is based on the irreducibility of ethical transcendence . . . (it) is an open, plural, opaque network of ethical relations which are non-totalisable . . . '.[51] It is not hard to feel that the political has here been more or less ousted by the ethical. One wonders in any case, with that 'open', 'plural' and 'non-totalisable' in mind, what a supposedly deconstructive ethics has contributed to the argument that a tediously familiar liberal pluralism does not. Kenneth Reinhard believes that Levinas posits an 'unbridgeable gap' or 'fundamental aporia' between ethics and politics, and that he is right to do so – even though 'it is only from the perspective of the political in its radical non-relationship with ethics that love as such can emerge . . . '.[52] It is instructive to learn that

---

[48] Derrida, 'Force of Law', p. 257.
[49] J. Hillis Miller, *The Ethics of Reading* (New York, 1987), p. 1.
[50] Ibid., p. 8.
[51] Simon Critchley, *The Ethics of Deconstruction* (Oxford, 1992), p. 225.
[52] Reinhard, 'Towards a Political Theology of the Neighbor', p. 49.

the non-relationship between ethics and politics is radical, rather than simply a non-relationship.

One might contrast these formulations with the views of the philosopher Herbert McCabe, who claims that there is no such thing as seeing something 'at the moral level' or 'in the light of morality'. The claim is perhaps rather dubious: we sometimes need to distinguish 'the moral point of view' from the technical or aesthetic or political point of view. But it is, so to speak, a generous error. Ethics for McCabe is more like literary criticism than it is like the application of codes or principles. Its purpose, he argues, 'is to enable us to enjoy life more by responding to it more sensitively, by entering into the significance of human action'.[53] And this investigation, like that of the analysis of a complex literary text, is in principle limitless. It is not that McCabe dismisses moral laws and principles (indeed, he is an absolutist where some of them are concerned), but that such precepts and prohibitions make sense only in the context of such a broader, conceptually thicker inquiry. Ethics concerns the texture and quality of a whole form of life. It is from this that we must start, not from absolute obligations and infinite responsibilities. Ethics and politics are distinct modes of investigation in the sense that each scrutinises social existence from a different angle – in the case of ethics, the values and qualities of human conduct and relationships; in the case of politics, public institutions and processes of power. Yet there is no clear ontological distinction at stake here. The difference is more methodological than real.

Slavoj Žižek rejects the privilege that Levinas assigns to the face-to-face Other.[54] Instead, he rightly insists that the political is the condition of the ethical, not *vice versa*. In his view, justice takes priority over love, the so-called third party over the one most proximate. Yet this is to invert Levinas's opposition, not to dismantle it. The love which Žižek demotes is still, as with Levinas, a face-to-face affair; whereas justice, which he prizes above love, is described as blind. But love, as we have seen already, is not in the first place a question of the *en face*. The second epistle of St Peter distinguishes between love, which is properly impersonal, and what it calls 'brotherly affection'. Far from contrasting with justice, love resembles it in being blind, in the sense that it refuses to privilege some people over others. On the other hand, as far as attending to the claims of flesh-and-blood men and women goes, justice is no more blind than love. Law, like love, must

---

[53]   Herbert McCabe, *Law, Love and Language* (London, 1968), p. 95.
[54]   Slavoj Žižek, 'Neighbors and Other Monsters: A Plea for Ethical Violence', in Žižek, Santner and Reinhard (eds), *The Neighbor*, p. 181.

be sensitive to the specific. Justice is not the opposite of love, but a dimension of it. It is that subset of our relations with others which concerns giving them their due so that they can flourish.

Kenneth Reinhard claims that 'The love of the neighbour cannot be generalised into a universal social love.'[55] But this, once more, is to think of love primarily as interpersonal, which is why it is hard to translate it into social terms. It overlooks the fact that one's relationship with one's neighbour is in an important sense impersonal. To love others 'for Christ's sake' means to love them for the sake of their sheer humanity – an abstraction which does not, however, mean not being attentive to *them*. 'Universal social love' sounds like some nebulous global philanthropy, an idea which Reinhard is quite right to find suspect; but he is wrong to imagine that the opposite of this is a love which is primarily interpersonal.

There might appear to be a tension between virtue ethics and an ethics of love. Aristotle, for example, notoriously fails to include charity among his list of virtues. As Alasdair MacIntyre puts it: 'For the love of the person, as against the goodness, pleasantness, or usefulness of the person, Aristotle can have no place.'[56] For Christians, this tension is resolved in the writings of Thomas Aquinas, whose concept of *beatitudo* is a version of Aristotle's *eudaimonia* or well-being, yet a well-being which, as we have seen, can ultimately be found only in the love of God. What the Aristotelians call virtue, or the spontaneous capacity for acting well, Christianity calls grace. To live the life of grace is to acquire the spontaneous habit of goodness in the manner of Aristotle's virtue, rather as a graceful dancer is one who performs without effort. It is the reverse of a laborious Kantian conformity to the law. It is also a great deal more pleasant.

For those of a less celestial turn of mind, the path from Aristotle to a more sociable ethics lies through Hegel and Marx. It is Hegel who places the individual's striving for realisation in the context of the same desire on the part of others, and who therefore concludes that in a just social order, each comes to self-fulfilment through and in terms of the self-fulfilment of the others. Others become the ground and condition of one's own coming to selfhood. The development of each, as Marx rephrases the point in the *Communist Manifesto*, becomes the condition of the development of all. And this is quite as much an instance of love as Levinas's encounter with the Other. The fact that it is political rather than interpersonal love makes no difference to this point. Lacan is thus mistaken to quote

---

[55]   Reinhard, 'Towards a Political Theology of the Neighbor', p. 49.
[56]   Alasdair MacIntyre, *A Short History of Ethics* (London, 1968), p. 80.

approvingly Mazarin's tag 'Politics is politics, but love always remains love.'[57] Marxism is simply an inquiry into what social transformation would be required for this form of life to thrive. When this reciprocal self-fulfilment occurs between two individuals – when each becomes the ground and means of the flourishing of the other – it is also known as love, whether erotic or not. Love is a practice, not in the first place a state of soul. It involves both freedom and autonomy, since it allows one to be set free from fear to become oneself. Fear, not hate, is the opposite of love. It also requires equality, since this process can really take place only among equals. It is a question of what Aristotle calls *philia* or friendship. There cannot be genuine friendship between oneself and one's valet, however much one's skin might glow and tingle whenever he enters the room.

To realise one's nature in ways which create the space for others to do so too is not an ethics of law, duty, conscience or obligation, yet it clearly implicates such issues. It rules out, for example, rape, torture and murder – indeed, any treatment of others which is not conducive either to their self-fulfilment or to one's own. It is just that its laws and prohibitions are derived from a positive conception of the good, rather than (like the Kantian moral law, or at least the will to obey it) figuring as a supreme good in themselves. The self-governing cooperatives we have glanced at already, in which matters are so arranged that as far as possible my own self-realisation promotes and is promoted by that of my fellow workers, might serve to bring this rather grandiose idea closer to earth. This, to be sure, is a utopian ethics, but it is none the worse for that. So for that matter is the moral idealism of Kant. There is no point in setting one's moral sights too timorously low. It is hard to think of a more precious goal to aim at, even if it might never be fully realisable. It is certainly a more desirable form of life than an ethics of the Real, even if that ethics has something of value to say about what it might take to achieve this sort of political friendship.

The prominence of Kantian thought in the work of thinkers like Lacan, Levinas, Deleuze, Lyotard, Foucault and Derrida, the extraordinary homage paid to his thought in Paris, is appropriate enough, given that he has a claim to be the greatest or second greatest philosopher of human history. For these thinkers, one feels, Kant *is* moral philosophy. Yet this veneration is also ironic, since there has been a decisive move in recent times to dethrone the deontological, of which Bernard Williams's *Ethics and the Limits of Philosophy* is an exemplary specimen. While Levinas, Derrida and

---

57   Lacan, *Ethics of Psychoanalysis*, p. 324.

others have been speaking of absolute obligations and infinite responsibilities, Williams and others have been pointing out just what a drastically impoverished version of ethics this cult of duty represents. In this sense, the option for Kant against Hegel has had some fairly disastrous consequences. The discourse known as morality mistakenly supposes that obligation lies at the core of ethical argument – a view that Levinas and Derrida, for all their scepticism of traditional moral thought, enthusiastically propagate. Much the same goes for the Lacanians, for whom, as we have seen, the absolute obligation in question is not a moral law but a desire peculiar to one's distinctive being. But you do not escape the despotism of the obligatory simply by substituting one sort of necessity for another. Obligations, like principles, certainly enter into moral discourse – but as one factor among several, and not necessarily as the one to which all others must invariably defer.

Much moral discourse is obsessed with principle and necessity, and its avant-gardist inheritors are scarcely different in this respect. It assumes that there is a special class of motives for acting called 'moral' motives which are radically different in kind from any other. It is also prone to imagine that the complexity of moral matters can be reduced to a single principle or set of principles. It revolves narrowly around a clutch of rather heavy-handed concepts of judgement and blame, approval and disapproval. The difference between morality and virtue ethics in this respect is one between a didactic novelist and a major realist. Because it mistakenly believes that any action worthy of moral judgement must be purely voluntary, and that the only alternative to such voluntarism is determinism, morality is a discourse sour with recrimination. It is the kind of legalistic view of human existence which provoked Jesus into calling down such frightful curses on the heads of the Pharisees – to whom, theologically speaking, he was in other respects fairly close.

Morality on this view is about remorse, self-reproach and absolute responsibility. It is what has landed so many individuals on death row in the United States. The view that one is absolutely responsible for one's own actions is one which American ideology shares with Emmanuel Levinas. The most powerful nation in history is in the grip of a crazed kind of voluntarism. In their devoutly Kantian way, the Lacanians, too, assume that blame, remorse, law, obligation and duty are indeed what morality is mostly about – but that the point is to find an exit from this unlovely mode of existence. This escape hatch is to be found beyond the law, in an ethics of the (positively conceived) Real. But if they had not signed on for such an arid variety of ethics in the first place, they might not have had to resort

to such ingenious (and sometimes improbable) manoeuvres to give it the
slip. What both morality and Realist ethics have in common is their purism.
It is a quasi-religious otherworldliness which the Lacanians inherit from
Kant – one to which both Judaism and Christianity can act as a much-
needed this-worldly corrective. When Slavoj Žižek writes that 'terrestrial
life (is) of ultimately secondary importance' for Christianity,[58] as though
Christians are sulphurous, multi-legged creatures from another galaxy, he
momentarily forgets that salvation is a this-worldly affair; that the risen
body is traditionally regarded as more, not less of a body than the historical
one; and that the kingdom of God is traditionally held to be a transfigured
earth, not a city in the stars.

There is something distinctly odd about post-structuralists like Derrida,
Lyotard, Hillis Miller and de Man turning for their moral truths to the sage
of Königsberg. For one thing, Kant promotes just the kind of universalism
which post-structuralism abhors. For another thing, this austere apologist
for duty and law would seem light years removed in tone and sensibility
from the ludic, laid-back, pleasure-hunting relativists of the *rive gauche*.
Iron necessities and unconditional decrees are hardly what we associate
with Roland Barthes or Jean Baudrillard. There are a number of respects,
however, in which the two camps see eye to eye. They share, for example,
a certain formalism. Just as the Kantian moral law lacks all substance
beyond itself, so substance for post-structuralism is subordinate to the
rules of discourse, the play of the signifier, the arbitrary act of positing or
the perpetual flickering of difference. The Kantian bestowal of the law on
oneself becomes in post-structuralist hands yet another instance of the
self-referential sign.

The two theories also share a certain anti-foundationalism. Kant's
moral law is founded not on divinity or human nature but on itself.
Post-structuralism is similarly prepared in Nietzschean fashion to live
without ultimate grounds. But the ethical, seen as a mysteriously coercive
law, can provide this unstable world with some sort of ballast from beyond.
'Ethics', writes Paul de Man, 'has nothing to do with the will (thwarted
or free) of a subject, nor *a fortiori* with a relationship between subjects.'[59]
Here then, in an ethics beyond subjectivity, is yet another affinity between
Kant and the post-structuralists, as the moral subject of the former,
who is no more than an obedient function of the law, converges with
the decentred subject of the latter. Just as pure randomness dissolves the

---

[58] Žižek, 'Neighbors and Other Monsters', p. 150.
[59] Paul de Man, *Allegories of Reading* (New Haven, CT and London, 1979), p. 206.

subject away, so does the kind of iron necessity which renders it largely superfluous.

The ethical, in this bleak de Manian scenario, has nothing to do with human agency or decision. It is rather a force which, like language, imposes itself upon us with all the arbitrary compulsion of an Aeschylean drama. Kant's moral law is translated into language or text: 'What makes a reading more or less true', de Man comments, 'is simply the predictability, the necessity of its occurrence, regardless of the reader or the author's wishes.'[60] If de Man means that moral absolutes are akin to being forced to read a text in a particular way, then he misunderstands the nature of such obligations, which can of course always be disobeyed. His necessity would seem more natural than ethical, more like an earthquake than a moral edict.

Like de Man, Hillis Miller also thinks of ethics in terms of absolutes and necessities. Like him, too, he rewrites Kant in a more modishly post-structuralist style. There are unconditional laws, but 'there is absolutely no foundation in knowledge (for them), that is in the epistemological realm governed by the category of truth and falsehood'.[61] As with Derrida's decisionism, the menial faculty of cognition is allowed no say in the question of moral value. Moral values cannot be grounded in whatever is the case, since whatever is the case is itself an ungrounded interpretation. It is not so much that pure and practical reason must be jealously discriminated, as with the Kantians; it is rather that there is really no pure reason in the first place.

For the Kantians, facts are one thing and values another; for the post-structuralists and their postmodern progeny, there is no rift at all between them, since facts are simply values in empirical guise. It is your values which will determine what you see. For Kant, the kind of knowledge we can have of the empirical world is just not of the sort that could ground our moral projects, not least because the world is a matter of determinism and morality is a question of freedom. For the post-structuralists, knowledge is simply too precarious an affair to ground anything much at all. Indeed, this is one reason for their turn to Kant. We noted in an earlier chapter that at the end of the nineteenth century, a number of positivists, scientific determinists and evolutionary Marxists found themselves unable to conjure moral value out of a world that they themselves had been busy bleaching

---

[60] Paul de Man, Foreword to Carol Jacobs, *The Dissimulating Harmony* (Baltimore, MD and London, 1978), p. xi.
[61] Hillis Miller, *Ethics of Reading*, p. 48.

clean of it. They were accordingly forced to import selective bits of Kant into their world-view, so as to fill in the very moral void they themselves had scooped out. Post-structuralism, having portrayed the world as ceaseless semiosis, libidinal intensity or the play of power, finds itself equally stumped for a way to generate values out of these accounts, and in reaching for its Kant repeats the manoeuvre of its *fin-de-siècle* forebears.

It is true that in one sense facts and values are linked in post-structuralist thought, since both are unmasked as baseless fictions. In another sense, however, they are cut adrift from each other, since the fictional status of facts is part of what prevents us from bringing epistemology to the aid of ethics. Ethical and political commitments must be independent of the facts, assuming that there are any facts in the first place. There is a surreptitious slide at work here from the reasonable claim that moral values cannot simply be read off from whatever is the case, to the implausible claim that the cognitive and the ethical are wholly autonomous of one another. This is not the case for virtue ethics, for which the virtuous person will actually perceive objective aspects of a situation which the less virtuous will not, and may regard these facts as constituting sufficient reason why some sort of action should be taken.[62]

For Hillis Miller, however, the less facts enter into the business of values, the purer our moral judgements become. 'No doubt the political and the ethical are always intimately intertwined', Miller remarks, in the guardedly concessionary tones of one just about to withdraw what he is perfunctorily granting, 'but an ethical act that is fully determined by political consider-ations or responsibilities is no longer ethical. It could even in a certain sense be said to be amoral.'[63] The more full-bloodedly political our actions become, the less moral they are, a case which might have come as some-thing of a surprise to Martin Luther King. The political sphere, as with the ethical Realists, is downgraded to drably utilitarian status, and as such is understandably hard to link to an ethics which has been defined in con-tradistinction to it. The more the political is debased, the more overween-ing the ethical appears. That this in itself is the effect of a certain political history would no doubt be dismissed by Hillis Miller as a less than purely ethical judgement.

The ethical, then, is at once arbitrary and absolute, rather like the rules of a game. It is a foundation, yet no foundation at all. It cannot be circum-

---

[62]   The latter case is argued by John McDowell in 'Are Moral Requirements Hypothetical Imperatives?', *Proceedings of the Aristotelian Society*, supp. vol. 52 (1978).
[63]   Hillis Miller, *Ethics of Reading*, p. 4.

vented, but neither can it be justified. Like language, at least on a post-structuralist view of it, moral decrees have all the unmotivated force of that which is grounded wholly in itself. They are commandingly self-identical edicts in a non-self-identical world. It is just because they seem to spring from nowhere, with no source in either knowledge, history, politics or nature, that they appear arbitrary; but this apparent lack of a context is also what invests them with a certain absolute or transcendent status. We feel obliged to treat such commands as enigmatic entities in themselves, and so as strangely absolute in force. They are absolute not because they are unquestionably well-founded, but precisely because they are not. Their absolutism is in proportion to their gratuitousness – so that, as with some reckless *acte gratuit*, their very groundlessness looms up as a perverse sort of ground. If there is no particular reason to obey them, there is no par-ticular reason to flout them either. Post-structuralism can thus avoid the embarrassments of moral relativism while preserving its faith in the anti-foundational. It can do so, however, only at the cost of confounding the unconditional with the unmotivated.

There is another reason why the false assumption that ethics consists chiefly in imperatives, prohibitions, promises, prescriptions and the like proves convenient for the post-structuralists. This is that it promises to reduce the question of ethics to the performative realm where they feel most at home. The law is rewritten as language, so that the inhuman nature of Kant's moral law, its icy disregard for the capacities of flesh-and-blood human subjects, is transmuted into the inhuman force of language itself. It is ethics for literary types. That what makes us human is itself inhuman is a motif of modernity from Kant to Derrida. This rewriting then has a bearing on the question of moral truth. Ethical propositions are really dis-cursive utterances, which can no more be assessed for their truth-value than any other kind of performative speech act. Moral judgements, Miller observes, are 'a baseless positing, always unjust and unjustified, therefore always likely to be displaced by another momentarily stronger or more persuasive but equally baseless positing of a different code of ethics'.[64] It would be intriguing to know how this *caveat* might apply to the judgement that Mao Zedong slaughtered millions of his fellow citizens. A moral code for Miller is absolute until it is toppled by one morally fitter, at which point it naturally ceases to be absolute. In a similar way, the Roman Catholic Church never changes its mind: it simply moves from one state of certainty to another, as it would if it were to alter its teaching on abortion or

[64] Ibid., p. 55.

contraception. There is a Nietzschean or social-Darwinist flavour to Miller's displacing of the weaker by the stronger, as there is to the decisionism of his and de Man's 'baseless positing'. In fact, the whole of this ethics is a curious amalgam of Nietzsche and Kant. 'Genuine philosophers', writes Nietzsche in one of his less self-effacing moods, '. . . are commanders and legislators; they say: *thus* shall it be!'[65] If moral judgements can no longer be supported by reason and evidence, one can always fall back on sheer rhetorical force instead. 'Just Do It!' is the form this sort of injunction takes. Because it is unsupported by any rational authority, it cannot be gainsaid because there is nothing there to be controverted. Such edicts are simply handed down mysteriously from on high. Once art after modernism has shed its numinous aura, ethics becomes the new form of transcendence for a post-religious era.

The same radical decisionism is to be found in Jean-François Lyotard's *Just Gaming*, which lends a post-structuralist twist to the customary philosophical ban on deriving a prescriptive from a descriptive statement. Neither ethics nor politics, Lyotard declares, can be based on a science of society. Michel Foucault concurs, insisting that 'it's not at all necessary to relate ethical problems to scientific knowledge . . . I think we have to get rid of this idea of an analytical or necessary link between ethics and other social or economic or political structures'.[66] The alternative case is advanced by Denys Turner: 'We want to know, because we want to be free; and from time to time we learn to call by the name of "knowledge" those forms of enquiry which we need if we are at all to free ourselves from those time-crusted conceptions which, in the course of history, have degenerated into the anachronism of ideology.'[67] Not all knowledge, to be sure, is of this political kind; but Turner sees that the vital kind of cognition we call emancipatory knowledge cannot easily be fitted into a rigorous division between the descriptive and prescriptive. Morality as classically conceived, he continues, is 'a scientific investigation of the social order that can generate norms for action'.[68] It is thus the reverse of ideology. What Marx pursues in his work, for example, is a moral inquiry in a traditional sense of the term, even if he himself for the most part failed to recognise it as

[65] Friedrich Nietzsche, *Beyond Good and Evil*, in W. Kaufmann (ed.), *Basic Writings of Nietzsche* (New York, 1968), p. 326.
[66] Michel Foucault, 'On the Genealogy of Ethics', in Paul Rabinow (ed.), *The Foucault Reader* (New York, 1984), pp. 349–50.
[67] Denys Turner, *Marxism and Christianity* (Oxford, 1983), p. 113.
[68] Ibid., p. 85.

such. He was too quick to identify such moral inquiry with moralism, and thus to write it off as so much ideological rhetoric. In this, he was unwittingly abetted by Kantians, sentimentalists, liberals and brutal-minded Evangelicals, all of whom had conspired to reduce ethics to just such a politically toothless affair.

Moral prescriptions must obviously implicate beliefs about how the world is. There is no point in pressing for the abolition of feudal serfdom in Hemel Hempstead. Pornographic video stores need not be banned among the Dinka, at least not yet. For Lyotard, however, it would seem that the empirical fails to enter the moral sphere even in this self-evident sense. We must judge, he declares, 'without criteria . . . It is decided, and that is all that can be said . . . I mean that, in each instance, I have a feeling, that is all . . . But if I am asked by what criteria do I judge, I will have no answer to give.'[69] A few pages later, this calculatedly outrageous appeal to the dogmatism of intuition is spelt out in more soberly Kantian terms: moral and political judgements, we are more moderately informed, can occur 'without going through a conceptual system that could serve as a criterion for practice'.[70] They resemble Kant's aesthetics more than they do his epistemology. Prescriptives cannot be justified, which for Lyotard is part of their unfathomable allure. The moral law is promulgated out of an empty transcendence. There is no principled, general or conceptual way of answering the question of why one is of one ethical or political party than the other. What obligates us is a kind of moral sublimity 'absolutely beyond our intelligence'.[71]

This captures in a mystified sort of way a genuine intuition – that fundamental moral commitments are not just conscious decisions, but have a smack of necessity about them. You cannot alter your aversion to genocide simply by willing to do so. In this sense, where we are most ourselves is not at all where we are most free, at least in one familiar sense of the word 'free'. This, perhaps, is one of several ways in which Kant's antithesis between freedom and determinism can be dismantled. The polarity is also taken apart in Christian belief, for which God is at once the necessary source of one's being, and the power which enables one to be a free agent. Only because men and women are dependent on him can they be self-determining. In Lyotard's view, the Kantian law 'guides

---

[69] Jean-François Lyotard and Jean-Loup Thébaud, *Just Gaming* (Minneapolis, 1985), pp. 14–15.
[70] Ibid., p. 18.
[71] Ibid., p. 71.

us in knowing what is just and not just. But guides us without, in the end, really guiding us, that is, without telling us what is just.'[72] As in the writings of Derrida, decisionism, Kantian formalism and the quasi-mystical appeal of the enigma converge with a post-Marxist distaste for determinate agendas.

The ethical, Hillis Miller rather grudgingly concedes, is intertwined with the political; but it is also contaminated by its mean-spirited presence, and like a hen-pecked husband is better off on its own. Here, with a vengeance, is a vision of politics, ethics and epistemology as autonomous (as opposed to distinct) domains. To salvage ethics from politics is to retrieve moral value from the corrupting climate of twentieth-century history. What has put paid to universal programmes and principles is above all the spectres of fascism and Stalinism. This then provides the last of our links between Kantianism and post-structuralism, two doctrines which for quite different reasons are deeply wary of the historical. For Aristotle, the idea of a non-political virtue would have been hard to grasp – not only because he has a different notion of virtue from, say, Miller or Lacan, but because he has a far less disenchanted conception of politics. How could one assess qualities of action and character in isolation from the *polis* which produces them? A judgement which failed to take account of such conditions would be not moral but moralistic. Ethics and politics are not separate spheres but different viewpoints on the same object – the former investigating such matters as needs, desires, qualities and values, the latter examining the conventions, forms of power, institutions and social relations within which alone such things are intelligible. It is for this reason that Aristotle regards ethics as a kind of sub-branch of politics. For some of the implications of this case, we can turn now to our Conclusion.

[72]   Ibid., p. 77.

Conclusion

There is a sense in which all strangers are blood strangers. St Paul speaks in his epistle to the Ephesians of the crumbling of the barriers between Israel and the Gentiles – those aliens who 'were once far off (but) have now been brought near in the blood of Christ'. Paul himself, so he remarks, 'has preached peace to you who were far off, and peace to those who were near'. Christ has reconfigured geographical space, erasing the distinction between those who are under and those who are outside the law. Physical terrains are no longer important.

It is mistaken to maintain that our spontaneous sympathies are confined to those we know, while our concern for those at a distance must be delegated to the rusty mechanism of abstract reason. Plenty of people feel more passionately about some remote phenomenon than they do about the people next door, or even about those who are closer to them than that. You may lose more sleep over a remote famine, or even over a centuries-old political defeat, than you do over your brother's bankruptcy. The benevolentists are wrong to imagine that emotions are largely domestic affairs. It is not true, as many conservatives suspect, that feeling is the enemy of cosmopolitanism. Feelings begin at home only in the literal sense that this is for the most part where we first learn them. Even then, however, our first fervent attachments may be to the Leader rather than to our kins-folk. Sentimentalism, one might suggest, is a form of affection which has never managed to leave home. In reaction to such provincialism, Kant holds that it is more worthy to treat those we cherish more or less as we behave to strangers. If he does not mean by this that we must treat our partners or children with emotional indifference, this is among other things because we are not always emotionally indifferent to strangers. Even the English can be brought to accept that.

Sylviane Agacinski maintains that 'In a case of ethical respect or dutiful loving, my relationship flows from a requirement which is indifferent to

the individuality of the other.' If this implies that we always act emotion-
lessly where strangers are concerned, the claim is clearly untrue. We have
seen, too, that to be indifferent to the individuality of another in the sense
of not confining one's love to certain persons (friends, for example, or
compatriots, or those with the same star sign or hair colour as oneself) does
not necessarily mean being indifferent to their individuality in the sense of
not attending to their specific needs. In any case, there are more ways of
respecting the individuality of others than feeling personal affection for
them. Law, Agacinski adds, always requires 'a dissolution of ties – of the
ties that attach us to finite individualities, the ties that bind individual
bodily existences together'.[1] But we have seen in the case of Shylock that
laws exist to protect bodily ties, not to annul them. One's bodily ties with
others are not simply face-to-face. Nor are the affective bonds between
ourselves and others necessarily dissolved by the laws which also hold
between us, whether they are the laws of the land or the law of love.
Agacincski makes the Humean mistake of assuming that feelings are inevitably local, and that laws are mere long-range stand-ins for them; whereas
the truth is not only that we can feel for those unknown to us, but that
one's feelings for those close at hand spring in part from what one has
learnt from one's dealings with strangers.

   To this extent, there is no obvious enmity between the imaginary and
the symbolic. We naturally feel deeper bonds of affection with those we
know rather than those who are unfamiliar; but affection is not the only
feeling at stake when it comes to strangers. As Bruce Robbins points out,
'You don't have to pull off the neat trick of relating to the world's distant
peoples with full imaginative and emotional intensity in order to lobby for
better policies with respect to their well-being.'[2] 'Thick' relations are not
always interpersonal ones: 'The thick, dense embodiedness that is so easily
accepted as a domestic fact', Robbins writes, 'cannot be refused to claims
and relationships that cross national borders.'[3] In any case, as Aquinas
points out, personal friendships can act as a kind of moral gymnasium for
less immediate relations. *Philia* or human friendship is not in the first place
for Aquinas a personal affair; but it is here that we can nurture the sort of

[1] Sylviane Agacinski, 'We Are Not Sublime: Love and Sacrifice, Abraham and Ourselves',
in Jonathan Rée and Jane Chamberlain (eds), *Kierkegaard: A Critical Reader* (Oxford, 1998),
p. 146.
[2] Bruce Robbins, *Feeling Global: Internationalism in Distress* (New York and London, 1999),
p. 152.
[3] Ibid., p. 172.

sensitivity which we also need to practise in more impersonal matters of justice and politics.

Symbolic relationships are ones mediated by law, politics and language; and these – Lacan's Other – are always as much media of division as of solidarity. Such relations can easily lapse into mere utility or contractualism. Yet in giving priority to our relations with strangers, the symbolic also reminds us that this, and not literal neighbours, is the paradigm of ethical conduct, including our behaviour towards literal neighbours. It is not that strangers are simply friends we have not yet made, but that friends are the alien creatures we happen to know. The definitive act of love is not a commingling of souls but taking the place of a stranger in the queue for the gas chambers. One can die for a friend, just as one can love a stranger; but to die for a stranger is the ultimate ethical 'event'. That Christians see such a death as demanded by God is one reason why he is not loving and terrible by turns, but why his love is a holy terror.

This is not, by and large, the conventional moral wisdom. Such stretching of our sympathies to countless anonymous others, observes the US right-winger Robert Sibley, 'strains to extend our concrete realities to include some distant and generalised "others" who, we are told, are our global neighbours'.[4] Extending its concrete realities to distant and generalised others, otherwise known as imperialism, has indeed involved the United States in a spot of strain from time to time. The symbolic insinuates an alienness into our affairs, including our proximate affairs, which is both deepening and potentially destructive. And this is where the thin edge of the Real is inserted. As far as the Real goes, the neighbour is the one who accepts us in our inhuman destitution, and whom we embrace in the same spirit. Neighbourhood is a practice rather than a locality. Only relationships rooted in our mortal weakness have a chance of evolving beyond the narcissistic.[5]

The Real, then, represents the symbolic order's point of inner fracture – the contradictions on which it threatens to founder, the trauma which skews it out of true, the negativity which it must exclude in order to flourish, the deathly encounter with its own limits which might allow it to remake itself. Flesh and blood may be the basis of the imaginary, in contrast to the disincarnate signifiers of the symbolic; but it is also the mark of the Real – of the animal, injurable, death-haunted humanity we share as a

---

[4] Quoted in Kwame Anthony Appiah, *Cosmopolitanism: Ethics in a World of Strangers* (London, 2006), p. 157.

[5] For an excellent discussion, see Martha Nussbaum, *For Love of Country: The Limits of Patriotism* (Boston, 1996).

species. What makes for intimacy is thus also what makes for universality. To encounter one another purely as companionable bodies is as palpable as it is abstract. Because flesh and blood is what constitutes us, the universality of the species enters into our every breath and gesture. It is this which postmodernism, a current of thought which has replaced the more classical forms of foundationalism with a new kind of absolute ground known as culture, most damagingly denies.

Flesh and blood is the degree zero of humanity, at once monstrous in its anonymity and the medium of our most cherished contact. It is because the mortal, afflicted body lies at the root of all culture that the local and the universal are not ultimately at odds. For the Jews of the so-called Old Testament, as we have seen, the body is not in the first place disciplined or erotic, emblazoned or aestheticised, but the principle which binds us into unity with bodies of our kind. It belongs to our creatureliness, as the benevolentists see, to grant a special status to what we can feel and perceive at first hand. But it is also part of our animal nature, as the benevolentists do not concede quite so readily, to feel for others simply because they have bodies in common with ours, however physically or culturally different those bodies may be. Difference in itself is simply not a sound enough foundation on which to construct either an ethics or a politics. It only appears so when the particular forms of universality we find to hand have for some reason gone awry.

We have seen that the near and the remote are allied in at least this sense, that the neighbour is simply whatever stranger happens to have strayed into our presence. This abstract exchangeability of individuals is made possible by the symbolic; but it exists, ethically speaking, to be exceeded. The indifference of charity is in the service of specific others, not a way of trampling roughshod over their distinctiveness. Because the symbolic sets us free from particularity, it can also free us for it. Anyone can now be cherished as inimitable, which is not the case with the imaginary. Enlightenment, as usual, progresses by its bad side.

For Christian doctrine, this symbolic truth is not incompatible with the Real – meaning, in this context, a disruptive excess or infinity, a transcendence of the finite which can prove both invigorating and injurious. The Christian version of this infinity is that there is no end to charity, which is a form of sharing in the *jouissance* of eternal life; so that while there is an identity or equivalence of a symbolic kind between the putative objects of that charity, the love devoted to any one of them recklessly overrides this equitable measure in the manner of the Real. Being prepared to lay down one's life for another – any other – presses this recklessness to a point of sublime absurdity, and in doing so captures something of the distinctive scandal and madness of Christianity. Yet this unthinkable Real is no more than the exchangeability of the symbolic order pressed to an extreme.

If Christian faith involves both the symbolic and the Real, it also proposes its own version of the imaginary. The mimesis in question is not some Burkeian imitation of the civilised figures around us, but the *imitatio Christi* – which is to say, in effect, the readiness to be murdered by the state in the pursuit of justice. It is to this grim fate that Jesus explicitly summons his comrades. What the eighteenth century knows as sympathy – the re-creation within oneself of the condition of another – is here given a rather more bloody twist, as we shift from love as social benevolence to love as sacrificial death. To say that Christians must share in the being-for-others of Christ is to claim that they must be ready to rehearse his foolish self-expenditure to the point of death. Even so, the foolhardy self-squandering demanded by the gospel, as opposed to a narrow ethic of tit-for-tat, is not to be confused with the Levinasian contrast between an infinity of personal responsibility and the prudential demands of the political. The fact that there is no end to charity should not be taken as a recipe for overriding prudence and realism, which are themselves desirable moral qualities. Charity, for example, must reckon with the need for justice, which is part of it. As Alasdair MacIntyre puts it, 'charity towards (our neighbour) goes beyond, but always includes justice'.[6] It is not that justice is on the side of the political, whereas love is a purely personal affair.

Nor is it the case, as the Levinasians tend to insist, that the personal relationship of love or responsibility is in every sense asymmetrical, in contrast with the strict equities of the symbolic order. This, to be sure, is true in the sense we have just noted – that charity is in principle without end. It is also true of one's dealings with one's enemies. Asymmetry here is a polite word for putting up with outrageous insults in return for generous deeds. But it is not true in the sense that the fullest kind of love, as we have noted already, must be equal and reciprocal. So there is no hard-and-fast distinction here between the ethical-Real and the political-symbolic. This is one reason why personal love probably comes more easily in a social order which fosters the virtues of mutuality and egalitarianism. And there are of course negative forms of asymmetry – the inequities of class or gender, for example, which Levinas characteristically overlooks – as well as positive ones.

---

[6] Alasdair MacIntyre, *Selected Essays, vol. 2: Ethics and Politics* (Cambridge, 2006), p. 146.

We need to be alert, ethically speaking, to the losses and gains of each of the Lacanian registers we have investigated. There is a quickness of sympathy about the imaginary which no authentic morality can easily dispense with. It is here that a purely juridical ethics falls down. In the end, law is not a thick enough medium of human communication. Yet shorn of this symbolic dimension, we seem at risk of lapsing into the extended egoism of the coterie, wary of strangers and nervous of the non-identical. An imaginary ethics also betrays an aversion to the Real, prudishly sceptical as it is, for example, of the reality of pure evil. If the Real is too unsociable an ethics, the imaginary is somewhat too clubbish.

The symbolic order, for its part, opens us up to the political, but exacts a tribute of flesh and blood from its members as their entry ticket to this precious universality. We must, so it appears, sacrifice our personal specificity to the impersonal ends of justice, freedom, equality and universality. If the imaginary is too fervid, the symbolic is too thin-blooded. The promptings of the heart give way to rational calculation, as an imaginary interplay between specular selves yields to a dialectic of difference and identity. We have already noted several times that one way of reconciling the unique and the universal in this respect is to attend to the peculiar needs of anyone whatsoever. It is this which the Angelos of this world – the more stiff-necked evangelists of the symbolic order – damagingly ignore.

There is a similar interplay of abstract and concrete about the Real. For one thing, as we have seen, flesh and blood is what is most palpable about us, but also most universal. For another thing, to know others most intimately is in a sense to encounter them as strangers, a truth of which D. H. Lawrence in his less rebarbative moods is finely conscious. Perhaps this is why Emerson speaks of the friend as a kind of 'beautiful enemy'. Moreover, if Lacan is to be credited, we tread a path through the abstract symbolic order only to discover on the far side of it the irreducibly specific desire which makes us what we are. Yet this desire remains as foreign to us as the inhuman law of the symbolic order itself. From this vantage-point, so Lacan obscurely suggests, we become capable of a limitless love. We are returned to the proximate presence of others, if not exactly to the imaginary; yet now we can love them with all the unyielding force of an anonymous symbolic law, one which has undergone a sea-change into the desire of the Real. We have seen already, however, that part of the price we pay for access to this domain is a species of spiritual elitism and tragic extremism.

There is a persistent Romantic dream of an object which has all the warmth and intimacy of the flesh, yet all the universal scope of a language. It is a fusion of the imaginary and symbolic to be found in the Romantic symbol or concrete universal. We have glimpsed it, too, in Kant's aesthetic fantasy of a body (the work of art) which seems to incarnate a universal law, yet which also appears as much fashioned for our pleasure as the ministrations of the mother. Christianity goes a step further, adding the Real to this unity of the other two registers. The risen Christ, the Word of God, is a human body with all the universal availability of a language.[7] We have seen already how in the Eucharistic meal, the 'Real' of this body, marked as it is by its sacrificial passage through death, is present in the universal 'language' of bread and wine, the medium of symbolic communication between the participants, in something like the way that a meaning is present in a word. The Real and symbolic orders are thus blended into a single action. The Eucharistic elements are shared as the form of a common life; but because to consume bread and wine is to reap life from an act of destruction, they signify at the same time the life-from-death *transitus* which is the Real or sacrificial structure of the event. Real and symbolic are also yoked to the imaginary, as the sharing of the bread and wine also involves a mutual exchange of identities in Christ. There is a kind of Christian imaginary, of which 'When you do it to the least of these my brethren, you do it to me' is exemplary. It is, so to speak, an instance of divine transitivism. The precept that one should do to others what you would have them do to you, a dangerous counsel for the masochistic, also turns on an imaginary exchange of positions. The Eucharist, then, celebrates a convivial being-with-others, as a love-feast which prefigures a future kingdom of peace and justice; but it is one founded on death, violence and revolutionary transformation, conditions which lie beyond the pleasure principle altogether.

It may well be, of course, that Christianity is not true. Certainly nothing in this study takes that truth for granted. It may also be the case that psychoanalysis is not true either. Perhaps one reason why neither of them is true is that they both posit a fictitious state known as the human condition. If this is the case, then one reason why both of them are false may be one reason why postmodernism is true. The problem arises if psychoanalysis is true but Christianity is not. If this is so, then it might reasonably be claimed that the tragic dimension of the human condition is finally irreparable. For the Christian gospel offers a radical solution to the terrors of the

---

[7]   See Terry Eagleton, *The Body as Language* (London, 1970).

Real and the ravages of the death drive – one which, far from disavowing these things in the manner of the liberal or socialist humanist, finds a redemptive truth precisely in this most unpropitious of places. Through the spiritual revolution known as faith, the obscene enjoyment of the death drive, which is 'good for nothing', is converted into the 'nothing to lose' recklessness of the good life.

If neither Christianity nor psychoanalysis is true, we can relax a little. There is no redemption, but no call for it either. There is no need for a solution because there is no problem. Or at least, there is no problem of the kind which psychoanalysis supposes there to be. If Christianity is true but psychoanalysis is false, we have been using the latter to misidentify the condition which the former promises to redeem. But what (to pose our first permutation once more) if Christianity is false but psychoanalysis is true? In that case, one might suggest, we are thrown back upon our political resources to repair the difficulties which the latter diagnoses. It is true that politics can do a great deal more to mitigate our condition than either of those two political sceptics, Freud and Lacan, would have credited. But it is doubtful that political change in itself is entirely capable of resolving the tragic condition they portray. For that, as Christianity holds, one would need a transformation which penetrated to the stuff of the body itself. If that is a myth, then the question is one of how tolerable our situation can be made without such miraculous interventions.

The relation between ethics and politics does not turn on a contrast between love and administration, the infinite and the finite, the near and the far, intimates and strangers or the asymmetrical and the symmetrical. The two are not related as spiritual to material, inward to outward, individual to society or singular to universal. Responsibility to others, *pace* Levinas and Derrida, is not absolute and infinite, but must be tempered by justice, prudence and realism. It is not that ethics deals with neighbours whereas politics deals with strangers. Ethics is not simply a reverent openness to the Other, but a question of, say, formulating policies on advertising or infanticide which affect those whom one does not know. It is not devalued by being thematised, as the Realists fastidiously imagine.

Ethics involves impersonal commands just as politics does. Conversely, political matters such as justice and equality apply to the relations between oneself and the Other just as much as they hold between strangers. Ethics and politics are not incommensurable realms, to be linked only by some deft deconstructive footwork, but different viewpoints on the same reality. There is no such thing as 'ethical' socialism, for example, as opposed to 'non-ethical' brands of the creed. The ethical is a matter of how we may live with each other most rewardingly, while the political is a question of what institutions will best promote this end. The ends of political association, Aristotle remarks in the *Politics*, are 'life and the good life'. If you see ethics and politics as separate spheres, or feel the need to retrieve the former from the grubby clutches of the latter, you are likely to end up denigrating the political and idealising the ethical. In a politically disenchanted age, the ethical is forced to abandon the *polis* and take up its home elsewhere: in art, faith, transcendence, the Other, the event, the infinite, the decision or the Real.

A certain view of the Holocaust can reinforce this split between the ethical and the political. Because the Holocaust would seem to demand absolute moral judgements, as well as pointing for some commentators to the transcendence of evil, the ethical question remains more pressing than ever in its wake. Yet because the grand political or historical narratives which supposedly gave birth to such a catastrophe must be abandoned for just that reason, or because no sheerly historical approach could account for such wickedness, these absolute judgements no longer have a foundation. They are as insistent as they are ungrounded. Moral judgements are both demanded and disarmed. We are left, then, with ethics as an empty transcendence.

The symbolic may indeed be too thin an atmosphere in which ethics can flourish. But this is not to say that law, politics, rights, the state and human welfare should be loftily disdained as so much inevitable but soul-killing technology. Only those who are privileged enough not to require their protection can view law and authority as inherently malign. The symbolic order is most effective when it has its roots in the body – in palpable human needs and wants, rather than in moral abstractions. Marx had lavish praise for bourgeois democracy, but considered that in this respect it did not go far enough. It incorporated men and women only as abstractly free and equal citizens, not in their unique particularity. Only socialist democracy, which had shrunk the gap between the political state and everyday life and labour, could do that.

As for the Real, one might claim that for all its manifest defects, the slogan 'Stick to your desire!' is an excellent political injunction at the present time. There is no point in the political left settling for half. What has made global capitalism more difficult to challenge in our day is the fact that it has grown more predatory, not less so. This means that the very changes in the system which have helped to dispirit and deplete the left are also why the need to combat that system remains more urgent than ever. The left should thus preserve its faith, rather than submitting to the lures of reformism or defeatism. It should respond to a political system which is incapable of either feeding humanity or yielding it sufficient justice with something of the implacable refusal of an Antigone – a refusal which is folly to conservatives and a stumbling-block to liberals. Even if it finally fails in this project, it can at least reap the bitter-sweet satisfaction of knowing that it was right all along.

Index